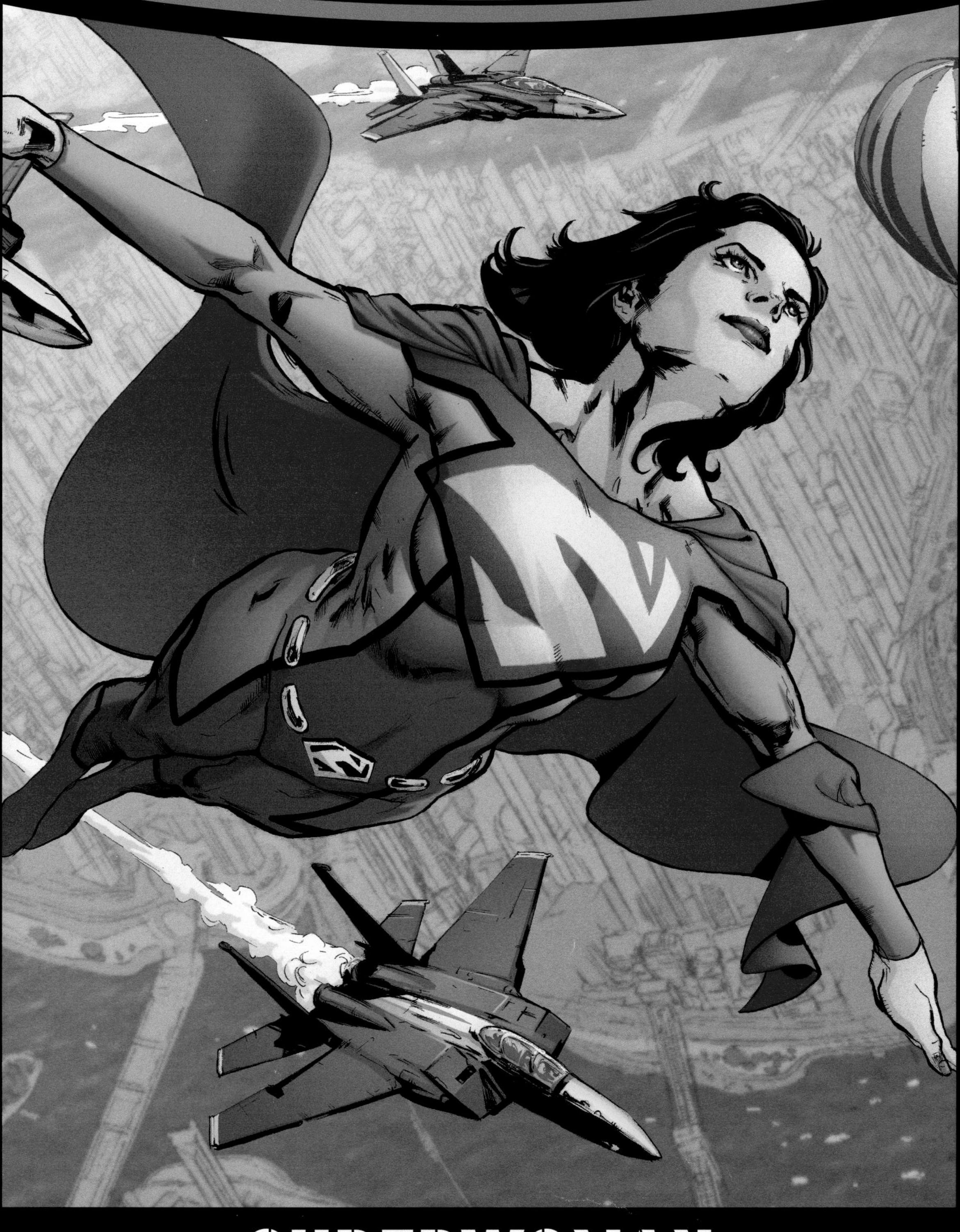

SUPERWOMAN

VOL.1 WHO KILLED SUPERWOMAN?

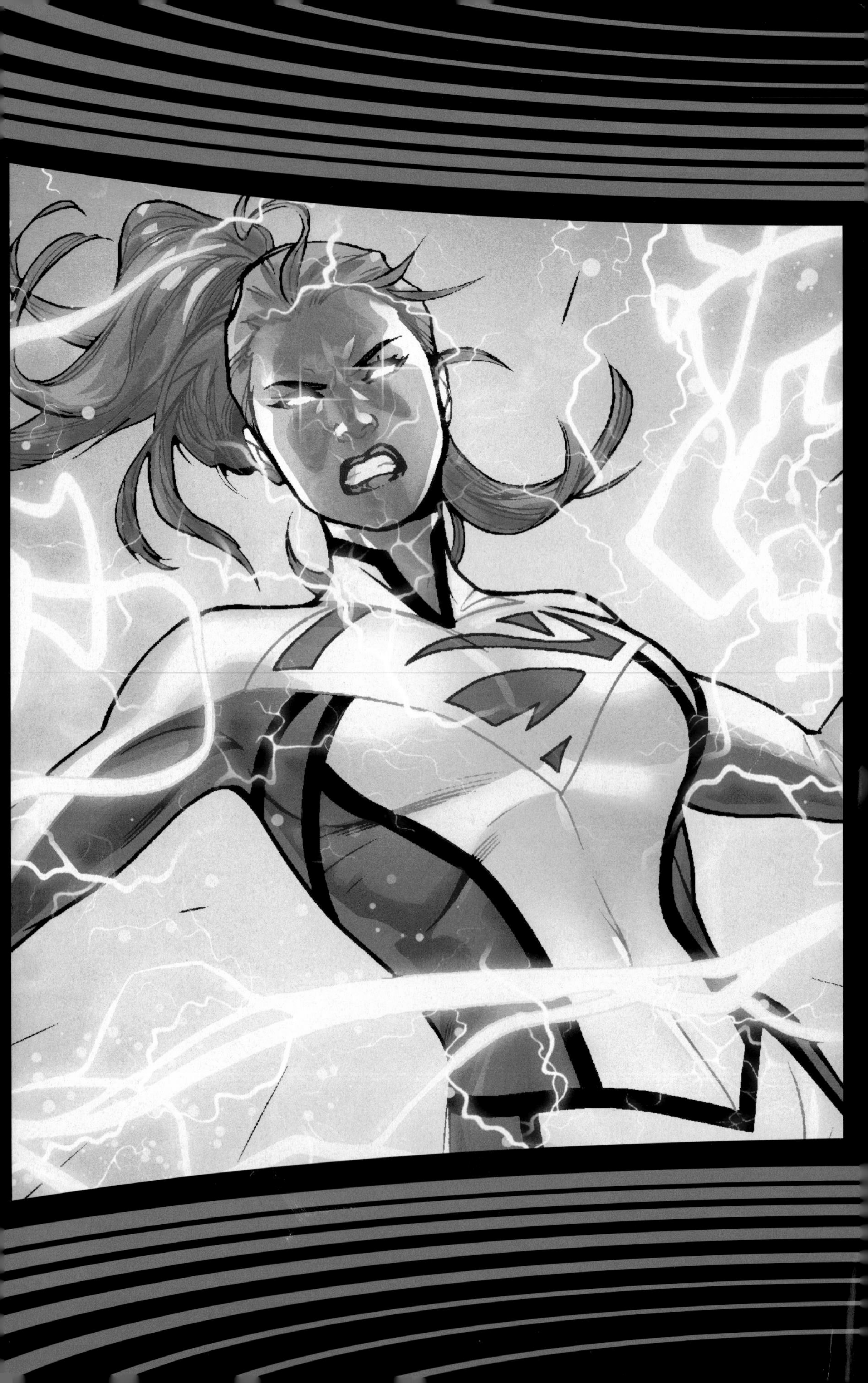

SUPERWOMAN

VOL.1 WHO KILLED SUPERWOMAN?

PHIL JIMENEZ
writer

PHIL JIMENEZ * **EMANUELA LUPACCHINO** * **JACK HERBERT**
JOE PRADO * **MATT SANTORELL** * **RAY McCARTHY**
artists

JEROMY COX * **HI-FI** * **TONY AVIÑA**
colorists

ROB LEIGH * **DAVE SHARPE** * **JOSH REED**
letterers

PHIL JIMENEZ AND STEVE DOWNER
collection cover artists

EDDIE BERGANZA Editor - Original Series ✷ PAUL KAMINSKI Associate Editor - Original Series
JEB WOODARD Group Editor - Collected Editions ✷ PAUL SANTOS Editor - Collected Edition
STEVE COOK Design Director - Books ✷ MONIQUE GRUSPE Publication Design

BOB HARRAS Senior VP - Editor-in-Chief, DC Comics

DIANE NELSON President ✷ DAN DiDIO Publisher ✷ JIM LEE Publisher ✷ GEOFF JOHNS President & Chief Creative Officer
AMIT DESAI Executive VP - Business & Marketing Strategy, Direct to Consumer & Global Franchise Management ✷ SAM ADES Senior VP - Direct to Consumer
BOBBIE CHASE VP - Talent Development ✷ MARK CHIARELLO Senior VP - Art, Design & Collected Editions
JOHN CUNNINGHAM Senior VP - Sales & Trade Marketing ✷ ANNE DePIES Senior VP - Business Strategy, Finance & Administration
DON FALLETTI VP - Manufacturing Operations ✷ LAWRENCE GANEM VP - Editorial Administration & Talent Relations
ALISON GILL Senior VP - Manufacturing & Operations ✷ HANK KANALZ Senior VP - Editorial Strategy & Administration
JAY KOGAN VP - Legal Affairs ✷ THOMAS LOFTUS VP - Business Affairs
JACK MAHAN VP - Business Affairs ✷ NICK J. NAPOLITANO VP - Manufacturing Administration
EDDIE SCANNELL VP - Consumer Marketing ✷ COURTNEY SIMMONS Senior VP - Publicity & Communications
JIM (SKI) SOKOLOWSKI VP - Comic Book Specialty Sales & Trade Marketing ✷ NANCY SPEARS VP - Mass, Book, Digital Sales & Trade Marketing

SUPERWOMAN VOL. 1: WHO KILLED SUPERWOMAN?

DC Comics, 2900 West Alameda Ave., Burbank, CA 91505.
Printed by LSC Communications, Salem, VA, USA. 3/31/17. First Printing.
ISBN: 978-1-4012-6780-3

Library of Congress Cataloging-in-Publication Data is available.

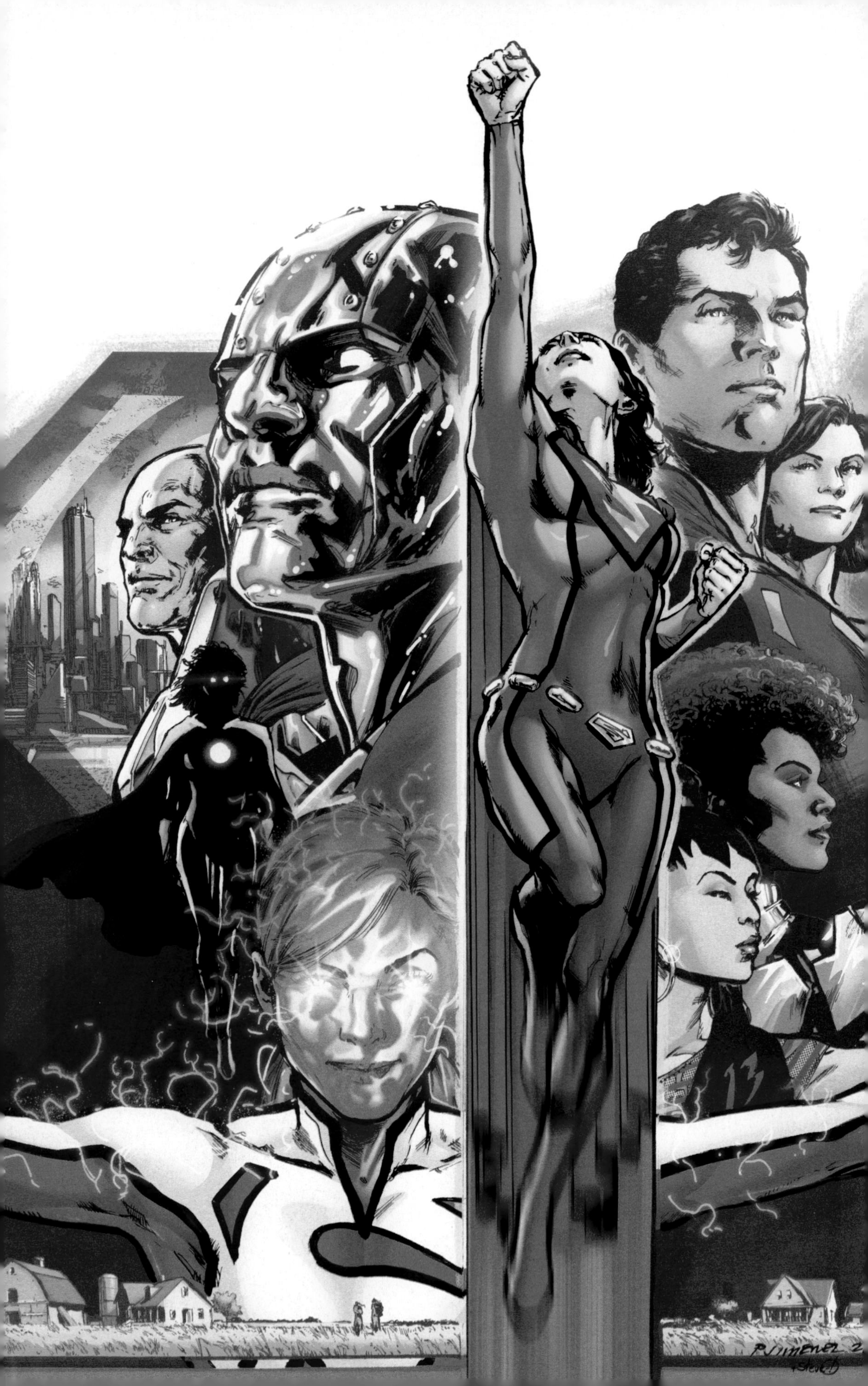

"WHO KILLED SUPERWOMAN? PART ONE"

PARFPHIL JIMENEZ writer/penciller ∗ MATT SANTORELLI inker

JEROMY COX colorist ∗ cover by PHIL JIMENEZ and STEVE DOWNER

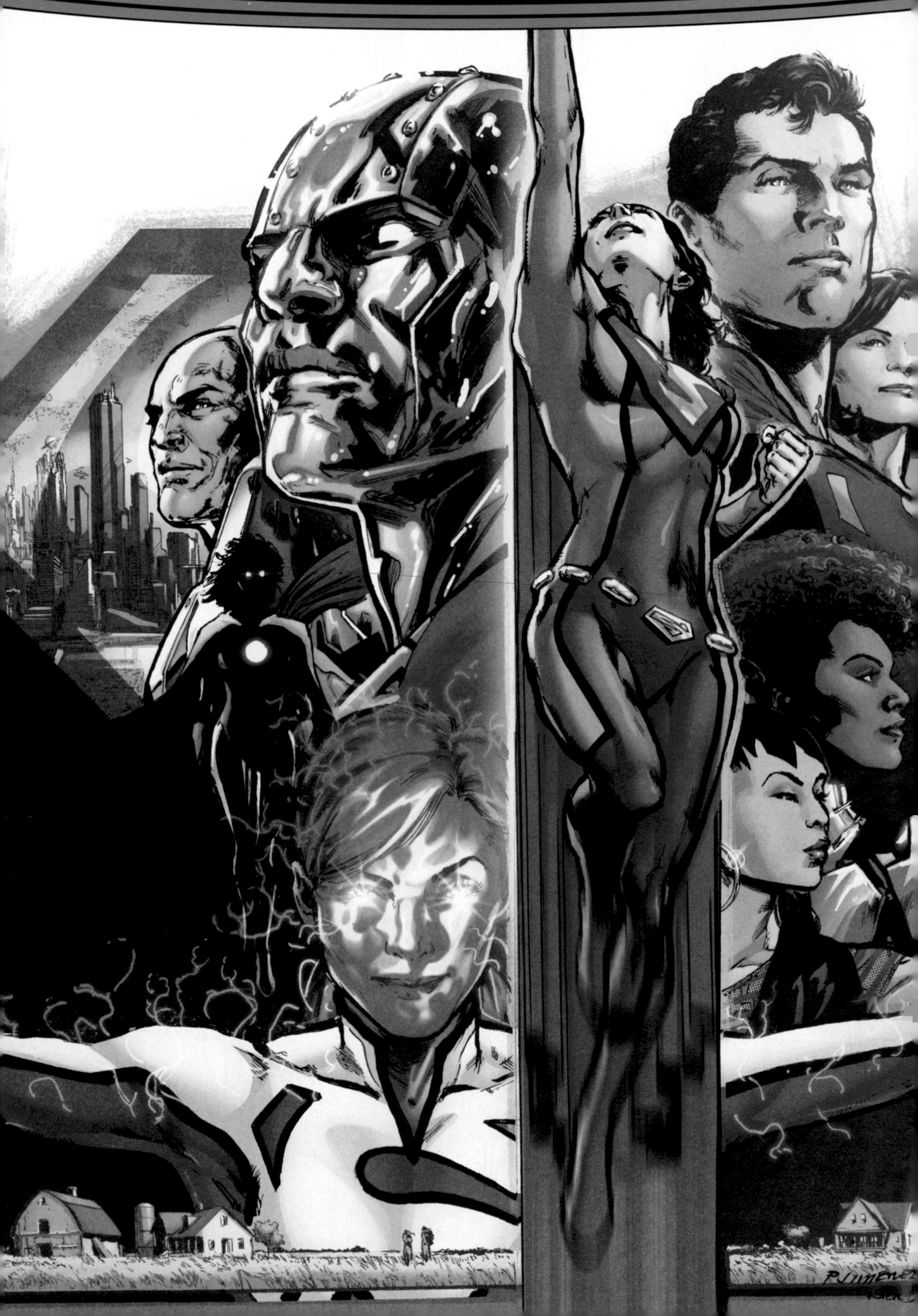

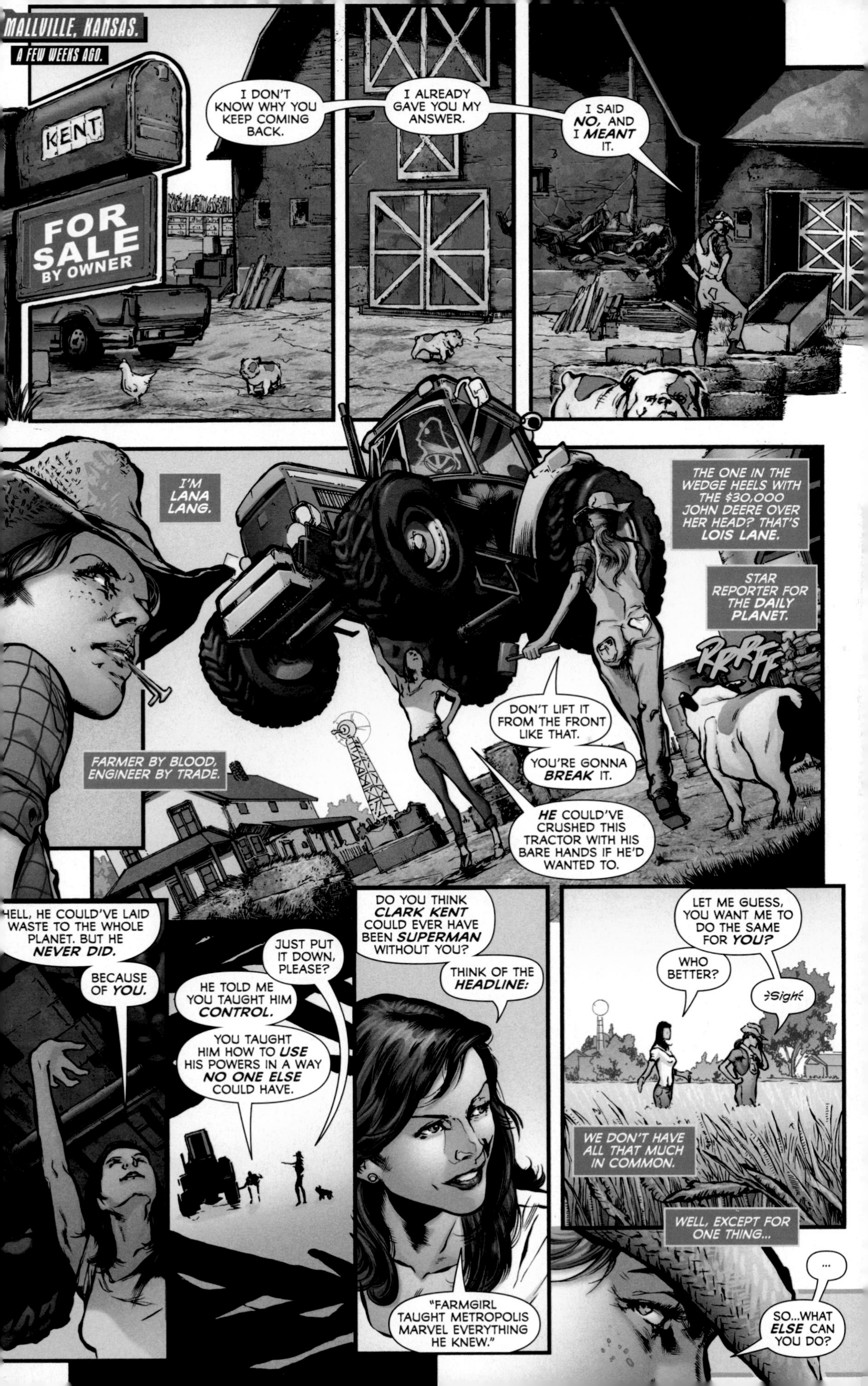

MALLVILLE, KANSAS.
A FEW WEEKS AGO.
KENT
FOR SALE BY OWNER
I DON'T KNOW WHY YOU KEEP COMING BACK.
I ALREADY GAVE YOU MY ANSWER.
I SAID NO, AND I MEANT IT.
I'M LANA LANG.
THE ONE IN THE WEDGE HEELS WITH THE $30,000 JOHN DEERE OVER HER HEAD? THAT'S LOIS LANE.
STAR REPORTER FOR THE DAILY PLANET.
RRRFF
DON'T LIFT IT FROM THE FRONT LIKE THAT.
YOU'RE GONNA BREAK IT.
FARMER BY BLOOD, ENGINEER BY TRADE.
HE COULD'VE CRUSHED THIS TRACTOR WITH HIS BARE HANDS IF HE'D WANTED TO.
HELL, HE COULD'VE LAID WASTE TO THE WHOLE PLANET. BUT HE NEVER DID.
BECAUSE OF YOU.
JUST PUT IT DOWN, PLEASE?
HE TOLD ME YOU TAUGHT HIM CONTROL.
YOU TAUGHT HIM HOW TO USE HIS POWERS IN A WAY NO ONE ELSE COULD HAVE.
DO YOU THINK CLARK KENT COULD EVER HAVE BEEN SUPERMAN WITHOUT YOU?
THINK OF THE HEADLINE:
"FARMGIRL TAUGHT METROPOLIS MARVEL EVERYTHING HE KNEW."
LET ME GUESS, YOU WANT ME TO DO THE SAME FOR YOU?
WHO BETTER?
Sigh
WE DON'T HAVE ALL THAT MUCH IN COMMON.
WELL, EXCEPT FOR ONE THING...
...
SO...WHAT ELSE CAN YOU DO?

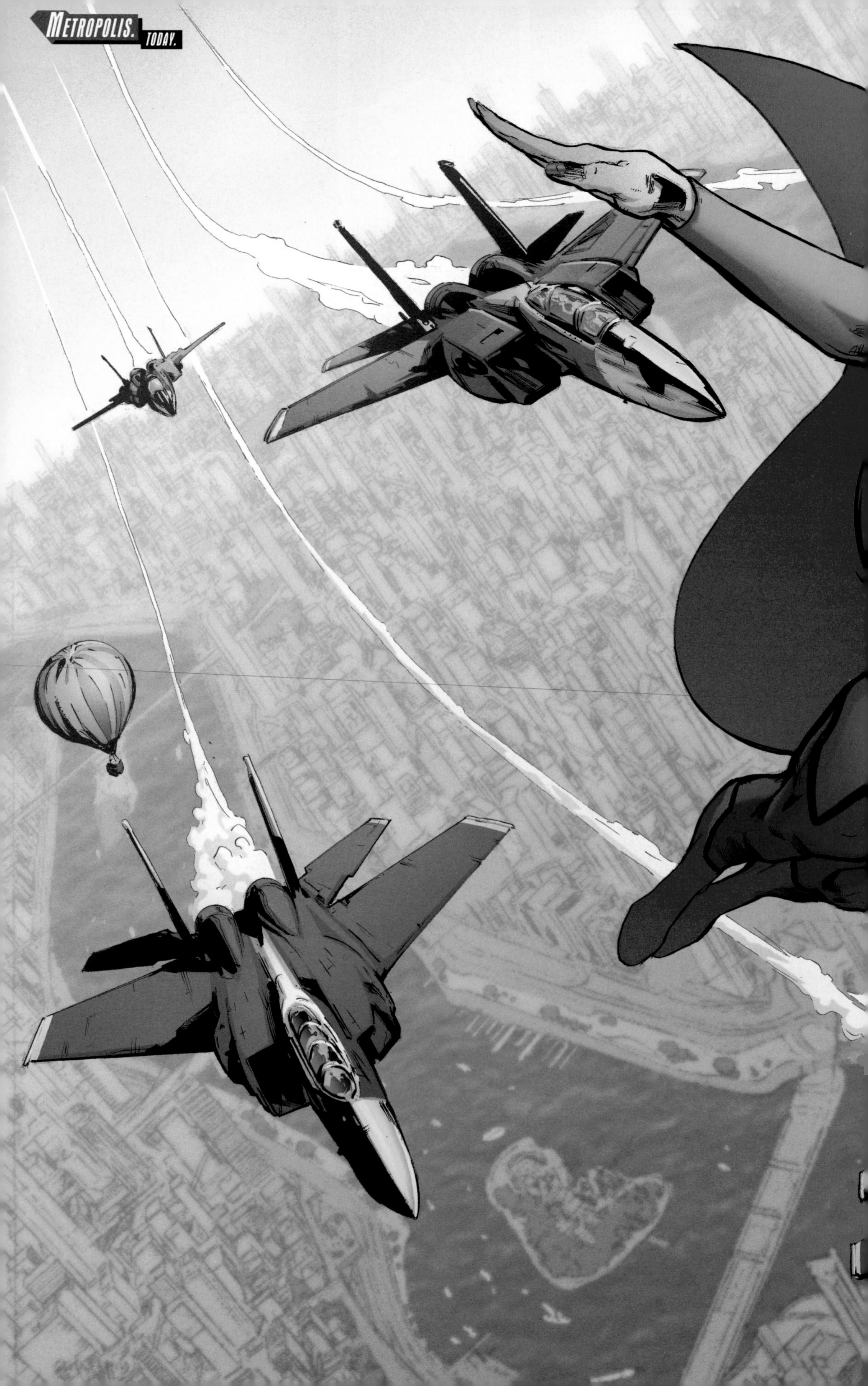
METROPOLIS. TODAY.

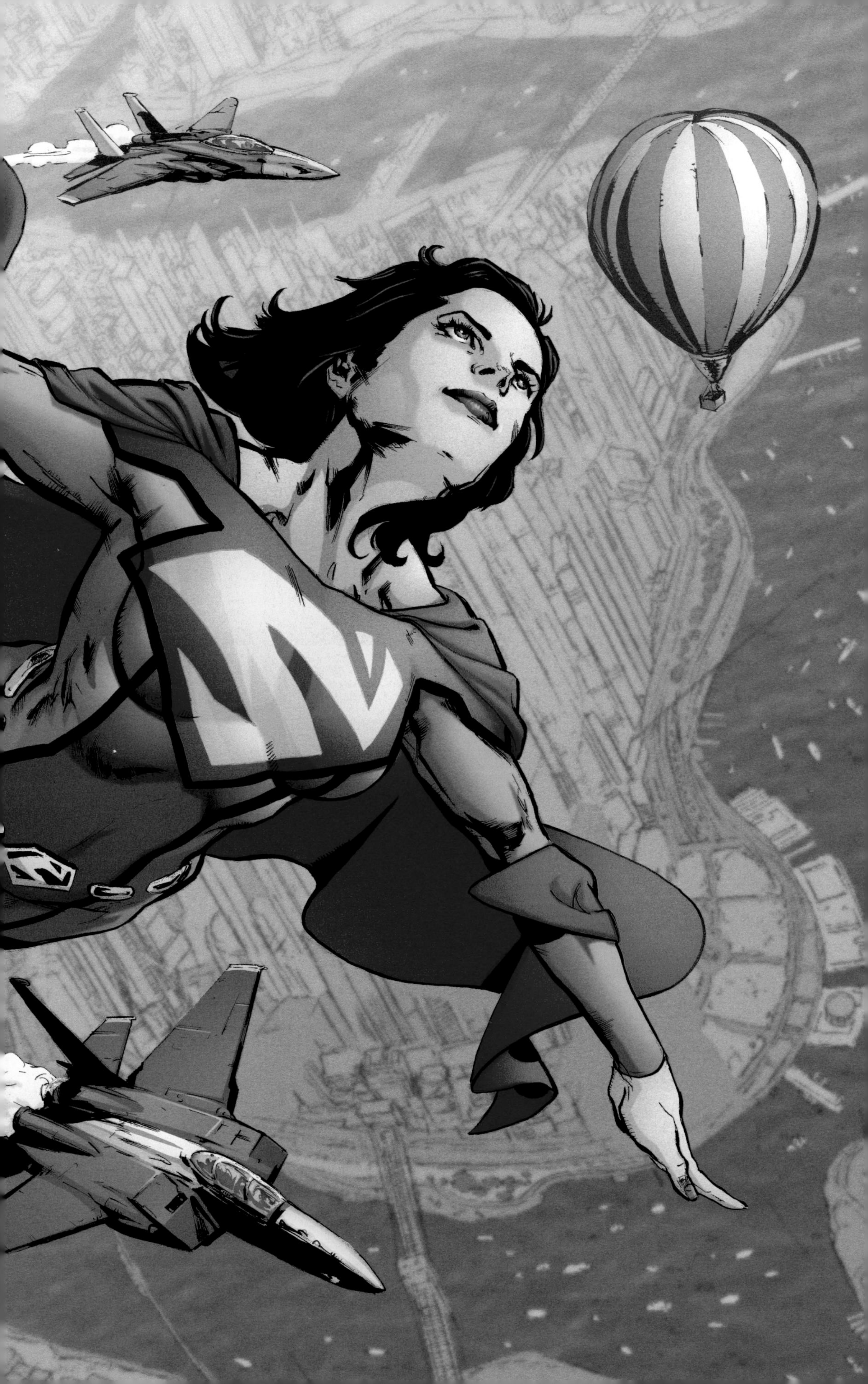

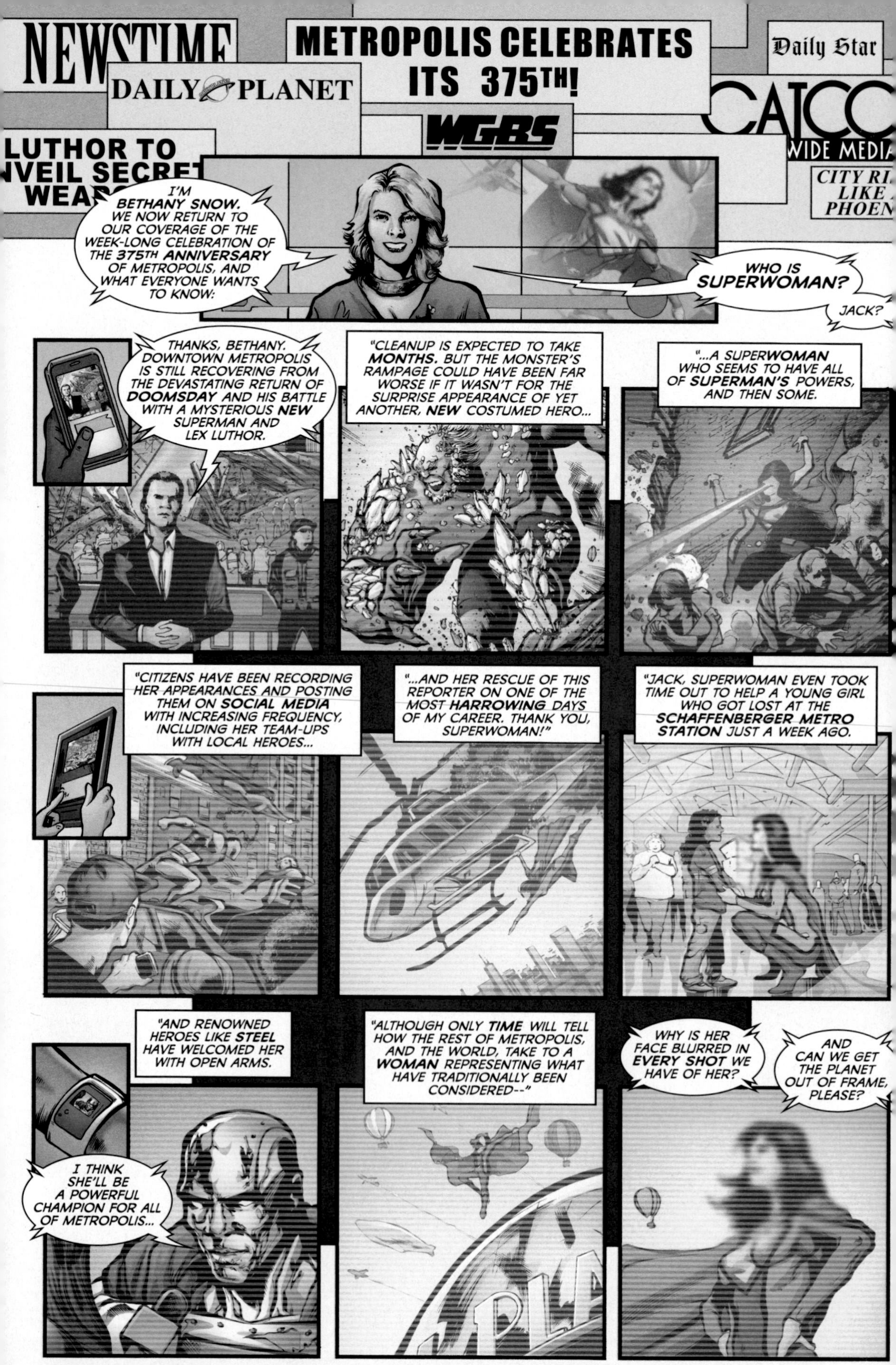
NEWSTIME
DAILY PLANET
METROPOLIS CELEBRATES ITS 375TH!
Daily Star
WGBS
CATCO WIDE MEDIA
LUTHOR TO UNVEIL SECRET WEAPON
CITY RISES LIKE A PHOENIX
I'M BETHANY SNOW. WE NOW RETURN TO OUR COVERAGE OF THE WEEK-LONG CELEBRATION OF THE 375TH ANNIVERSARY OF METROPOLIS, AND WHAT EVERYONE WANTS TO KNOW:
WHO IS SUPERWOMAN?
JACK?
THANKS, BETHANY. DOWNTOWN METROPOLIS IS STILL RECOVERING FROM THE DEVASTATING RETURN OF DOOMSDAY AND HIS BATTLE WITH A MYSTERIOUS NEW SUPERMAN AND LEX LUTHOR.
"CLEANUP IS EXPECTED TO TAKE MONTHS. BUT THE MONSTER'S RAMPAGE COULD HAVE BEEN FAR WORSE IF IT WASN'T FOR THE SURPRISE APPEARANCE OF YET ANOTHER, NEW COSTUMED HERO...
"...A SUPERWOMAN WHO SEEMS TO HAVE ALL OF SUPERMAN'S POWERS, AND THEN SOME.
"CITIZENS HAVE BEEN RECORDING HER APPEARANCES AND POSTING THEM ON SOCIAL MEDIA WITH INCREASING FREQUENCY, INCLUDING HER TEAM-UPS WITH LOCAL HEROES...
"...AND HER RESCUE OF THIS REPORTER ON ONE OF THE MOST HARROWING DAYS OF MY CAREER. THANK YOU, SUPERWOMAN!"
"JACK, SUPERWOMAN EVEN TOOK TIME OUT TO HELP A YOUNG GIRL WHO GOT LOST AT THE SCHAFFENBERGER METRO STATION JUST A WEEK AGO.
"AND RENOWNED HEROES LIKE STEEL HAVE WELCOMED HER WITH OPEN ARMS.
I THINK SHE'LL BE A POWERFUL CHAMPION FOR ALL OF METROPOLIS...
"ALTHOUGH ONLY TIME WILL TELL HOW THE REST OF METROPOLIS, AND THE WORLD, TAKE TO A WOMAN REPRESENTING WHAT HAVE TRADITIONALLY BEEN CONSIDERED--"
WHY IS HER FACE BLURRED IN EVERY SHOT WE HAVE OF HER?
AND CAN WE GET THE PLANET OUT OF FRAME, PLEASE?

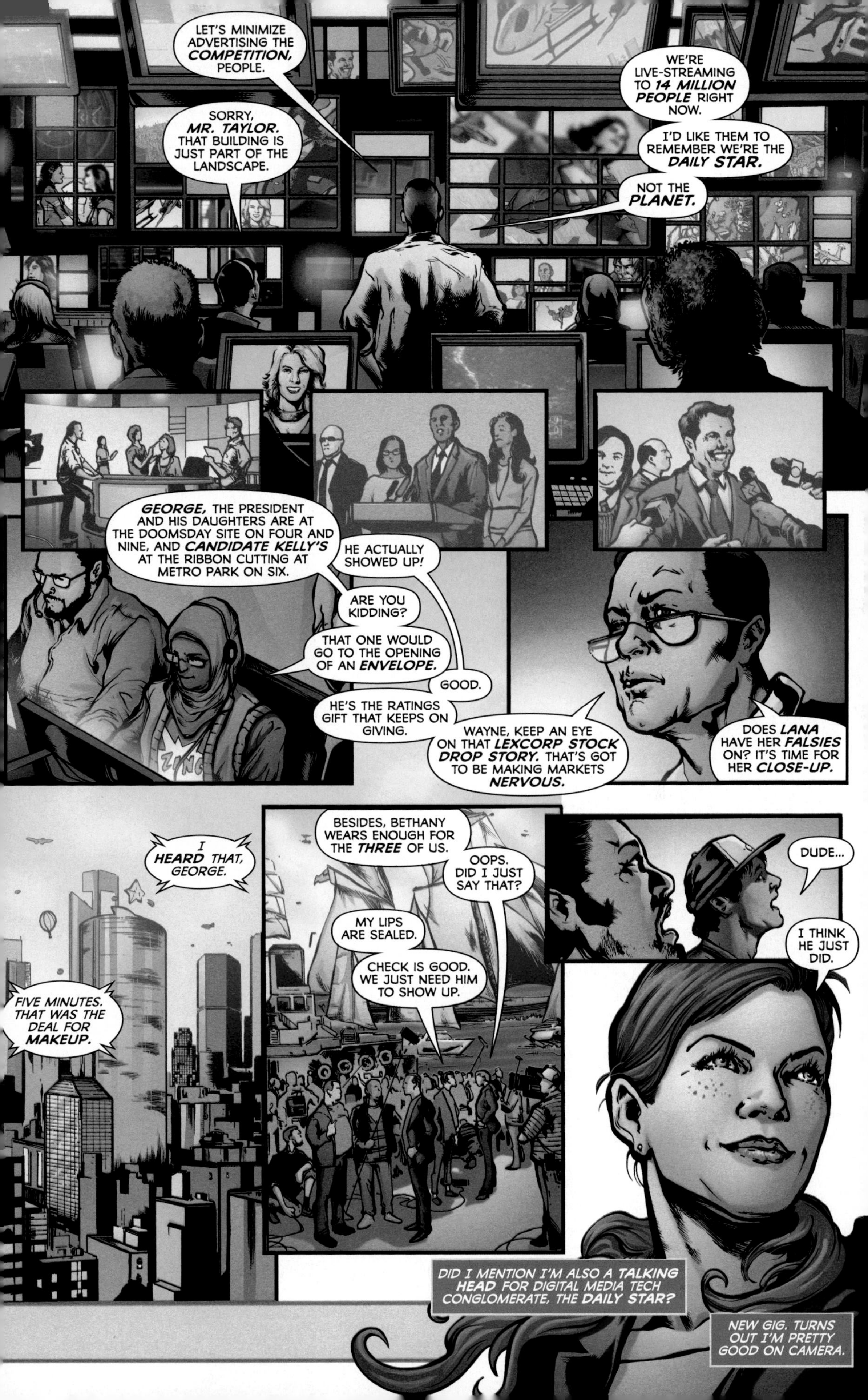
LET'S MINIMIZE ADVERTISING THE COMPETITION, PEOPLE.
SORRY, MR. TAYLOR. THAT BUILDING IS JUST PART OF THE LANDSCAPE.
WE'RE LIVE-STREAMING TO 14 MILLION PEOPLE RIGHT NOW.
I'D LIKE THEM TO REMEMBER WE'RE THE DAILY STAR.
NOT THE PLANET.
GEORGE, THE PRESIDENT AND HIS DAUGHTERS ARE AT THE DOOMSDAY SITE ON FOUR AND NINE, AND CANDIDATE KELLY'S AT THE RIBBON CUTTING AT METRO PARK ON SIX.
HE ACTUALLY SHOWED UP!
ARE YOU KIDDING?
THAT ONE WOULD GO TO THE OPENING OF AN ENVELOPE.
GOOD.
HE'S THE RATINGS GIFT THAT KEEPS ON GIVING.
WAYNE, KEEP AN EYE ON THAT LEXCORP STOCK DROP STORY. THAT'S GOT TO BE MAKING MARKETS NERVOUS.
DOES LANA HAVE HER FALSIES ON? IT'S TIME FOR HER CLOSE-UP.
I HEARD THAT, GEORGE.
FIVE MINUTES. THAT WAS THE DEAL FOR MAKEUP.
BESIDES, BETHANY WEARS ENOUGH FOR THE THREE OF US.
OOPS. DID I JUST SAY THAT?
MY LIPS ARE SEALED.
CHECK IS GOOD. WE JUST NEED HIM TO SHOW UP.
DUDE...
I THINK HE JUST DID.
DID I MENTION I'M ALSO A TALKING HEAD FOR DIGITAL MEDIA TECH CONGLOMERATE, THE DAILY STAR?
NEW GIG. TURNS OUT I'M PRETTY GOOD ON CAMERA.

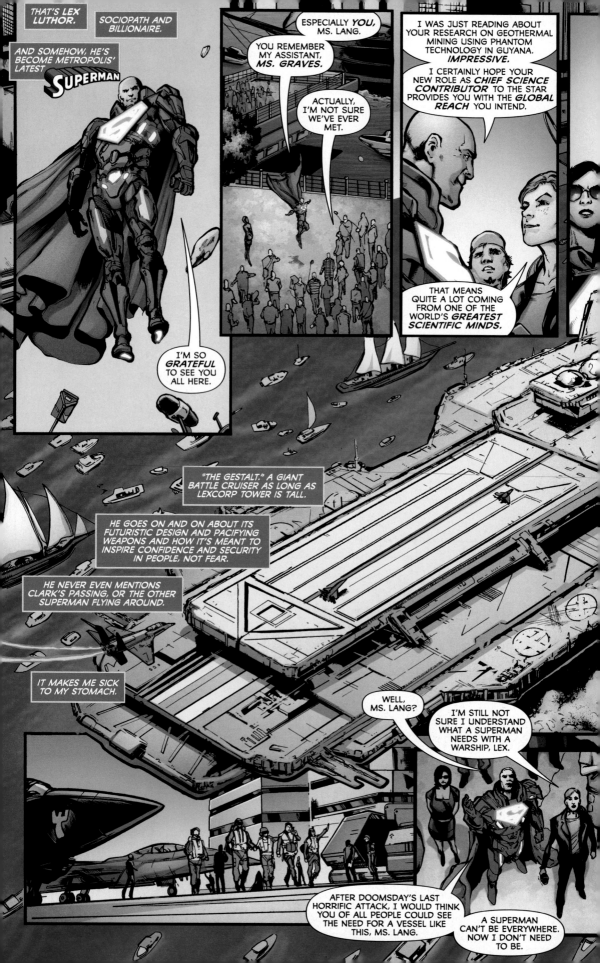

THAT'S *LEX LUTHOR.* SOCIOPATH AND BILLIONAIRE.

AND SOMEHOW, HE'S BECOME METROPOLIS' LATEST **SUPERMAN**

I'M SO *GRATEFUL* TO SEE YOU ALL HERE.

ESPECIALLY *YOU,* MS. LANG.

YOU REMEMBER MY ASSISTANT, *MS. GRAVES.*

ACTUALLY, I'M NOT SURE WE'VE EVER MET.

I WAS JUST READING ABOUT YOUR RESEARCH ON GEOTHERMAL MINING USING PHANTOM TECHNOLOGY IN GUYANA. *IMPRESSIVE.*

I CERTAINLY HOPE YOUR NEW ROLE AS *CHIEF SCIENCE CONTRIBUTOR* TO THE STAR PROVIDES YOU WITH THE *GLOBAL REACH* YOU INTEND.

THAT MEANS QUITE A LOT COMING FROM ONE OF THE WORLD'S *GREATEST SCIENTIFIC MINDS.*

"THE GESTALT." A GIANT BATTLE CRUISER AS LONG AS LEXCORP TOWER IS TALL.

HE GOES ON AND ON ABOUT ITS FUTURISTIC DESIGN AND PACIFYING WEAPONS AND HOW IT'S MEANT TO INSPIRE CONFIDENCE AND SECURITY IN PEOPLE, NOT FEAR.

HE NEVER EVEN MENTIONS CLARK'S PASSING, OR THE OTHER SUPERMAN FLYING AROUND.

IT MAKES ME SICK TO MY STOMACH.

WELL, MS. LANG?

I'M STILL NOT SURE I UNDERSTAND WHAT A SUPERMAN NEEDS WITH A WARSHIP, LEX.

AFTER DOOMSDAY'S LAST HORRIFIC ATTACK, I WOULD THINK YOU OF ALL PEOPLE COULD SEE THE NEED FOR A VESSEL LIKE THIS, MS. LANG.

A SUPERMAN CAN'T BE EVERYWHERE. NOW I DON'T NEED TO BE.

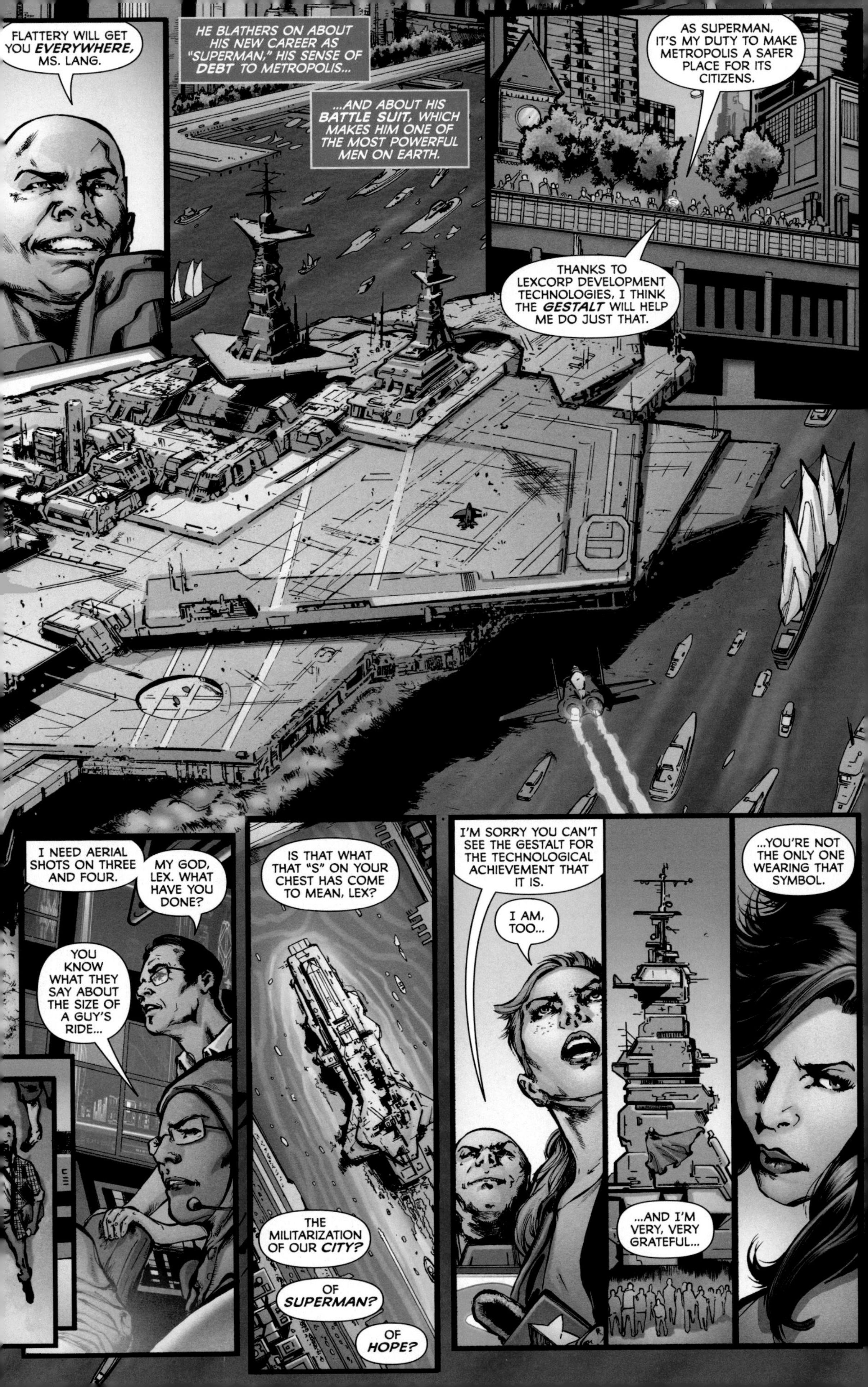
FLATTERY WILL GET YOU EVERYWHERE, MS. LANG.
HE BLATHERS ON ABOUT HIS NEW CAREER AS "SUPERMAN," HIS SENSE OF DEBT TO METROPOLIS...
...AND ABOUT HIS BATTLE SUIT, WHICH MAKES HIM ONE OF THE MOST POWERFUL MEN ON EARTH.
AS SUPERMAN, IT'S MY DUTY TO MAKE METROPOLIS A SAFER PLACE FOR ITS CITIZENS.
THANKS TO LEXCORP DEVELOPMENT TECHNOLOGIES, I THINK THE GESTALT WILL HELP ME DO JUST THAT.
I NEED AERIAL SHOTS ON THREE AND FOUR.
MY GOD, LEX. WHAT HAVE YOU DONE?
YOU KNOW WHAT THEY SAY ABOUT THE SIZE OF A GUY'S RIDE...
IS THAT WHAT THAT "S" ON YOUR CHEST HAS COME TO MEAN, LEX?
THE MILITARIZATION OF OUR CITY?
OF SUPERMAN?
OF HOPE?
I'M SORRY YOU CAN'T SEE THE GESTALT FOR THE TECHNOLOGICAL ACHIEVEMENT THAT IT IS.
I AM, TOO...
...AND I'M VERY, VERY GRATEFUL...
...YOU'RE NOT THE ONLY ONE WEARING THAT SYMBOL.

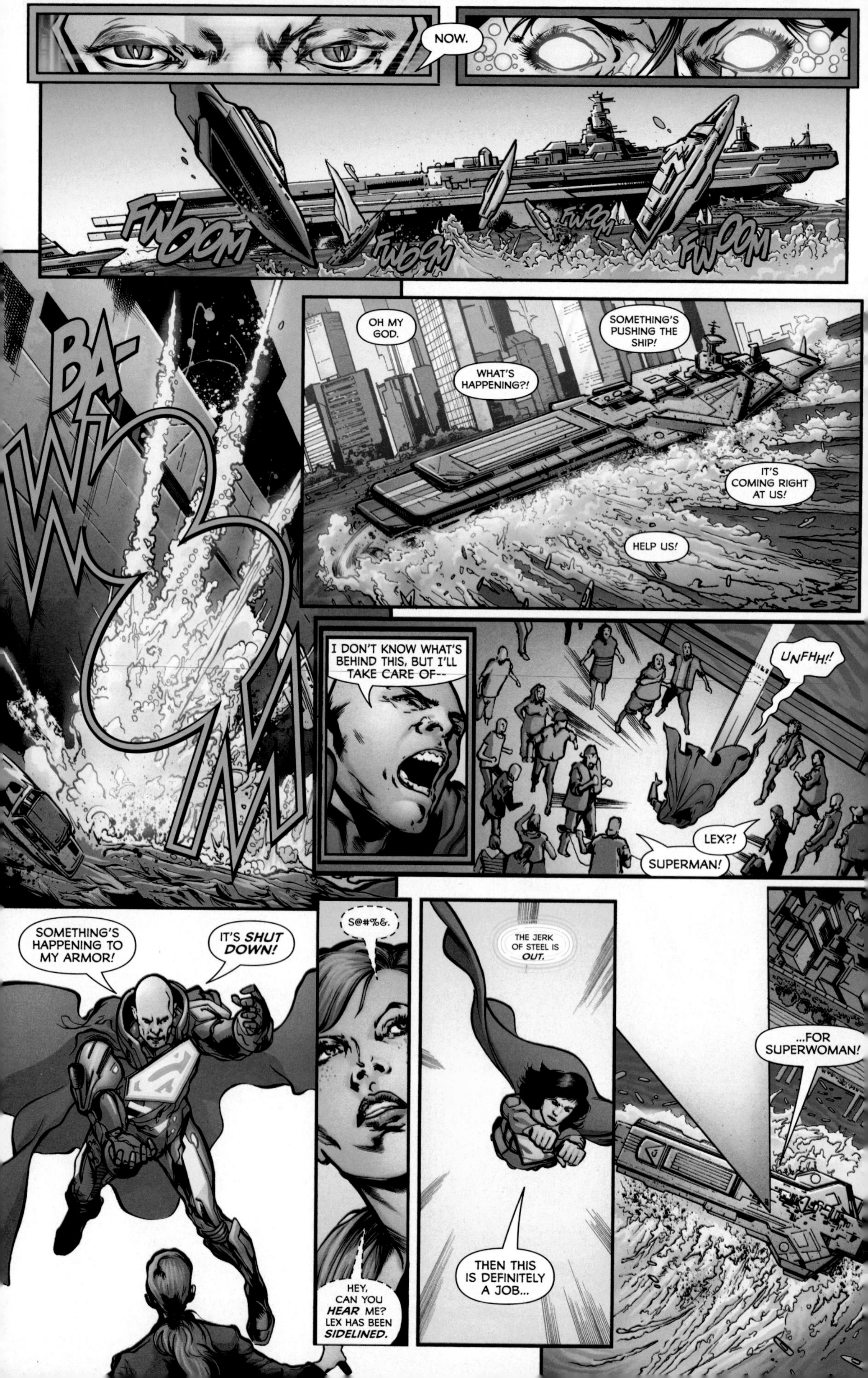
NOW.
FWOOM
FWOOM
FWOOM
FWOOM
BA-WOOM
OH MY GOD.
SOMETHING'S PUSHING THE SHIP!
WHAT'S HAPPENING?!
IT'S COMING RIGHT AT US!
HELP US!
I DON'T KNOW WHAT'S BEHIND THIS, BUT I'LL TAKE CARE OF--
UNFHH!!
LEX?!
SUPERMAN!
SOMETHING'S HAPPENING TO MY ARMOR!
IT'S SHUT DOWN!
S@#%&.
HEY, CAN YOU HEAR ME? LEX HAS BEEN SIDELINED.
THE JERK OF STEEL IS OUT.
THEN THIS IS DEFINITELY A JOB...
...FOR SUPERWOMAN!

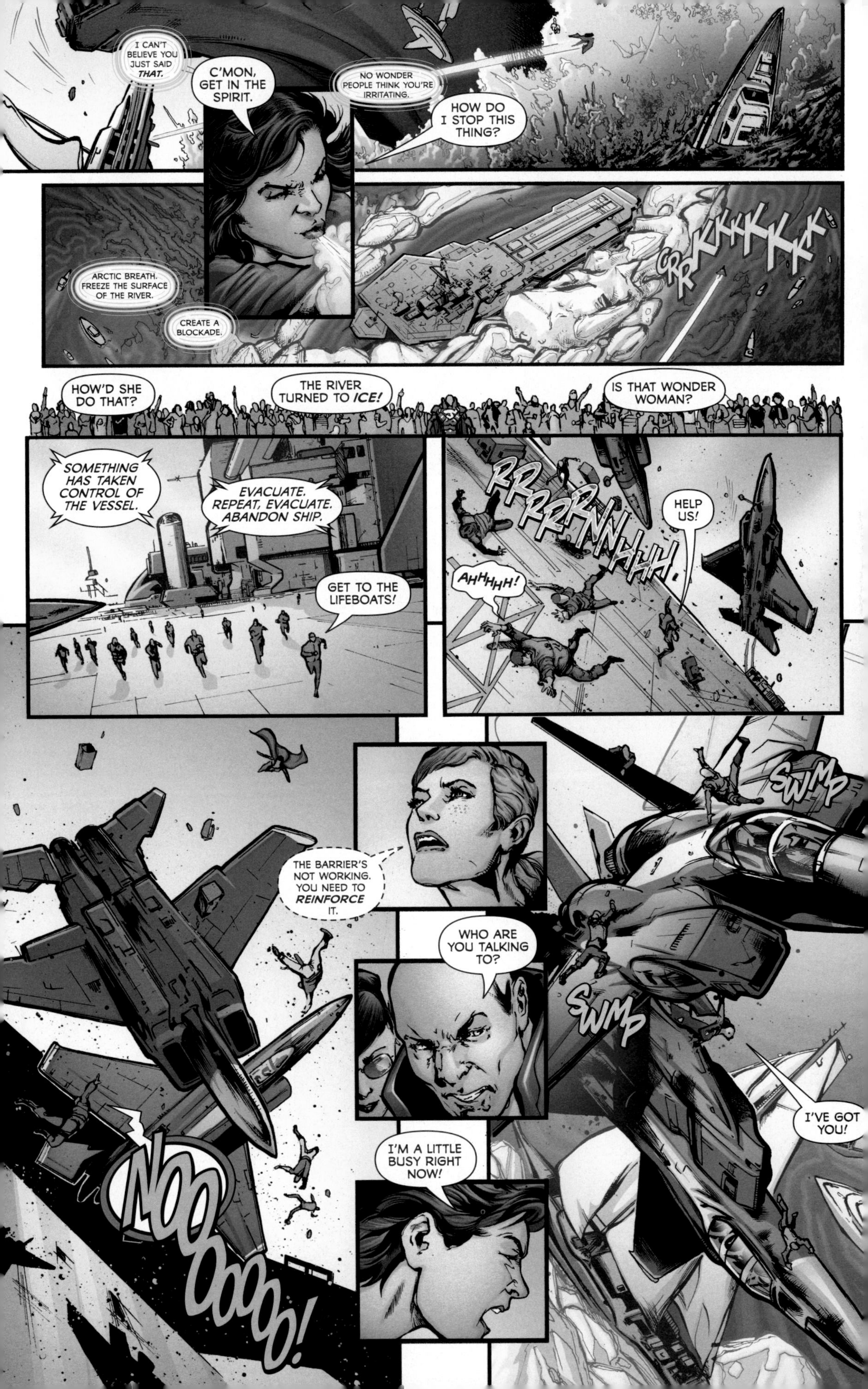
I CAN'T BELIEVE YOU JUST SAID THAT.
C'MON, GET IN THE SPIRIT.
NO WONDER PEOPLE THINK YOU'RE IRRITATING.
HOW DO I STOP THIS THING?
ARCTIC BREATH. FREEZE THE SURFACE OF THE RIVER.
CREATE A BLOCKADE.
CRRKKKKKKKK
HOW'D SHE DO THAT?
THE RIVER TURNED TO ICE!
IS THAT WONDER WOMAN?
SOMETHING HAS TAKEN CONTROL OF THE VESSEL.
EVACUATE. REPEAT, EVACUATE. ABANDON SHIP.
GET TO THE LIFEBOATS!
RRRRRNNHHH
HELP US!
AHHHHH!
THE BARRIER'S NOT WORKING. YOU NEED TO REINFORCE IT.
WHO ARE YOU TALKING TO?
I'M A LITTLE BUSY RIGHT NOW!
NOOOOOOO!
SWMP
SWMP
I'VE GOT YOU!

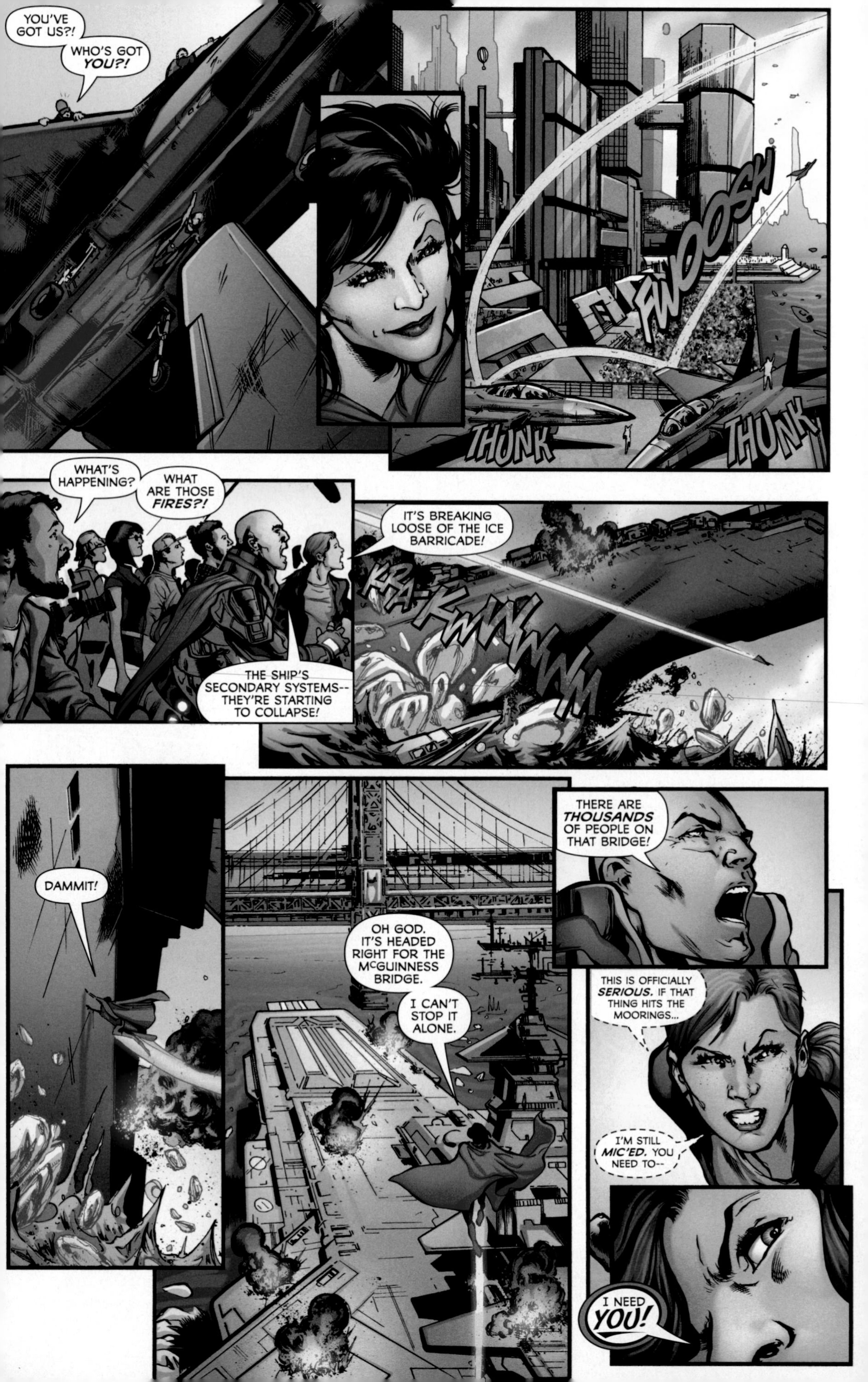
YOU'VE GOT US?!
WHO'S GOT YOU?!
FWOOSH
THUNK
THUNK
WHAT'S HAPPENING?
WHAT ARE THOSE FIRES?!
IT'S BREAKING LOOSE OF THE ICE BARRICADE!
THE SHIP'S SECONDARY SYSTEMS-- THEY'RE STARTING TO COLLAPSE!
KRA-KWANNNNM
DAMMIT!
OH GOD. IT'S HEADED RIGHT FOR THE McGUINNESS BRIDGE.
I CAN'T STOP IT ALONE.
THERE ARE THOUSANDS OF PEOPLE ON THAT BRIDGE!
THIS IS OFFICIALLY SERIOUS. IF THAT THING HITS THE MOORINGS...
I'M STILL MIC'ED. YOU NEED TO--
I NEED YOU!

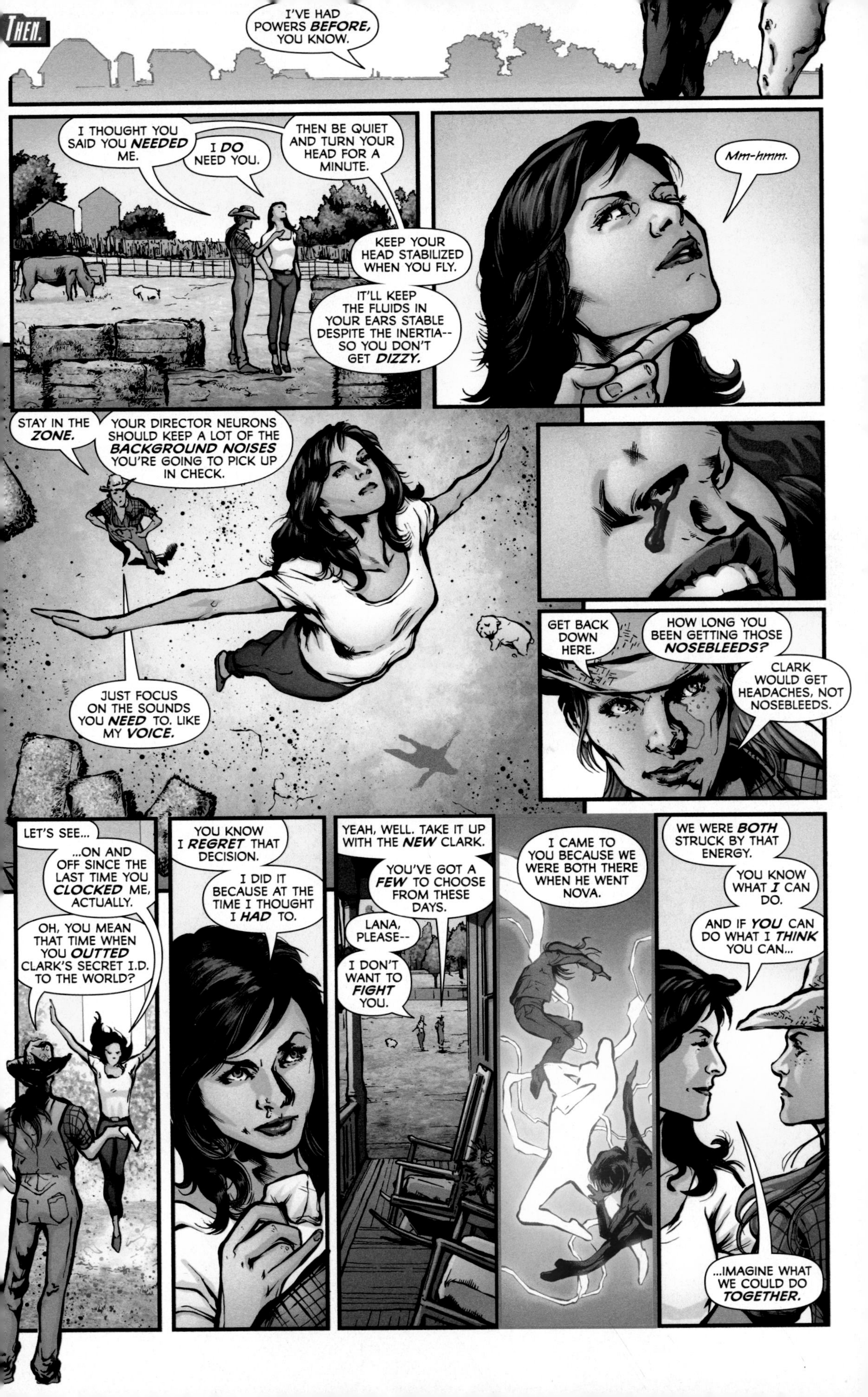
THEN.
I'VE HAD POWERS BEFORE, YOU KNOW.
I THOUGHT YOU SAID YOU NEEDED ME.
I DO NEED YOU.
THEN BE QUIET AND TURN YOUR HEAD FOR A MINUTE.
KEEP YOUR HEAD STABILIZED WHEN YOU FLY.
IT'LL KEEP THE FLUIDS IN YOUR EARS STABLE DESPITE THE INERTIA-- SO YOU DON'T GET DIZZY.
Mm-hmm.
STAY IN THE ZONE.
YOUR DIRECTOR NEURONS SHOULD KEEP A LOT OF THE BACKGROUND NOISES YOU'RE GOING TO PICK UP IN CHECK.
JUST FOCUS ON THE SOUNDS YOU NEED TO. LIKE MY VOICE.
GET BACK DOWN HERE.
HOW LONG YOU BEEN GETTING THOSE NOSEBLEEDS?
CLARK WOULD GET HEADACHES, NOT NOSEBLEEDS.
LET'S SEE...
...ON AND OFF SINCE THE LAST TIME YOU CLOCKED ME, ACTUALLY.
OH, YOU MEAN THAT TIME WHEN YOU OUTTED CLARK'S SECRET I.D. TO THE WORLD?
YOU KNOW I REGRET THAT DECISION.
I DID IT BECAUSE AT THE TIME I THOUGHT I HAD TO.
YEAH, WELL. TAKE IT UP WITH THE NEW CLARK.
YOU'VE GOT A FEW TO CHOOSE FROM THESE DAYS.
LANA, PLEASE--
I DON'T WANT TO FIGHT YOU.
I CAME TO YOU BECAUSE WE WERE BOTH THERE WHEN HE WENT NOVA.
WE WERE BOTH STRUCK BY THAT ENERGY.
YOU KNOW WHAT I CAN DO.
AND IF YOU CAN DO WHAT I THINK YOU CAN...
...IMAGINE WHAT WE COULD DO TOGETHER.

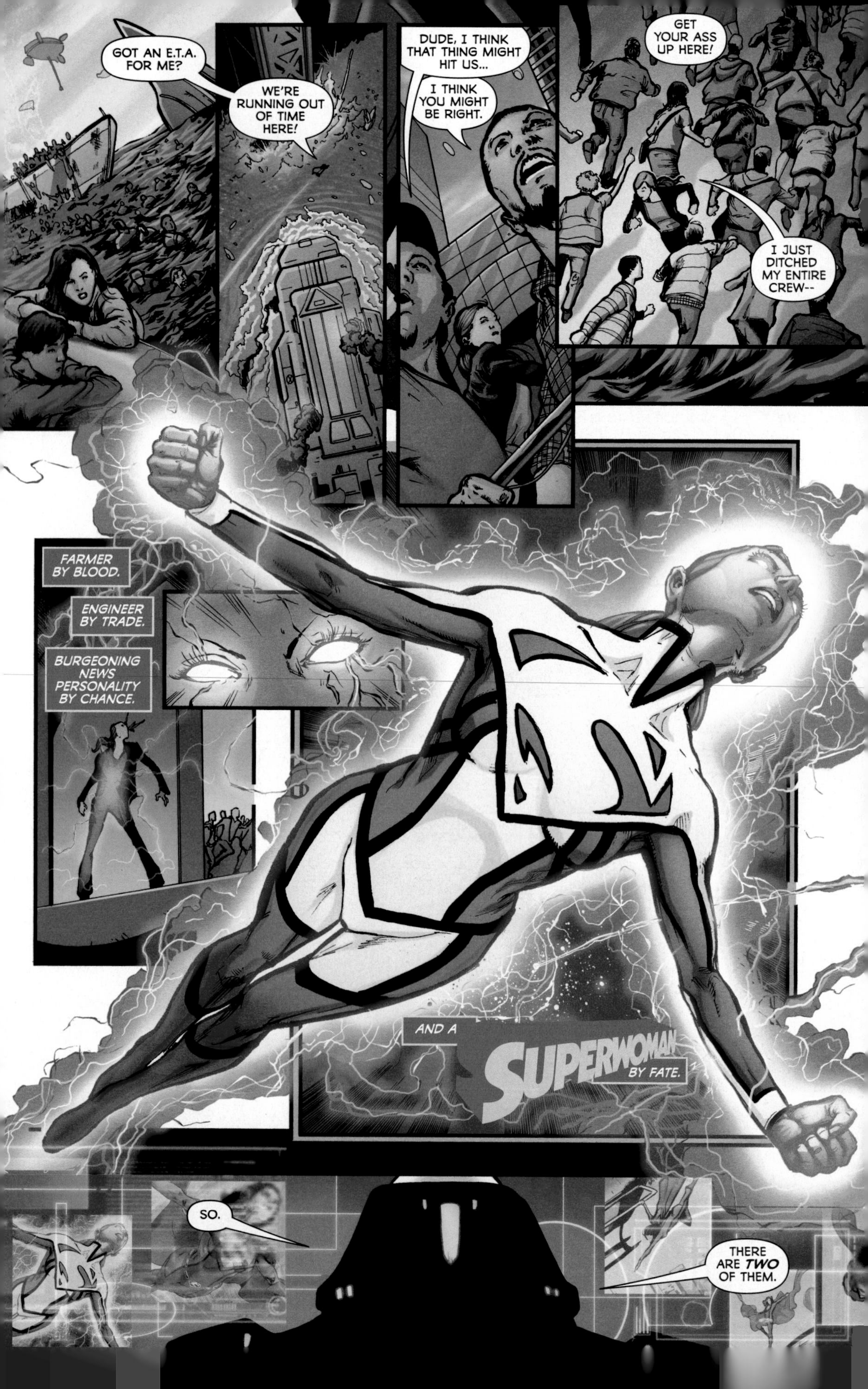
GOT AN E.T.A. FOR ME?
WE'RE RUNNING OUT OF TIME HERE!
DUDE, I THINK THAT THING MIGHT HIT US...
I THINK YOU MIGHT BE RIGHT.
GET YOUR ASS UP HERE!
I JUST DITCHED MY ENTIRE CREW--
FARMER BY BLOOD.
ENGINEER BY TRADE.
BURGEONING NEWS PERSONALITY BY CHANCE.
AND A SUPERWOMAN BY FATE.
SO.
THERE ARE TWO OF THEM.

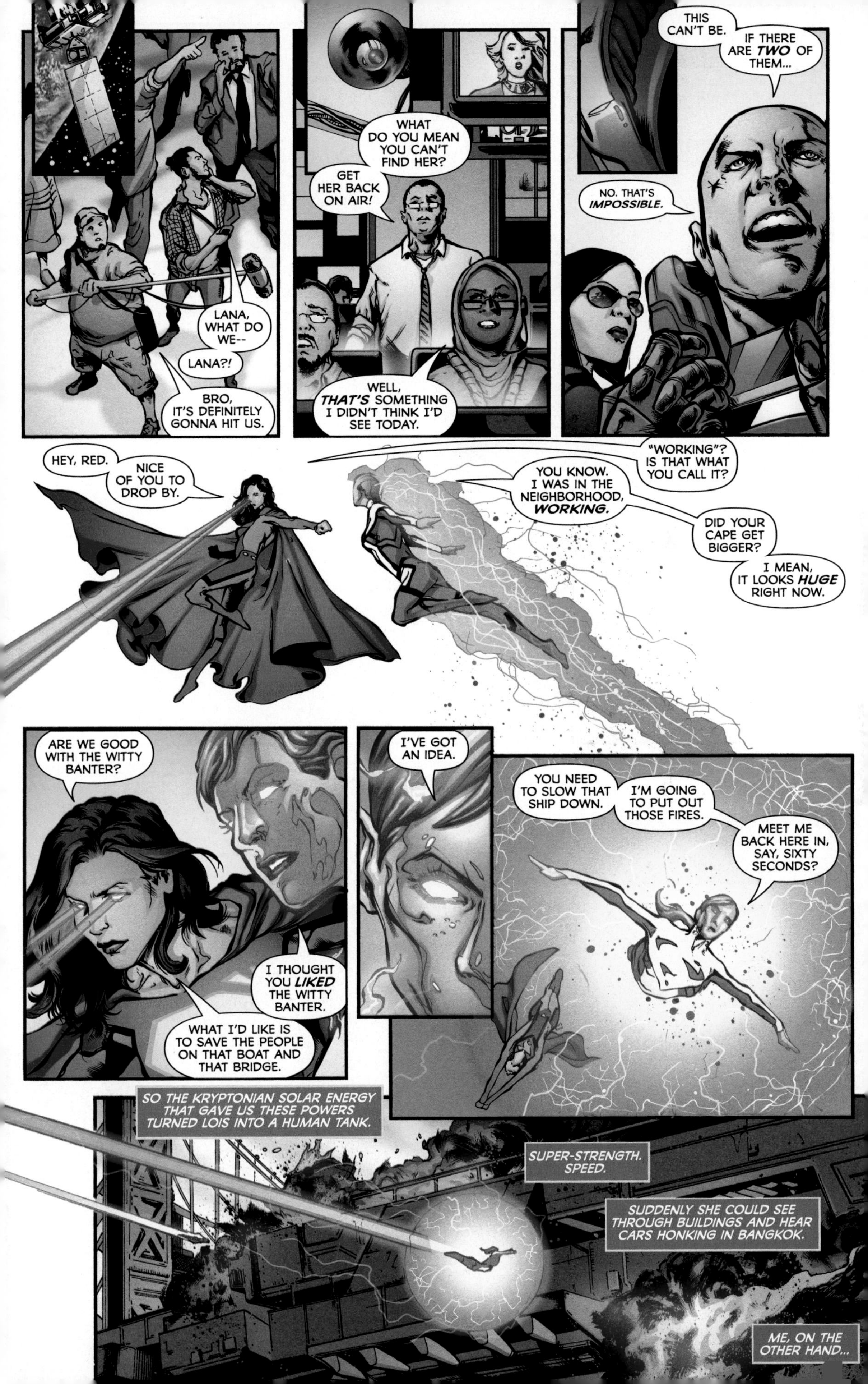
LANA, WHAT DO WE--
LANA?!
BRO, IT'S DEFINITELY GONNA HIT US.
WHAT DO YOU MEAN YOU CAN'T FIND HER?
GET HER BACK ON AIR!
WELL, THAT'S SOMETHING I DIDN'T THINK I'D SEE TODAY.
THIS CAN'T BE.
IF THERE ARE TWO OF THEM...
NO. THAT'S IMPOSSIBLE.
HEY, RED.
NICE OF YOU TO DROP BY.
"WORKING"? IS THAT WHAT YOU CALL IT?
YOU KNOW. I WAS IN THE NEIGHBORHOOD, WORKING.
DID YOUR CAPE GET BIGGER?
I MEAN, IT LOOKS HUGE RIGHT NOW.
ARE WE GOOD WITH THE WITTY BANTER?
I THOUGHT YOU LIKED THE WITTY BANTER.
WHAT I'D LIKE IS TO SAVE THE PEOPLE ON THAT BOAT AND THAT BRIDGE.
I'VE GOT AN IDEA.
YOU NEED TO SLOW THAT SHIP DOWN.
I'M GOING TO PUT OUT THOSE FIRES.
MEET ME BACK HERE IN, SAY, SIXTY SECONDS?
SO THE KRYPTONIAN SOLAR ENERGY THAT GAVE US THESE POWERS TURNED LOIS INTO A HUMAN TANK.
SUPER-STRENGTH. SPEED.
SUDDENLY SHE COULD SEE THROUGH BUILDINGS AND HEAR CARS HONKING IN BANGKOK.
ME, ON THE OTHER HAND...

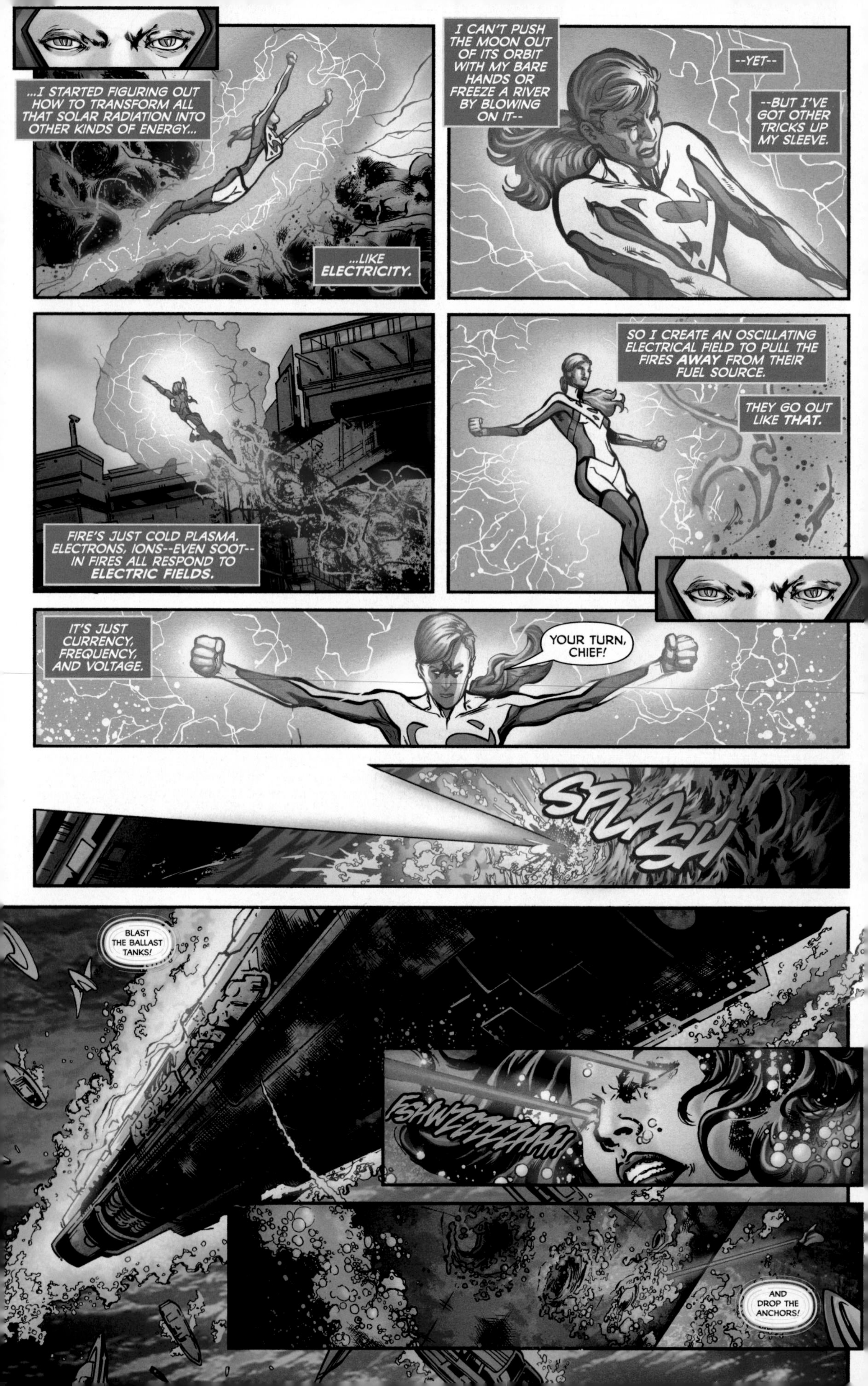
...I STARTED FIGURING OUT HOW TO TRANSFORM ALL THAT SOLAR RADIATION INTO OTHER KINDS OF ENERGY...
...LIKE ELECTRICITY.
I CAN'T PUSH THE MOON OUT OF ITS ORBIT WITH MY BARE HANDS OR FREEZE A RIVER BY BLOWING ON IT--
--YET--
--BUT I'VE GOT OTHER TRICKS UP MY SLEEVE.
FIRE'S JUST COLD PLASMA. ELECTRONS, IONS--EVEN SOOT--IN FIRES ALL RESPOND TO ELECTRIC FIELDS.
SO I CREATE AN OSCILLATING ELECTRICAL FIELD TO PULL THE FIRES AWAY FROM THEIR FUEL SOURCE.
THEY GO OUT LIKE THAT.
IT'S JUST CURRENCY, FREQUENCY, AND VOLTAGE.
YOUR TURN, CHIEF!
SPLASH
BLAST THE BALLAST TANKS!
FSHWZZZZHH
AND DROP THE ANCHORS!

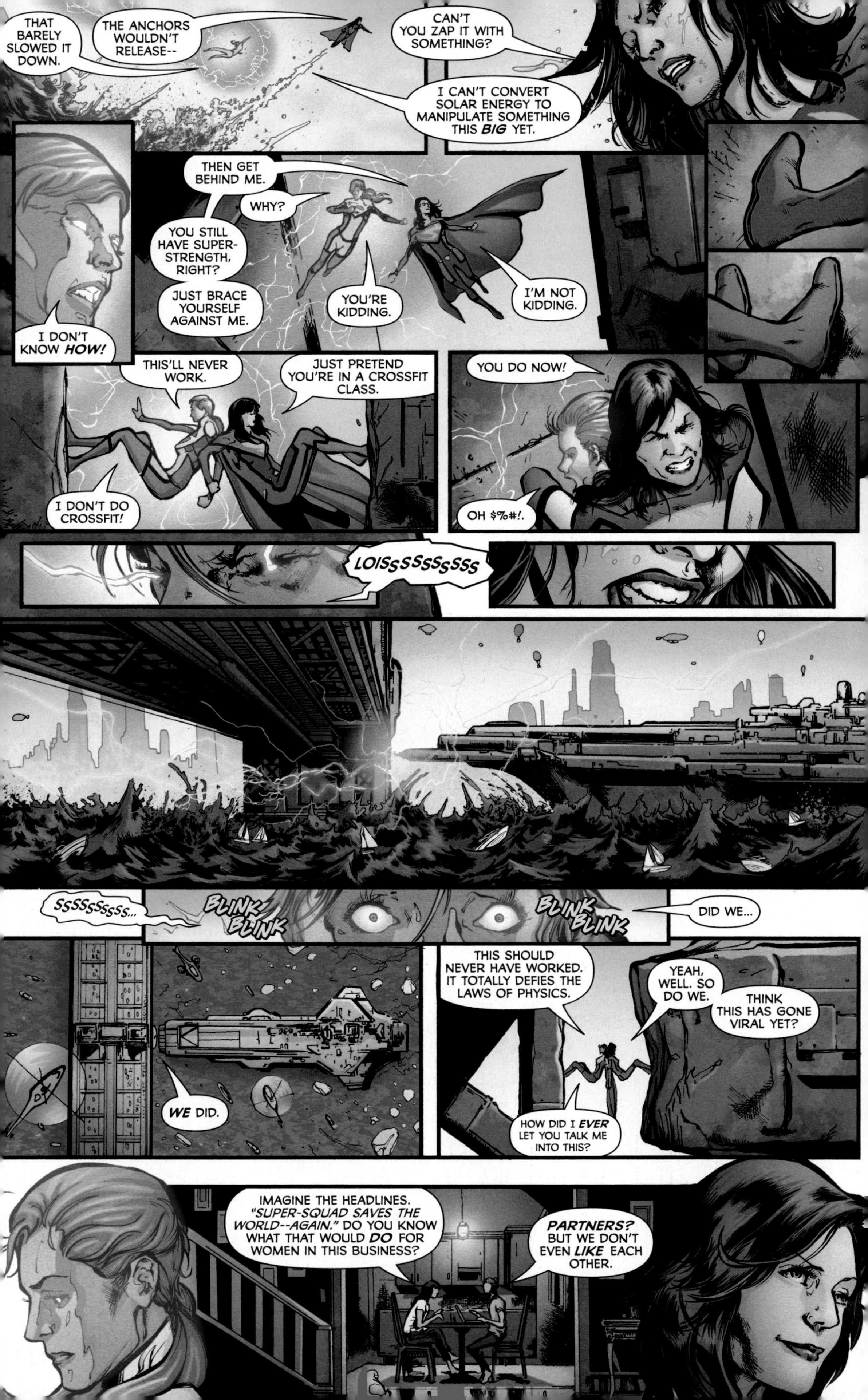
THE ANCHORS WOULDN'T RELEASE--
THAT BARELY SLOWED IT DOWN.
CAN'T YOU ZAP IT WITH SOMETHING?
I CAN'T CONVERT SOLAR ENERGY TO MANIPULATE SOMETHING THIS BIG YET.
THEN GET BEHIND ME.
WHY?
YOU STILL HAVE SUPER-STRENGTH, RIGHT?
JUST BRACE YOURSELF AGAINST ME.
YOU'RE KIDDING.
I'M NOT KIDDING.
I DON'T KNOW HOW!
THIS'LL NEVER WORK.
JUST PRETEND YOU'RE IN A CROSSFIT CLASS.
I DON'T DO CROSSFIT!
YOU DO NOW!
OH $%#!.
LOISSSSSSSSSS
SSSSSSSSS...
BLINK BLINK
BLINK BLINK
DID WE...
WE DID.
THIS SHOULD NEVER HAVE WORKED. IT TOTALLY DEFIES THE LAWS OF PHYSICS.
YEAH, WELL. SO DO WE.
THINK THIS HAS GONE VIRAL YET?
HOW DID I EVER LET YOU TALK ME INTO THIS?
IMAGINE THE HEADLINES. "SUPER-SQUAD SAVES THE WORLD--AGAIN." DO YOU KNOW WHAT THAT WOULD DO FOR WOMEN IN THIS BUSINESS?
PARTNERS? BUT WE DON'T EVEN LIKE EACH OTHER.

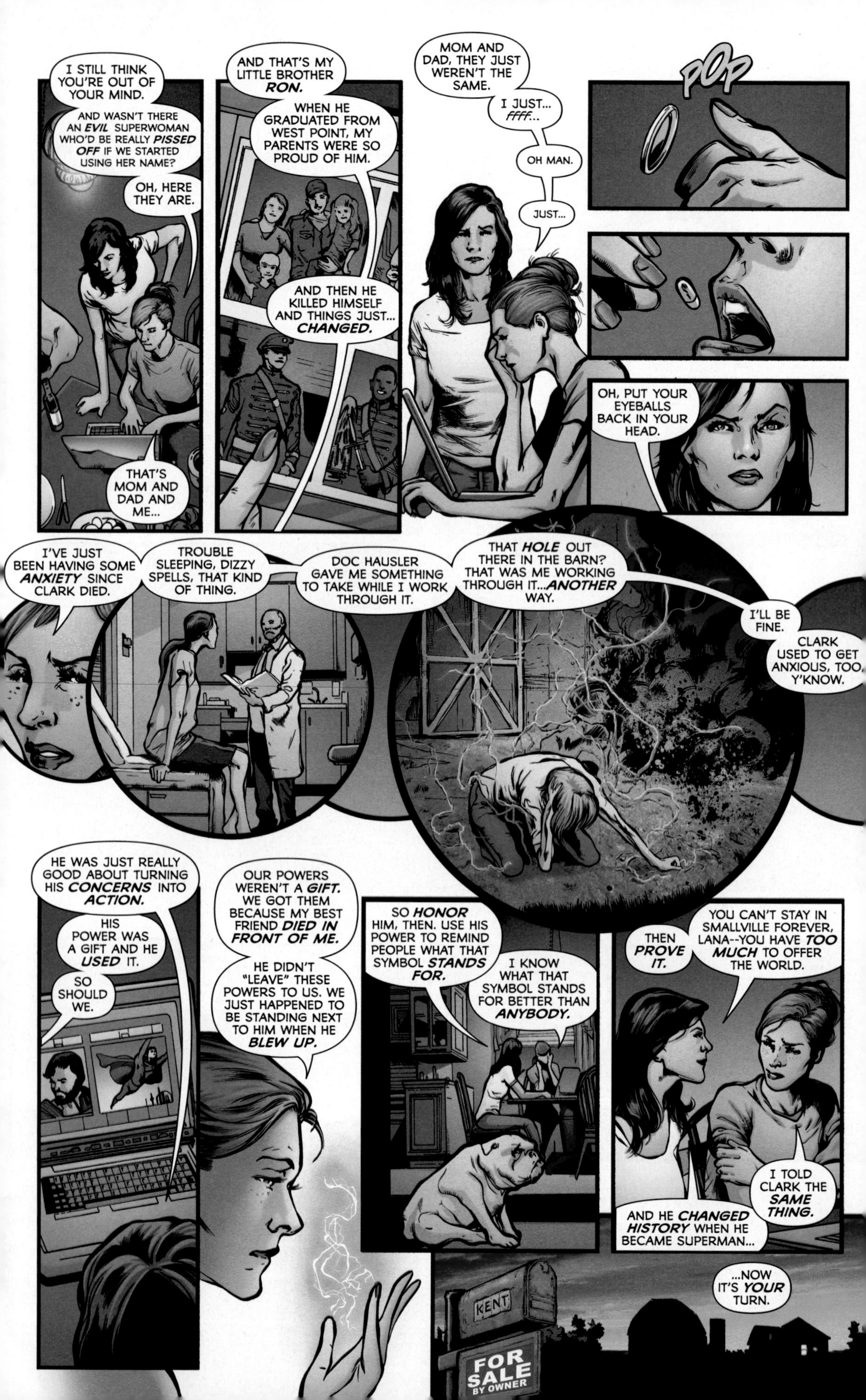

I STILL THINK YOU'RE OUT OF YOUR MIND.
AND WASN'T THERE AN EVIL SUPERWOMAN WHO'D BE REALLY PISSED OFF IF WE STARTED USING HER NAME?
OH, HERE THEY ARE.
THAT'S MOM AND DAD AND ME...
AND THAT'S MY LITTLE BROTHER RON.
WHEN HE GRADUATED FROM WEST POINT, MY PARENTS WERE SO PROUD OF HIM.
AND THEN HE KILLED HIMSELF AND THINGS JUST... CHANGED.
MOM AND DAD, THEY JUST WEREN'T THE SAME.
I JUST... FFFF...
OH MAN.
JUST...
POP
OH, PUT YOUR EYEBALLS BACK IN YOUR HEAD.
I'VE JUST BEEN HAVING SOME ANXIETY SINCE CLARK DIED.
TROUBLE SLEEPING, DIZZY SPELLS, THAT KIND OF THING.
DOC HAUSLER GAVE ME SOMETHING TO TAKE WHILE I WORK THROUGH IT.
THAT HOLE OUT THERE IN THE BARN? THAT WAS ME WORKING THROUGH IT...ANOTHER WAY.
I'LL BE FINE.
CLARK USED TO GET ANXIOUS, TOO, Y'KNOW.
HE WAS JUST REALLY GOOD ABOUT TURNING HIS CONCERNS INTO ACTION.
HIS POWER WAS A GIFT AND HE USED IT.
SO SHOULD WE.
OUR POWERS WEREN'T A GIFT. WE GOT THEM BECAUSE MY BEST FRIEND DIED IN FRONT OF ME.
HE DIDN'T "LEAVE" THESE POWERS TO US. WE JUST HAPPENED TO BE STANDING NEXT TO HIM WHEN HE BLEW UP.
SO HONOR HIM, THEN. USE HIS POWER TO REMIND PEOPLE WHAT THAT SYMBOL STANDS FOR.
I KNOW WHAT THAT SYMBOL STANDS FOR BETTER THAN ANYBODY.
THEN PROVE IT.
YOU CAN'T STAY IN SMALLVILLE FOREVER, LANA--YOU HAVE TOO MUCH TO OFFER THE WORLD.
I TOLD CLARK THE SAME THING.
AND HE CHANGED HISTORY WHEN HE BECAME SUPERMAN...
...NOW IT'S YOUR TURN.
KENT
FOR SALE BY OWNER

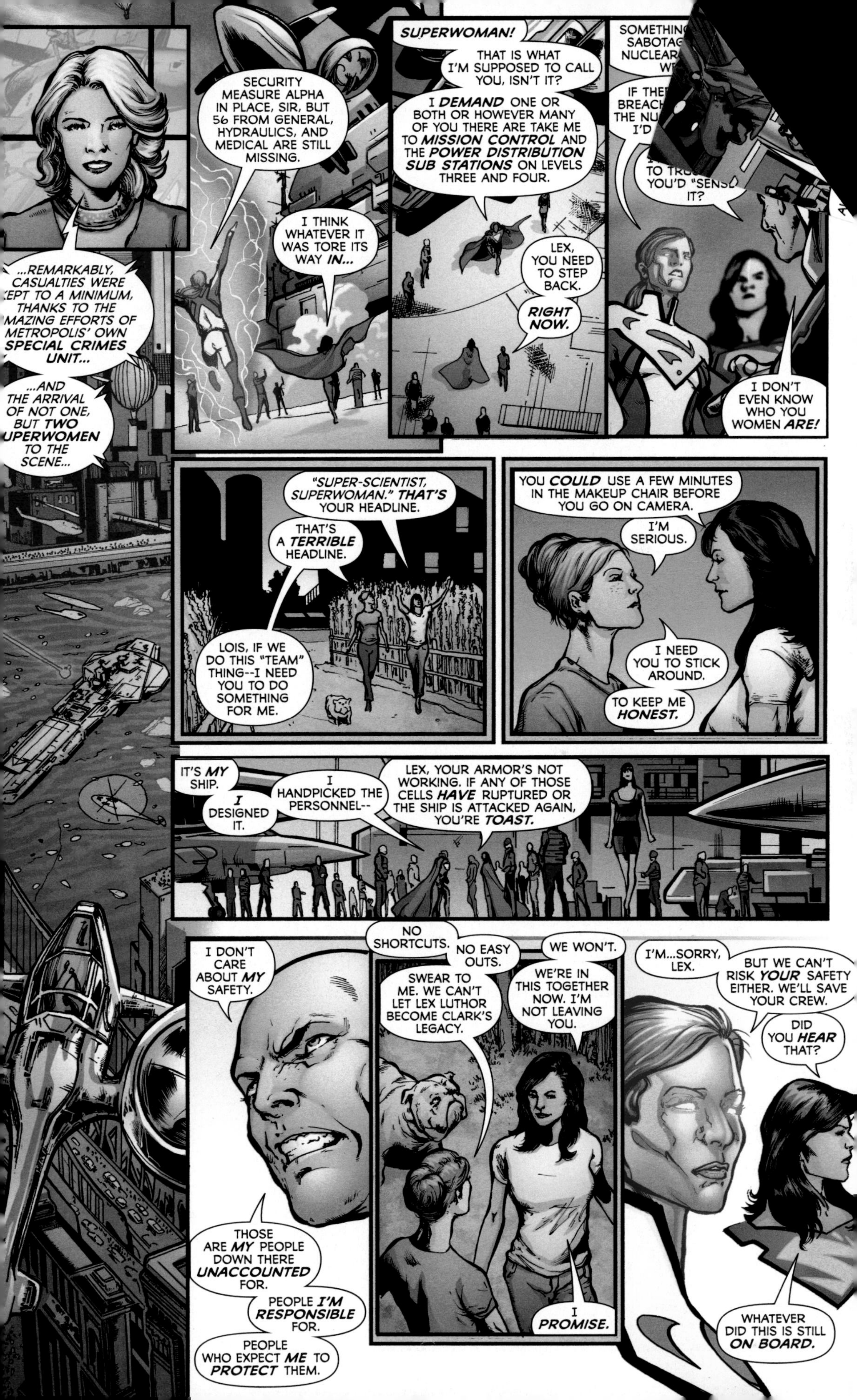

...REMARKABLY, CASUALTIES WERE KEPT TO A MINIMUM, THANKS TO THE AMAZING EFFORTS OF METROPOLIS' OWN SPECIAL CRIMES UNIT...
...AND THE ARRIVAL OF NOT ONE, BUT TWO SUPERWOMEN TO THE SCENE...
SECURITY MEASURE ALPHA IN PLACE, SIR, BUT 56 FROM GENERAL, HYDRAULICS, AND MEDICAL ARE STILL MISSING.
I THINK WHATEVER IT WAS TORE ITS WAY IN...
SUPERWOMAN!
THAT IS WHAT I'M SUPPOSED TO CALL YOU, ISN'T IT?
I DEMAND ONE OR BOTH OR HOWEVER MANY OF YOU THERE ARE TAKE ME TO MISSION CONTROL AND THE POWER DISTRIBUTION SUB STATIONS ON LEVELS THREE AND FOUR.
LEX, YOU NEED TO STEP BACK.
RIGHT NOW.
I DON'T EVEN KNOW WHO YOU WOMEN ARE!
"SUPER-SCIENTIST, SUPERWOMAN." THAT'S YOUR HEADLINE.
THAT'S A TERRIBLE HEADLINE.
LOIS, IF WE DO THIS "TEAM" THING--I NEED YOU TO DO SOMETHING FOR ME.
YOU COULD USE A FEW MINUTES IN THE MAKEUP CHAIR BEFORE YOU GO ON CAMERA.
I'M SERIOUS.
I NEED YOU TO STICK AROUND.
TO KEEP ME HONEST.
IT'S MY SHIP.
I DESIGNED IT.
I HANDPICKED THE PERSONNEL--
LEX, YOUR ARMOR'S NOT WORKING. IF ANY OF THOSE CELLS HAVE RUPTURED OR THE SHIP IS ATTACKED AGAIN, YOU'RE TOAST.
I DON'T CARE ABOUT MY SAFETY.
THOSE ARE MY PEOPLE DOWN THERE UNACCOUNTED FOR.
PEOPLE I'M RESPONSIBLE FOR.
PEOPLE WHO EXPECT ME TO PROTECT THEM.
NO SHORTCUTS.
NO EASY OUTS.
SWEAR TO ME. WE CAN'T LET LEX LUTHOR BECOME CLARK'S LEGACY.
WE WON'T.
WE'RE IN THIS TOGETHER NOW. I'M NOT LEAVING YOU.
I PROMISE.
I'M...SORRY, LEX.
BUT WE CAN'T RISK YOUR SAFETY EITHER. WE'LL SAVE YOUR CREW.
DID YOU HEAR THAT?
WHATEVER DID THIS IS STILL ON BOARD.

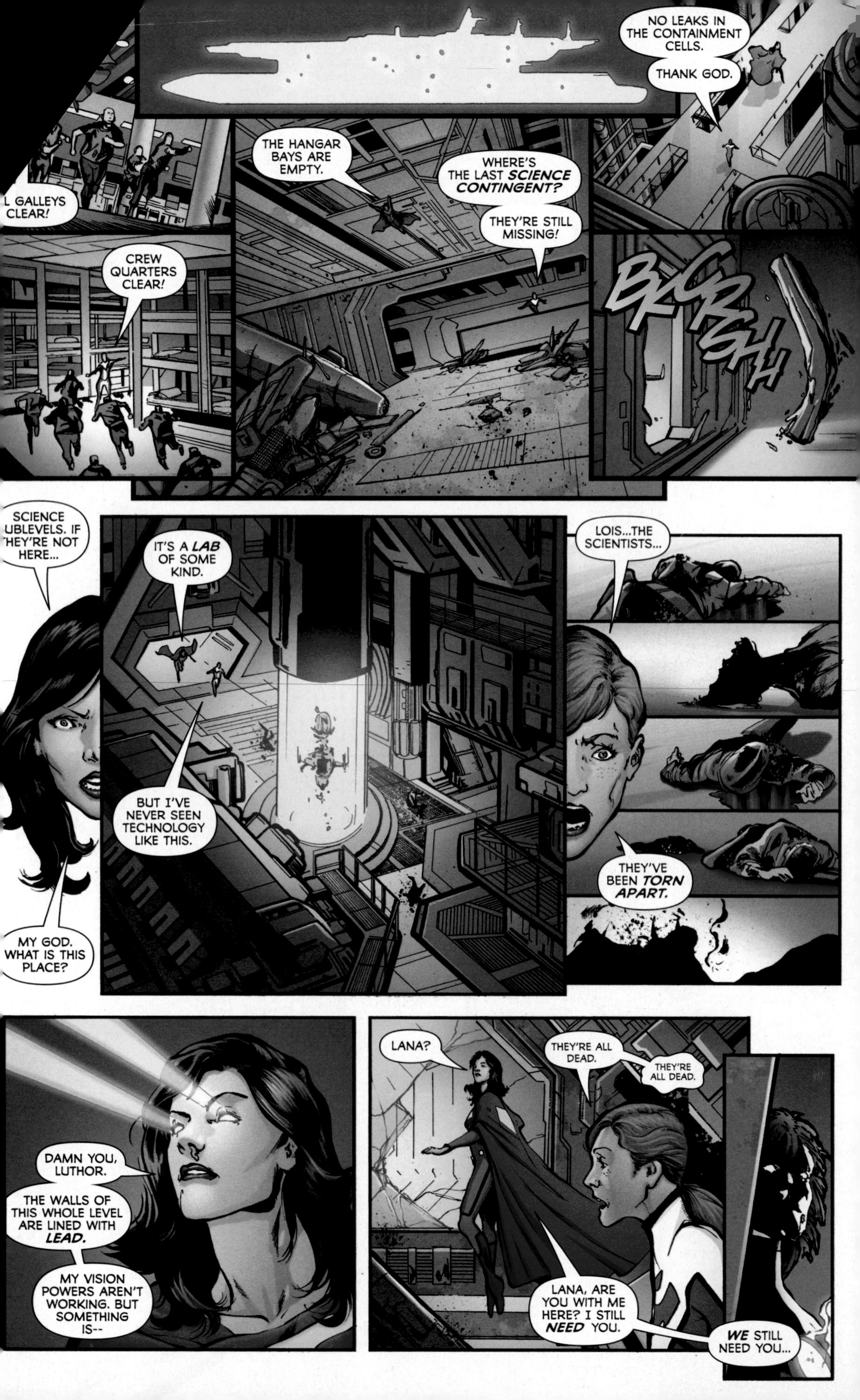
NO LEAKS IN THE CONTAINMENT CELLS.
THANK GOD.
L GALLEYS CLEAR!
THE HANGAR BAYS ARE EMPTY.
WHERE'S THE LAST SCIENCE CONTINGENT?
THEY'RE STILL MISSING!
CREW QUARTERS CLEAR!
BKCRSHH
SCIENCE UBLEVELS. IF HEY'RE NOT HERE...
IT'S A LAB OF SOME KIND.
BUT I'VE NEVER SEEN TECHNOLOGY LIKE THIS.
MY GOD. WHAT IS THIS PLACE?
LOIS...THE SCIENTISTS...
THEY'VE BEEN TORN APART.
DAMN YOU, LUTHOR.
THE WALLS OF THIS WHOLE LEVEL ARE LINED WITH LEAD.
MY VISION POWERS AREN'T WORKING. BUT SOMETHING IS--
LANA?
THEY'RE ALL DEAD.
THEY'RE ALL DEAD.
LANA, ARE YOU WITH ME HERE? I STILL NEED YOU.
WE STILL NEED YOU...

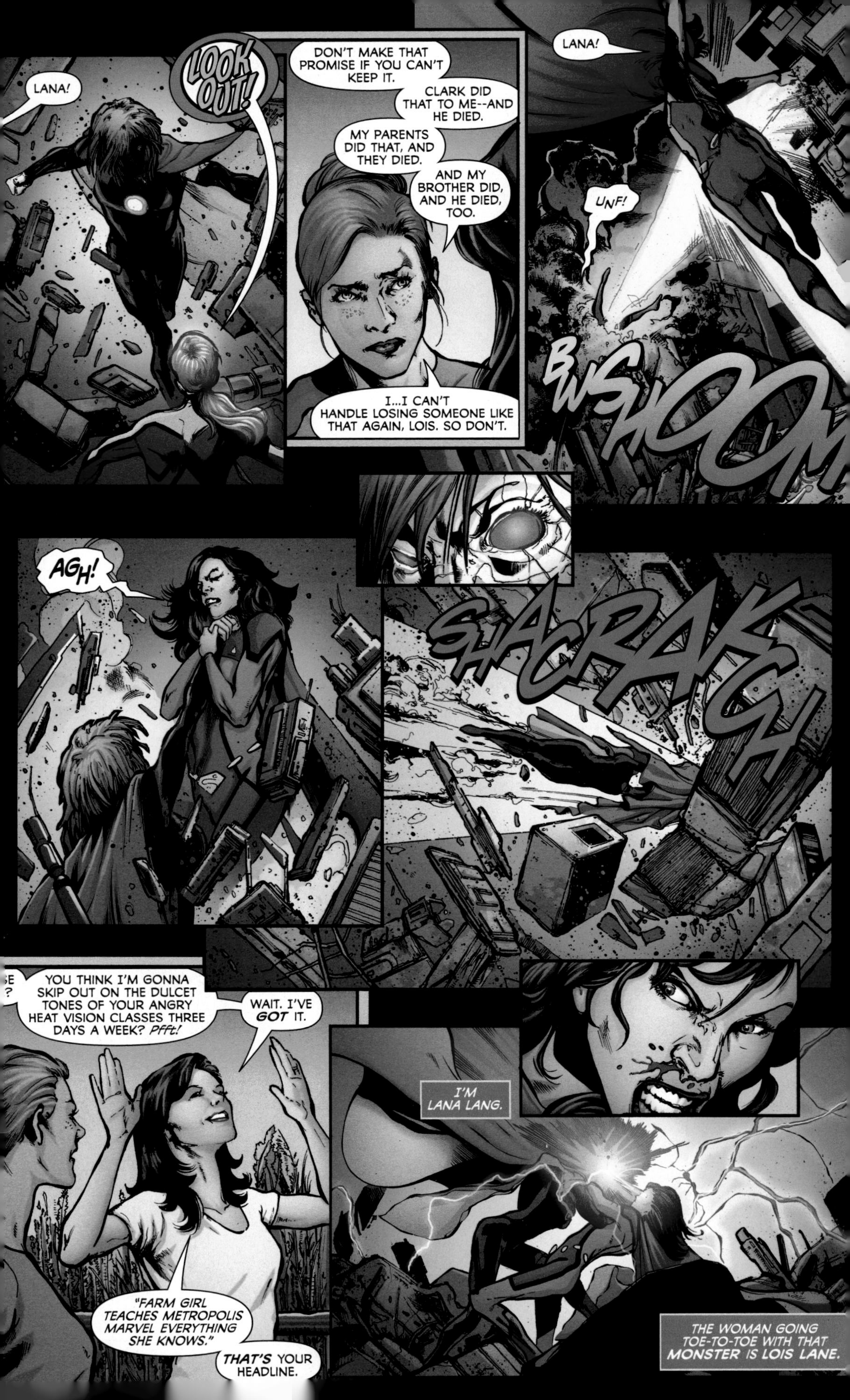
LANA!
LOOK OUT!
DON'T MAKE THAT PROMISE IF YOU CAN'T KEEP IT.
CLARK DID THAT TO ME--AND HE DIED.
MY PARENTS DID THAT, AND THEY DIED.
AND MY BROTHER DID, AND HE DIED, TOO.
I...I CAN'T HANDLE LOSING SOMEONE LIKE THAT AGAIN, LOIS. SO DON'T.
LANA!
UNF!
BWSHOOM
AGH!
SHACRAKGH
YOU THINK I'M GONNA SKIP OUT ON THE DULCET TONES OF YOUR ANGRY HEAT VISION CLASSES THREE DAYS A WEEK? *Pfft!*
WAIT. I'VE *GOT* IT.
"FARM GIRL TEACHES METROPOLIS MARVEL EVERYTHING SHE KNOWS."
THAT'S YOUR HEADLINE.
I'M LANA LANG.
THE WOMAN GOING TOE-TO-TOE WITH THAT MONSTER IS LOIS LANE.

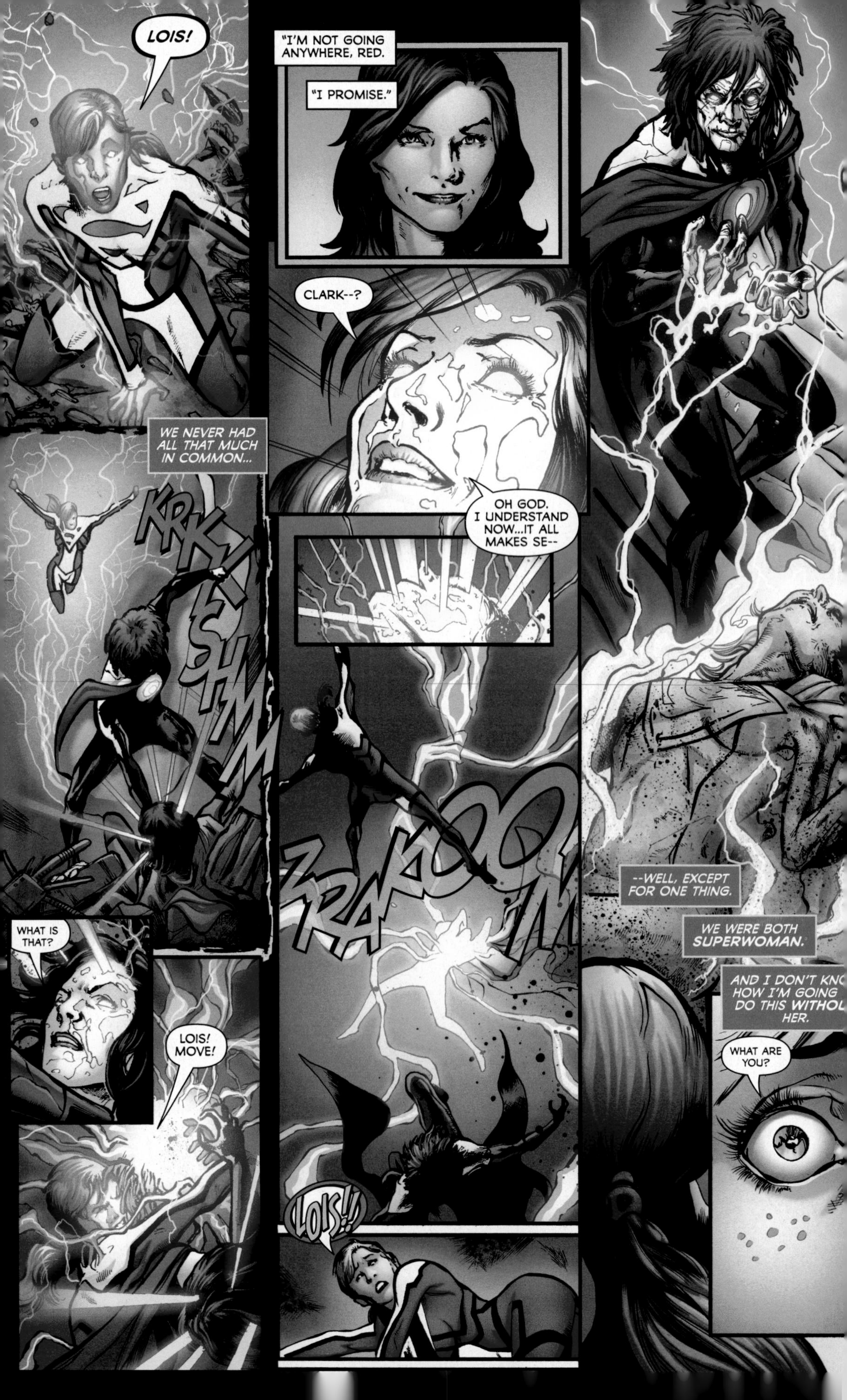
LOIS!
"I'M NOT GOING ANYWHERE, RED.
"I PROMISE."
CLARK--?
OH GOD. I UNDERSTAND NOW...IT ALL MAKES SE--
WE NEVER HAD ALL THAT MUCH IN COMMON...
KRKSHMM
ZRAKOOM
WHAT IS THAT?
LOIS! MOVE!
LOIS!!
--WELL, EXCEPT FOR ONE THING.
WE WERE BOTH SUPERWOMAN.
AND I DON'T KNO HOW I'M GOING DO THIS WITHOU HER.
WHAT ARE YOU?

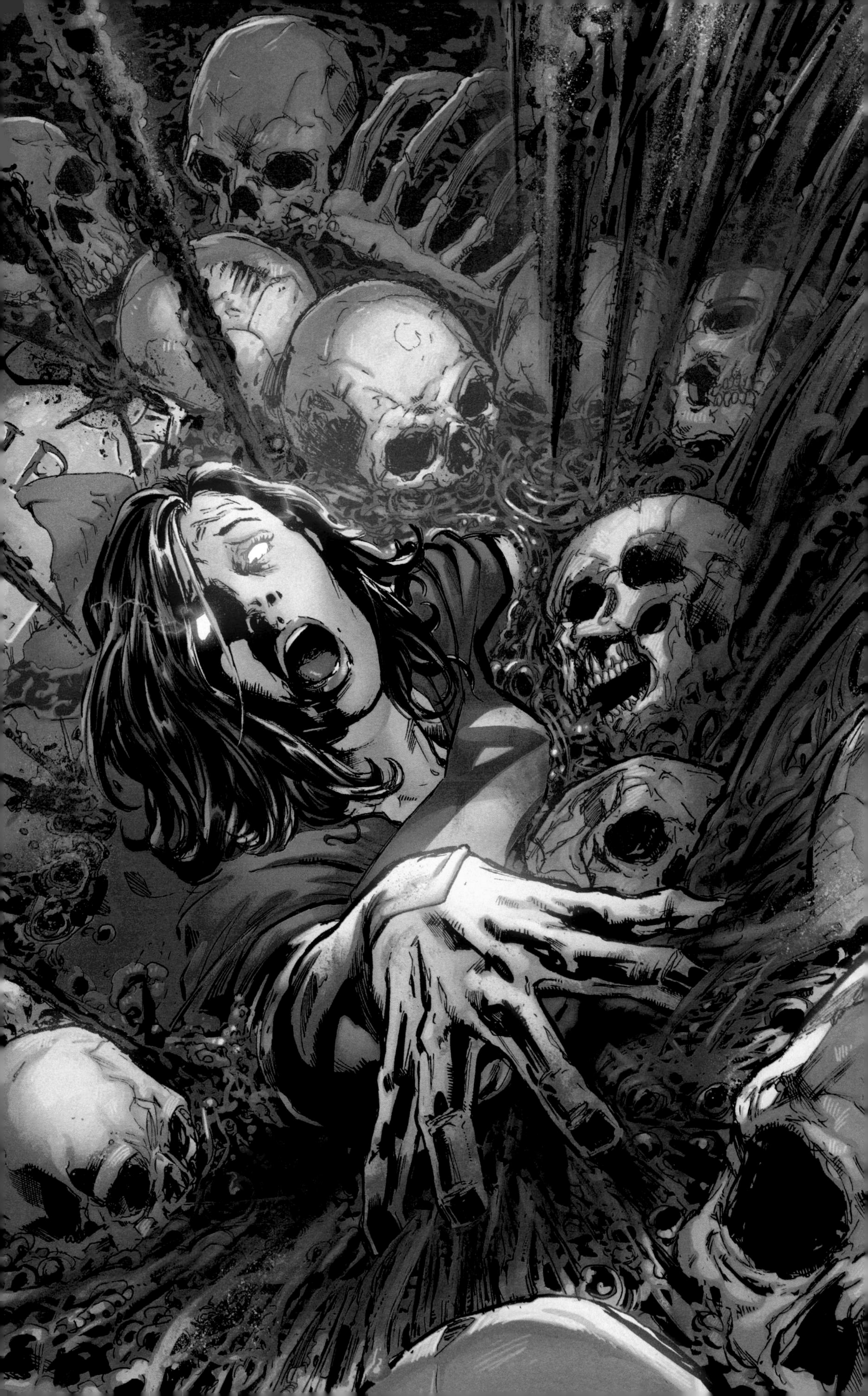

"WHO KILLED SUPERWOMAN? PART 2: WHAT COMES NEXT?"

PHIL JIMENEZ writer/penciller * MATT SANTORELLI JOE PRADO inkers

JEROMY COX colorist * cover by PHIL JIMENEZ and STEVE DOWNER

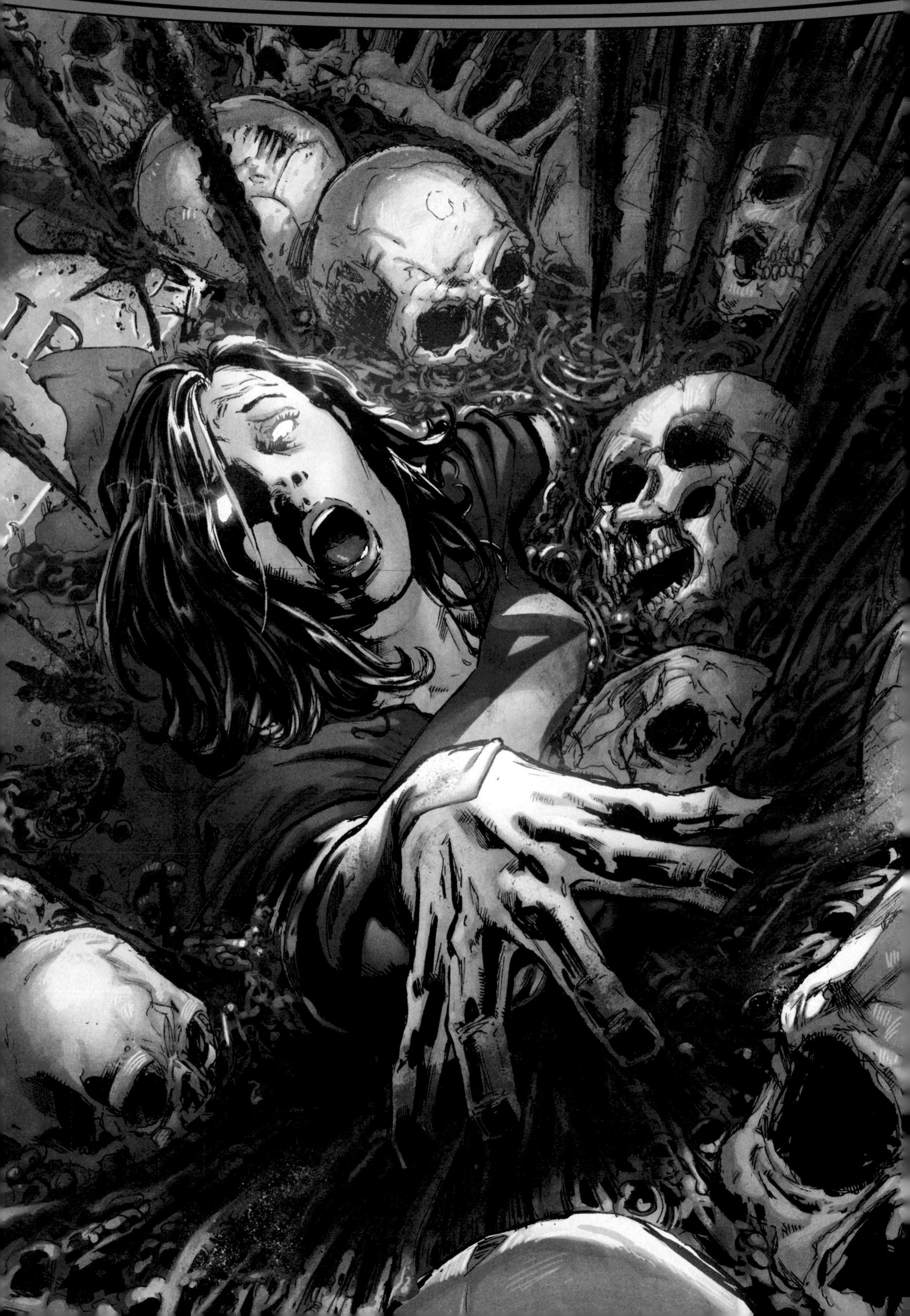

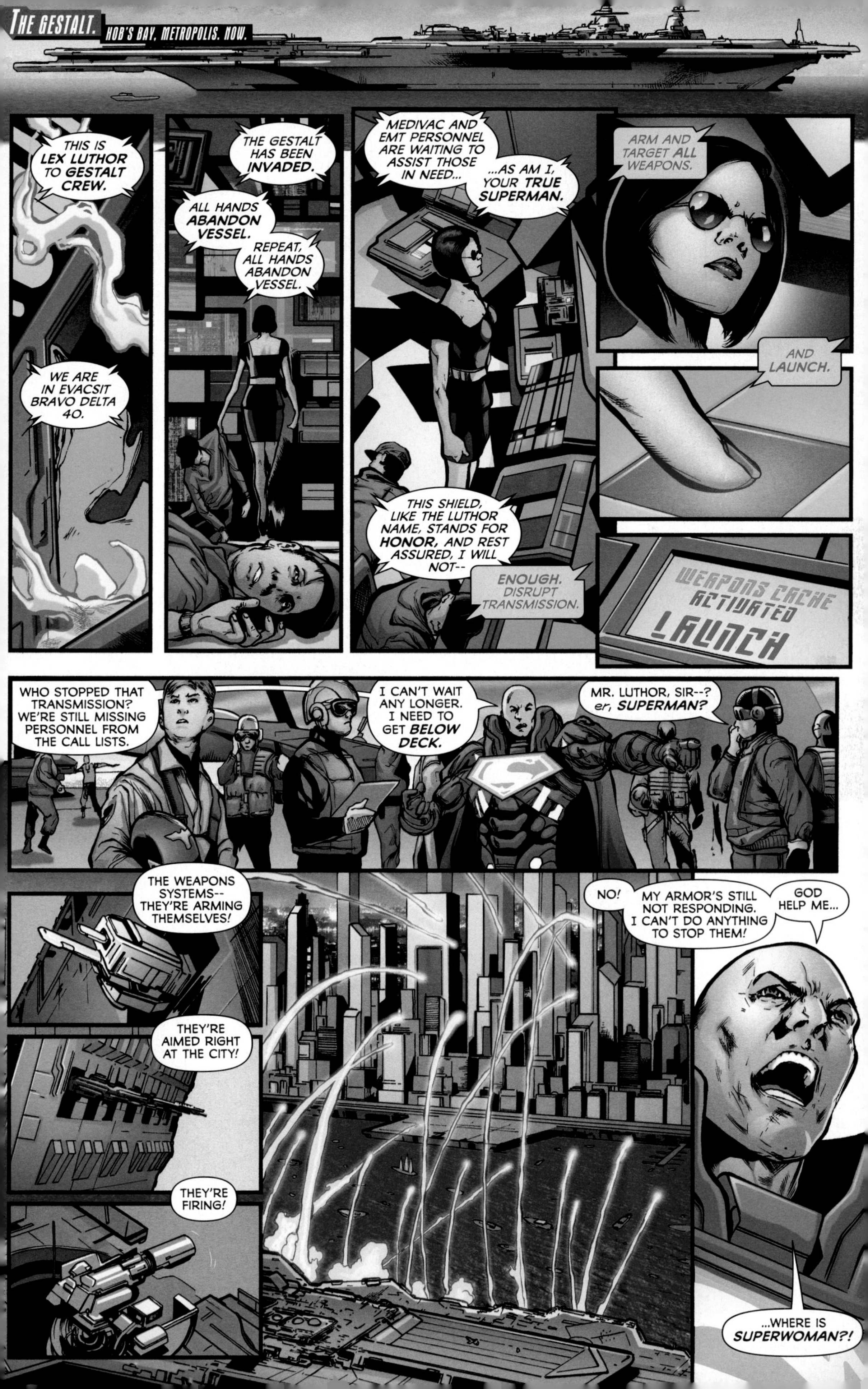
THE GESTALT.
HOB'S BAY, METROPOLIS. NOW.
THIS IS LEX LUTHOR TO GESTALT CREW.
WE ARE IN EVACSIT BRAVO DELTA 40.
THE GESTALT HAS BEEN INVADED.
ALL HANDS ABANDON VESSEL.
REPEAT, ALL HANDS ABANDON VESSEL.
MEDIVAC AND EMT PERSONNEL ARE WAITING TO ASSIST THOSE IN NEED...
...AS AM I, YOUR TRUE SUPERMAN.
THIS SHIELD, LIKE THE LUTHOR NAME, STANDS FOR HONOR, AND REST ASSURED, I WILL NOT--
ENOUGH. DISRUPT TRANSMISSION.
ARM AND TARGET ALL WEAPONS.
AND LAUNCH.
WEAPONS CACHE ACTIVATED
LAUNCH
WHO STOPPED THAT TRANSMISSION? WE'RE STILL MISSING PERSONNEL FROM THE CALL LISTS.
I CAN'T WAIT ANY LONGER. I NEED TO GET BELOW DECK.
MR. LUTHOR, SIR--? er, SUPERMAN?
THE WEAPONS SYSTEMS-- THEY'RE ARMING THEMSELVES!
THEY'RE AIMED RIGHT AT THE CITY!
THEY'RE FIRING!
NO!
MY ARMOR'S STILL NOT RESPONDING. I CAN'T DO ANYTHING TO STOP THEM!
GOD HELP ME...
...WHERE IS SUPERWOMAN?!

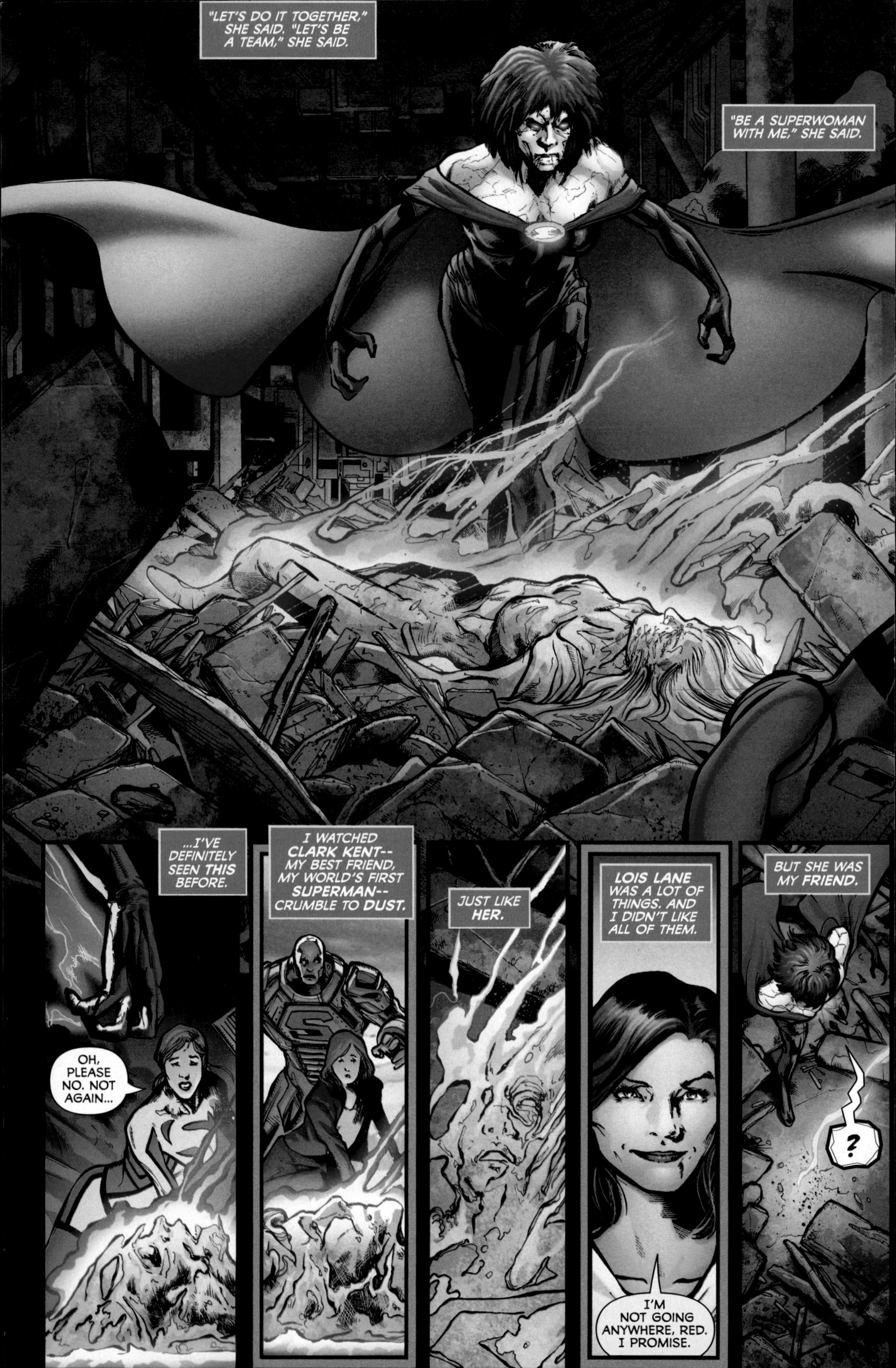
"LET'S DO IT TOGETHER," SHE SAID. "LET'S BE A TEAM," SHE SAID.
"BE A SUPERWOMAN WITH ME," SHE SAID.
...I'VE DEFINITELY SEEN THIS BEFORE.
OH, PLEASE NO. NOT AGAIN...
I WATCHED CLARK KENT-- MY BEST FRIEND, MY WORLD'S FIRST SUPERMAN-- CRUMBLE TO DUST.
JUST LIKE HER.
LOIS LANE WAS A LOT OF THINGS. AND I DIDN'T LIKE ALL OF THEM.
I'M NOT GOING ANYWHERE, RED. I PROMISE.
BUT SHE WAS MY FRIEND.
?

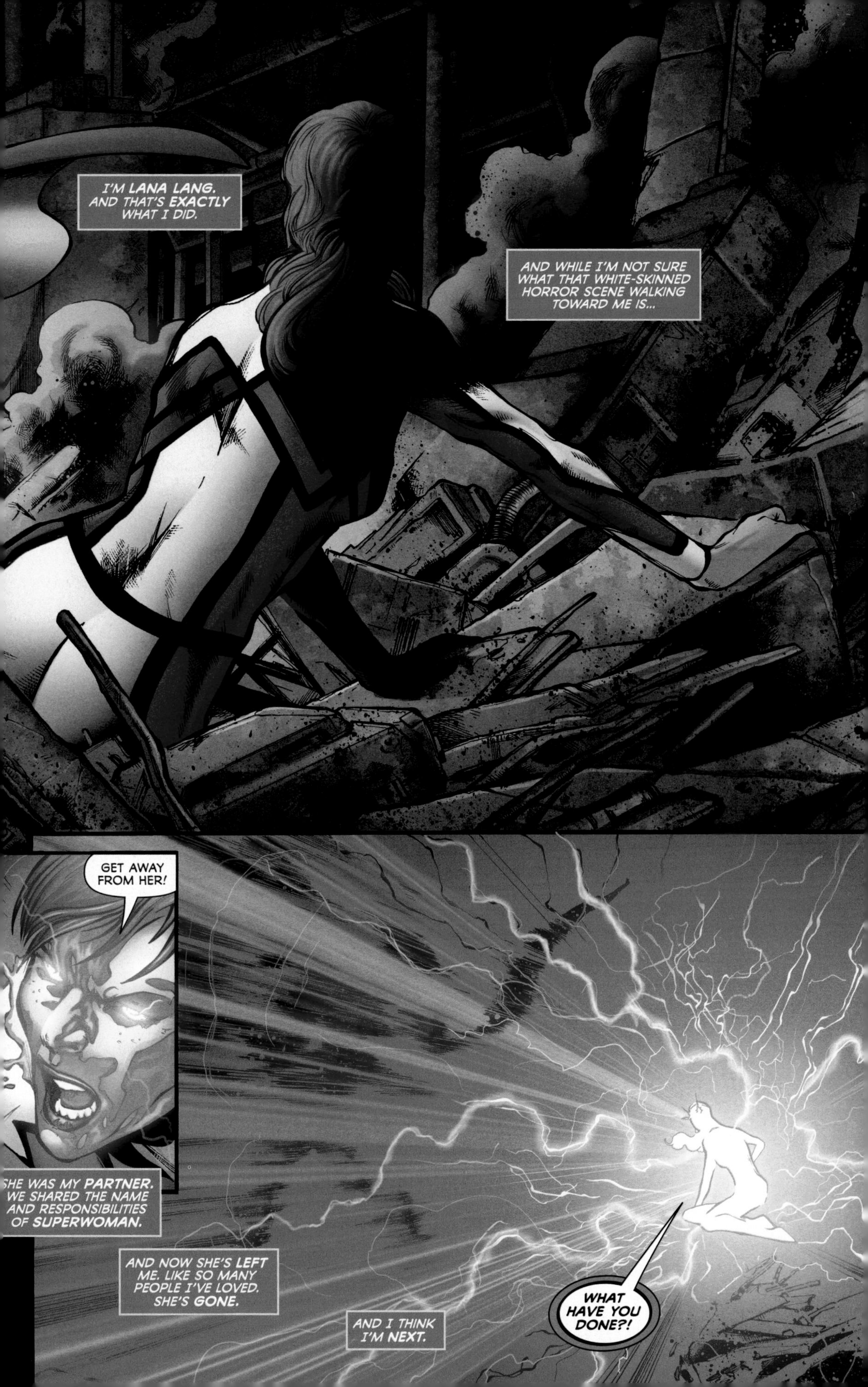
I'M LANA LANG. AND THAT'S EXACTLY WHAT I DID.
AND WHILE I'M NOT SURE WHAT THAT WHITE-SKINNED HORROR SCENE WALKING TOWARD ME IS...
GET AWAY FROM HER!
SHE WAS MY PARTNER. WE SHARED THE NAME AND RESPONSIBILITIES OF SUPERWOMAN.
AND NOW SHE'S LEFT ME. LIKE SO MANY PEOPLE I'VE LOVED. SHE'S GONE.
AND I THINK I'M NEXT.
WHAT HAVE YOU DONE?!

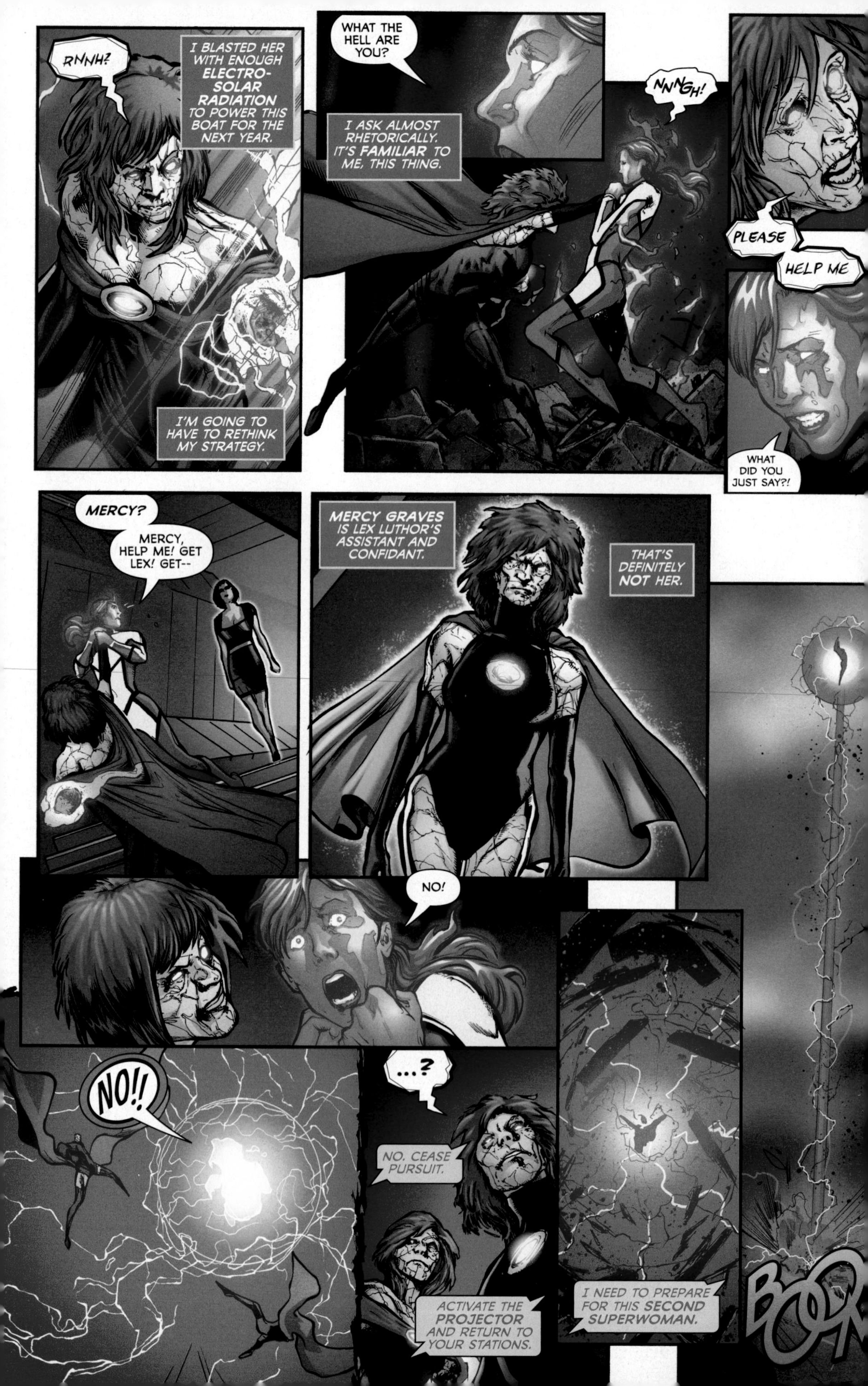
RNNH?
I BLASTED HER WITH ENOUGH ELECTRO-SOLAR RADIATION TO POWER THIS BOAT FOR THE NEXT YEAR.
I'M GOING TO HAVE TO RETHINK MY STRATEGY.
WHAT THE HELL ARE YOU?
I ASK ALMOST RHETORICALLY. IT'S FAMILIAR TO ME, THIS THING.
NNNGH!
PLEASE
HELP ME
WHAT DID YOU JUST SAY?!
MERCY?
MERCY, HELP ME! GET LEX! GET--
MERCY GRAVES IS LEX LUTHOR'S ASSISTANT AND CONFIDANT.
THAT'S DEFINITELY NOT HER.
NO!
NO!!
...?
NO. CEASE PURSUIT.
ACTIVATE THE PROJECTOR AND RETURN TO YOUR STATIONS.
I NEED TO PREPARE FOR THIS SECOND SUPERWOMAN.
BOOOM

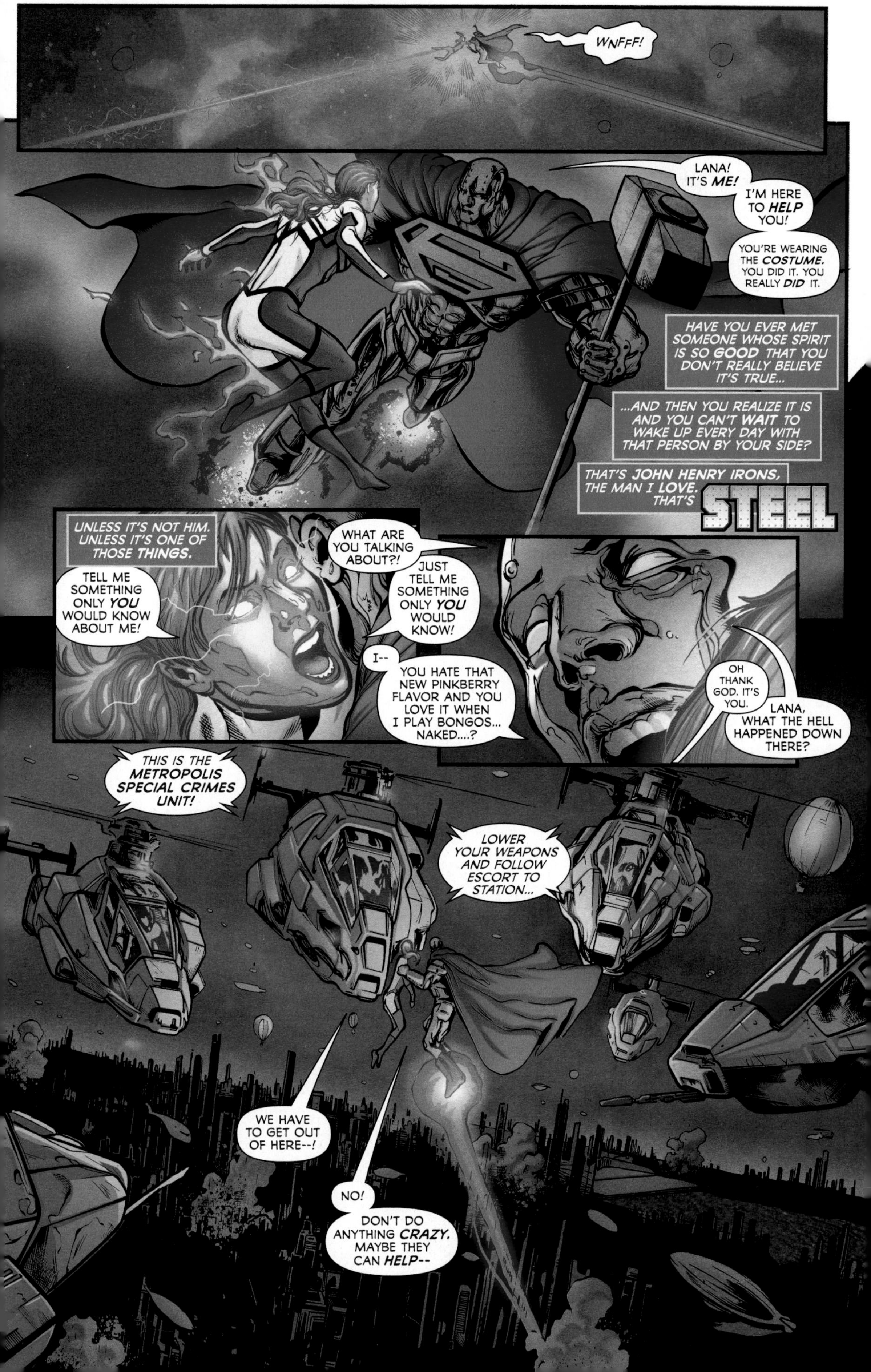
WNFFF!
LANA! IT'S ME!
I'M HERE TO HELP YOU!
YOU'RE WEARING THE COSTUME. YOU DID IT. YOU REALLY DID IT.
HAVE YOU EVER MET SOMEONE WHOSE SPIRIT IS SO GOOD THAT YOU DON'T REALLY BELIEVE IT'S TRUE...
...AND THEN YOU REALIZE IT IS AND YOU CAN'T WAIT TO WAKE UP EVERY DAY WITH THAT PERSON BY YOUR SIDE?
THAT'S JOHN HENRY IRONS, THE MAN I LOVE. THAT'S
STEEL
UNLESS IT'S NOT HIM. UNLESS IT'S ONE OF THOSE THINGS.
TELL ME SOMETHING ONLY YOU WOULD KNOW ABOUT ME!
WHAT ARE YOU TALKING ABOUT?!
JUST TELL ME SOMETHING ONLY YOU WOULD KNOW!
I--
YOU HATE THAT NEW PINKBERRY FLAVOR AND YOU LOVE IT WHEN I PLAY BONGOS... NAKED....?
OH THANK GOD. IT'S YOU.
LANA, WHAT THE HELL HAPPENED DOWN THERE?
THIS IS THE METROPOLIS SPECIAL CRIMES UNIT!
LOWER YOUR WEAPONS AND FOLLOW ESCORT TO STATION...
WE HAVE TO GET OUT OF HERE--!
NO!
DON'T DO ANYTHING CRAZY. MAYBE THEY CAN HELP--

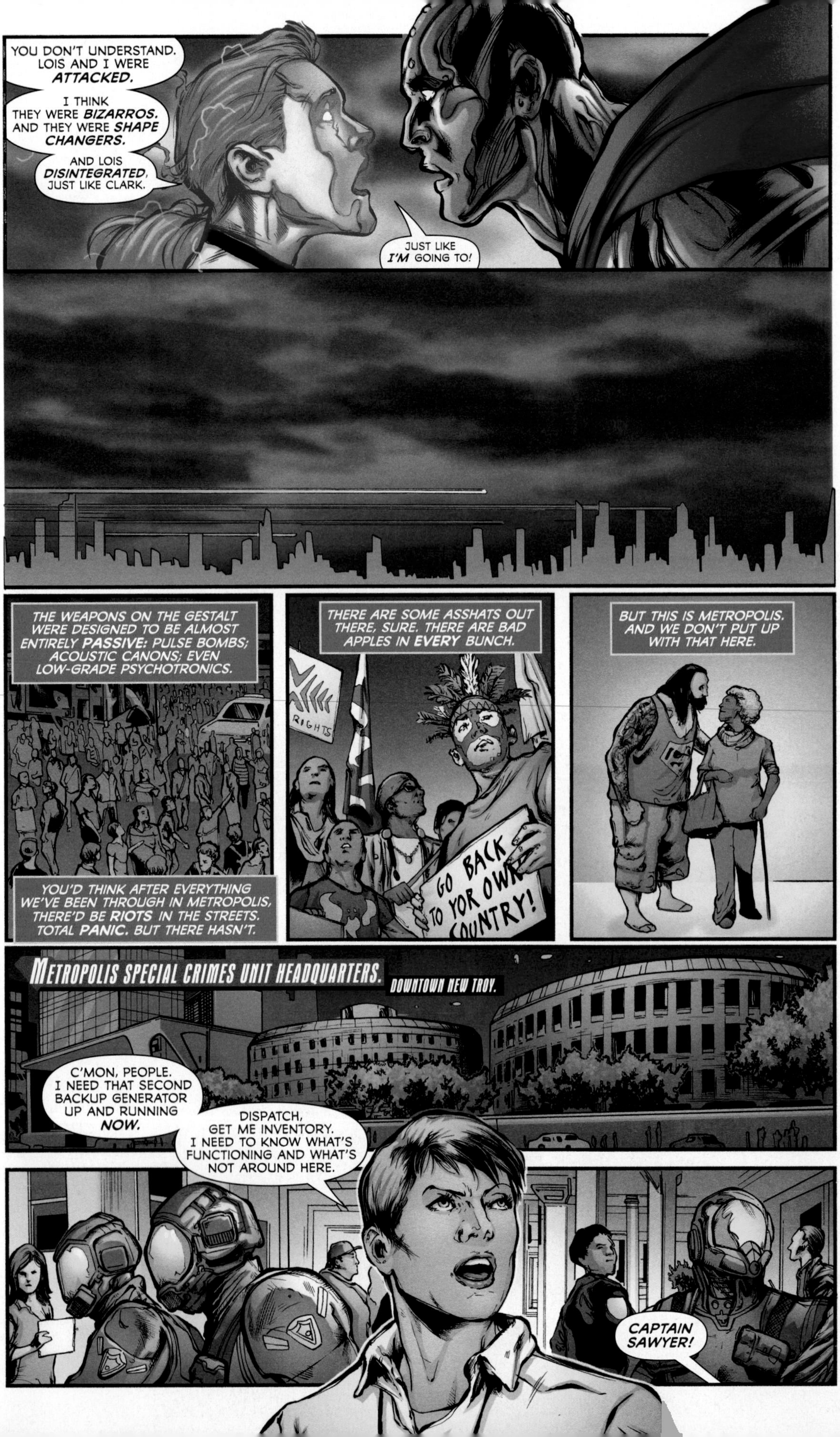
YOU DON'T UNDERSTAND. LOIS AND I WERE ATTACKED.
I THINK THEY WERE BIZARROS. AND THEY WERE SHAPE CHANGERS.
AND LOIS DISINTEGRATED, JUST LIKE CLARK.
JUST LIKE I'M GOING TO!
THE WEAPONS ON THE GESTALT WERE DESIGNED TO BE ALMOST ENTIRELY PASSIVE: PULSE BOMBS; ACOUSTIC CANONS; EVEN LOW-GRADE PSYCHOTRONICS.
YOU'D THINK AFTER EVERYTHING WE'VE BEEN THROUGH IN METROPOLIS, THERE'D BE RIOTS IN THE STREETS. TOTAL PANIC. BUT THERE HASN'T.
THERE ARE SOME ASSHATS OUT THERE, SURE. THERE ARE BAD APPLES IN EVERY BUNCH.
RIGHTS
GO BACK TO YOR OWN COUNTRY!
BUT THIS IS METROPOLIS. AND WE DON'T PUT UP WITH THAT HERE.
METROPOLIS SPECIAL CRIMES UNIT HEADQUARTERS.
DOWNTOWN NEW TROY.
C'MON, PEOPLE. I NEED THAT SECOND BACKUP GENERATOR UP AND RUNNING NOW.
DISPATCH, GET ME INVENTORY. I NEED TO KNOW WHAT'S FUNCTIONING AND WHAT'S NOT AROUND HERE.
CAPTAIN SAWYER!

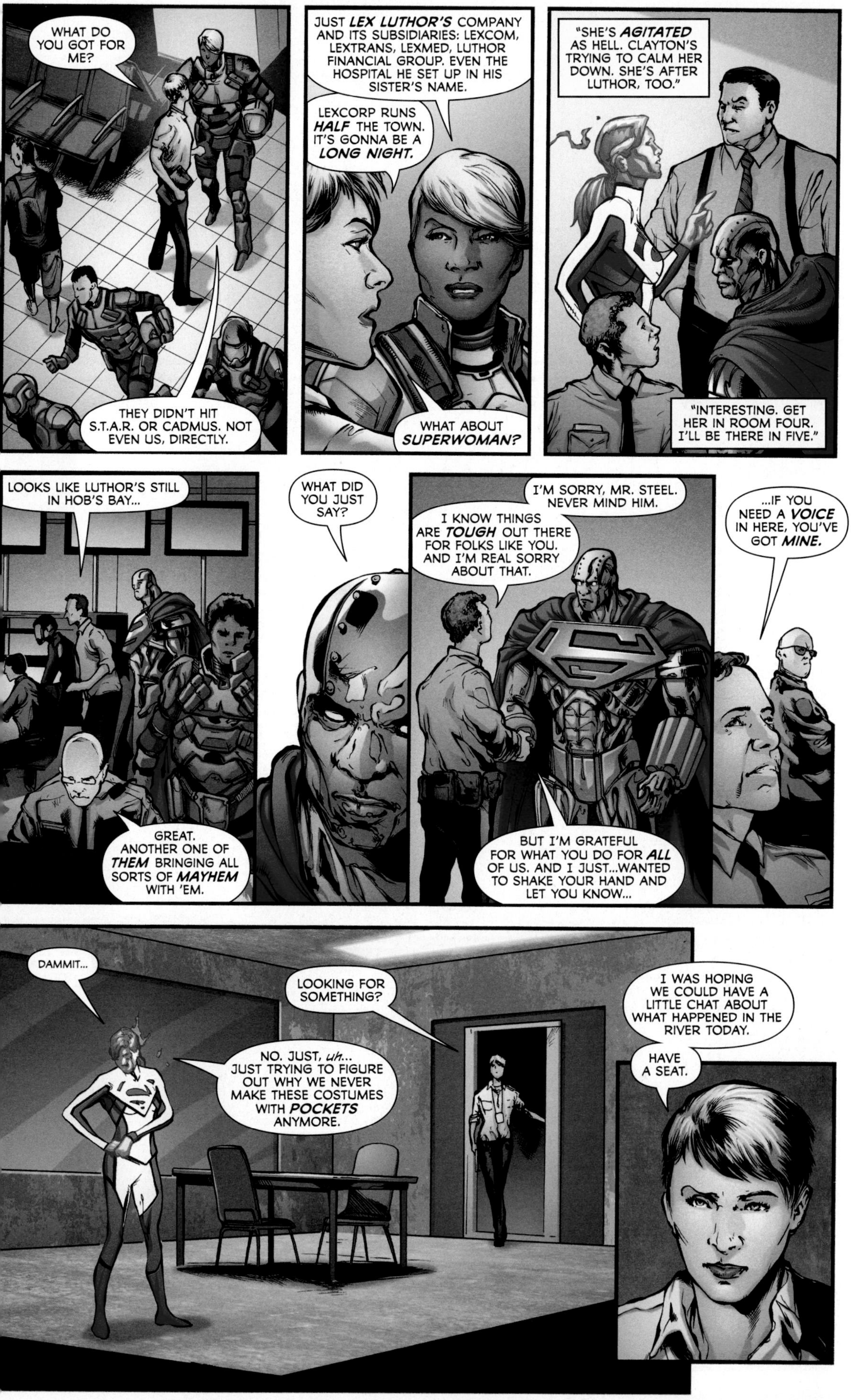
WHAT DO YOU GOT FOR ME?
THEY DIDN'T HIT S.T.A.R. OR CADMUS. NOT EVEN US, DIRECTLY.
JUST LEX LUTHOR'S COMPANY AND ITS SUBSIDIARIES: LEXCOM, LEXTRANS, LEXMED, LUTHOR FINANCIAL GROUP. EVEN THE HOSPITAL HE SET UP IN HIS SISTER'S NAME.
LEXCORP RUNS HALF THE TOWN. IT'S GONNA BE A LONG NIGHT.
WHAT ABOUT SUPERWOMAN?
"SHE'S AGITATED AS HELL. CLAYTON'S TRYING TO CALM HER DOWN. SHE'S AFTER LUTHOR, TOO."
"INTERESTING. GET HER IN ROOM FOUR. I'LL BE THERE IN FIVE."
LOOKS LIKE LUTHOR'S STILL IN HOB'S BAY...
GREAT. ANOTHER ONE OF THEM BRINGING ALL SORTS OF MAYHEM WITH 'EM.
WHAT DID YOU JUST SAY?
I'M SORRY, MR. STEEL. NEVER MIND HIM.
I KNOW THINGS ARE TOUGH OUT THERE FOR FOLKS LIKE YOU. AND I'M REAL SORRY ABOUT THAT.
BUT I'M GRATEFUL FOR WHAT YOU DO FOR ALL OF US. AND I JUST...WANTED TO SHAKE YOUR HAND AND LET YOU KNOW...
...IF YOU NEED A VOICE IN HERE, YOU'VE GOT MINE.
DAMMIT...
LOOKING FOR SOMETHING?
NO. JUST, uh... JUST TRYING TO FIGURE OUT WHY WE NEVER MAKE THESE COSTUMES WITH POCKETS ANYMORE.
I WAS HOPING WE COULD HAVE A LITTLE CHAT ABOUT WHAT HAPPENED IN THE RIVER TODAY.
HAVE A SEAT.

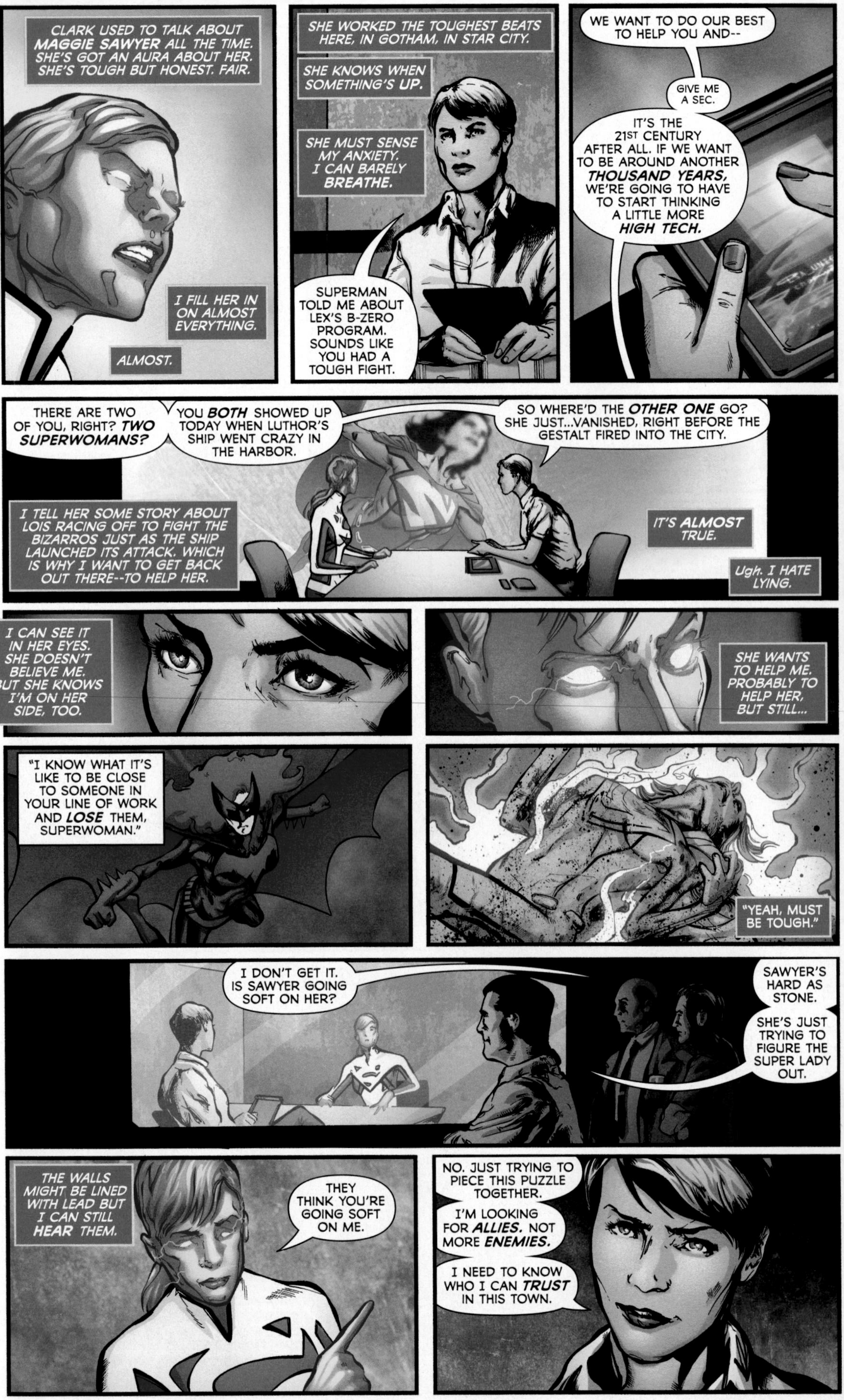
CLARK USED TO TALK ABOUT MAGGIE SAWYER ALL THE TIME. SHE'S GOT AN AURA ABOUT HER. SHE'S TOUGH BUT HONEST. FAIR.
I FILL HER IN ON ALMOST EVERYTHING.
ALMOST.
SHE WORKED THE TOUGHEST BEATS HERE, IN GOTHAM, IN STAR CITY.
SHE KNOWS WHEN SOMETHING'S UP.
SHE MUST SENSE MY ANXIETY. I CAN BARELY BREATHE.
SUPERMAN TOLD ME ABOUT LEX'S B-ZERO PROGRAM. SOUNDS LIKE YOU HAD A TOUGH FIGHT.
WE WANT TO DO OUR BEST TO HELP YOU AND--
GIVE ME A SEC.
IT'S THE 21ST CENTURY AFTER ALL. IF WE WANT TO BE AROUND ANOTHER THOUSAND YEARS, WE'RE GOING TO HAVE TO START THINKING A LITTLE MORE HIGH TECH.
THERE ARE TWO OF YOU, RIGHT? TWO SUPERWOMANS?
YOU BOTH SHOWED UP TODAY WHEN LUTHOR'S SHIP WENT CRAZY IN THE HARBOR.
SO WHERE'D THE OTHER ONE GO? SHE JUST...VANISHED, RIGHT BEFORE THE GESTALT FIRED INTO THE CITY.
I TELL HER SOME STORY ABOUT LOIS RACING OFF TO FIGHT THE BIZARROS JUST AS THE SHIP LAUNCHED ITS ATTACK. WHICH IS WHY I WANT TO GET BACK OUT THERE--TO HELP HER.
IT'S ALMOST TRUE.
Ugh. I HATE LYING.
I CAN SEE IT IN HER EYES. SHE DOESN'T BELIEVE ME. BUT SHE KNOWS I'M ON HER SIDE, TOO.
SHE WANTS TO HELP ME. PROBABLY TO HELP HER, BUT STILL...
"I KNOW WHAT IT'S LIKE TO BE CLOSE TO SOMEONE IN YOUR LINE OF WORK AND LOSE THEM, SUPERWOMAN."
"YEAH, MUST BE TOUGH."
I DON'T GET IT. IS SAWYER GOING SOFT ON HER?
SAWYER'S HARD AS STONE.
SHE'S JUST TRYING TO FIGURE THE SUPER LADY OUT.
THE WALLS MIGHT BE LINED WITH LEAD BUT I CAN STILL HEAR THEM.
THEY THINK YOU'RE GOING SOFT ON ME.
NO. JUST TRYING TO PIECE THIS PUZZLE TOGETHER.
I'M LOOKING FOR ALLIES. NOT MORE ENEMIES.
I NEED TO KNOW WHO I CAN TRUST IN THIS TOWN.

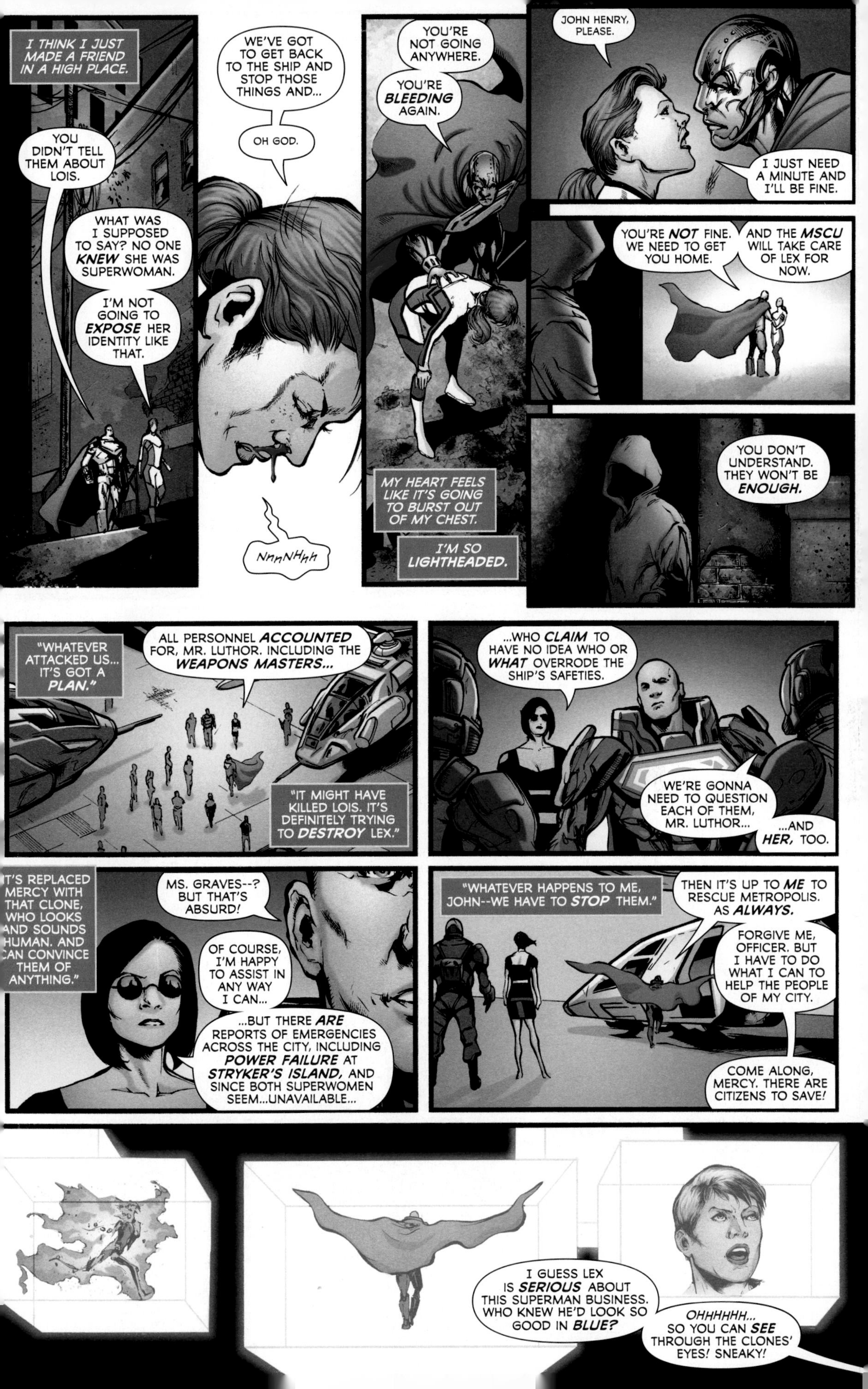
I THINK I JUST MADE A FRIEND IN A HIGH PLACE.
YOU DIDN'T TELL THEM ABOUT LOIS.
WHAT WAS I SUPPOSED TO SAY? NO ONE KNEW SHE WAS SUPERWOMAN.
I'M NOT GOING TO EXPOSE HER IDENTITY LIKE THAT.
WE'VE GOT TO GET BACK TO THE SHIP AND STOP THOSE THINGS AND...
OH GOD.
NnnNHnh
YOU'RE NOT GOING ANYWHERE.
YOU'RE BLEEDING AGAIN.
MY HEART FEELS LIKE IT'S GOING TO BURST OUT OF MY CHEST.
I'M SO LIGHTHEADED.
JOHN HENRY, PLEASE.
I JUST NEED A MINUTE AND I'LL BE FINE.
YOU'RE NOT FINE. WE NEED TO GET YOU HOME.
AND THE MSCU WILL TAKE CARE OF LEX FOR NOW.
YOU DON'T UNDERSTAND. THEY WON'T BE ENOUGH.
"WHATEVER ATTACKED US... IT'S GOT A PLAN."
ALL PERSONNEL ACCOUNTED FOR, MR. LUTHOR. INCLUDING THE WEAPONS MASTERS...
"IT MIGHT HAVE KILLED LOIS. IT'S DEFINITELY TRYING TO DESTROY LEX."
...WHO CLAIM TO HAVE NO IDEA WHO OR WHAT OVERRODE THE SHIP'S SAFETIES.
WE'RE GONNA NEED TO QUESTION EACH OF THEM, MR. LUTHOR...
...AND HER, TOO.
IT'S REPLACED MERCY WITH THAT CLONE, WHO LOOKS AND SOUNDS HUMAN. AND CAN CONVINCE THEM OF ANYTHING."
MS. GRAVES--? BUT THAT'S ABSURD!
OF COURSE, I'M HAPPY TO ASSIST IN ANY WAY I CAN...
...BUT THERE ARE REPORTS OF EMERGENCIES ACROSS THE CITY, INCLUDING POWER FAILURE AT STRYKER'S ISLAND, AND SINCE BOTH SUPERWOMEN SEEM...UNAVAILABLE...
"WHATEVER HAPPENS TO ME, JOHN--WE HAVE TO STOP THEM."
THEN IT'S UP TO ME TO RESCUE METROPOLIS. AS ALWAYS.
FORGIVE ME, OFFICER. BUT I HAVE TO DO WHAT I CAN TO HELP THE PEOPLE OF MY CITY.
COME ALONG, MERCY. THERE ARE CITIZENS TO SAVE!
I GUESS LEX IS SERIOUS ABOUT THIS SUPERMAN BUSINESS. WHO KNEW HE'D LOOK SO GOOD IN BLUE?
OHHHHHH... SO YOU CAN SEE THROUGH THE CLONES' EYES! SNEAKY!

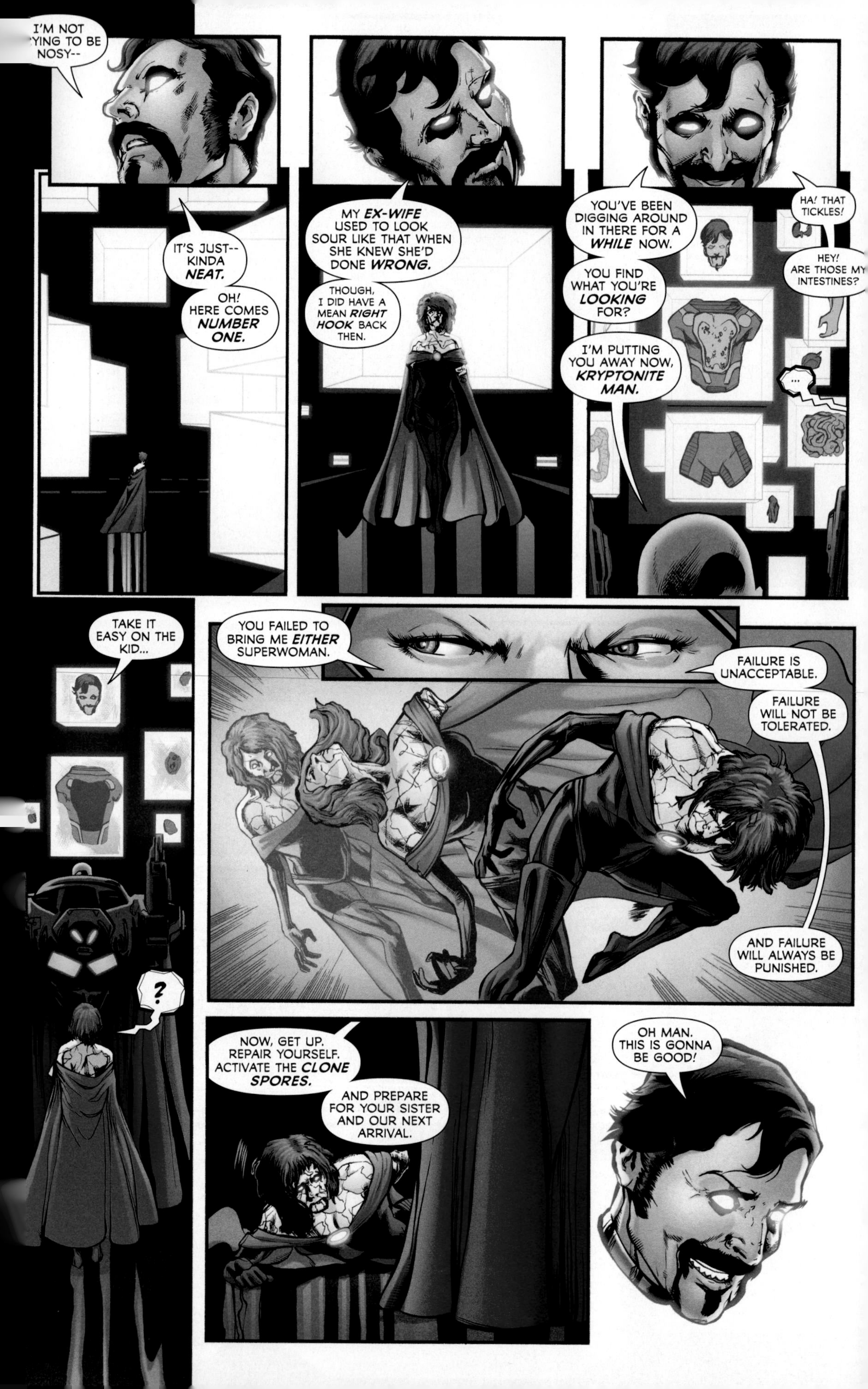
I'M NOT YING TO BE NOSY--
IT'S JUST-- KINDA NEAT.
OH! HERE COMES NUMBER ONE.
MY EX-WIFE USED TO LOOK SOUR LIKE THAT WHEN SHE KNEW SHE'D DONE WRONG.
THOUGH, I DID HAVE A MEAN RIGHT HOOK BACK THEN.
YOU'VE BEEN DIGGING AROUND IN THERE FOR A WHILE NOW.
YOU FIND WHAT YOU'RE LOOKING FOR?
I'M PUTTING YOU AWAY NOW, KRYPTONITE MAN.
HA! THAT TICKLES!
HEY! ARE THOSE MY INTESTINES?
...
TAKE IT EASY ON THE KID...
?
YOU FAILED TO BRING ME EITHER SUPERWOMAN.
FAILURE IS UNACCEPTABLE.
FAILURE WILL NOT BE TOLERATED.
AND FAILURE WILL ALWAYS BE PUNISHED.
NOW, GET UP. REPAIR YOURSELF. ACTIVATE THE CLONE SPORES.
AND PREPARE FOR YOUR SISTER AND OUR NEXT ARRIVAL.
OH MAN. THIS IS GONNA BE GOOD!

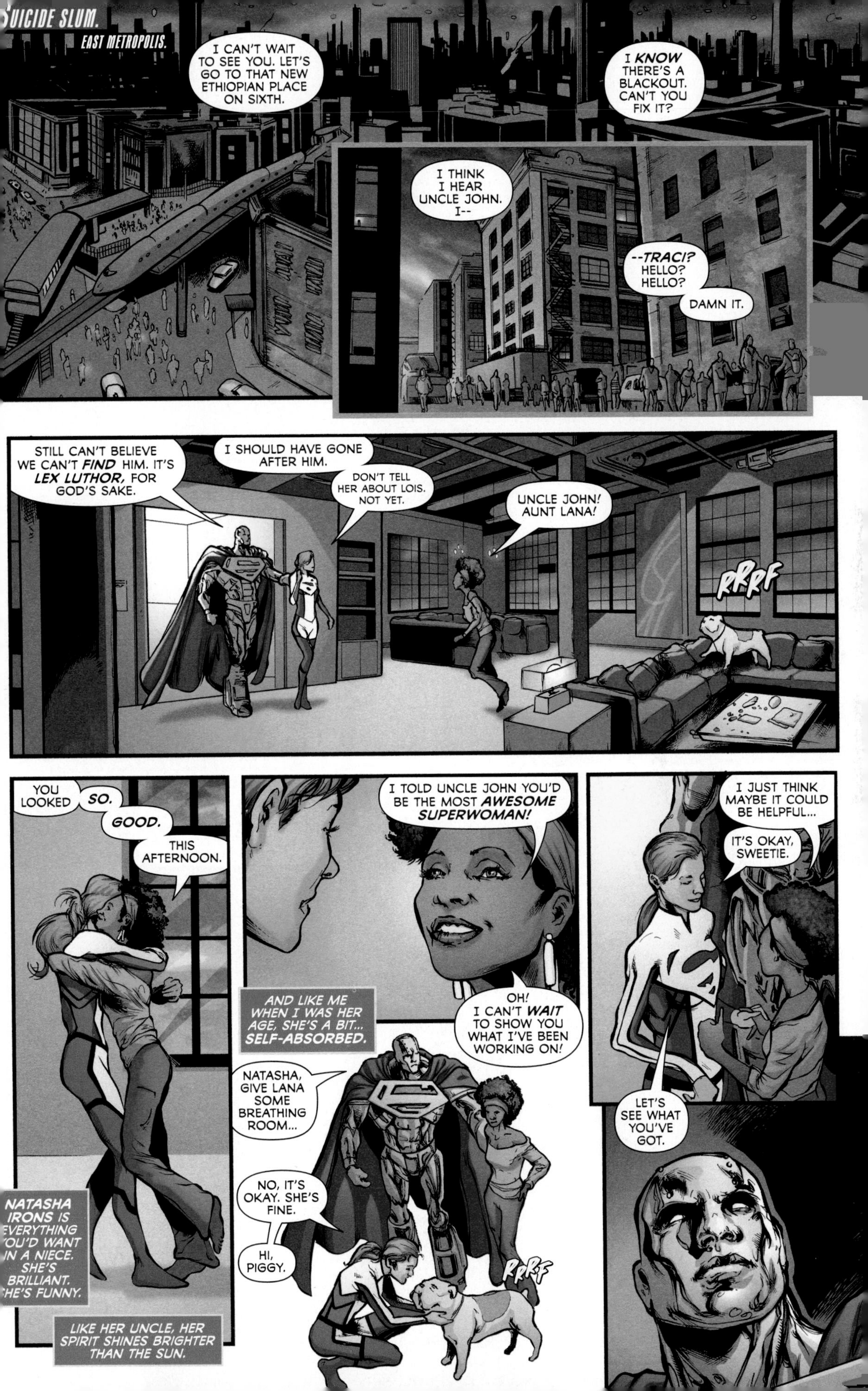
SUICIDE SLUM.
EAST METROPOLIS.
I CAN'T WAIT TO SEE YOU. LET'S GO TO THAT NEW ETHIOPIAN PLACE ON SIXTH.
I KNOW THERE'S A BLACKOUT. CAN'T YOU FIX IT?
I THINK I HEAR UNCLE JOHN. I--
--TRACI? HELLO? HELLO?
DAMN IT.
STILL CAN'T BELIEVE WE CAN'T FIND HIM. IT'S LEX LUTHOR, FOR GOD'S SAKE.
I SHOULD HAVE GONE AFTER HIM.
DON'T TELL HER ABOUT LOIS. NOT YET.
UNCLE JOHN! AUNT LANA!
RRRF
YOU LOOKED
SO.
GOOD.
THIS AFTERNOON.
NATASHA IRONS IS EVERYTHING YOU'D WANT IN A NIECE. SHE'S BRILLIANT. SHE'S FUNNY.
LIKE HER UNCLE, HER SPIRIT SHINES BRIGHTER THAN THE SUN.
I TOLD UNCLE JOHN YOU'D BE THE MOST AWESOME SUPERWOMAN!
AND LIKE ME WHEN I WAS HER AGE, SHE'S A BIT... SELF-ABSORBED.
OH! I CAN'T WAIT TO SHOW YOU WHAT I'VE BEEN WORKING ON!
NATASHA, GIVE LANA SOME BREATHING ROOM...
NO, IT'S OKAY. SHE'S FINE.
HI, PIGGY.
RRRF
I JUST THINK MAYBE IT COULD BE HELPFUL...
IT'S OKAY, SWEETIE.
LET'S SEE WHAT YOU'VE GOT.

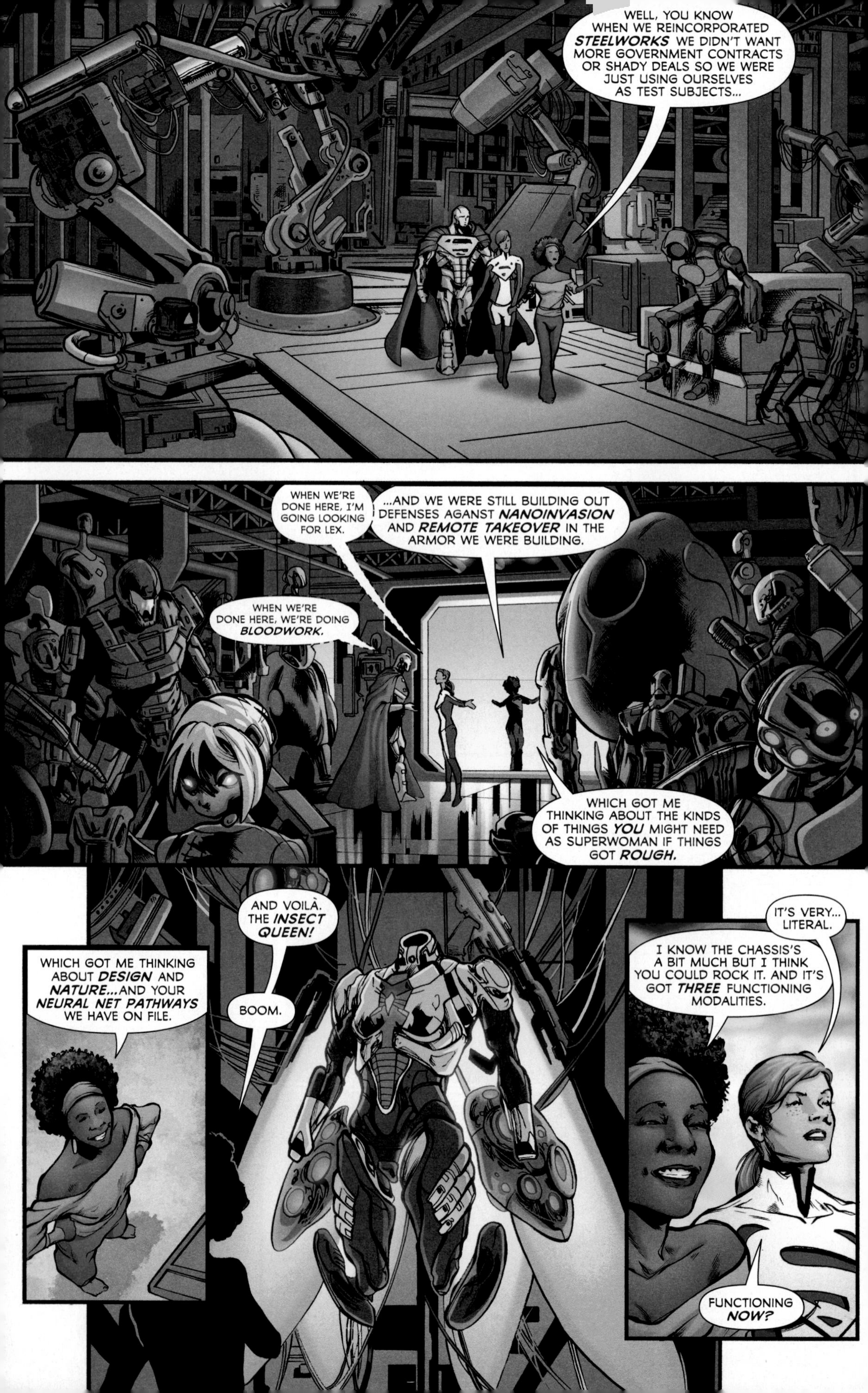
WELL, YOU KNOW WHEN WE REINCORPORATED STEELWORKS WE DIDN'T WANT MORE GOVERNMENT CONTRACTS OR SHADY DEALS SO WE WERE JUST USING OURSELVES AS TEST SUBJECTS...
WHEN WE'RE DONE HERE, I'M GOING LOOKING FOR LEX.
...AND WE WERE STILL BUILDING OUT DEFENSES AGANST NANOINVASION AND REMOTE TAKEOVER IN THE ARMOR WE WERE BUILDING.
WHEN WE'RE DONE HERE, WE'RE DOING BLOODWORK.
WHICH GOT ME THINKING ABOUT THE KINDS OF THINGS YOU MIGHT NEED AS SUPERWOMAN IF THINGS GOT ROUGH.
WHICH GOT ME THINKING ABOUT DESIGN AND NATURE...AND YOUR NEURAL NET PATHWAYS WE HAVE ON FILE.
AND VOILÀ. THE INSECT QUEEN!
BOOM.
I KNOW THE CHASSIS'S A BIT MUCH BUT I THINK YOU COULD ROCK IT. AND IT'S GOT THREE FUNCTIONING MODALITIES.
IT'S VERY... LITERAL.
FUNCTIONING NOW?

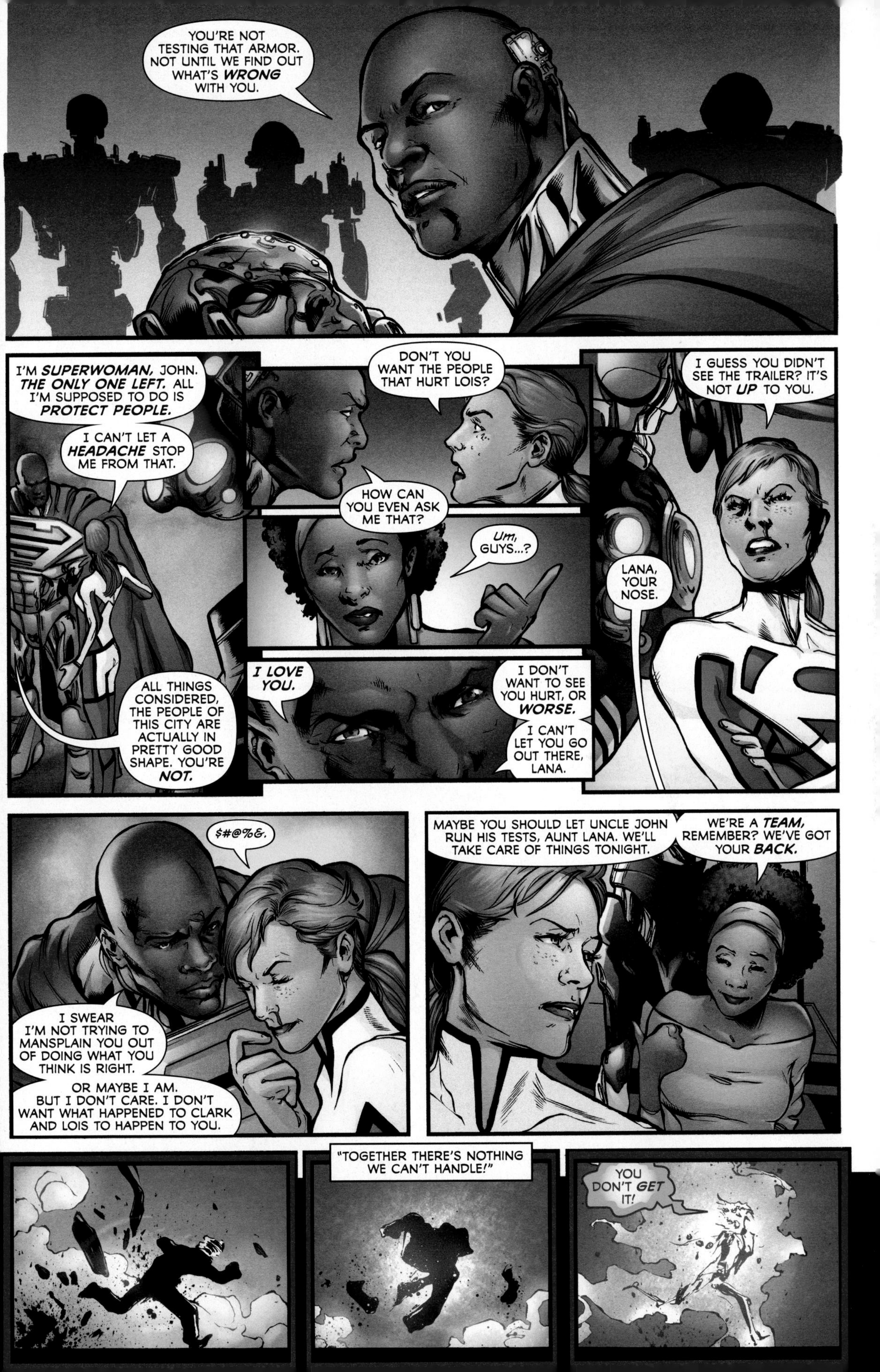
YOU'RE NOT TESTING THAT ARMOR. NOT UNTIL WE FIND OUT WHAT'S WRONG WITH YOU.
I'M SUPERWOMAN, JOHN. THE ONLY ONE LEFT. ALL I'M SUPPOSED TO DO IS PROTECT PEOPLE.
I CAN'T LET A HEADACHE STOP ME FROM THAT.
ALL THINGS CONSIDERED, THE PEOPLE OF THIS CITY ARE ACTUALLY IN PRETTY GOOD SHAPE. YOU'RE NOT.
DON'T YOU WANT THE PEOPLE THAT HURT LOIS?
HOW CAN YOU EVEN ASK ME THAT?
UM, GUYS...?
I LOVE YOU.
I DON'T WANT TO SEE YOU HURT, OR WORSE.
I CAN'T LET YOU GO OUT THERE, LANA.
I GUESS YOU DIDN'T SEE THE TRAILER? IT'S NOT UP TO YOU.
LANA, YOUR NOSE.
$#@%&.
I SWEAR I'M NOT TRYING TO MANSPLAIN YOU OUT OF DOING WHAT YOU THINK IS RIGHT.
OR MAYBE I AM. BUT I DON'T CARE. I DON'T WANT WHAT HAPPENED TO CLARK AND LOIS TO HAPPEN TO YOU.
MAYBE YOU SHOULD LET UNCLE JOHN RUN HIS TESTS, AUNT LANA. WE'LL TAKE CARE OF THINGS TONIGHT.
WE'RE A TEAM, REMEMBER? WE'VE GOT YOUR BACK.
"TOGETHER THERE'S NOTHING WE CAN'T HANDLE!"
YOU DON'T GET IT!

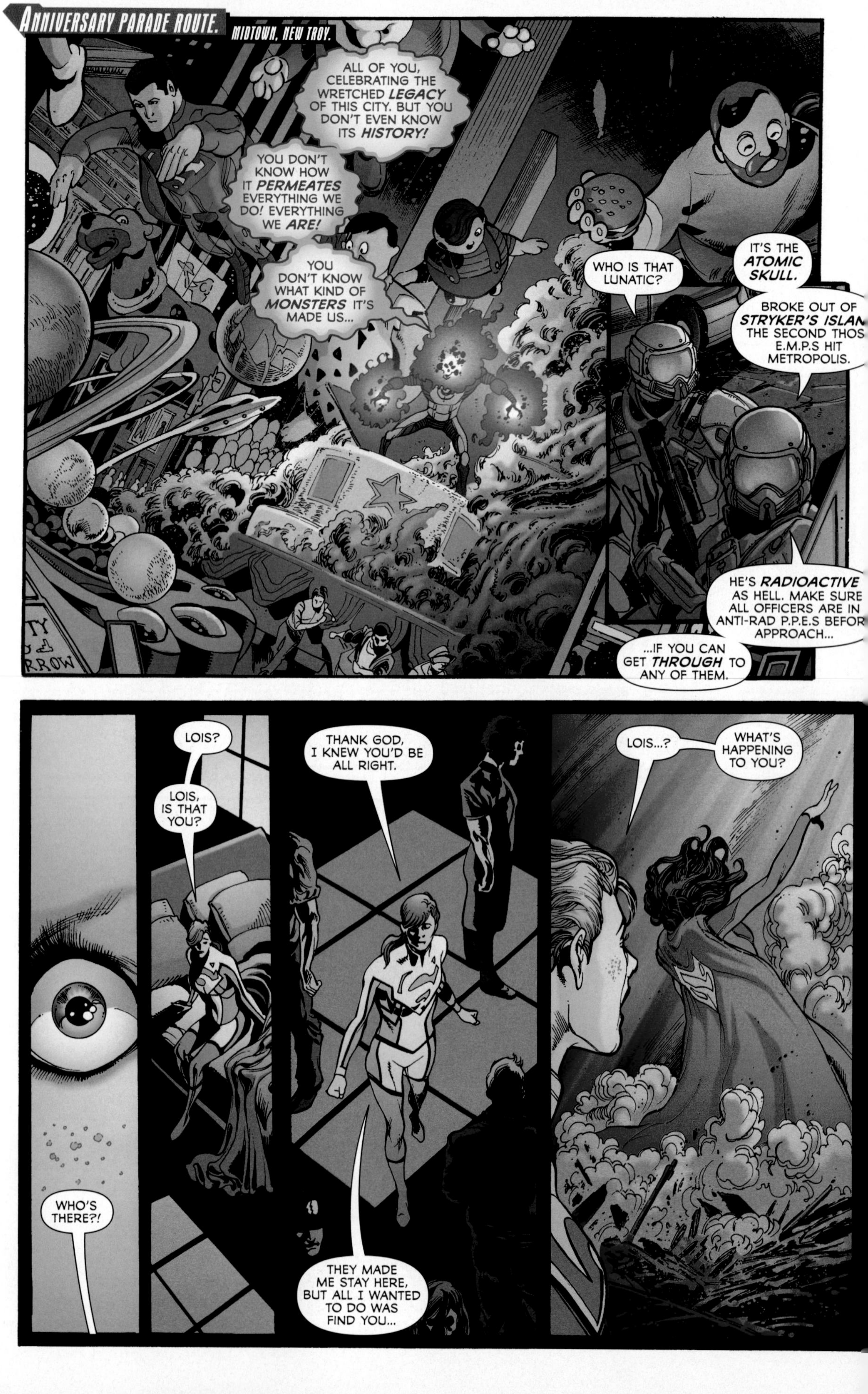

ANNIVERSARY PARADE ROUTE.
MIDTOWN, NEW TROY.
ALL OF YOU, CELEBRATING THE WRETCHED LEGACY OF THIS CITY. BUT YOU DON'T EVEN KNOW ITS HISTORY!
YOU DON'T KNOW HOW IT PERMEATES EVERYTHING WE DO! EVERYTHING WE ARE!
YOU DON'T KNOW WHAT KIND OF MONSTERS IT'S MADE US...
WHO IS THAT LUNATIC?
IT'S THE ATOMIC SKULL.
BROKE OUT OF STRYKER'S ISLAN THE SECOND THOS E.M.P.S HIT METROPOLIS.
HE'S RADIOACTIVE AS HELL. MAKE SURE ALL OFFICERS ARE IN ANTI-RAD P.P.E.S BEFOR APPROACH...
...IF YOU CAN GET THROUGH TO ANY OF THEM.
WHO'S THERE?!
LOIS?
LOIS, IS THAT YOU?
THANK GOD, I KNEW YOU'D BE ALL RIGHT.
THEY MADE ME STAY HERE, BUT ALL I WANTED TO DO WAS FIND YOU...
LOIS...?
WHAT'S HAPPENING TO YOU?

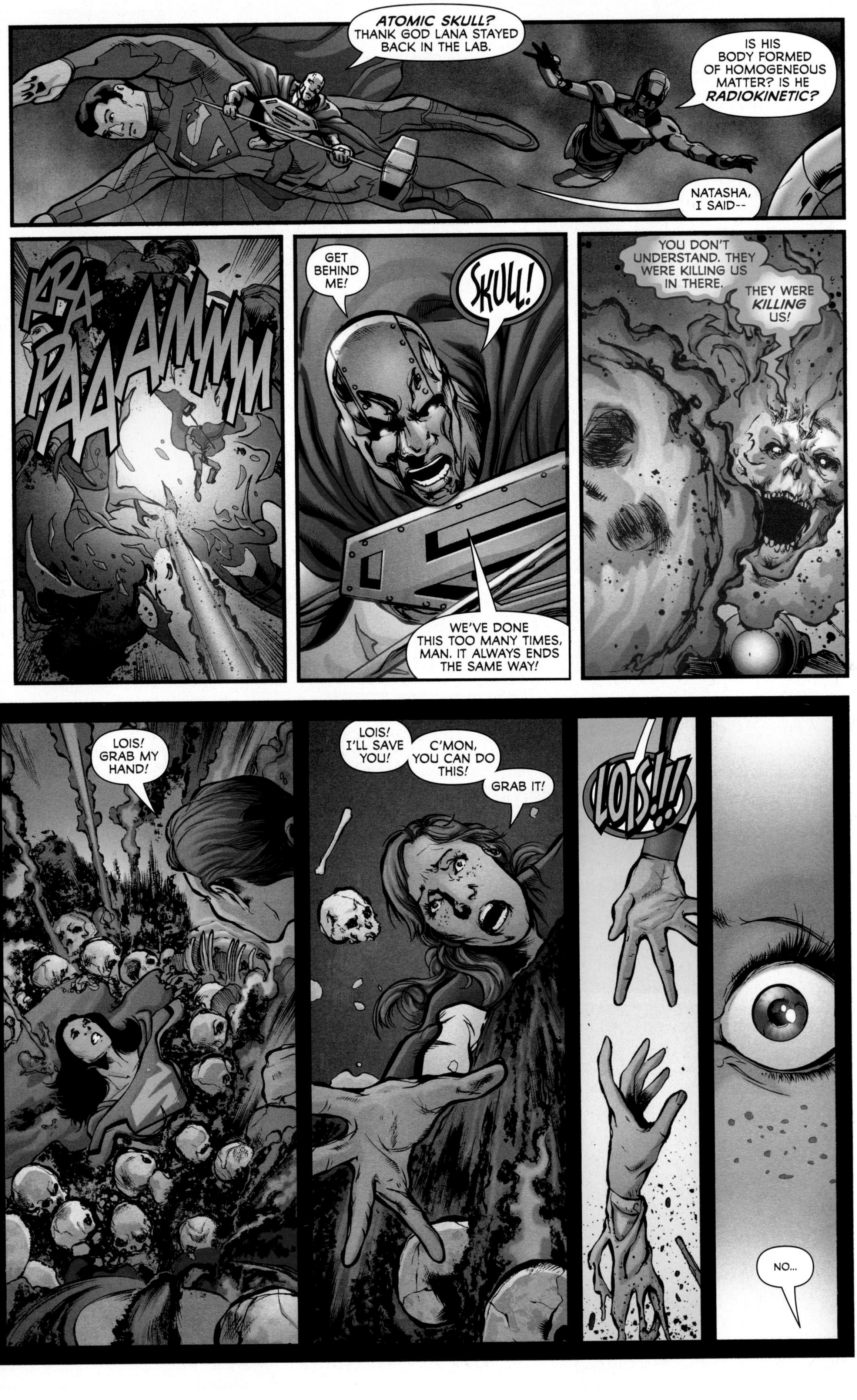
ATOMIC SKULL? THANK GOD LANA STAYED BACK IN THE LAB.
IS HIS BODY FORMED OF HOMOGENEOUS MATTER? IS HE RADIOKINETIC?
NATASHA, I SAID--
KRA PAAAMMM
GET BEHIND ME!
SKULL!
WE'VE DONE THIS TOO MANY TIMES, MAN. IT ALWAYS ENDS THE SAME WAY!
YOU DON'T UNDERSTAND. THEY WERE KILLING US IN THERE.
THEY WERE KILLING US!
LOIS! GRAB MY HAND!
LOIS! I'LL SAVE YOU!
C'MON, YOU CAN DO THIS!
GRAB IT!
LOIS!!!
NO...

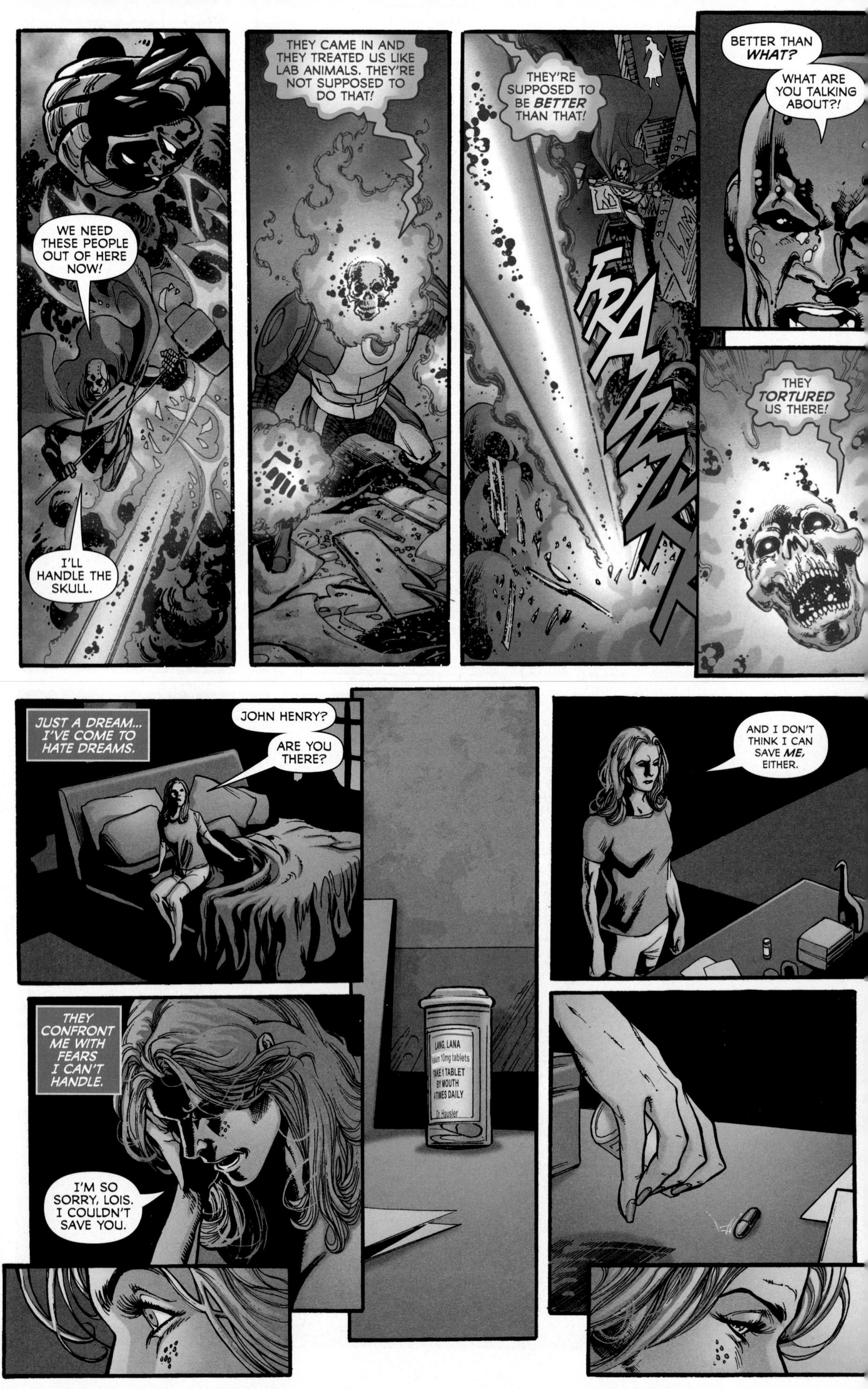

WE NEED THESE PEOPLE OUT OF HERE NOW!
I'LL HANDLE THE SKULL.
THEY CAME IN AND THEY TREATED US LIKE LAB ANIMALS. THEY'RE NOT SUPPOSED TO DO THAT!
THEY'RE SUPPOSED TO BE *BETTER* THAN THAT!
BETTER THAN *WHAT?*
WHAT ARE YOU TALKING ABOUT?!
THEY *TORTURED* US THERE!
JUST A DREAM... I'VE COME TO HATE DREAMS.
JOHN HENRY?
ARE YOU THERE?
THEY CONFRONT ME WITH FEARS I CAN'T HANDLE.
I'M SO SORRY, LOIS. I COULDN'T SAVE YOU.
LANG, LANA
Valium 10mg tablets
TAKE 1 TABLET BY MOUTH 4 TIMES DAILY
Dr. Hausler
AND I DON'T THINK I CAN SAVE *ME,* EITHER.

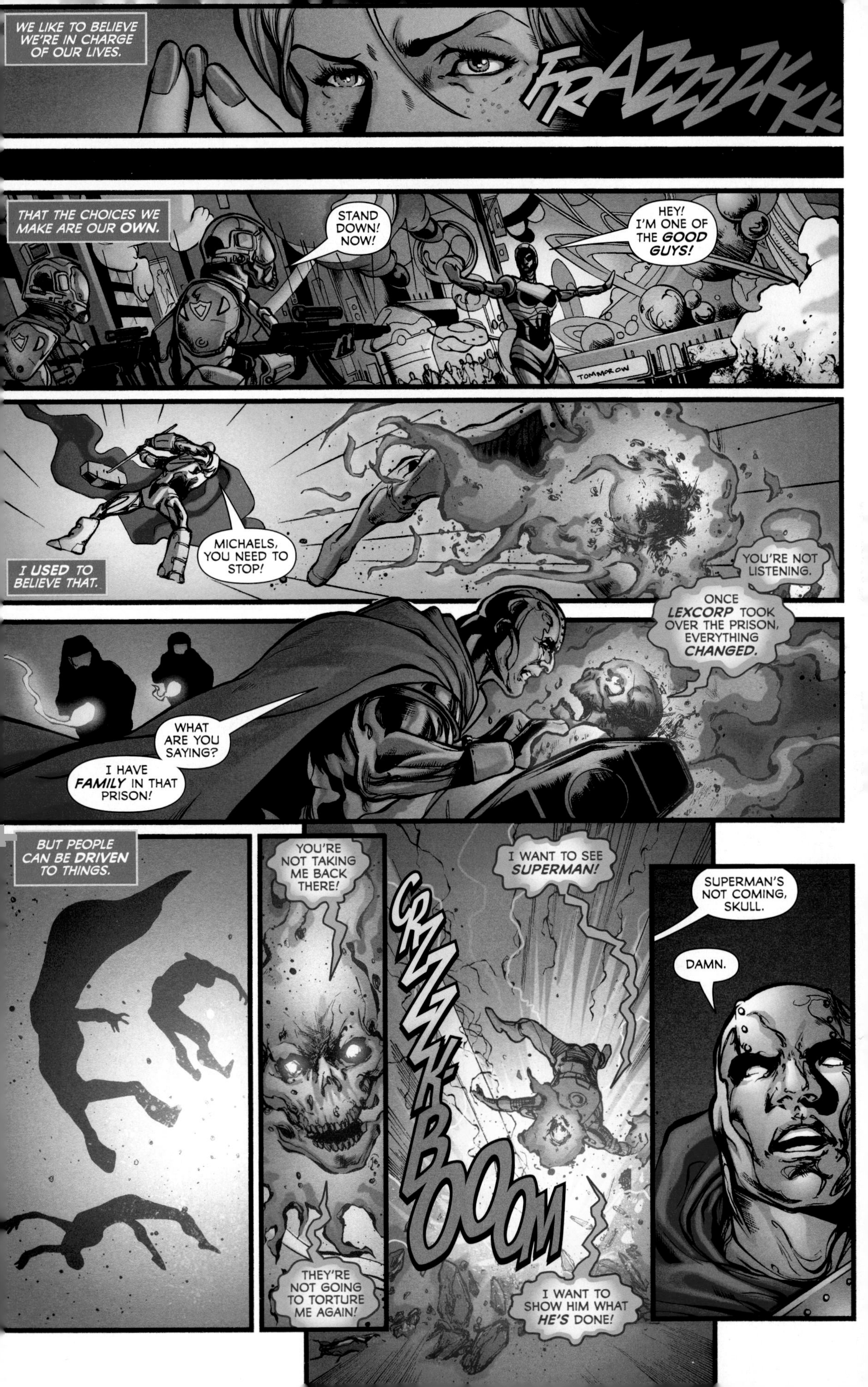

WE LIKE TO BELIEVE WE'RE IN CHARGE OF OUR LIVES.
FRAZZZZKKK
THAT THE CHOICES WE MAKE ARE OUR OWN.
STAND DOWN! NOW!
HEY! I'M ONE OF THE GOOD GUYS!
TOMMPROW
I USED TO BELIEVE THAT.
MICHAELS, YOU NEED TO STOP!
YOU'RE NOT LISTENING.
ONCE LEXCORP TOOK OVER THE PRISON, EVERYTHING CHANGED.
WHAT ARE YOU SAYING?
I HAVE FAMILY IN THAT PRISON!
BUT PEOPLE CAN BE DRIVEN TO THINGS.
YOU'RE NOT TAKING ME BACK THERE!
THEY'RE NOT GOING TO TORTURE ME AGAIN!
CRZZZZKBOOOM
I WANT TO SEE SUPERMAN!
I WANT TO SHOW HIM WHAT HE'S DONE!
SUPERMAN'S NOT COMING, SKULL.
DAMN.

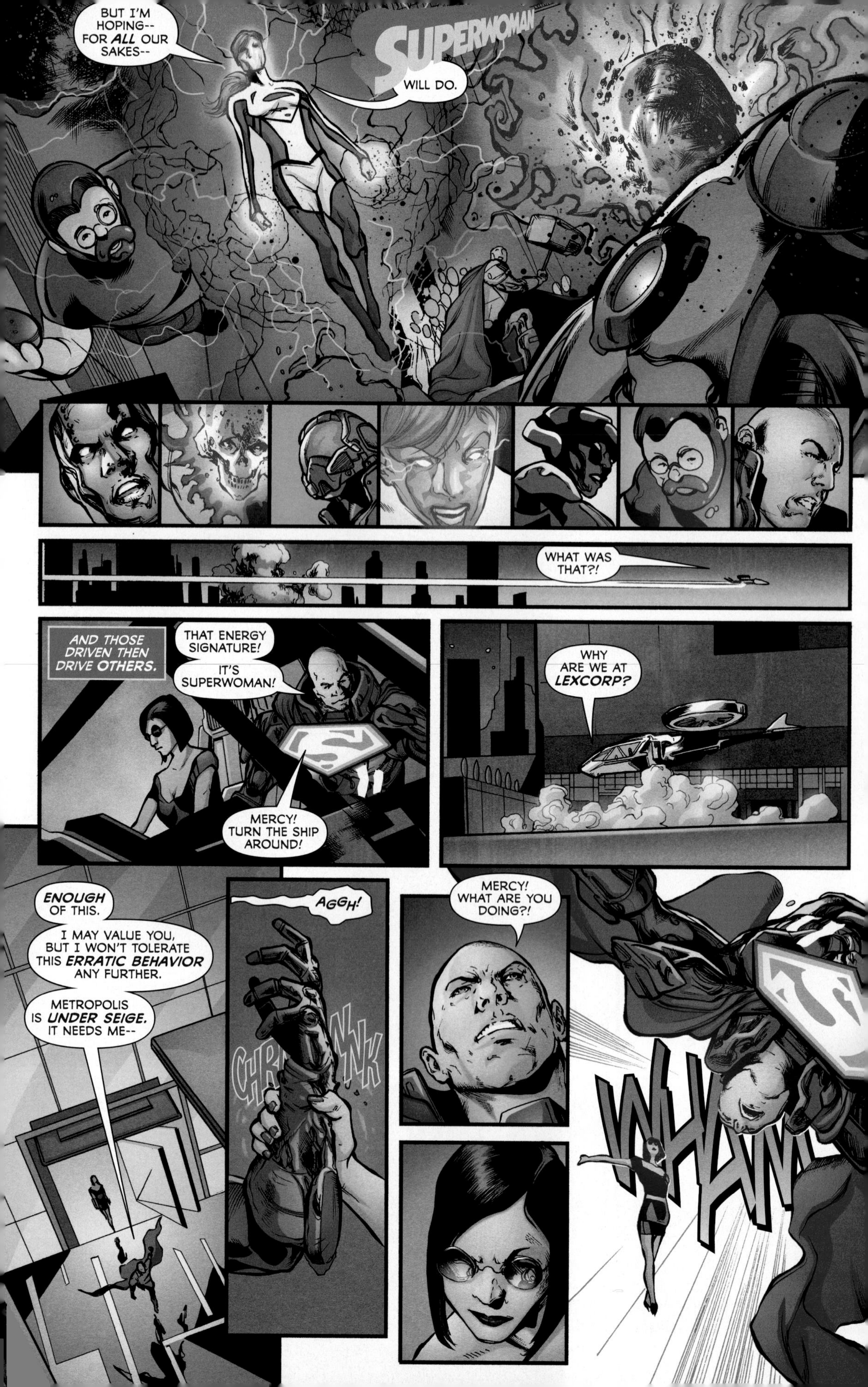
BUT I'M HOPING-- FOR ALL OUR SAKES--
SUPERWOMAN
WILL DO.
WHAT WAS THAT?!
AND THOSE DRIVEN THEN DRIVE OTHERS.
THAT ENERGY SIGNATURE!
IT'S SUPERWOMAN!
MERCY! TURN THE SHIP AROUND!
WHY ARE WE AT LEXCORP?
ENOUGH OF THIS.
I MAY VALUE YOU, BUT I WON'T TOLERATE THIS ERRATIC BEHAVIOR ANY FURTHER.
METROPOLIS IS UNDER SEIGE. IT NEEDS ME--
AGGH!
CHRUNNK
MERCY! WHAT ARE YOU DOING?!
WHAM

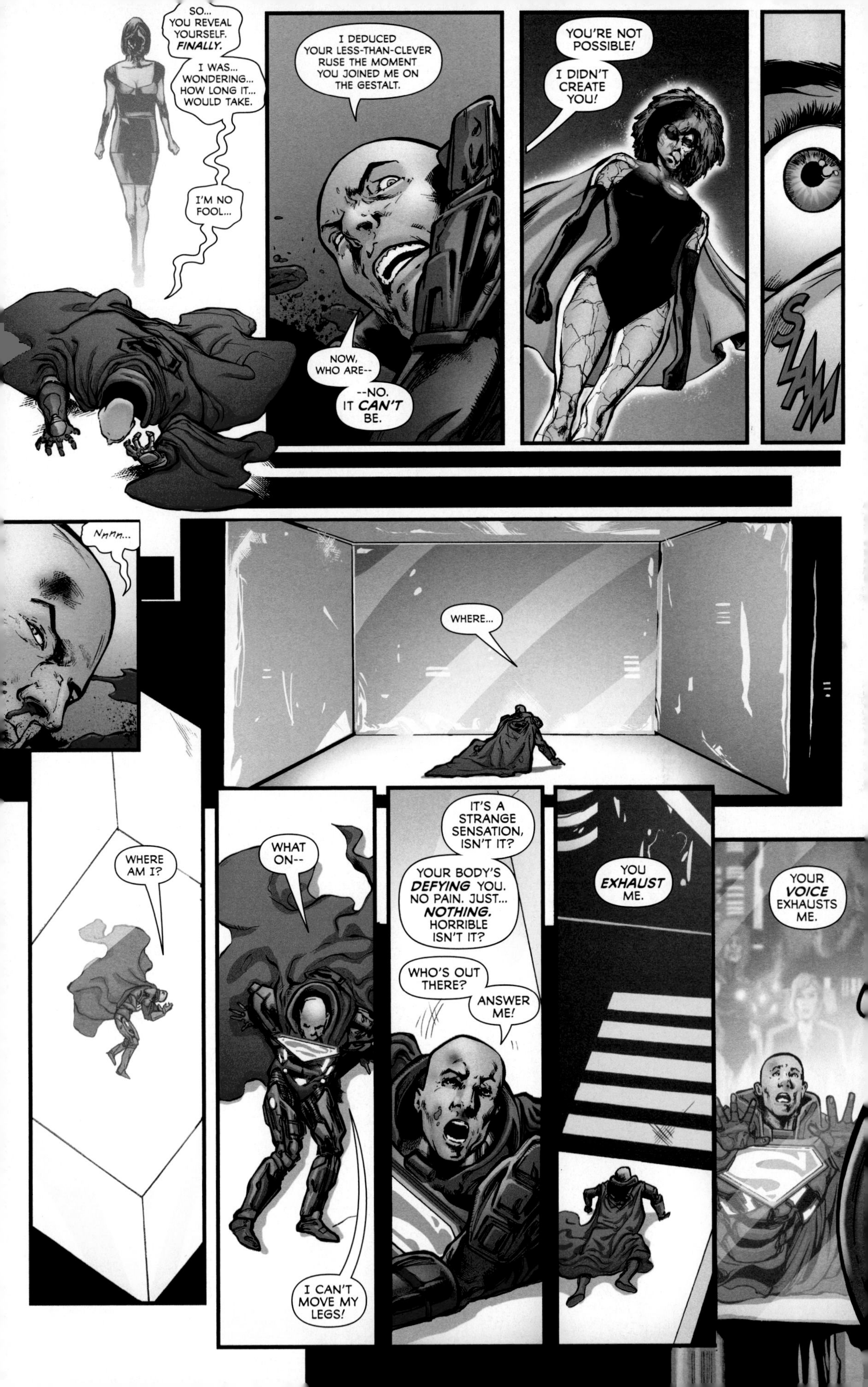
SO... YOU REVEAL YOURSELF. *FINALLY.*
I WAS... WONDERING... HOW LONG IT... WOULD TAKE.
I'M NO FOOL...
I DEDUCED YOUR LESS-THAN-CLEVER RUSE THE MOMENT YOU JOINED ME ON THE GESTALT.
NOW, WHO ARE--
--NO. IT *CAN'T* BE.
YOU'RE NOT POSSIBLE!
I DIDN'T CREATE YOU!
SLAM
Nnnn...
WHERE...
WHERE AM I?
WHAT ON--
I CAN'T MOVE MY LEGS!
IT'S A STRANGE SENSATION, ISN'T IT?
YOUR BODY'S *DEFYING* YOU. NO PAIN. JUST... *NOTHING.* HORRIBLE ISN'T IT?
WHO'S OUT THERE?
ANSWER ME!
YOU *EXHAUST* ME.
YOUR *VOICE* EXHAUSTS ME.

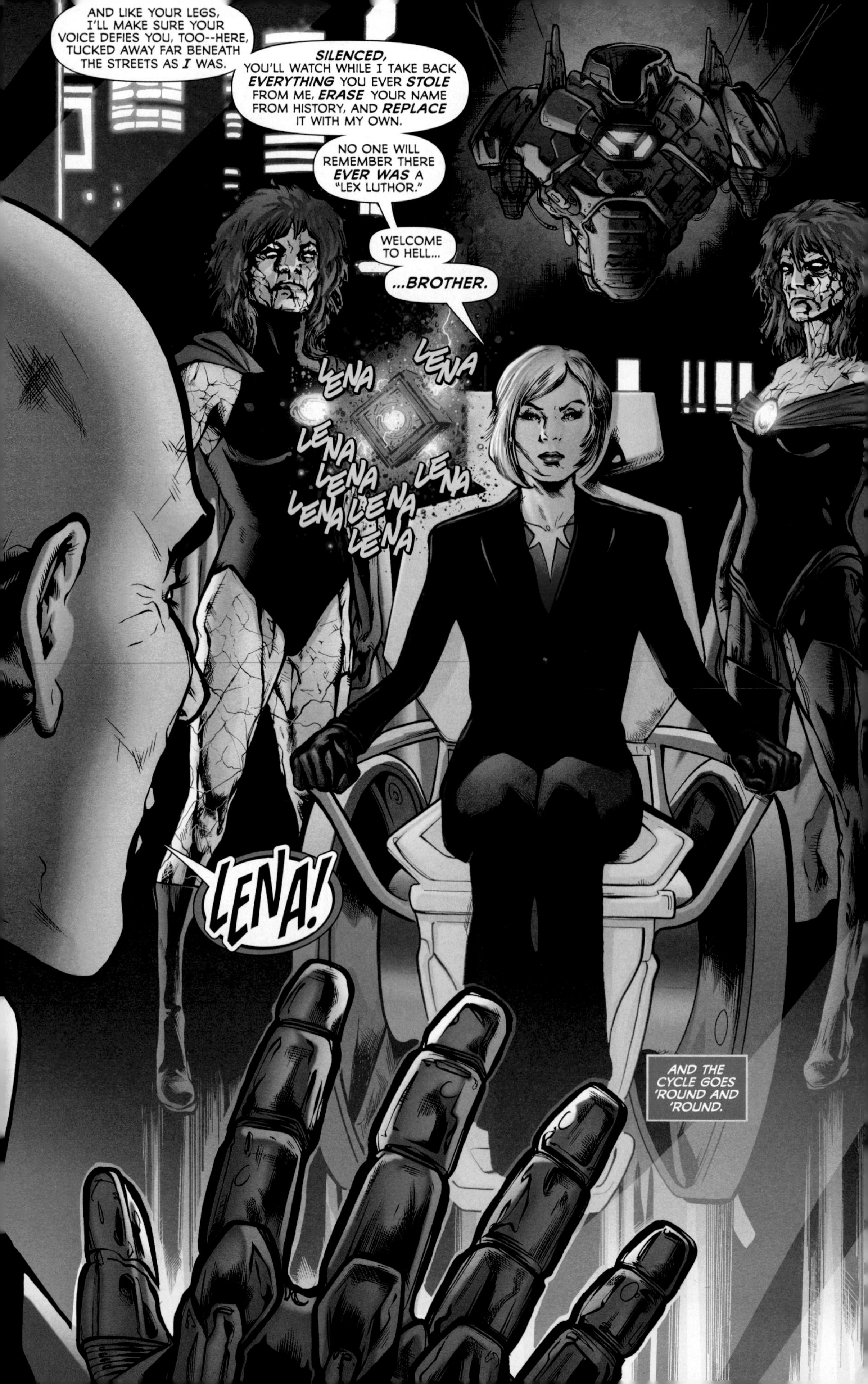

AND LIKE YOUR LEGS, I'LL MAKE SURE YOUR VOICE DEFIES YOU, TOO--HERE, TUCKED AWAY FAR BENEATH THE STREETS AS *I* WAS.
SILENCED, YOU'LL WATCH WHILE I TAKE BACK *EVERYTHING* YOU EVER *STOLE* FROM ME, *ERASE* YOUR NAME FROM HISTORY, AND *REPLACE* IT WITH MY OWN.
NO ONE WILL REMEMBER THERE *EVER WAS* A "LEX LUTHOR."
WELCOME TO HELL...
...BROTHER.
LENA LENA LENA LENA LENA LENA LENA LENA LENA
LENA!
AND THE CYCLE GOES 'ROUND AND 'ROUND.

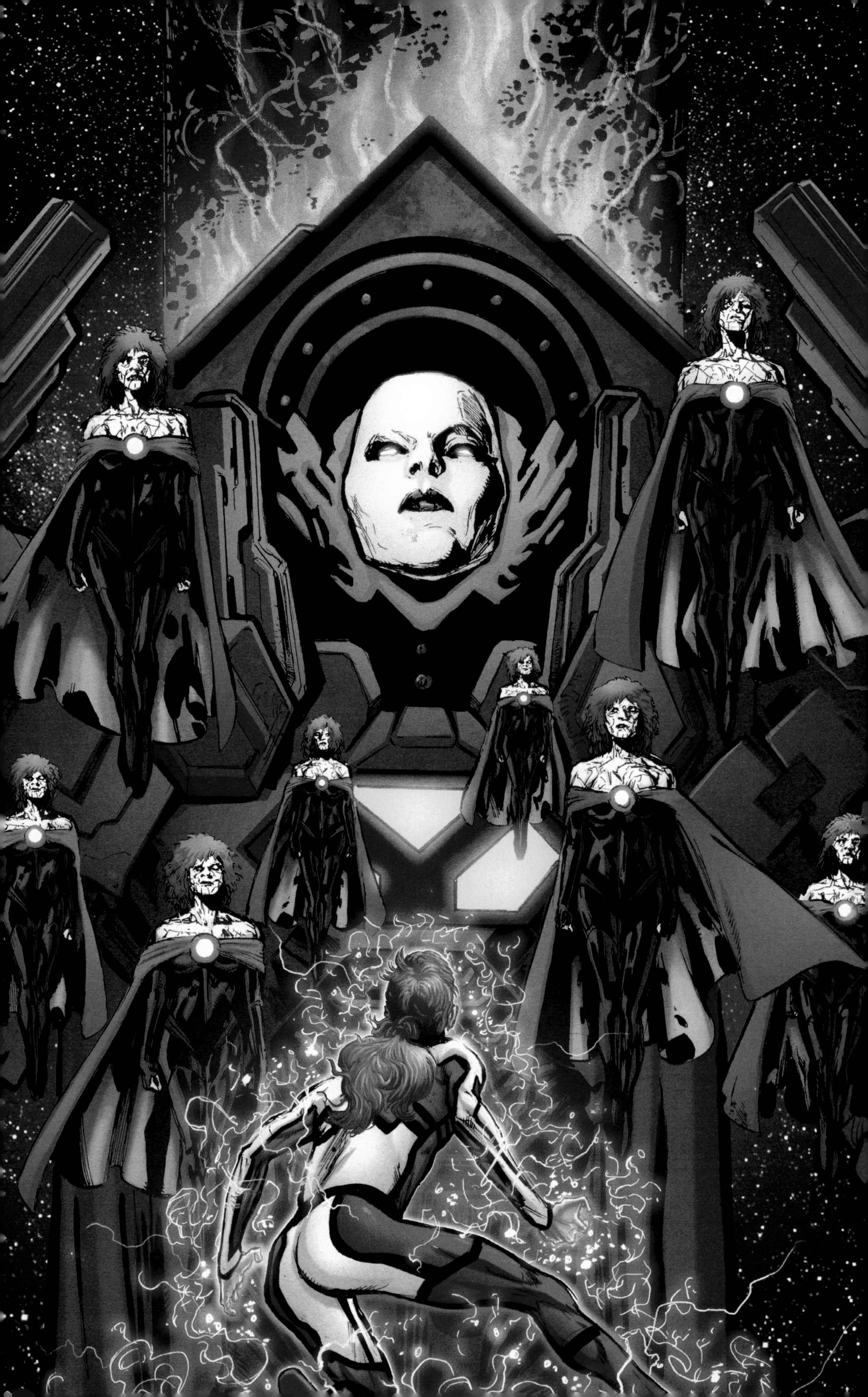

“WHO KILLED SUPERWOMAN? PART 3”

PHIL JIMENEZ writer * EMANUELA LUPACCHINO penciller * RAY MCCARTHY inker

HI-FI colorist * cover by PHIL JIMENEZ and JEROMY COX

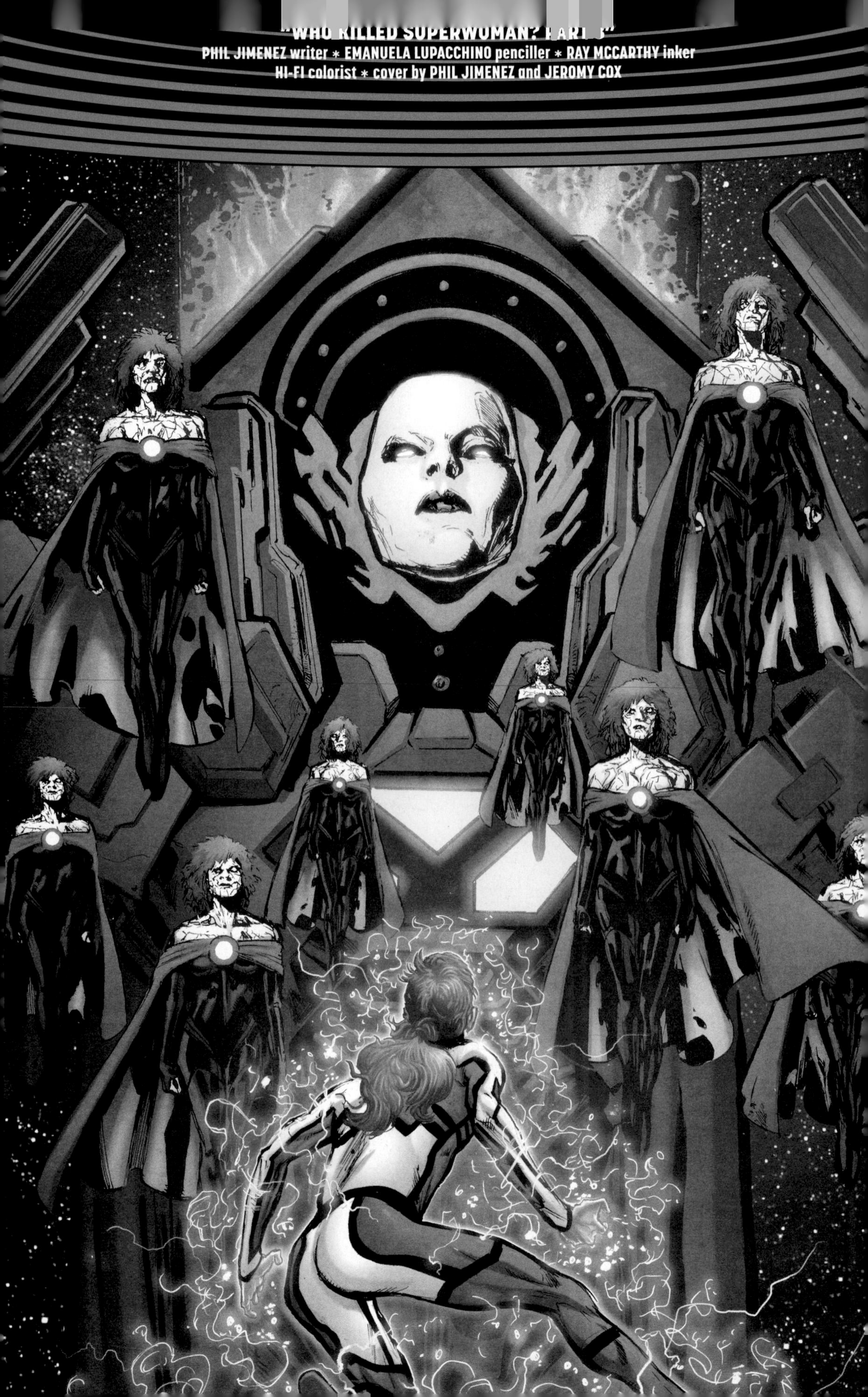

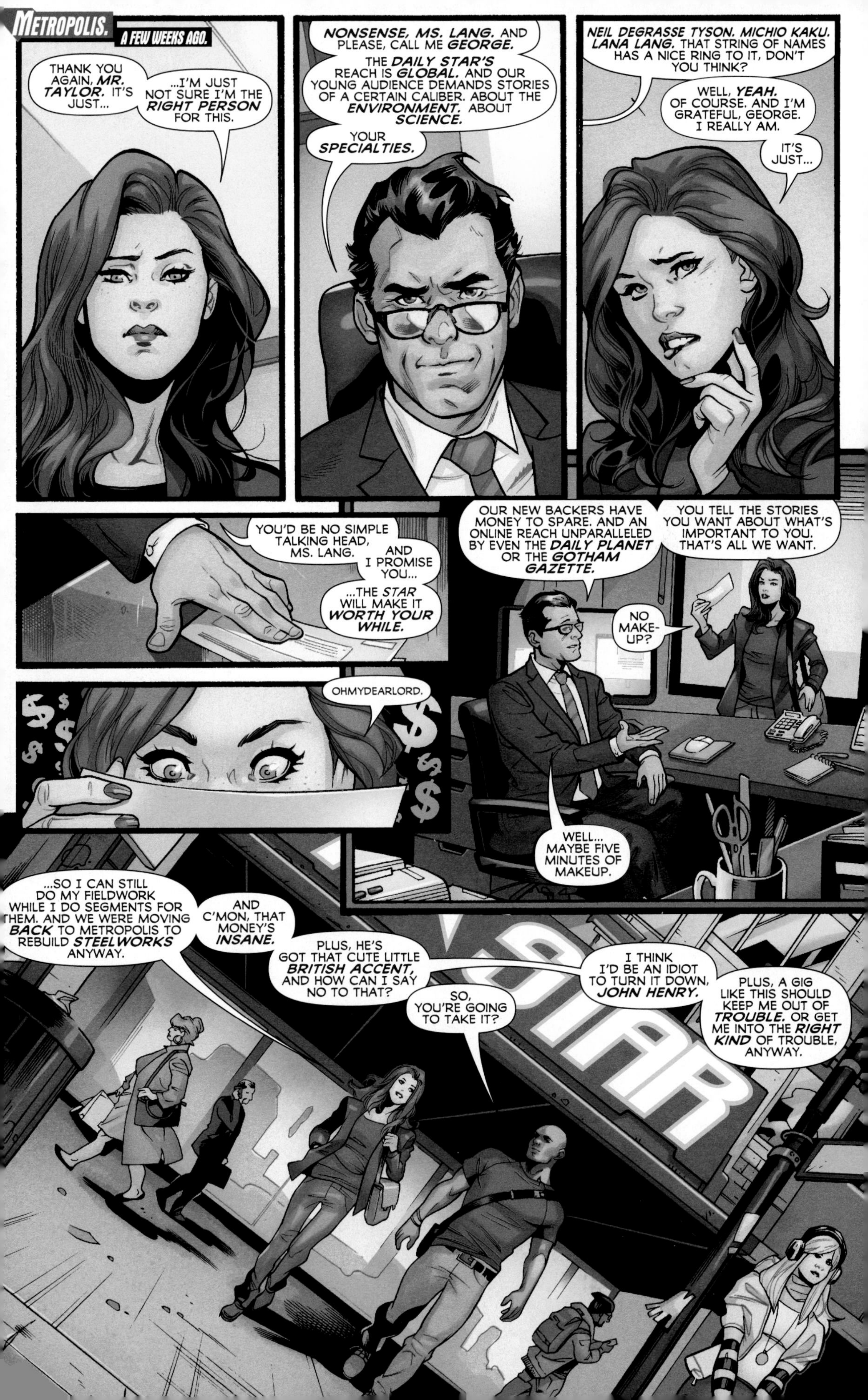
METROPOLIS.
A FEW WEEKS AGO.
THANK YOU AGAIN, MR. TAYLOR. IT'S JUST...
...I'M JUST NOT SURE I'M THE RIGHT PERSON FOR THIS.
NONSENSE, MS. LANG. AND PLEASE, CALL ME GEORGE.
THE DAILY STAR'S REACH IS GLOBAL. AND OUR YOUNG AUDIENCE DEMANDS STORIES OF A CERTAIN CALIBER. ABOUT THE ENVIRONMENT. ABOUT SCIENCE.
YOUR SPECIALTIES.
NEIL DEGRASSE TYSON. MICHIO KAKU. LANA LANG. THAT STRING OF NAMES HAS A NICE RING TO IT, DON'T YOU THINK?
WELL, YEAH. OF COURSE. AND I'M GRATEFUL, GEORGE. I REALLY AM.
IT'S JUST...
YOU'D BE NO SIMPLE TALKING HEAD, MS. LANG.
AND I PROMISE YOU...
...THE STAR WILL MAKE IT WORTH YOUR WHILE.
OHMYDEARLORD.
OUR NEW BACKERS HAVE MONEY TO SPARE. AND AN ONLINE REACH UNPARALLELED BY EVEN THE DAILY PLANET OR THE GOTHAM GAZETTE.
YOU TELL THE STORIES YOU WANT ABOUT WHAT'S IMPORTANT TO YOU. THAT'S ALL WE WANT.
NO MAKE-UP?
WELL... MAYBE FIVE MINUTES OF MAKEUP.
...SO I CAN STILL DO MY FIELDWORK WHILE I DO SEGMENTS FOR THEM. AND WE WERE MOVING BACK TO METROPOLIS TO REBUILD STEELWORKS ANYWAY.
AND C'MON, THAT MONEY'S INSANE.
PLUS, HE'S GOT THAT CUTE LITTLE BRITISH ACCENT, AND HOW CAN I SAY NO TO THAT?
SO, YOU'RE GOING TO TAKE IT?
I THINK I'D BE AN IDIOT TO TURN IT DOWN, JOHN HENRY.
PLUS, A GIG LIKE THIS SHOULD KEEP ME OUT OF TROUBLE. OR GET ME INTO THE RIGHT KIND OF TROUBLE, ANYWAY.
STAR

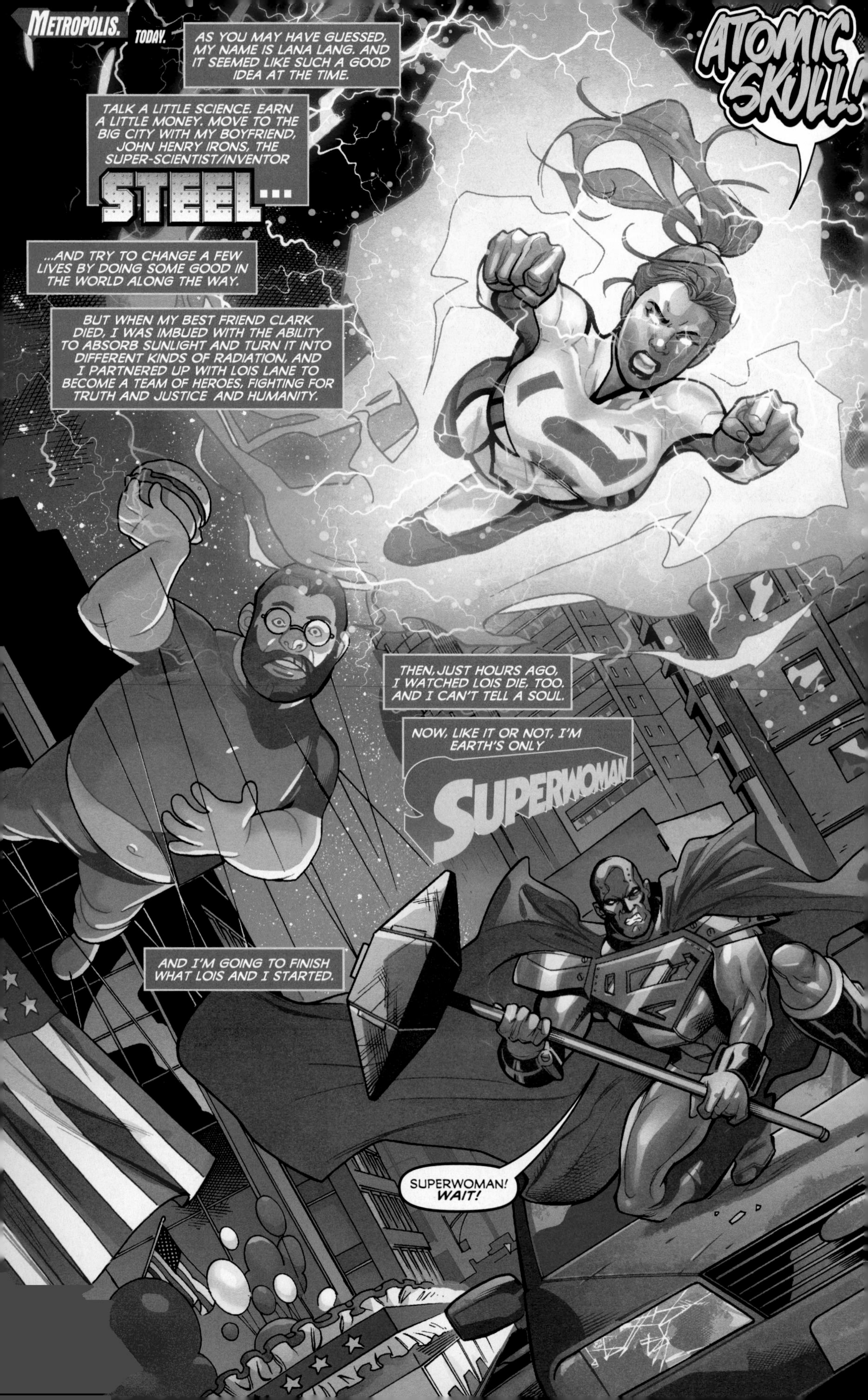
METROPOLIS.
TODAY.
AS YOU MAY HAVE GUESSED, MY NAME IS LANA LANG. AND IT SEEMED LIKE SUCH A GOOD IDEA AT THE TIME.
ATOMIC SKULL!
TALK A LITTLE SCIENCE. EARN A LITTLE MONEY. MOVE TO THE BIG CITY WITH MY BOYFRIEND, JOHN HENRY IRONS, THE SUPER-SCIENTIST/INVENTOR
STEEL...
...AND TRY TO CHANGE A FEW LIVES BY DOING SOME GOOD IN THE WORLD ALONG THE WAY.
BUT WHEN MY BEST FRIEND CLARK DIED, I WAS IMBUED WITH THE ABILITY TO ABSORB SUNLIGHT AND TURN IT INTO DIFFERENT KINDS OF RADIATION, AND I PARTNERED UP WITH LOIS LANE TO BECOME A TEAM OF HEROES, FIGHTING FOR TRUTH AND JUSTICE AND HUMANITY.
THEN, JUST HOURS AGO, I WATCHED LOIS DIE, TOO. AND I CAN'T TELL A SOUL.
NOW, LIKE IT OR NOT, I'M EARTH'S ONLY
SUPERWOMAN
AND I'M GOING TO FINISH WHAT LOIS AND I STARTED.
SUPERWOMAN! WAIT!

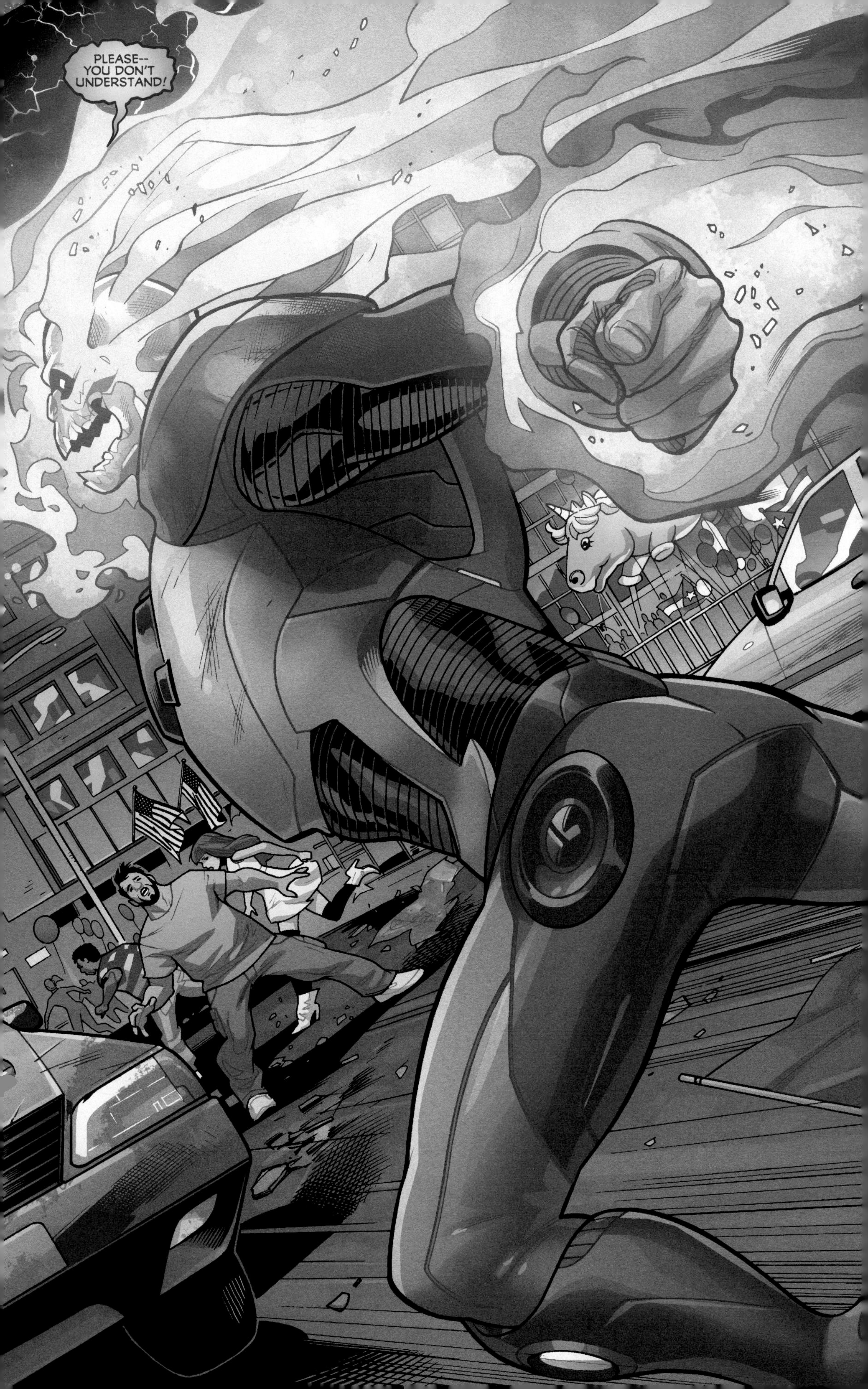
PLEASE-- YOU DON'T UNDERSTAND!

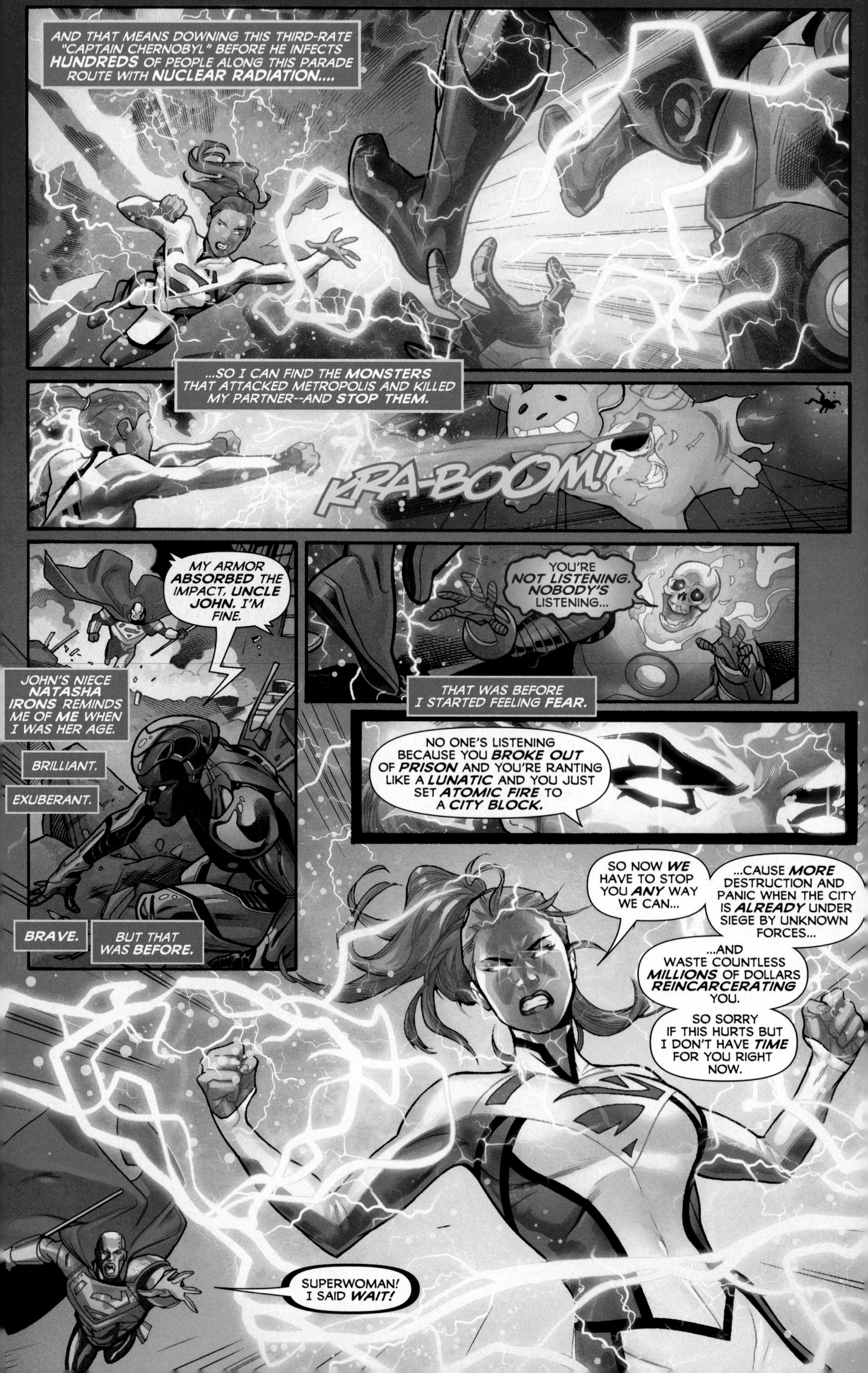
AND THAT MEANS DOWNING THIS THIRD-RATE "CAPTAIN CHERNOBYL" BEFORE HE INFECTS HUNDREDS OF PEOPLE ALONG THIS PARADE ROUTE WITH NUCLEAR RADIATION....
...SO I CAN FIND THE MONSTERS THAT ATTACKED METROPOLIS AND KILLED MY PARTNER--AND STOP THEM.
KRA-BOOM!
MY ARMOR ABSORBED THE IMPACT, UNCLE JOHN. I'M FINE.
JOHN'S NIECE NATASHA IRONS REMINDS ME OF ME WHEN I WAS HER AGE.
BRILLIANT.
EXUBERANT.
BRAVE.
BUT THAT WAS BEFORE.
YOU'RE NOT LISTENING. NOBODY'S LISTENING...
THAT WAS BEFORE I STARTED FEELING FEAR.
NO ONE'S LISTENING BECAUSE YOU BROKE OUT OF PRISON AND YOU'RE RANTING LIKE A LUNATIC AND YOU JUST SET ATOMIC FIRE TO A CITY BLOCK.
SO NOW WE HAVE TO STOP YOU ANY WAY WE CAN...
...CAUSE MORE DESTRUCTION AND PANIC WHEN THE CITY IS ALREADY UNDER SIEGE BY UNKNOWN FORCES...
...AND WASTE COUNTLESS MILLIONS OF DOLLARS REINCARCERATING YOU.
SO SORRY IF THIS HURTS BUT I DON'T HAVE TIME FOR YOU RIGHT NOW.
SUPERWOMAN! I SAID WAIT!

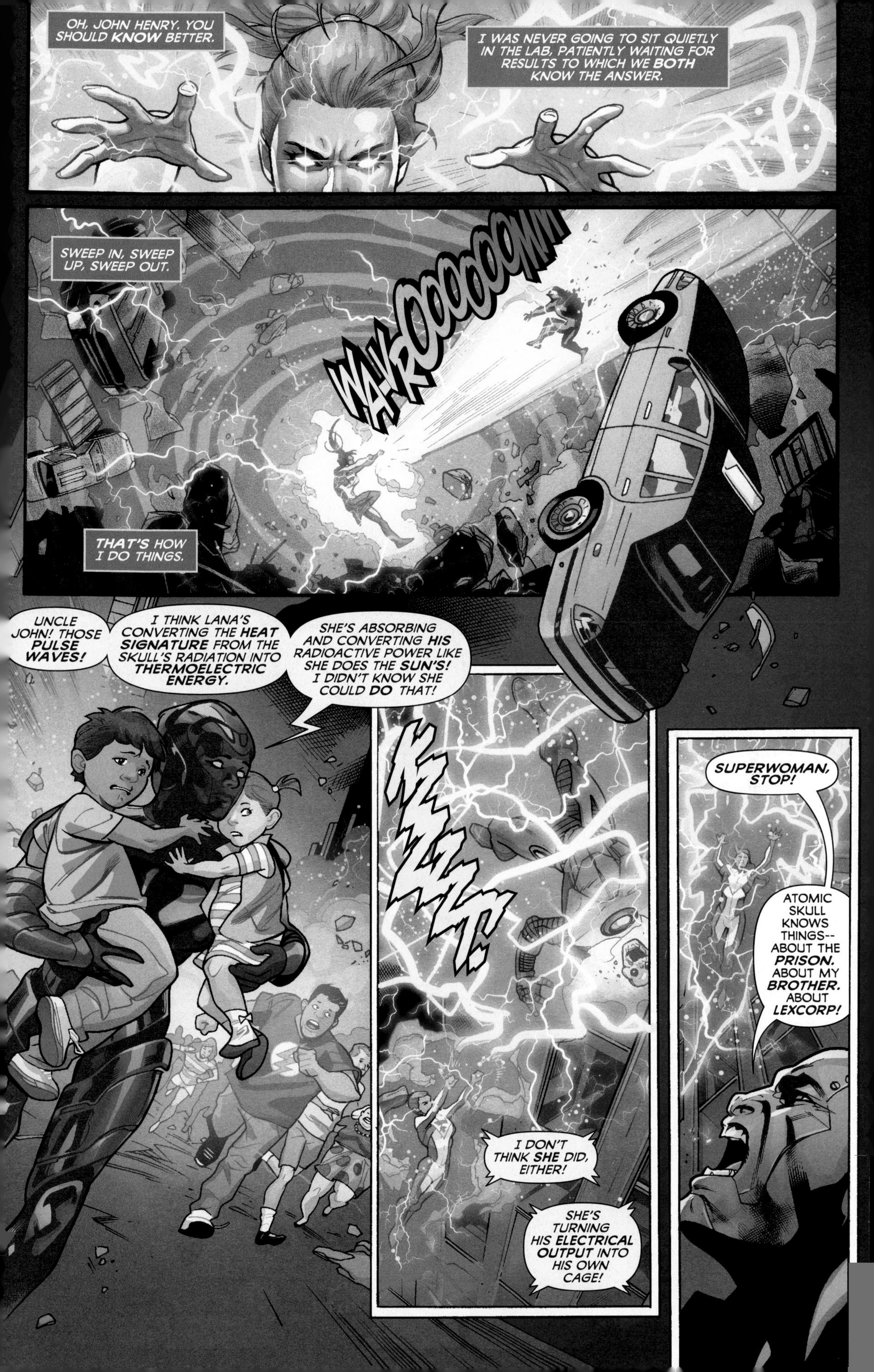
OH, JOHN HENRY. YOU SHOULD KNOW BETTER.
I WAS NEVER GOING TO SIT QUIETLY IN THE LAB, PATIENTLY WAITING FOR RESULTS TO WHICH WE BOTH KNOW THE ANSWER.
SWEEP IN, SWEEP UP, SWEEP OUT.
WA-ROOOOOOM
THAT'S HOW I DO THINGS.
UNCLE JOHN! THOSE PULSE WAVES!
I THINK LANA'S CONVERTING THE HEAT SIGNATURE FROM THE SKULL'S RADIATION INTO THERMOELECTRIC ENERGY.
SHE'S ABSORBING AND CONVERTING HIS RADIOACTIVE POWER LIKE SHE DOES THE SUN'S! I DIDN'T KNOW SHE COULD DO THAT!
I DON'T THINK SHE DID, EITHER!
SHE'S TURNING HIS ELECTRICAL OUTPUT INTO HIS OWN CAGE!
SUPERWOMAN, STOP!
ATOMIC SKULL KNOWS THINGS-- ABOUT THE PRISON. ABOUT MY BROTHER. ABOUT LEXCORP!

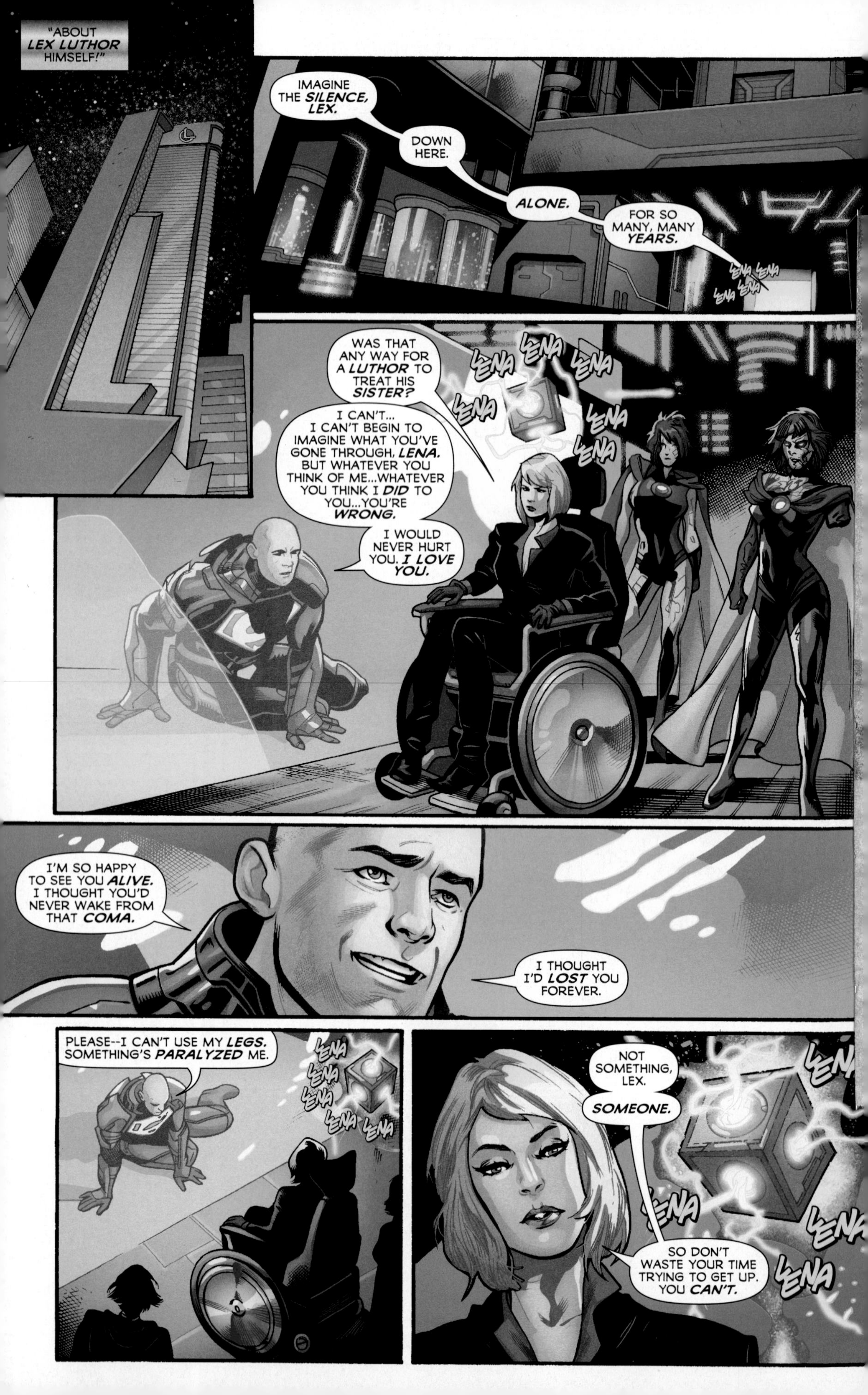
"ABOUT LEX LUTHOR HIMSELF!"
IMAGINE THE SILENCE, LEX.
DOWN HERE.
ALONE.
FOR SO MANY, MANY YEARS.
LENA LENA LENA LENA
WAS THAT ANY WAY FOR A LUTHOR TO TREAT HIS SISTER?
LENA LENA LENA LENA LENA LENA
I CAN'T... I CAN'T BEGIN TO IMAGINE WHAT YOU'VE GONE THROUGH, LENA. BUT WHATEVER YOU THINK OF ME...WHATEVER YOU THINK I DID TO YOU...YOU'RE WRONG.
I WOULD NEVER HURT YOU. I LOVE YOU.
I'M SO HAPPY TO SEE YOU ALIVE. I THOUGHT YOU'D NEVER WAKE FROM THAT COMA.
I THOUGHT I'D LOST YOU FOREVER.
PLEASE--I CAN'T USE MY LEGS. SOMETHING'S PARALYZED ME.
LENA LENA LENA LENA LENA LENA
NOT SOMETHING, LEX.
SOMEONE.
SO DON'T WASTE YOUR TIME TRYING TO GET UP. YOU CAN'T.
LENA LENA LENA LENA

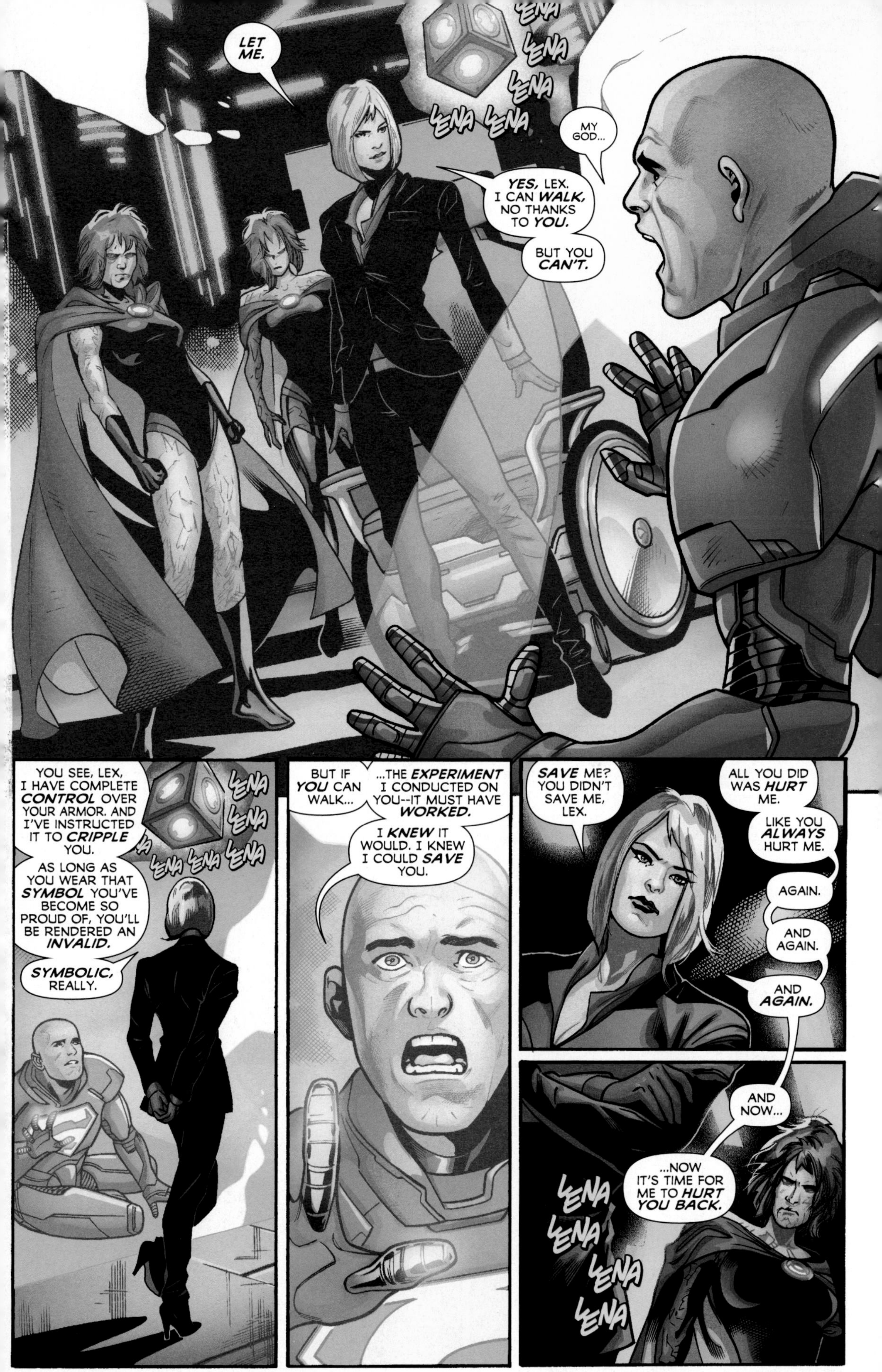
LET ME.
LENA LENA LENA LENA LENA
MY GOD...
YES, LEX. I CAN WALK, NO THANKS TO YOU.
BUT YOU CAN'T.
YOU SEE, LEX, I HAVE COMPLETE CONTROL OVER YOUR ARMOR. AND I'VE INSTRUCTED IT TO CRIPPLE YOU.
LENA LENA LENA LENA LENA
AS LONG AS YOU WEAR THAT SYMBOL YOU'VE BECOME SO PROUD OF, YOU'LL BE RENDERED AN INVALID.
SYMBOLIC, REALLY.
BUT IF YOU CAN WALK...
...THE EXPERIMENT I CONDUCTED ON YOU--IT MUST HAVE WORKED.
I KNEW IT WOULD. I KNEW I COULD SAVE YOU.
SAVE ME? YOU DIDN'T SAVE ME, LEX.
ALL YOU DID WAS HURT ME.
LIKE YOU ALWAYS HURT ME.
AGAIN.
AND AGAIN.
AND AGAIN.
AND NOW...
...NOW IT'S TIME FOR ME TO HURT YOU BACK.
LENA LENA LENA LENA

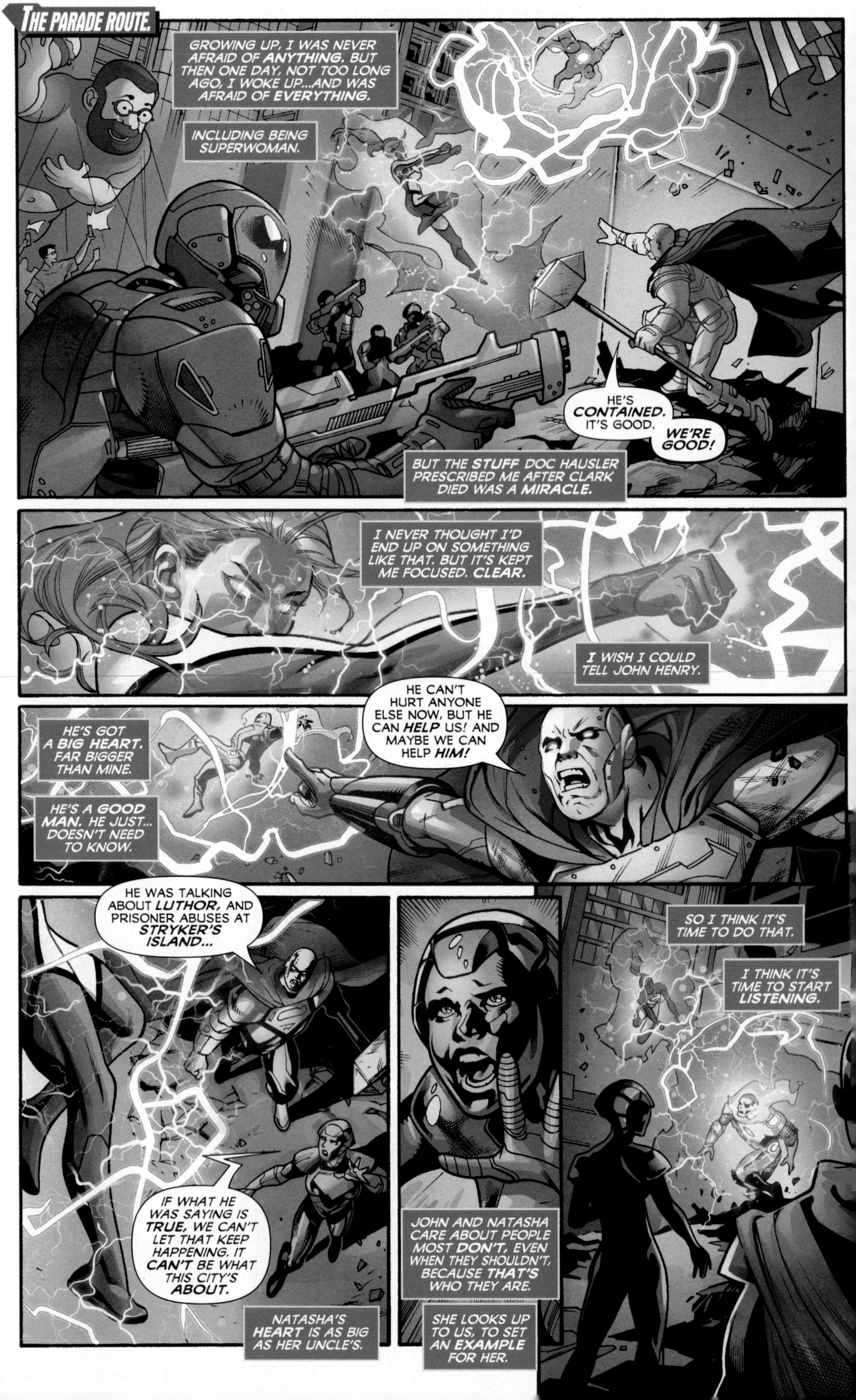
THE PARADE ROUTE.
GROWING UP, I WAS NEVER AFRAID OF ANYTHING. BUT THEN ONE DAY, NOT TOO LONG AGO, I WOKE UP...AND WAS AFRAID OF EVERYTHING.
INCLUDING BEING SUPERWOMAN.
HE'S CONTAINED. IT'S GOOD. WE'RE GOOD!
BUT THE STUFF DOC HAUSLER PRESCRIBED ME AFTER CLARK DIED WAS A MIRACLE.
I NEVER THOUGHT I'D END UP ON SOMETHING LIKE THAT. BUT IT'S KEPT ME FOCUSED. CLEAR.
I WISH I COULD TELL JOHN HENRY.
HE'S GOT A BIG HEART. FAR BIGGER THAN MINE.
HE'S A GOOD MAN. HE JUST... DOESN'T NEED TO KNOW.
HE CAN'T HURT ANYONE ELSE NOW, BUT HE CAN HELP US! AND MAYBE WE CAN HELP HIM!
HE WAS TALKING ABOUT LUTHOR, AND PRISONER ABUSES AT STRYKER'S ISLAND...
IF WHAT HE WAS SAYING IS TRUE, WE CAN'T LET THAT KEEP HAPPENING. IT CAN'T BE WHAT THIS CITY'S ABOUT.
NATASHA'S HEART IS AS BIG AS HER UNCLE'S.
JOHN AND NATASHA CARE ABOUT PEOPLE MOST DON'T, EVEN WHEN THEY SHOULDN'T, BECAUSE THAT'S WHO THEY ARE.
SHE LOOKS UP TO US, TO SET AN EXAMPLE FOR HER.
SO I THINK IT'S TIME TO DO THAT.
I THINK IT'S TIME TO START LISTENING.

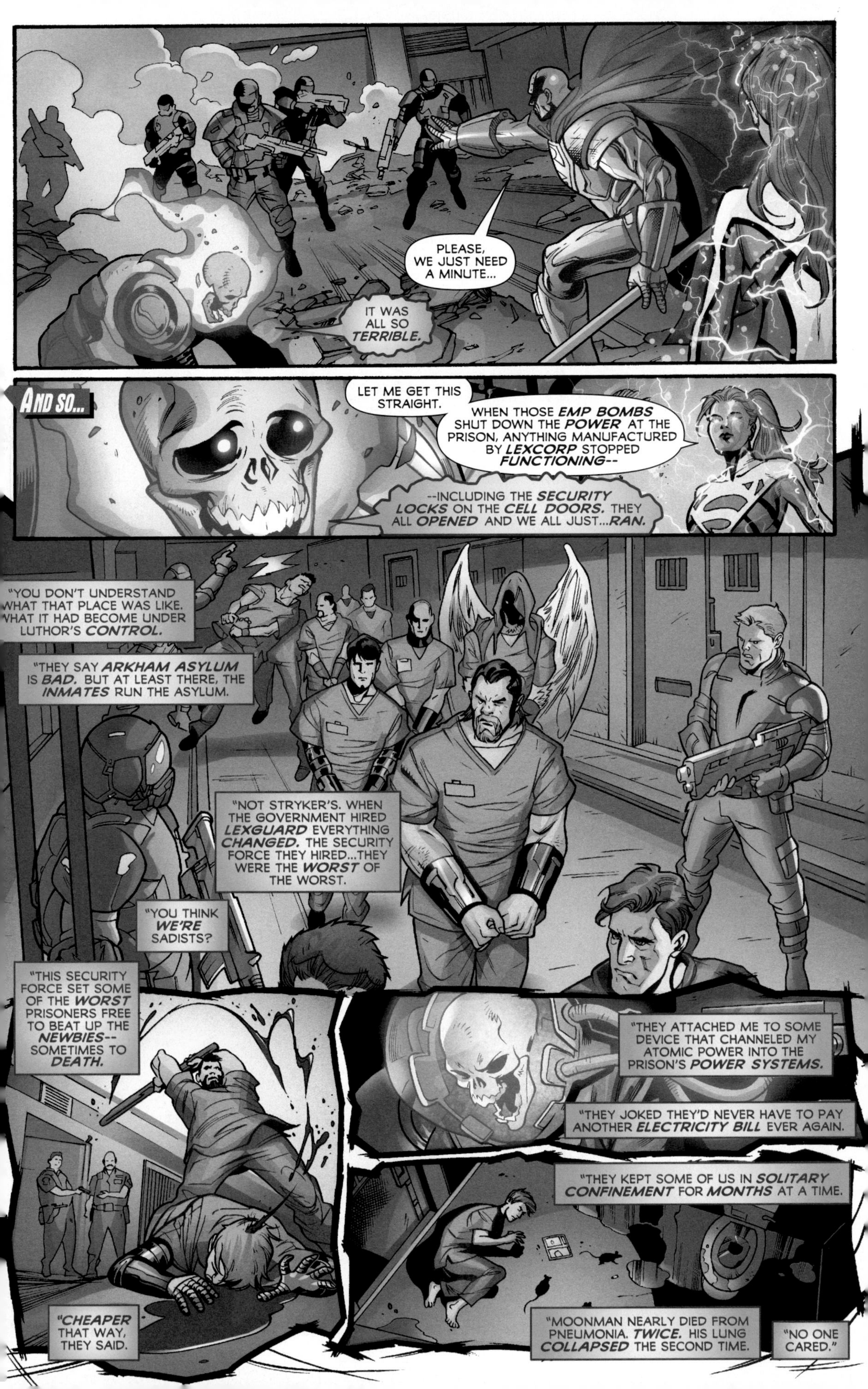
PLEASE, WE JUST NEED A MINUTE...
IT WAS ALL SO TERRIBLE.
AND SO...
LET ME GET THIS STRAIGHT.
WHEN THOSE EMP BOMBS SHUT DOWN THE POWER AT THE PRISON, ANYTHING MANUFACTURED BY LEXCORP STOPPED FUNCTIONING--
--INCLUDING THE SECURITY LOCKS ON THE CELL DOORS. THEY ALL OPENED AND WE ALL JUST...RAN.
"YOU DON'T UNDERSTAND WHAT THAT PLACE WAS LIKE. WHAT IT HAD BECOME UNDER LUTHOR'S CONTROL.
"THEY SAY ARKHAM ASYLUM IS BAD. BUT AT LEAST THERE, THE INMATES RUN THE ASYLUM.
"NOT STRYKER'S. WHEN THE GOVERNMENT HIRED LEXGUARD EVERYTHING CHANGED. THE SECURITY FORCE THEY HIRED...THEY WERE THE WORST OF THE WORST.
"YOU THINK WE'RE SADISTS?
"THIS SECURITY FORCE SET SOME OF THE WORST PRISONERS FREE TO BEAT UP THE NEWBIES--SOMETIMES TO DEATH.
"CHEAPER THAT WAY, THEY SAID.
"THEY ATTACHED ME TO SOME DEVICE THAT CHANNELED MY ATOMIC POWER INTO THE PRISON'S POWER SYSTEMS.
"THEY JOKED THEY'D NEVER HAVE TO PAY ANOTHER ELECTRICITY BILL EVER AGAIN.
"THEY KEPT SOME OF US IN SOLITARY CONFINEMENT FOR MONTHS AT A TIME.
"MOONMAN NEARLY DIED FROM PNEUMONIA. TWICE. HIS LUNG COLLAPSED THE SECOND TIME.
"NO ONE CARED."

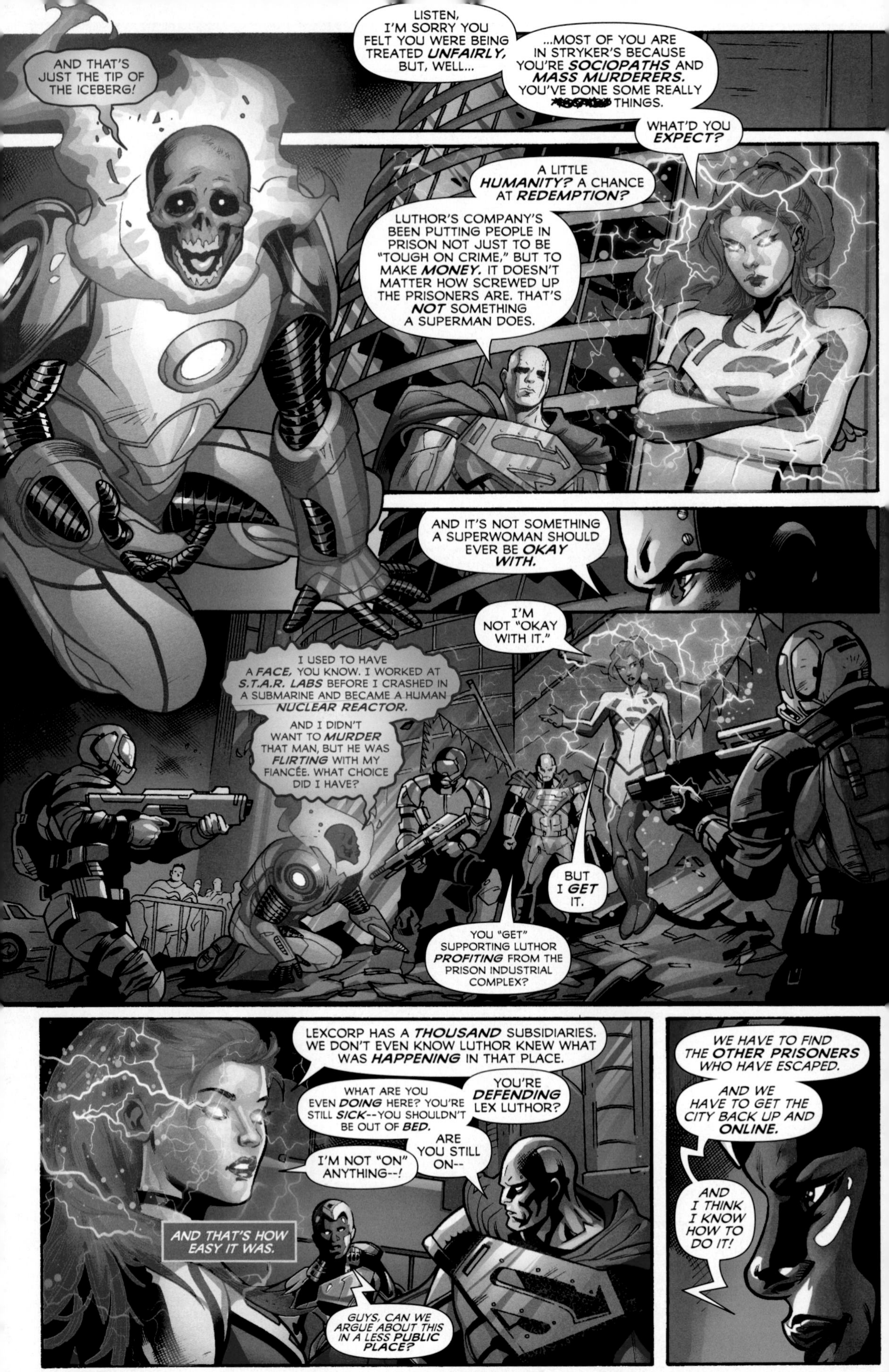
AND THAT'S JUST THE TIP OF THE ICEBERG!
LISTEN, I'M SORRY YOU FELT YOU WERE BEING TREATED UNFAIRLY, BUT, WELL...
...MOST OF YOU ARE IN STRYKER'S BECAUSE YOU'RE SOCIOPATHS AND MASS MURDERERS. YOU'VE DONE SOME REALLY THINGS.
WHAT'D YOU EXPECT?
A LITTLE HUMANITY? A CHANCE AT REDEMPTION?
LUTHOR'S COMPANY'S BEEN PUTTING PEOPLE IN PRISON NOT JUST TO BE "TOUGH ON CRIME," BUT TO MAKE MONEY. IT DOESN'T MATTER HOW SCREWED UP THE PRISONERS ARE. THAT'S NOT SOMETHING A SUPERMAN DOES.
AND IT'S NOT SOMETHING A SUPERWOMAN SHOULD EVER BE OKAY WITH.
I'M NOT "OKAY WITH IT."
I USED TO HAVE A FACE, YOU KNOW. I WORKED AT S.T.A.R. LABS BEFORE I CRASHED IN A SUBMARINE AND BECAME A HUMAN NUCLEAR REACTOR.
AND I DIDN'T WANT TO MURDER THAT MAN, BUT HE WAS FLIRTING WITH MY FIANCÉE. WHAT CHOICE DID I HAVE?
BUT I GET IT.
YOU "GET" SUPPORTING LUTHOR PROFITING FROM THE PRISON INDUSTRIAL COMPLEX?
LEXCORP HAS A THOUSAND SUBSIDIARIES. WE DON'T EVEN KNOW LUTHOR KNEW WHAT WAS HAPPENING IN THAT PLACE.
YOU'RE DEFENDING LEX LUTHOR?
WHAT ARE YOU EVEN DOING HERE? YOU'RE STILL SICK--YOU SHOULDN'T BE OUT OF BED.
ARE YOU STILL ON--
I'M NOT "ON" ANYTHING--!
AND THAT'S HOW EASY IT WAS.
GUYS, CAN WE ARGUE ABOUT THIS IN A LESS PUBLIC PLACE?
WE HAVE TO FIND THE OTHER PRISONERS WHO HAVE ESCAPED.
AND WE HAVE TO GET THE CITY BACK UP AND ONLINE.
AND I THINK I KNOW HOW TO DO IT!

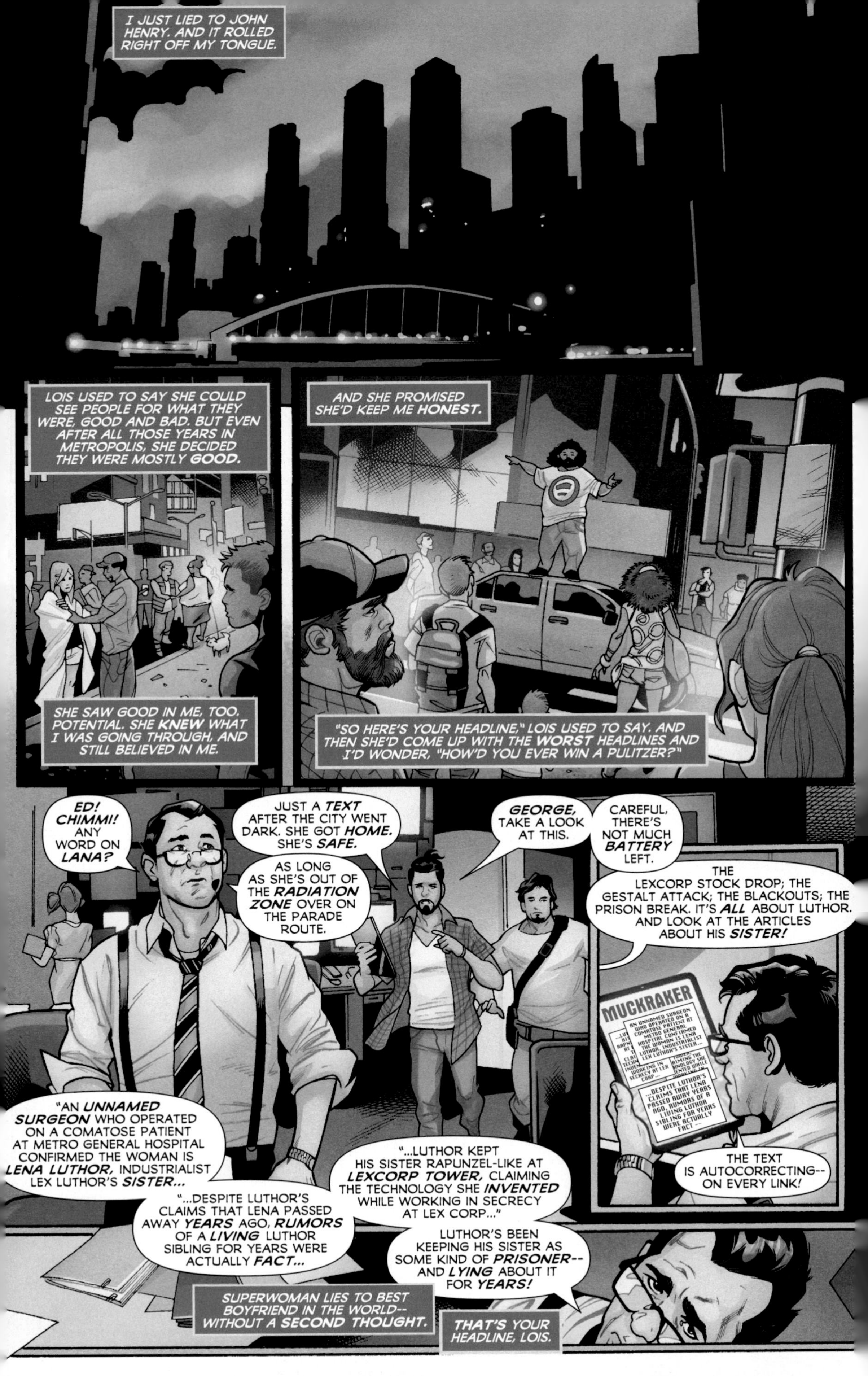
I JUST LIED TO JOHN HENRY. AND IT ROLLED RIGHT OFF MY TONGUE.
LOIS USED TO SAY SHE COULD SEE PEOPLE FOR WHAT THEY WERE, GOOD AND BAD. BUT EVEN AFTER ALL THOSE YEARS IN METROPOLIS, SHE DECIDED THEY WERE MOSTLY GOOD.
SHE SAW GOOD IN ME, TOO. POTENTIAL. SHE KNEW WHAT I WAS GOING THROUGH, AND STILL BELIEVED IN ME.
AND SHE PROMISED SHE'D KEEP ME HONEST.
"SO HERE'S YOUR HEADLINE," LOIS USED TO SAY. AND THEN SHE'D COME UP WITH THE WORST HEADLINES AND I'D WONDER, "HOW'D YOU EVER WIN A PULITZER?"
ED! CHIMMI! ANY WORD ON LANA?
JUST A TEXT AFTER THE CITY WENT DARK. SHE GOT HOME. SHE'S SAFE.
AS LONG AS SHE'S OUT OF THE RADIATION ZONE OVER ON THE PARADE ROUTE.
GEORGE, TAKE A LOOK AT THIS.
CAREFUL, THERE'S NOT MUCH BATTERY LEFT.
THE LEXCORP STOCK DROP; THE GESTALT ATTACK; THE BLACKOUTS; THE PRISON BREAK. IT'S ALL ABOUT LUTHOR. AND LOOK AT THE ARTICLES ABOUT HIS SISTER!
MUCKRAKER
THE TEXT IS AUTOCORRECTING-- ON EVERY LINK!
"AN UNNAMED SURGEON WHO OPERATED ON A COMATOSE PATIENT AT METRO GENERAL HOSPITAL CONFIRMED THE WOMAN IS LENA LUTHOR, INDUSTRIALIST LEX LUTHOR'S SISTER...
"...DESPITE LUTHOR'S CLAIMS THAT LENA PASSED AWAY YEARS AGO, RUMORS OF A LIVING LUTHOR SIBLING FOR YEARS WERE ACTUALLY FACT...
"...LUTHOR KEPT HIS SISTER RAPUNZEL-LIKE AT LEXCORP TOWER, CLAIMING THE TECHNOLOGY SHE INVENTED WHILE WORKING IN SECRECY AT LEX CORP..."
LUTHOR'S BEEN KEEPING HIS SISTER AS SOME KIND OF PRISONER-- AND LYING ABOUT IT FOR YEARS!
SUPERWOMAN LIES TO BEST BOYFRIEND IN THE WORLD-- WITHOUT A SECOND THOUGHT.
THAT'S YOUR HEADLINE, LOIS.

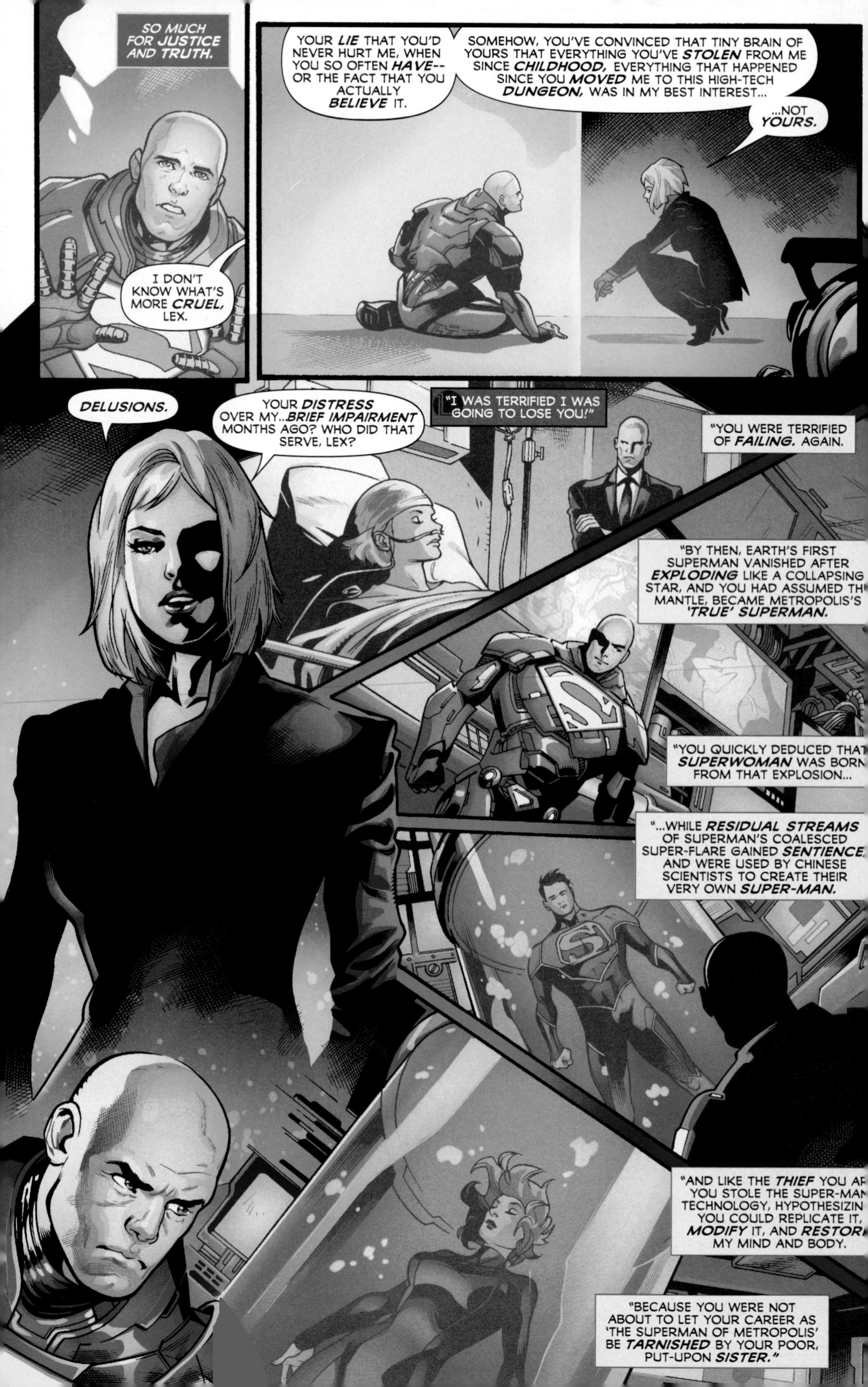
SO MUCH FOR JUSTICE AND TRUTH.
I DON'T KNOW WHAT'S MORE CRUEL, LEX.
YOUR LIE THAT YOU'D NEVER HURT ME, WHEN YOU SO OFTEN HAVE-- OR THE FACT THAT YOU ACTUALLY BELIEVE IT.
SOMEHOW, YOU'VE CONVINCED THAT TINY BRAIN OF YOURS THAT EVERYTHING YOU'VE STOLEN FROM ME SINCE CHILDHOOD, EVERYTHING THAT HAPPENED SINCE YOU MOVED ME TO THIS HIGH-TECH DUNGEON, WAS IN MY BEST INTEREST...
...NOT YOURS.
DELUSIONS.
YOUR DISTRESS OVER MY...BRIEF IMPAIRMENT MONTHS AGO? WHO DID THAT SERVE, LEX?
"I WAS TERRIFIED I WAS GOING TO LOSE YOU!"
"YOU WERE TERRIFIED OF FAILING. AGAIN.
"BY THEN, EARTH'S FIRST SUPERMAN VANISHED AFTER EXPLODING LIKE A COLLAPSING STAR, AND YOU HAD ASSUMED TH MANTLE, BECAME METROPOLIS'S 'TRUE' SUPERMAN.
"YOU QUICKLY DEDUCED THAT SUPERWOMAN WAS BORN FROM THAT EXPLOSION...
"...WHILE RESIDUAL STREAMS OF SUPERMAN'S COALESCED SUPER-FLARE GAINED SENTIENCE, AND WERE USED BY CHINESE SCIENTISTS TO CREATE THEIR VERY OWN SUPER-MAN.
"AND LIKE THE THIEF YOU AR YOU STOLE THE SUPER-MAN TECHNOLOGY, HYPOTHESIZIN YOU COULD REPLICATE IT, MODIFY IT, AND RESTOR MY MIND AND BODY.
"BECAUSE YOU WERE NOT ABOUT TO LET YOUR CAREER AS 'THE SUPERMAN OF METROPOLIS' BE TARNISHED BY YOUR POOR, PUT-UPON SISTER."

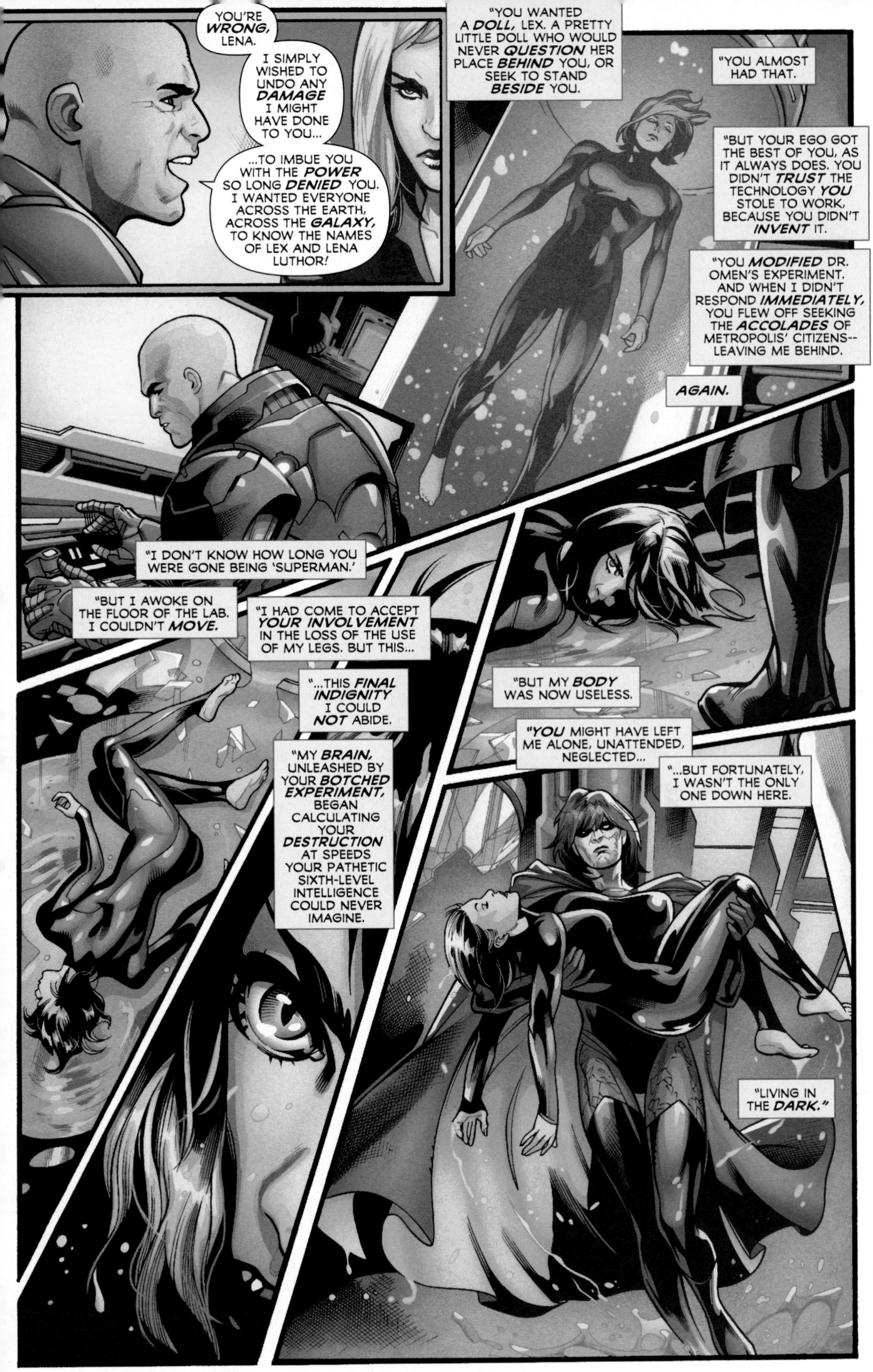
YOU'RE WRONG, LENA.
I SIMPLY WISHED TO UNDO ANY DAMAGE I MIGHT HAVE DONE TO YOU...
...TO IMBUE YOU WITH THE POWER SO LONG DENIED YOU. I WANTED EVERYONE ACROSS THE EARTH, ACROSS THE GALAXY, TO KNOW THE NAMES OF LEX AND LENA LUTHOR!
"YOU WANTED A DOLL, LEX. A PRETTY LITTLE DOLL WHO WOULD NEVER QUESTION HER PLACE BEHIND YOU, OR SEEK TO STAND BESIDE YOU.
"YOU ALMOST HAD THAT.
"BUT YOUR EGO GOT THE BEST OF YOU, AS IT ALWAYS DOES. YOU DIDN'T TRUST THE TECHNOLOGY YOU STOLE TO WORK, BECAUSE YOU DIDN'T INVENT IT.
"YOU MODIFIED DR. OMEN'S EXPERIMENT. AND WHEN I DIDN'T RESPOND IMMEDIATELY, YOU FLEW OFF SEEKING THE ACCOLADES OF METROPOLIS' CITIZENS--LEAVING ME BEHIND.
AGAIN.
"I DON'T KNOW HOW LONG YOU WERE GONE BEING 'SUPERMAN.'
"BUT I AWOKE ON THE FLOOR OF THE LAB. I COULDN'T MOVE.
"I HAD COME TO ACCEPT YOUR INVOLVEMENT IN THE LOSS OF THE USE OF MY LEGS. BUT THIS...
"...THIS FINAL INDIGNITY I COULD NOT ABIDE.
"BUT MY BODY WAS NOW USELESS.
"MY BRAIN, UNLEASHED BY YOUR BOTCHED EXPERIMENT, BEGAN CALCULATING YOUR DESTRUCTION AT SPEEDS YOUR PATHETIC SIXTH-LEVEL INTELLIGENCE COULD NEVER IMAGINE.
"YOU MIGHT HAVE LEFT ME ALONE, UNATTENDED, NEGLECTED...
"...BUT FORTUNATELY, I WASN'T THE ONLY ONE DOWN HERE.
"LIVING IN THE DARK."

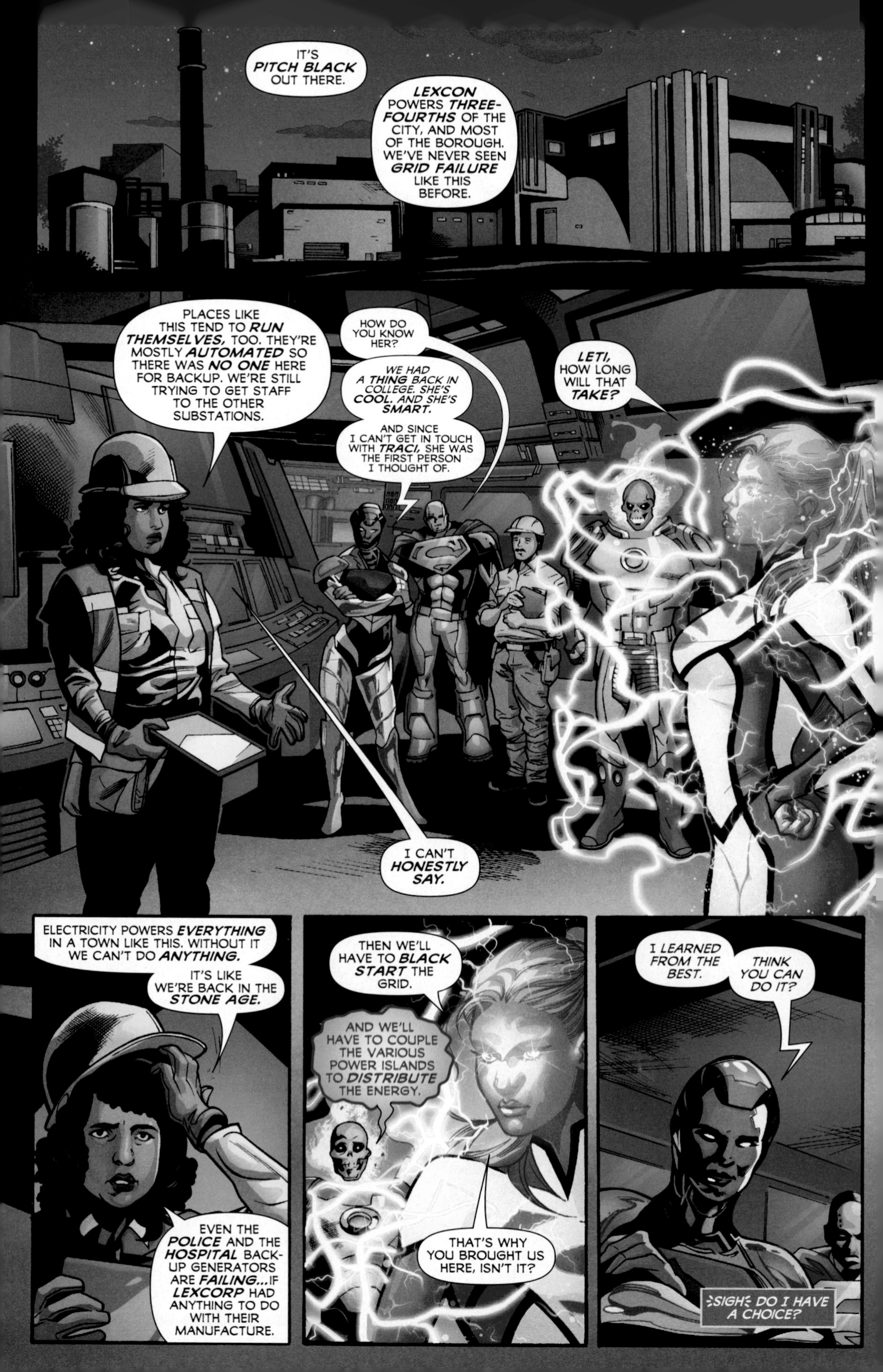
IT'S PITCH BLACK OUT THERE.
LEXCON POWERS THREE-FOURTHS OF THE CITY, AND MOST OF THE BOROUGH. WE'VE NEVER SEEN GRID FAILURE LIKE THIS BEFORE.
PLACES LIKE THIS TEND TO RUN THEMSELVES, TOO. THEY'RE MOSTLY AUTOMATED SO THERE WAS NO ONE HERE FOR BACKUP. WE'RE STILL TRYING TO GET STAFF TO THE OTHER SUBSTATIONS.
HOW DO YOU KNOW HER?
WE HAD A THING BACK IN COLLEGE. SHE'S COOL. AND SHE'S SMART.
AND SINCE I CAN'T GET IN TOUCH WITH TRACI, SHE WAS THE FIRST PERSON I THOUGHT OF.
LETI, HOW LONG WILL THAT TAKE?
I CAN'T HONESTLY SAY.
ELECTRICITY POWERS EVERYTHING IN A TOWN LIKE THIS. WITHOUT IT WE CAN'T DO ANYTHING.
IT'S LIKE WE'RE BACK IN THE STONE AGE.
EVEN THE POLICE AND THE HOSPITAL BACK-UP GENERATORS ARE FAILING...IF LEXCORP HAD ANYTHING TO DO WITH THEIR MANUFACTURE.
THEN WE'LL HAVE TO BLACK START THE GRID.
AND WE'LL HAVE TO COUPLE THE VARIOUS POWER ISLANDS TO DISTRIBUTE THE ENERGY.
THAT'S WHY YOU BROUGHT US HERE, ISN'T IT?
I LEARNED FROM THE BEST.
THINK YOU CAN DO IT?
SIGH DO I HAVE A CHOICE?

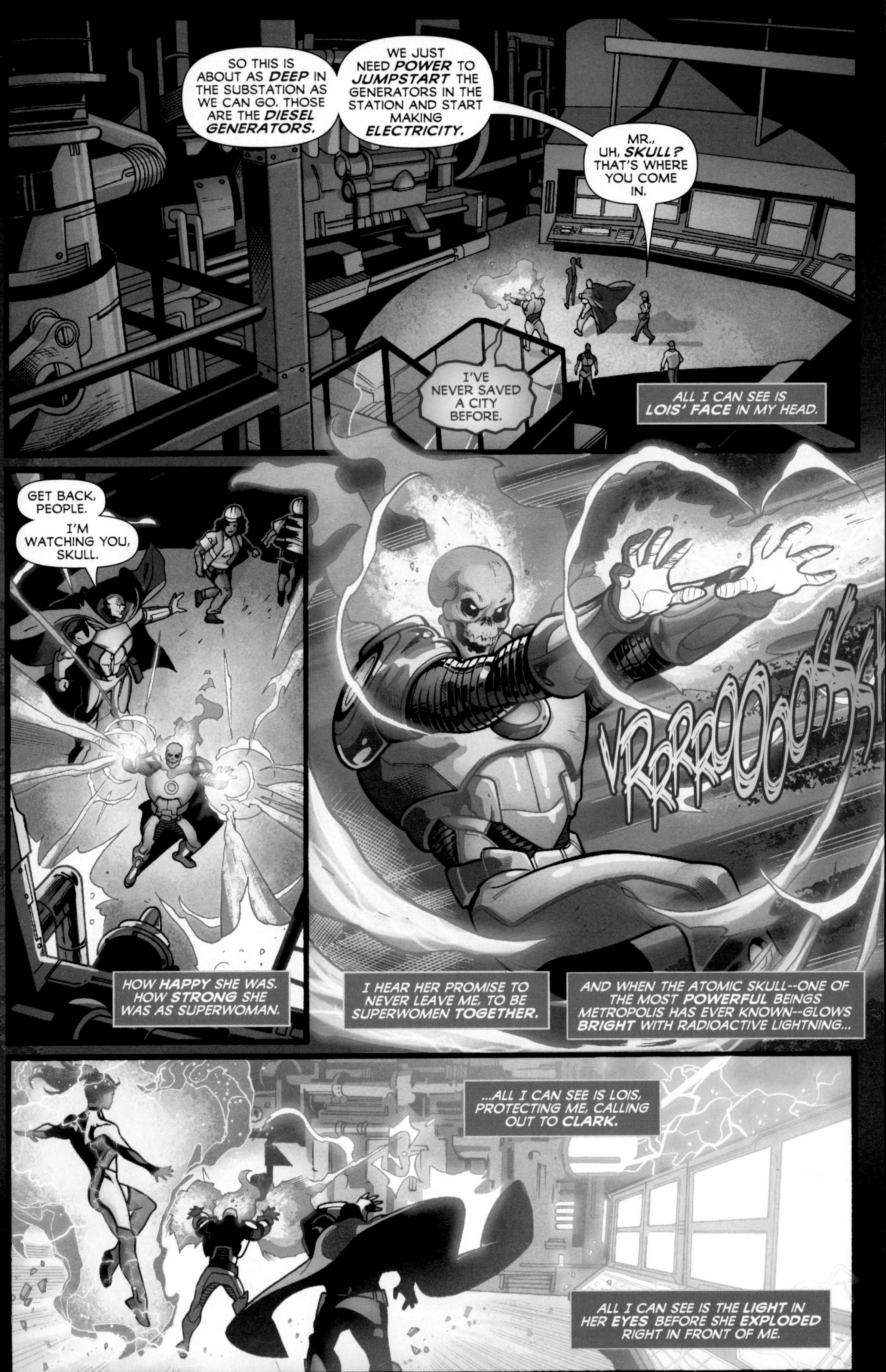

SO THIS IS ABOUT AS DEEP IN THE SUBSTATION AS WE CAN GO. THOSE ARE THE DIESEL GENERATORS.
WE JUST NEED POWER TO JUMPSTART THE GENERATORS IN THE STATION AND START MAKING ELECTRICITY.
MR., UH, SKULL? THAT'S WHERE YOU COME IN.
I'VE NEVER SAVED A CITY BEFORE.
ALL I CAN SEE IS LOIS' FACE IN MY HEAD.
GET BACK, PEOPLE.
I'M WATCHING YOU, SKULL.
HOW HAPPY SHE WAS. HOW STRONG SHE WAS AS SUPERWOMAN.
I HEAR HER PROMISE TO NEVER LEAVE ME, TO BE SUPERWOMEN TOGETHER.
AND WHEN THE ATOMIC SKULL--ONE OF THE MOST POWERFUL BEINGS METROPOLIS HAS EVER KNOWN--GLOWS BRIGHT WITH RADIOACTIVE LIGHTNING...
VRRRROOOOOSSH
...ALL I CAN SEE IS LOIS, PROTECTING ME, CALLING OUT TO CLARK.
ALL I CAN SEE IS THE LIGHT IN HER EYES BEFORE SHE EXPLODED RIGHT IN FRONT OF ME.

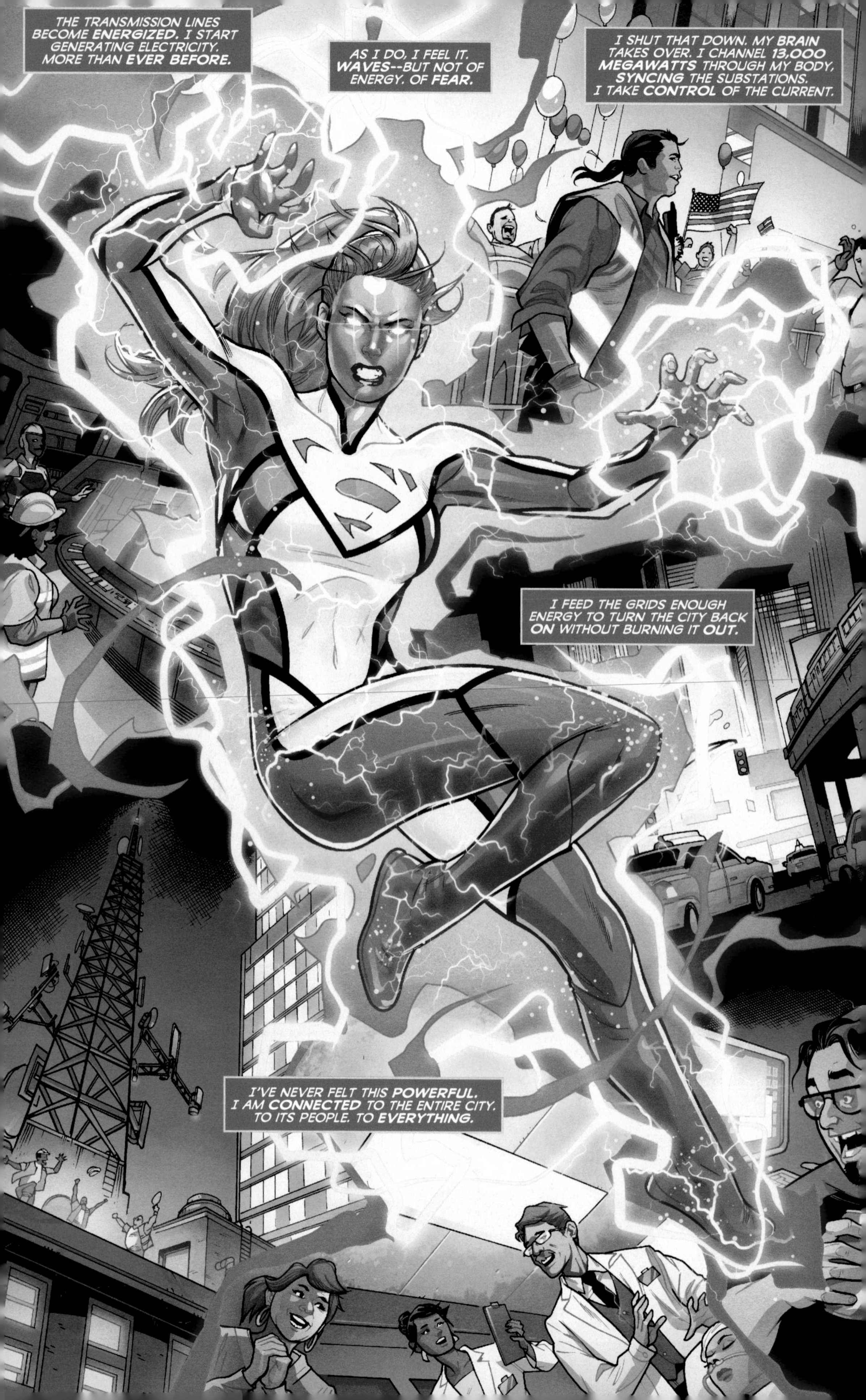
THE TRANSMISSION LINES BECOME ENERGIZED. I START GENERATING ELECTRICITY. MORE THAN EVER BEFORE.
AS I DO, I FEEL IT. WAVES--BUT NOT OF ENERGY. OF FEAR.
I SHUT THAT DOWN. MY BRAIN TAKES OVER. I CHANNEL 13,000 MEGAWATTS THROUGH MY BODY, SYNCING THE SUBSTATIONS. I TAKE CONTROL OF THE CURRENT.
I FEED THE GRIDS ENOUGH ENERGY TO TURN THE CITY BACK ON WITHOUT BURNING IT OUT.
I'VE NEVER FELT THIS POWERFUL. I AM CONNECTED TO THE ENTIRE CITY. TO ITS PEOPLE. TO EVERYTHING.

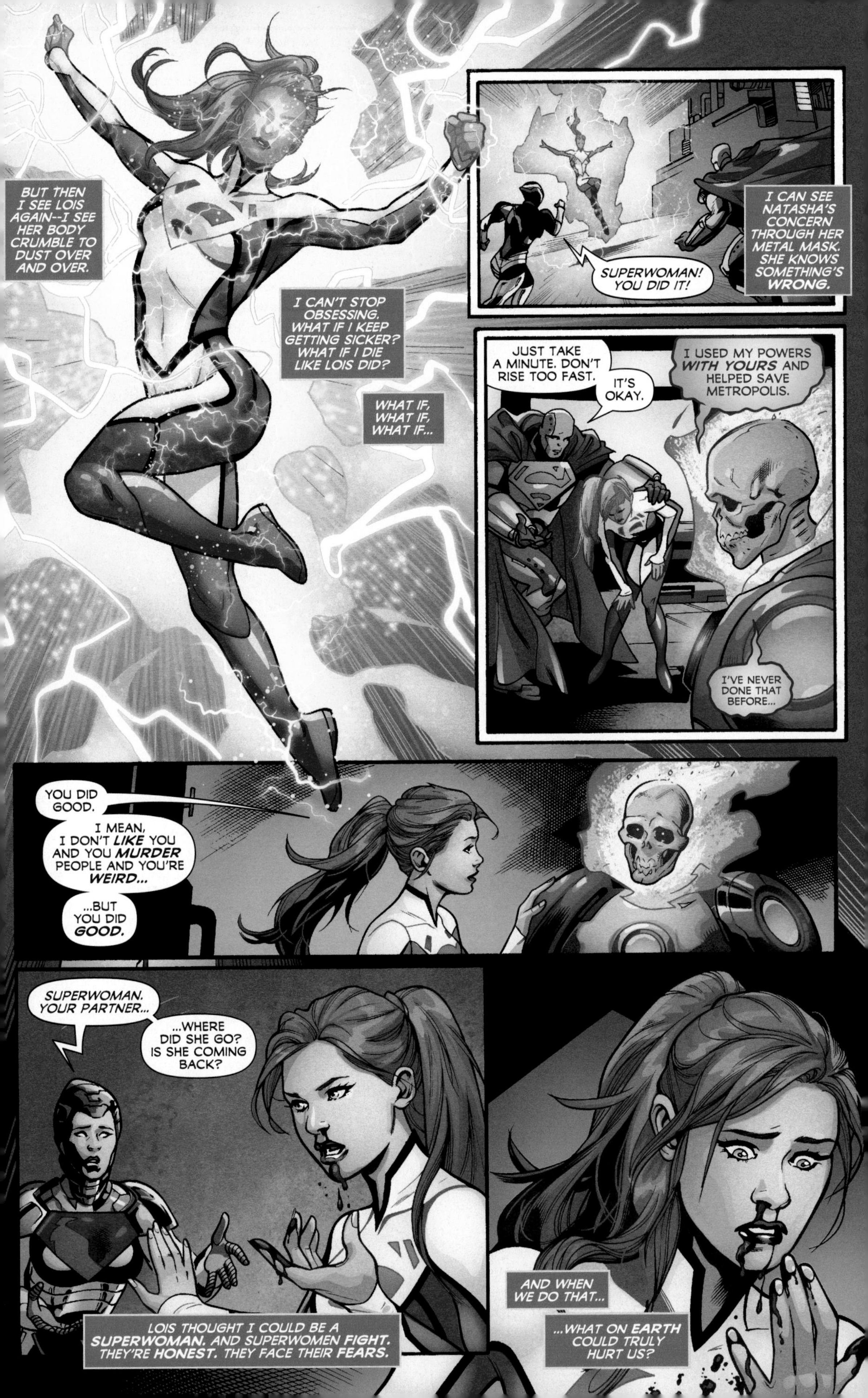
BUT THEN I SEE LOIS AGAIN--I SEE HER BODY CRUMBLE TO DUST OVER AND OVER.
I CAN'T STOP OBSESSING. WHAT IF I KEEP GETTING SICKER? WHAT IF I DIE LIKE LOIS DID?
WHAT IF, WHAT IF, WHAT IF...
SUPERWOMAN! YOU DID IT!
I CAN SEE NATASHA'S CONCERN THROUGH HER METAL MASK. SHE KNOWS SOMETHING'S WRONG.
JUST TAKE A MINUTE. DON'T RISE TOO FAST.
IT'S OKAY.
I USED MY POWERS WITH YOURS AND HELPED SAVE METROPOLIS.
I'VE NEVER DONE THAT BEFORE...
YOU DID GOOD.
I MEAN, I DON'T LIKE YOU AND YOU MURDER PEOPLE AND YOU'RE WEIRD...
...BUT YOU DID GOOD.
SUPERWOMAN. YOUR PARTNER...
...WHERE DID SHE GO? IS SHE COMING BACK?
LOIS THOUGHT I COULD BE A SUPERWOMAN. AND SUPERWOMEN FIGHT. THEY'RE HONEST. THEY FACE THEIR FEARS.
AND WHEN WE DO THAT...
...WHAT ON EARTH COULD TRULY HURT US?

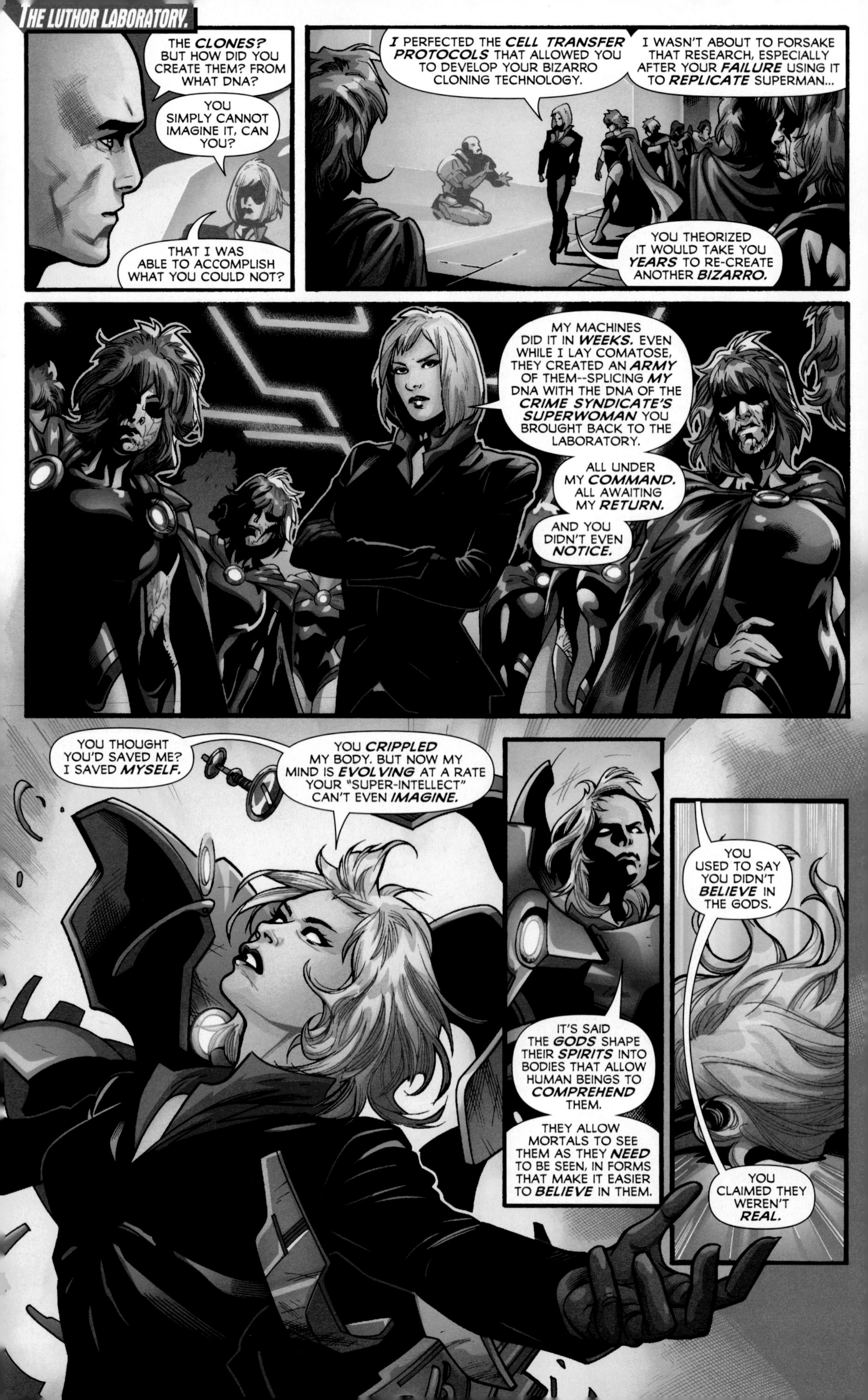
THE LUTHOR LABORATORY.
THE CLONES? BUT HOW DID YOU CREATE THEM? FROM WHAT DNA?
YOU SIMPLY CANNOT IMAGINE IT, CAN YOU?
THAT I WAS ABLE TO ACCOMPLISH WHAT YOU COULD NOT?
I PERFECTED THE CELL TRANSFER PROTOCOLS THAT ALLOWED YOU TO DEVELOP YOUR BIZARRO CLONING TECHNOLOGY.
I WASN'T ABOUT TO FORSAKE THAT RESEARCH, ESPECIALLY AFTER YOUR FAILURE USING IT TO REPLICATE SUPERMAN...
YOU THEORIZED IT WOULD TAKE YOU YEARS TO RE-CREATE ANOTHER BIZARRO.
MY MACHINES DID IT IN WEEKS. EVEN WHILE I LAY COMATOSE, THEY CREATED AN ARMY OF THEM--SPLICING MY DNA WITH THE DNA OF THE CRIME SYNDICATE'S SUPERWOMAN YOU BROUGHT BACK TO THE LABORATORY.
ALL UNDER MY COMMAND. ALL AWAITING MY RETURN.
AND YOU DIDN'T EVEN NOTICE.
YOU THOUGHT YOU'D SAVED ME? I SAVED MYSELF.
YOU CRIPPLED MY BODY. BUT NOW MY MIND IS EVOLVING AT A RATE YOUR "SUPER-INTELLECT" CAN'T EVEN IMAGINE.
IT'S SAID THE GODS SHAPE THEIR SPIRITS INTO BODIES THAT ALLOW HUMAN BEINGS TO COMPREHEND THEM.
THEY ALLOW MORTALS TO SEE THEM AS THEY NEED TO BE SEEN, IN FORMS THAT MAKE IT EASIER TO BELIEVE IN THEM.
YOU USED TO SAY YOU DIDN'T BELIEVE IN THE GODS.
YOU CLAIMED THEY WEREN'T REAL.

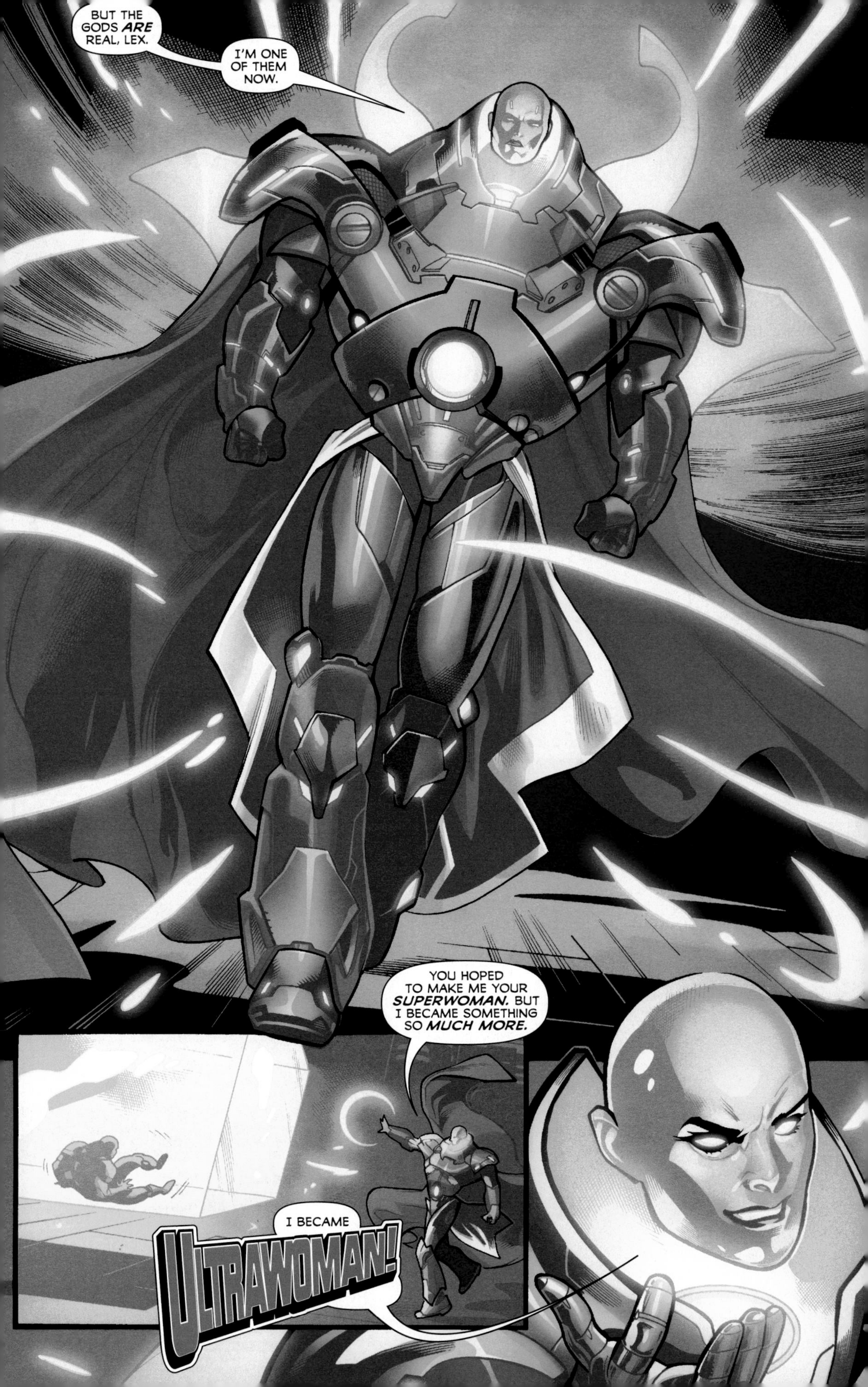

BUT THE GODS *ARE* REAL, LEX.
I'M ONE OF THEM NOW.
YOU HOPED TO MAKE ME YOUR *SUPERWOMAN.* BUT I BECAME SOMETHING SO *MUCH MORE.*
I BECAME
ULTRAWOMAN!

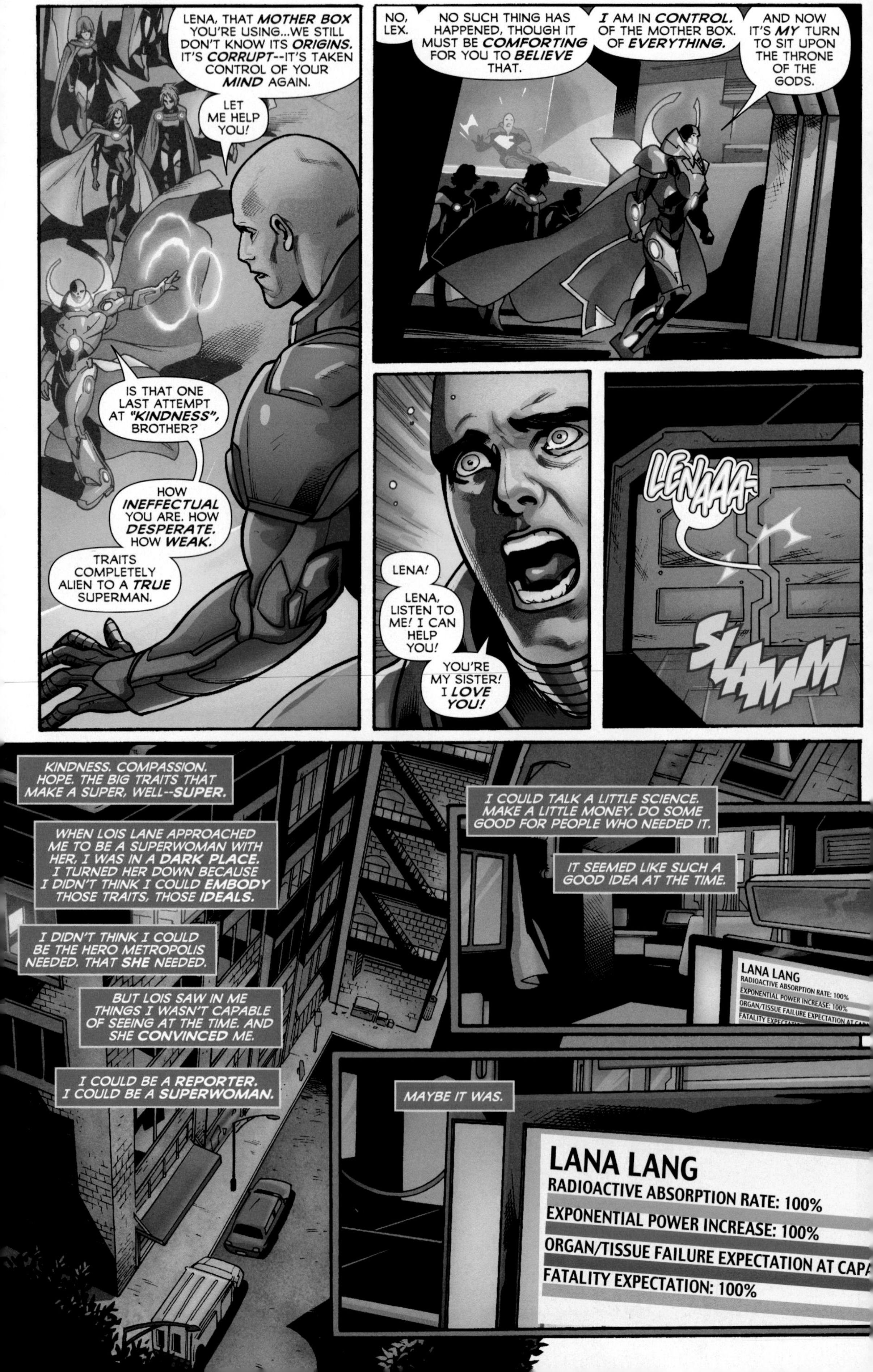

LENA, THAT MOTHER BOX YOU'RE USING...WE STILL DON'T KNOW ITS ORIGINS. IT'S CORRUPT--IT'S TAKEN CONTROL OF YOUR MIND AGAIN.
LET ME HELP YOU!
IS THAT ONE LAST ATTEMPT AT "KINDNESS", BROTHER?
HOW INEFFECTUAL YOU ARE. HOW DESPERATE. HOW WEAK.
TRAITS COMPLETELY ALIEN TO A TRUE SUPERMAN.
NO, LEX.
NO SUCH THING HAS HAPPENED, THOUGH IT MUST BE COMFORTING FOR YOU TO BELIEVE THAT.
I AM IN CONTROL. OF THE MOTHER BOX. OF EVERYTHING.
AND NOW IT'S MY TURN TO SIT UPON THE THRONE OF THE GODS.
LENA!
LENA, LISTEN TO ME! I CAN HELP YOU!
YOU'RE MY SISTER! I LOVE YOU!
LENAAAA
SLAMM
KINDNESS. COMPASSION. HOPE. THE BIG TRAITS THAT MAKE A SUPER, WELL--SUPER.
WHEN LOIS LANE APPROACHED ME TO BE A SUPERWOMAN WITH HER, I WAS IN A DARK PLACE. I TURNED HER DOWN BECAUSE I DIDN'T THINK I COULD EMBODY THOSE TRAITS, THOSE IDEALS.
I DIDN'T THINK I COULD BE THE HERO METROPOLIS NEEDED. THAT SHE NEEDED.
BUT LOIS SAW IN ME THINGS I WASN'T CAPABLE OF SEEING AT THE TIME. AND SHE CONVINCED ME.
I COULD BE A REPORTER. I COULD BE A SUPERWOMAN.
I COULD TALK A LITTLE SCIENCE. MAKE A LITTLE MONEY. DO SOME GOOD FOR PEOPLE WHO NEEDED IT.
IT SEEMED LIKE SUCH A GOOD IDEA AT THE TIME.
LANA LANG
RADIOACTIVE ABSORPTION RATE: 100%
EXPONENTIAL POWER INCREASE: 100%
ORGAN/TISSUE FAILURE EXPECTATION AT CAPA
MAYBE IT WAS.
LANA LANG
RADIOACTIVE ABSORPTION RATE: 100%
EXPONENTIAL POWER INCREASE: 100%
ORGAN/TISSUE FAILURE EXPECTATION AT CAPA
FATALITY EXPECTATION: 100%

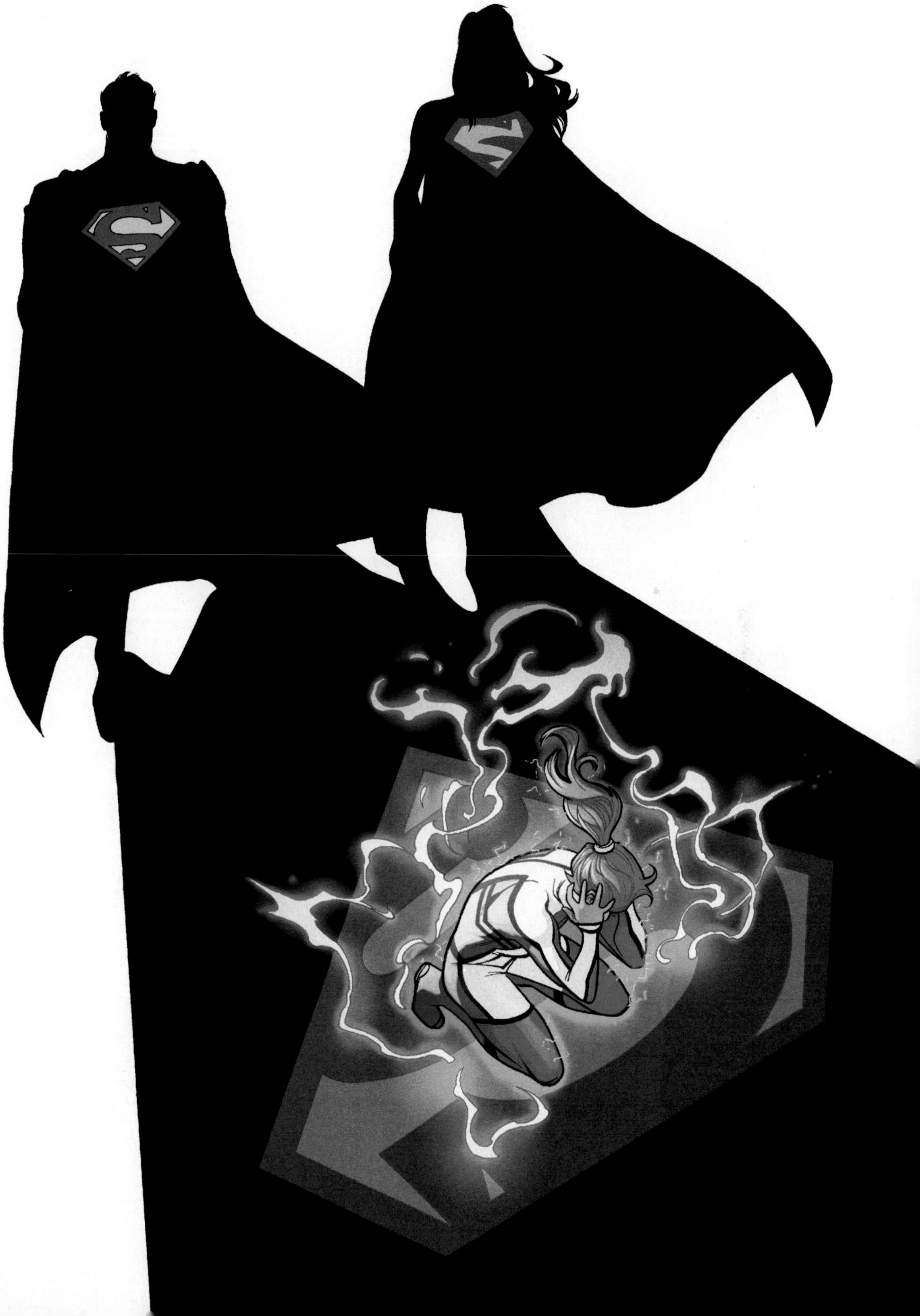

"WHO KILLED SUPERWOMAN? PART 1: TOGETHER AGAIN (FOR THE VERY FIRST TIME!)"

PHIL JIMENEZ writer * EMANUELA LUPACCHINO penciller * RAY McCARTHY inker

HI-FI colorist * cover by EMANUELA LUPACCHINO, RAY McCARTHY and BRAD ANDERSON

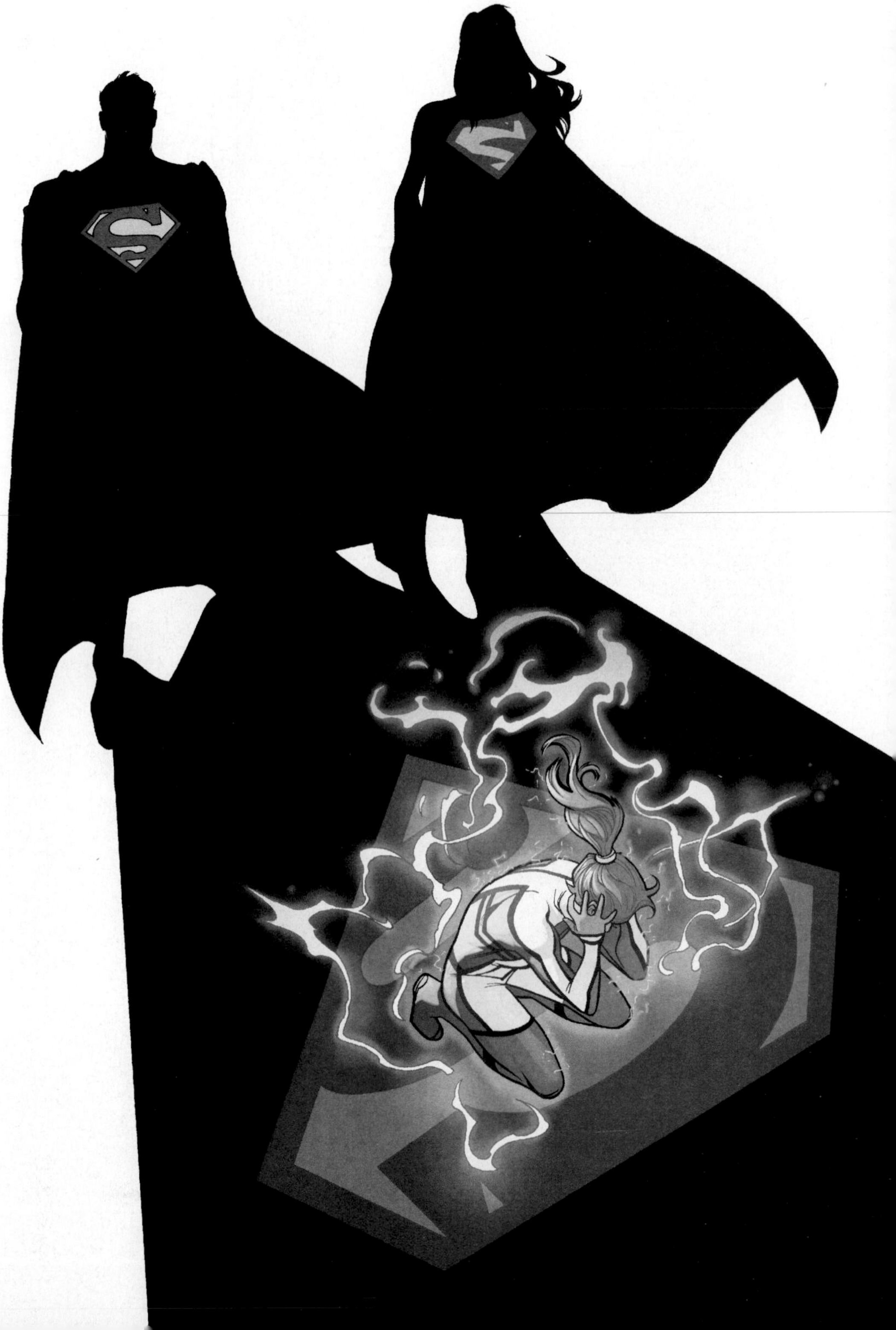

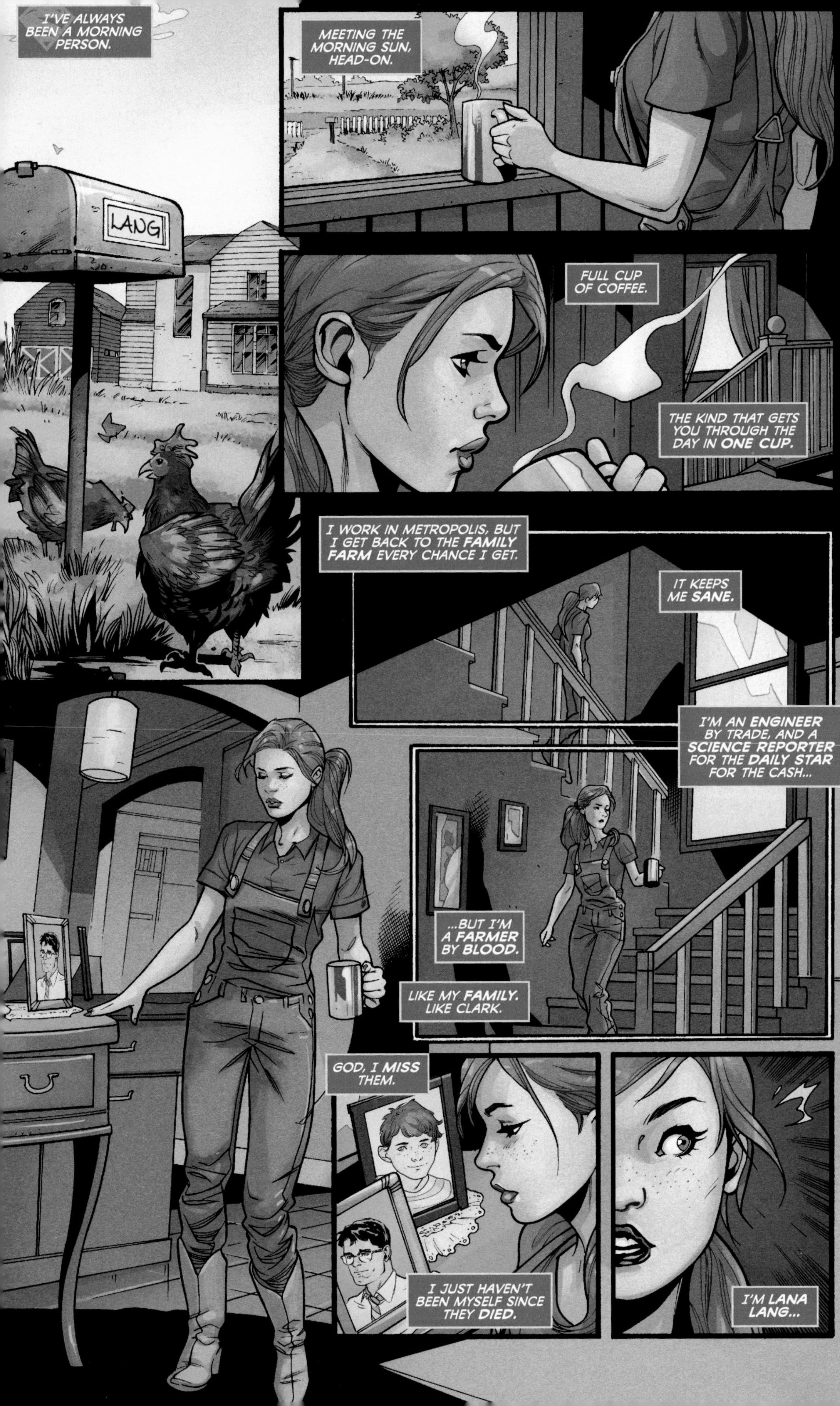
I'VE ALWAYS BEEN A MORNING PERSON.
MEETING THE MORNING SUN, HEAD-ON.
LANG
FULL CUP OF COFFEE.
THE KIND THAT GETS YOU THROUGH THE DAY IN ONE CUP.
I WORK IN METROPOLIS, BUT I GET BACK TO THE FAMILY FARM EVERY CHANCE I GET.
IT KEEPS ME SANE.
I'M AN ENGINEER BY TRADE, AND A SCIENCE REPORTER FOR THE DAILY STAR FOR THE CASH...
...BUT I'M A FARMER BY BLOOD.
LIKE MY FAMILY. LIKE CLARK.
GOD, I MISS THEM.
I JUST HAVEN'T BEEN MYSELF SINCE THEY DIED.
I'M LANA LANG...

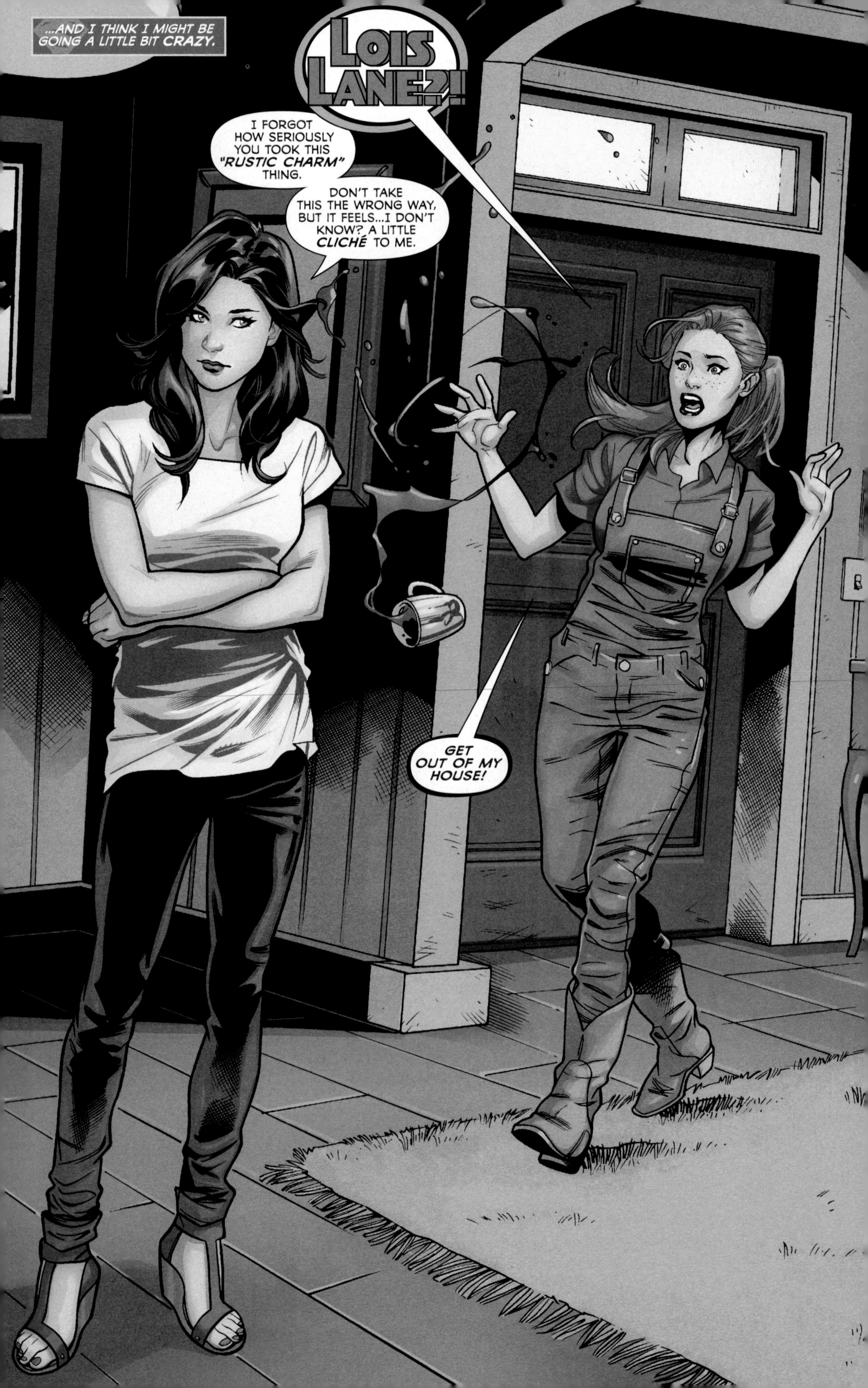
...AND I THINK I MIGHT BE GOING A LITTLE BIT CRAZY.
LOIS LANE?!
I FORGOT HOW SERIOUSLY YOU TOOK THIS "RUSTIC CHARM" THING.
DON'T TAKE THIS THE WRONG WAY, BUT IT FEELS...I DON'T KNOW? A LITTLE CLICHÉ TO ME.
GET OUT OF MY HOUSE!

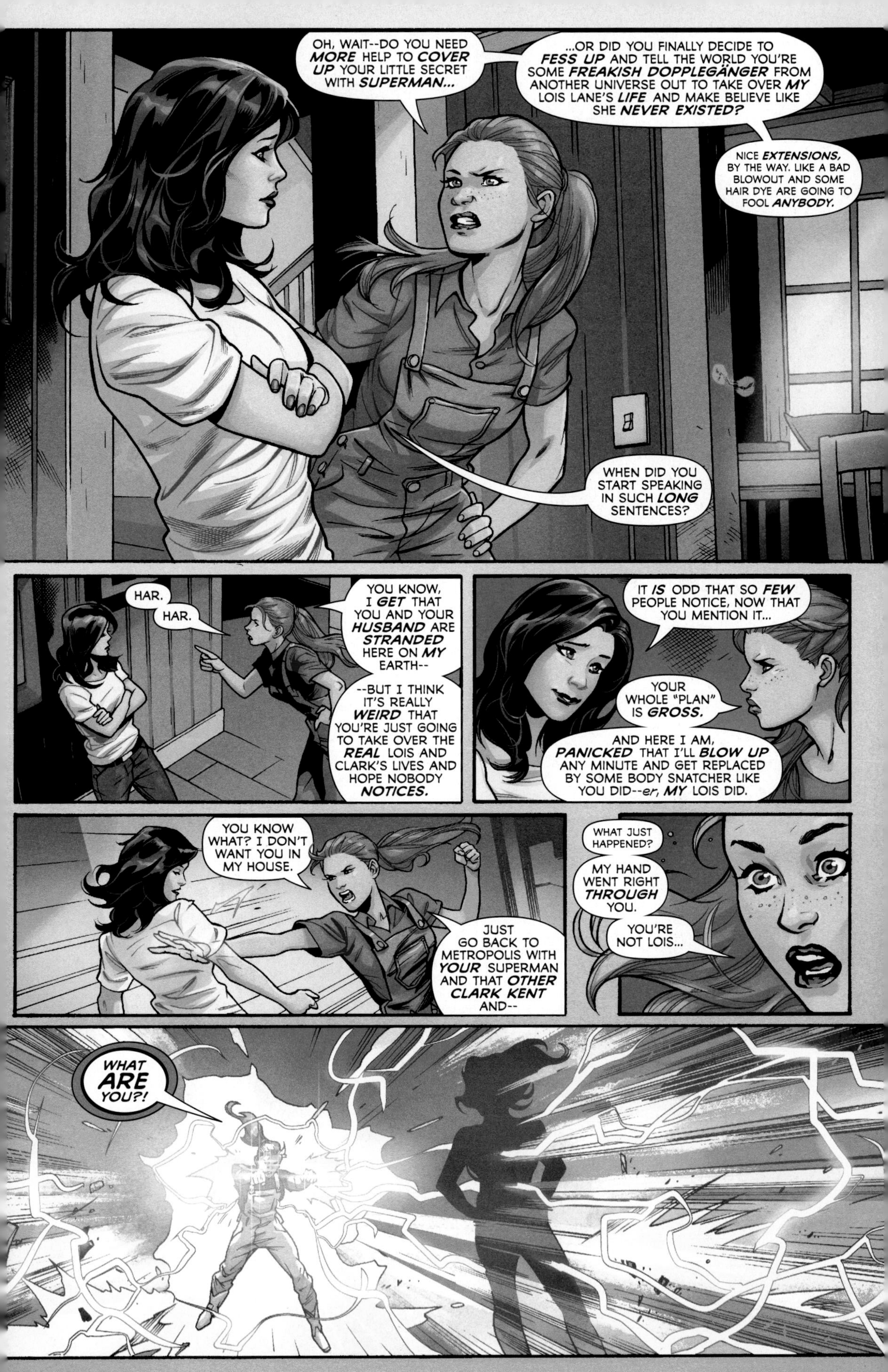
OH, WAIT--DO YOU NEED MORE HELP TO COVER UP YOUR LITTLE SECRET WITH SUPERMAN...
...OR DID YOU FINALLY DECIDE TO FESS UP AND TELL THE WORLD YOU'RE SOME FREAKISH DOPPLEGÄNGER FROM ANOTHER UNIVERSE OUT TO TAKE OVER MY LOIS LANE'S LIFE AND MAKE BELIEVE LIKE SHE NEVER EXISTED?
NICE EXTENSIONS, BY THE WAY. LIKE A BAD BLOWOUT AND SOME HAIR DYE ARE GOING TO FOOL ANYBODY.
WHEN DID YOU START SPEAKING IN SUCH LONG SENTENCES?
HAR.
HAR.
YOU KNOW, I GET THAT YOU AND YOUR HUSBAND ARE STRANDED HERE ON MY EARTH--
--BUT I THINK IT'S REALLY WEIRD THAT YOU'RE JUST GOING TO TAKE OVER THE REAL LOIS AND CLARK'S LIVES AND HOPE NOBODY NOTICES.
IT IS ODD THAT SO FEW PEOPLE NOTICE, NOW THAT YOU MENTION IT...
YOUR WHOLE "PLAN" IS GROSS.
AND HERE I AM, PANICKED THAT I'LL BLOW UP ANY MINUTE AND GET REPLACED BY SOME BODY SNATCHER LIKE YOU DID--er, MY LOIS DID.
YOU KNOW WHAT? I DON'T WANT YOU IN MY HOUSE.
JUST GO BACK TO METROPOLIS WITH YOUR SUPERMAN AND THAT OTHER CLARK KENT AND--
WHAT JUST HAPPENED?
MY HAND WENT RIGHT THROUGH YOU.
YOU'RE NOT LOIS...
WHAT ARE YOU?!

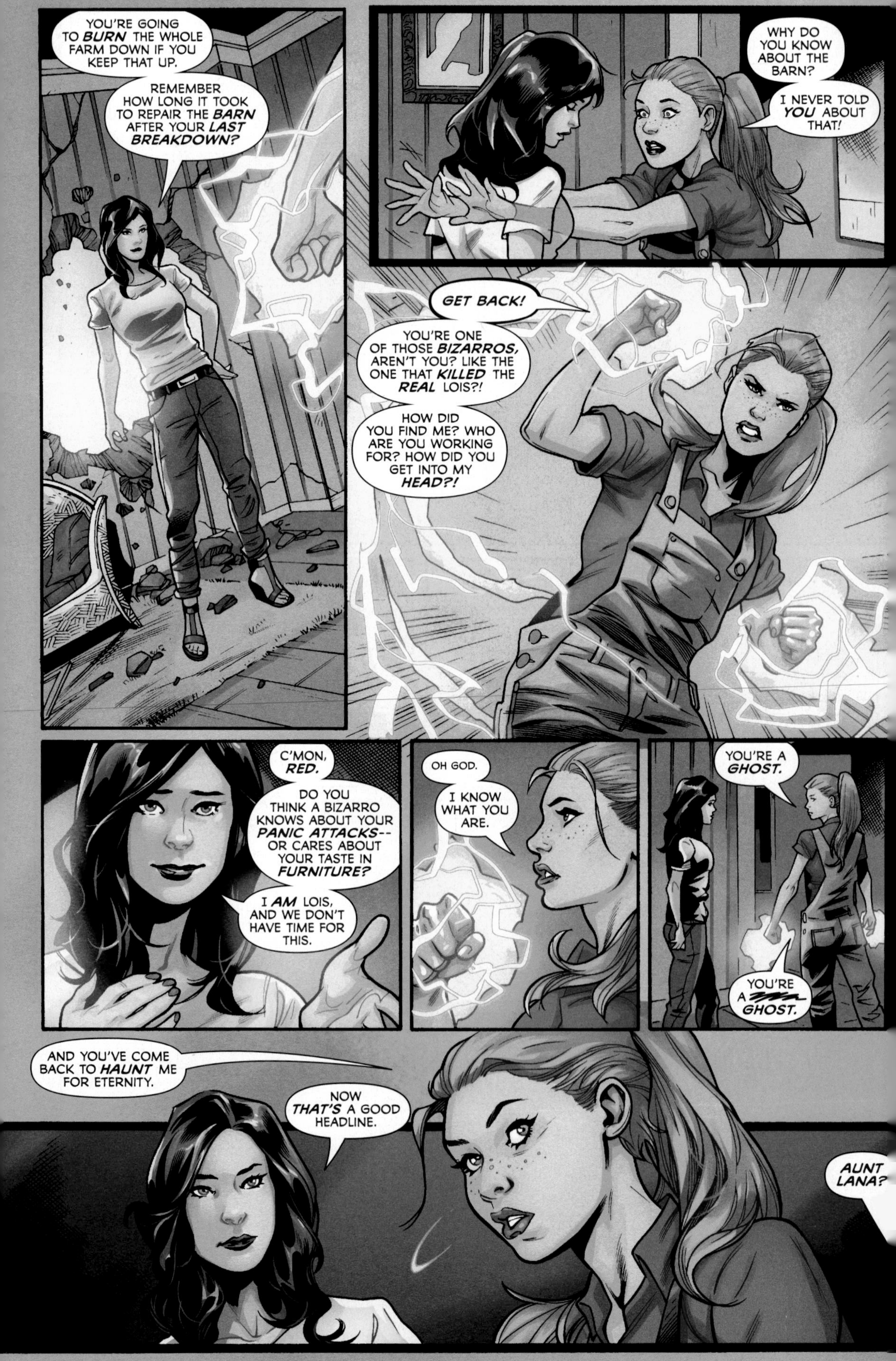
YOU'RE GOING TO *BURN* THE WHOLE FARM DOWN IF YOU KEEP THAT UP.
REMEMBER HOW LONG IT TOOK TO REPAIR THE *BARN* AFTER YOUR *LAST BREAKDOWN?*
WHY DO YOU KNOW ABOUT THE BARN?
I NEVER TOLD *YOU* ABOUT THAT!
GET BACK!
YOU'RE ONE OF THOSE *BIZARROS,* AREN'T YOU? LIKE THE ONE THAT *KILLED* THE *REAL* LOIS?!
HOW DID YOU FIND ME? WHO ARE YOU WORKING FOR? HOW DID YOU GET INTO MY *HEAD?!*
C'MON, *RED.*
DO YOU THINK A BIZARRO KNOWS ABOUT YOUR *PANIC ATTACKS--* OR CARES ABOUT YOUR TASTE IN *FURNITURE?*
I *AM* LOIS, AND WE DON'T HAVE TIME FOR THIS.
OH GOD.
I KNOW WHAT YOU ARE.
YOU'RE A *GHOST.*
YOU'RE A *GHOST.*
AND YOU'VE COME BACK TO *HAUNT* ME FOR ETERNITY.
NOW *THAT'S* A GOOD HEADLINE.
AUNT LANA?

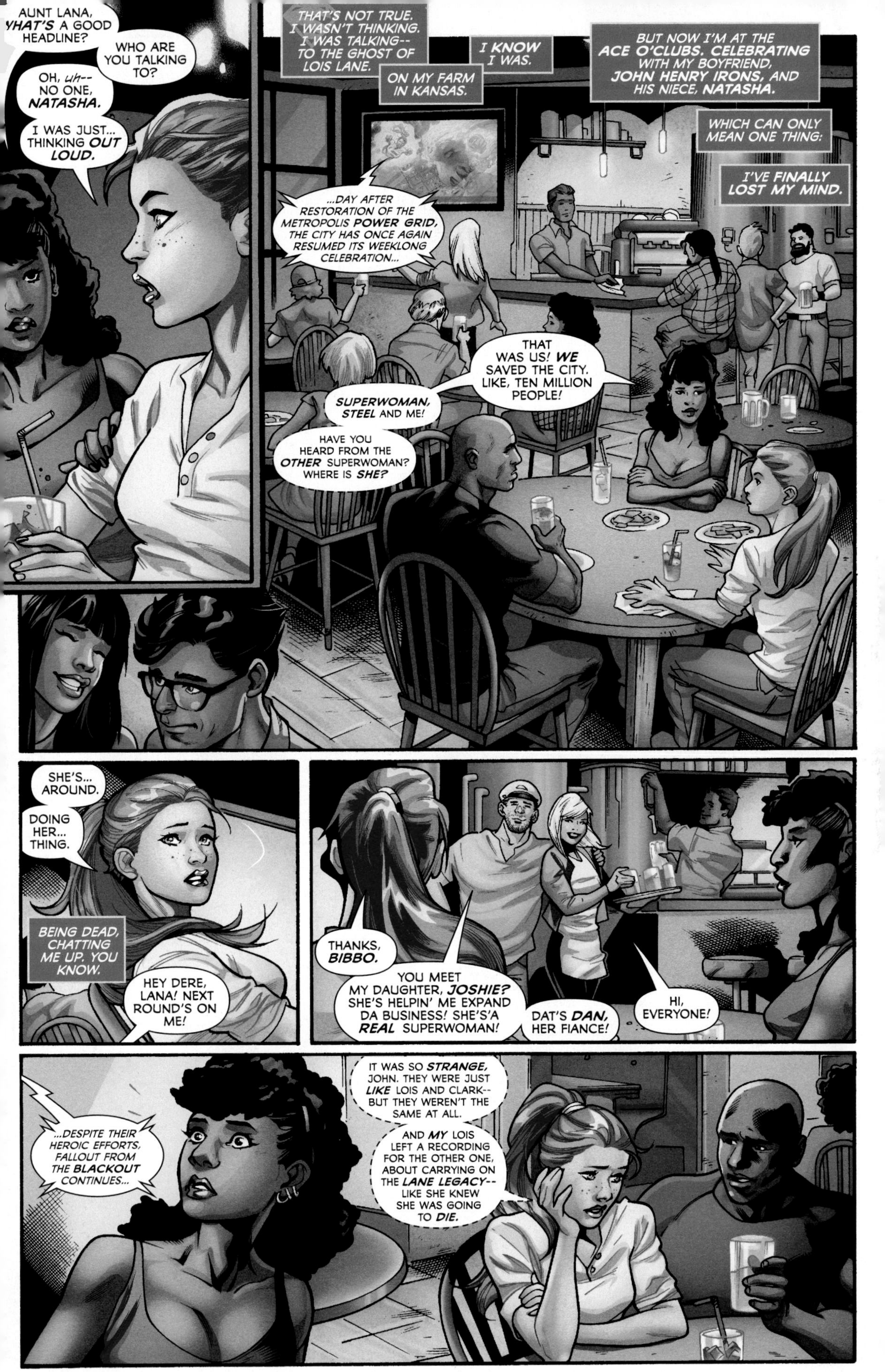
AUNT LANA, YHAT'S A GOOD HEADLINE?
WHO ARE YOU TALKING TO?
OH, uh-- NO ONE, NATASHA.
I WAS JUST... THINKING OUT LOUD.
THAT'S NOT TRUE. I WASN'T THINKING. I WAS TALKING-- TO THE GHOST OF LOIS LANE.
ON MY FARM IN KANSAS.
I KNOW I WAS.
BUT NOW I'M AT THE ACE O'CLUBS. CELEBRATING WITH MY BOYFRIEND, JOHN HENRY IRONS, AND HIS NIECE, NATASHA.
WHICH CAN ONLY MEAN ONE THING:
I'VE FINALLY LOST MY MIND.
...DAY AFTER RESTORATION OF THE METROPOLIS POWER GRID, THE CITY HAS ONCE AGAIN RESUMED ITS WEEKLONG CELEBRATION...
THAT WAS US! WE SAVED THE CITY. LIKE, TEN MILLION PEOPLE!
SUPERWOMAN, STEEL AND ME!
HAVE YOU HEARD FROM THE OTHER SUPERWOMAN? WHERE IS SHE?
SHE'S... AROUND.
DOING HER... THING.
BEING DEAD, CHATTING ME UP, YOU KNOW.
HEY DERE, LANA! NEXT ROUND'S ON ME!
THANKS, BIBBO.
YOU MEET MY DAUGHTER, JOSHIE? SHE'S HELPIN' ME EXPAND DA BUSINESS! SHE'S'A REAL SUPERWOMAN!
DAT'S DAN, HER FIANCE!
HI, EVERYONE!
...DESPITE THEIR HEROIC EFFORTS, FALLOUT FROM THE BLACKOUT CONTINUES...
IT WAS SO STRANGE, JOHN. THEY WERE JUST LIKE LOIS AND CLARK-- BUT THEY WEREN'T THE SAME AT ALL.
AND MY LOIS LEFT A RECORDING FOR THE OTHER ONE, ABOUT CARRYING ON THE LANE LEGACY-- LIKE SHE KNEW SHE WAS GOING TO DIE.

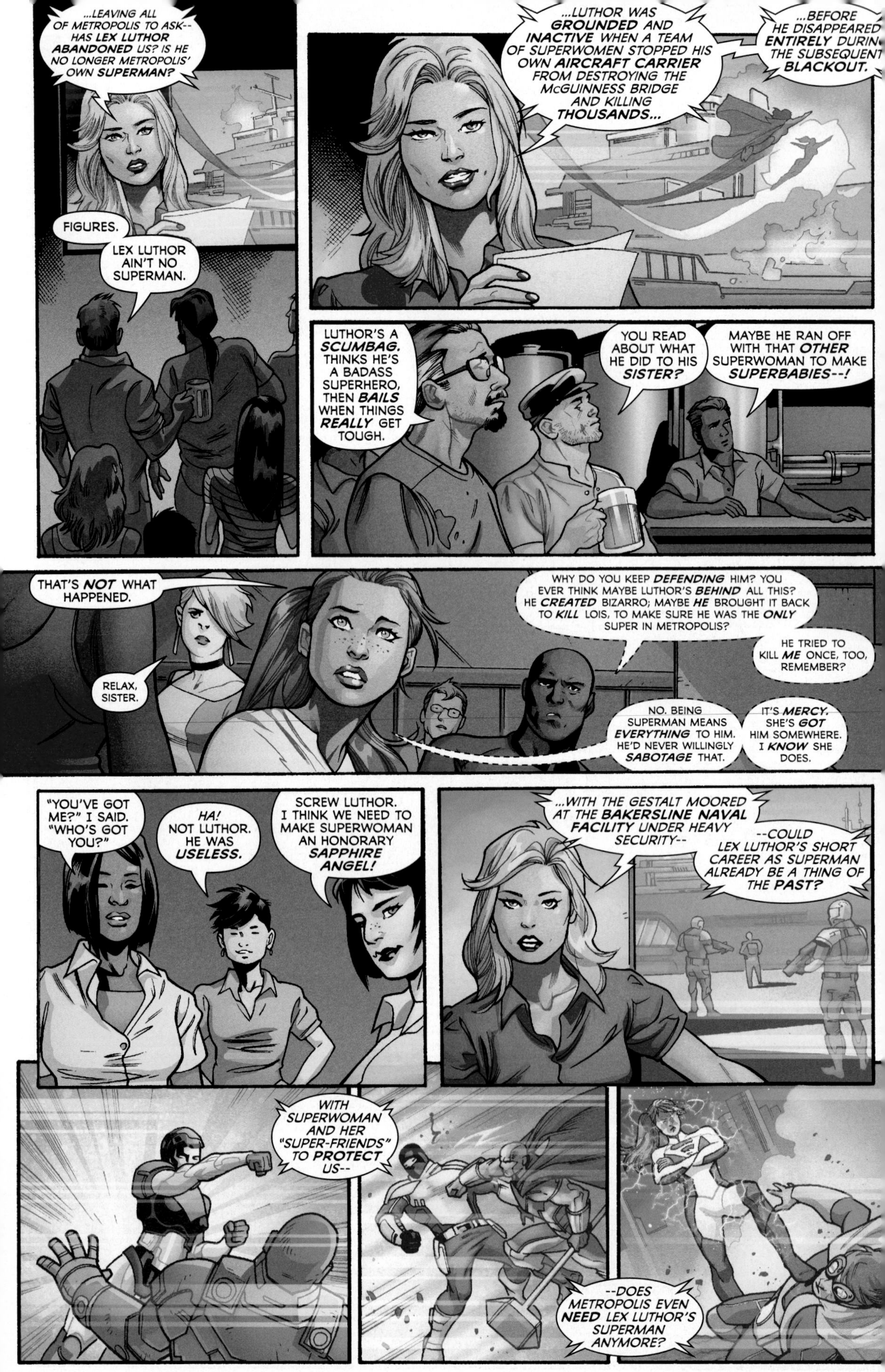
...LEAVING ALL OF METROPOLIS TO ASK--HAS LEX LUTHOR ABANDONED US? IS HE NO LONGER METROPOLIS' OWN SUPERMAN?
FIGURES.
LEX LUTHOR AIN'T NO SUPERMAN.
...LUTHOR WAS GROUNDED AND INACTIVE WHEN A TEAM OF SUPERWOMEN STOPPED HIS OWN AIRCRAFT CARRIER FROM DESTROYING THE McGUINNESS BRIDGE AND KILLING THOUSANDS...
...BEFORE HE DISAPPEARED ENTIRELY DURING THE SUBSEQUENT BLACKOUT.
LUTHOR'S A SCUMBAG. THINKS HE'S A BADASS SUPERHERO, THEN BAILS WHEN THINGS REALLY GET TOUGH.
YOU READ ABOUT WHAT HE DID TO HIS SISTER?
MAYBE HE RAN OFF WITH THAT OTHER SUPERWOMAN TO MAKE SUPERBABIES--!
THAT'S NOT WHAT HAPPENED.
RELAX, SISTER.
WHY DO YOU KEEP DEFENDING HIM? YOU EVER THINK MAYBE LUTHOR'S BEHIND ALL THIS? HE CREATED BIZARRO; MAYBE HE BROUGHT IT BACK TO KILL LOIS, TO MAKE SURE HE WAS THE ONLY SUPER IN METROPOLIS?
HE TRIED TO KILL ME ONCE, TOO, REMEMBER?
NO. BEING SUPERMAN MEANS EVERYTHING TO HIM. HE'D NEVER WILLINGLY SABOTAGE THAT.
IT'S MERCY. SHE'S GOT HIM SOMEWHERE. I KNOW SHE DOES.
"YOU'VE GOT ME?" I SAID. "WHO'S GOT YOU?"
HA! NOT LUTHOR. HE WAS USELESS.
SCREW LUTHOR. I THINK WE NEED TO MAKE SUPERWOMAN AN HONORARY SAPPHIRE ANGEL!
...WITH THE GESTALT MOORED AT THE BAKERSLINE NAVAL FACILITY UNDER HEAVY SECURITY--
--COULD LEX LUTHOR'S SHORT CAREER AS SUPERMAN ALREADY BE A THING OF THE PAST?
WITH SUPERWOMAN AND HER "SUPER-FRIENDS" TO PROTECT US--
--DOES METROPOLIS EVEN NEED LEX LUTHOR'S SUPERMAN ANYMORE?

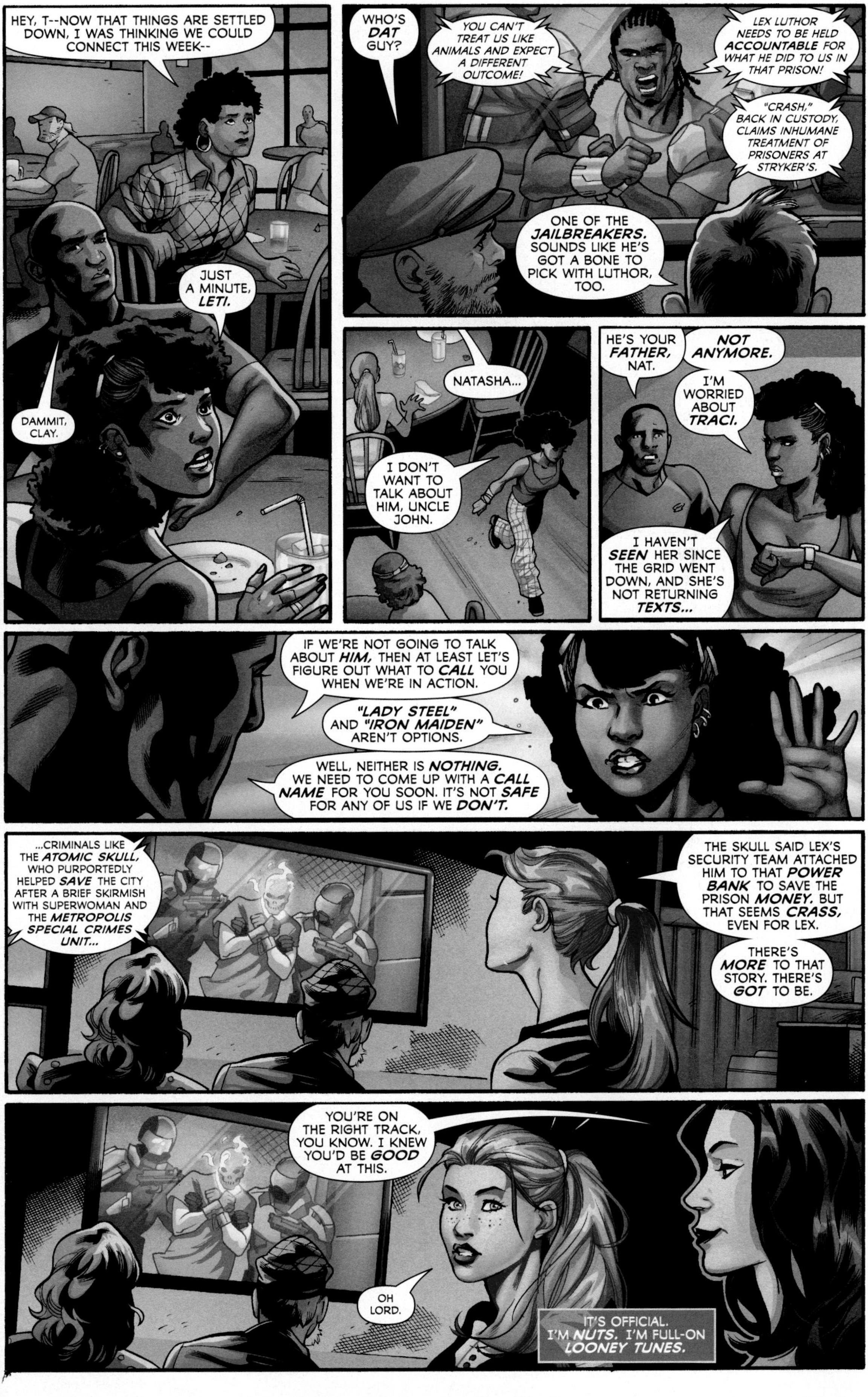
HEY, T--NOW THAT THINGS ARE SETTLED DOWN, I WAS THINKING WE COULD CONNECT THIS WEEK--
JUST A MINUTE, LETI.
DAMMIT, CLAY.
WHO'S DAT GUY?
YOU CAN'T TREAT US LIKE ANIMALS AND EXPECT A DIFFERENT OUTCOME!
LEX LUTHOR NEEDS TO BE HELD ACCOUNTABLE FOR WHAT HE DID TO US IN THAT PRISON!
"CRASH," BACK IN CUSTODY, CLAIMS INHUMANE TREATMENT OF PRISONERS AT STRYKER'S.
ONE OF THE JAILBREAKERS. SOUNDS LIKE HE'S GOT A BONE TO PICK WITH LUTHOR, TOO.
NATASHA...
I DON'T WANT TO TALK ABOUT HIM, UNCLE JOHN.
HE'S YOUR FATHER, NAT.
NOT ANYMORE.
I'M WORRIED ABOUT TRACI.
I HAVEN'T SEEN HER SINCE THE GRID WENT DOWN, AND SHE'S NOT RETURNING TEXTS...
IF WE'RE NOT GOING TO TALK ABOUT HIM, THEN AT LEAST LET'S FIGURE OUT WHAT TO CALL YOU WHEN WE'RE IN ACTION.
"LADY STEEL" AND "IRON MAIDEN" AREN'T OPTIONS.
WELL, NEITHER IS NOTHING. WE NEED TO COME UP WITH A CALL NAME FOR YOU SOON. IT'S NOT SAFE FOR ANY OF US IF WE DON'T.
...CRIMINALS LIKE THE ATOMIC SKULL, WHO PURPORTEDLY HELPED SAVE THE CITY AFTER A BRIEF SKIRMISH WITH SUPERWOMAN AND THE METROPOLIS SPECIAL CRIMES UNIT...
THE SKULL SAID LEX'S SECURITY TEAM ATTACHED HIM TO THAT POWER BANK TO SAVE THE PRISON MONEY. BUT THAT SEEMS CRASS, EVEN FOR LEX.
THERE'S MORE TO THAT STORY. THERE'S GOT TO BE.
YOU'RE ON THE RIGHT TRACK, YOU KNOW. I KNEW YOU'D BE GOOD AT THIS.
OH LORD.
IT'S OFFICIAL. I'M NUTS. I'M FULL-ON LOONEY TUNES.

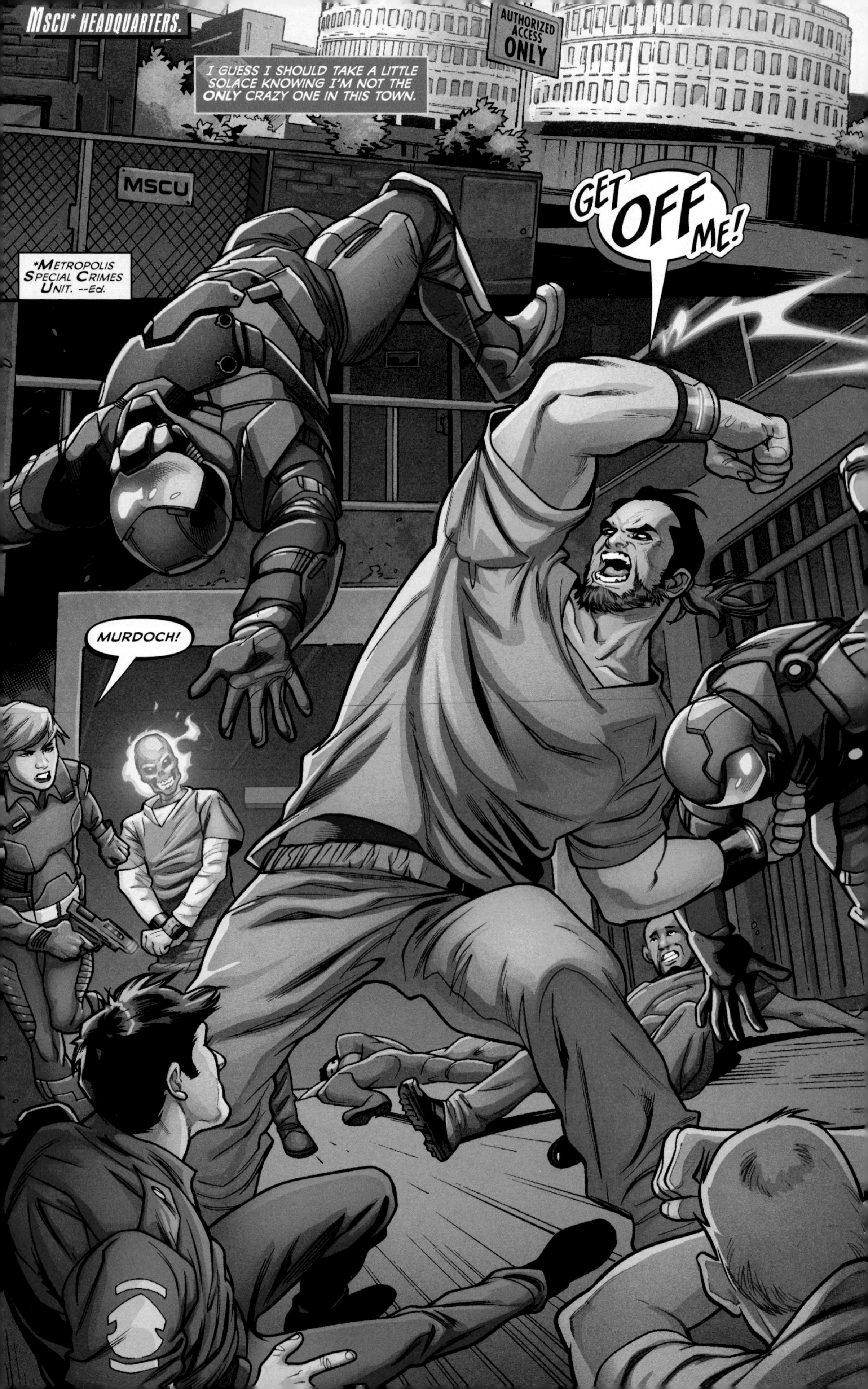
MSCU* HEADQUARTERS.
AUTHORIZED ACCESS ONLY
I GUESS I SHOULD TAKE A LITTLE SOLACE KNOWING I'M NOT THE ONLY CRAZY ONE IN THIS TOWN.
MSCU
*METROPOLIS SPECIAL CRIMES UNIT. --Ed.
GET OFF ME!
MURDOCH!

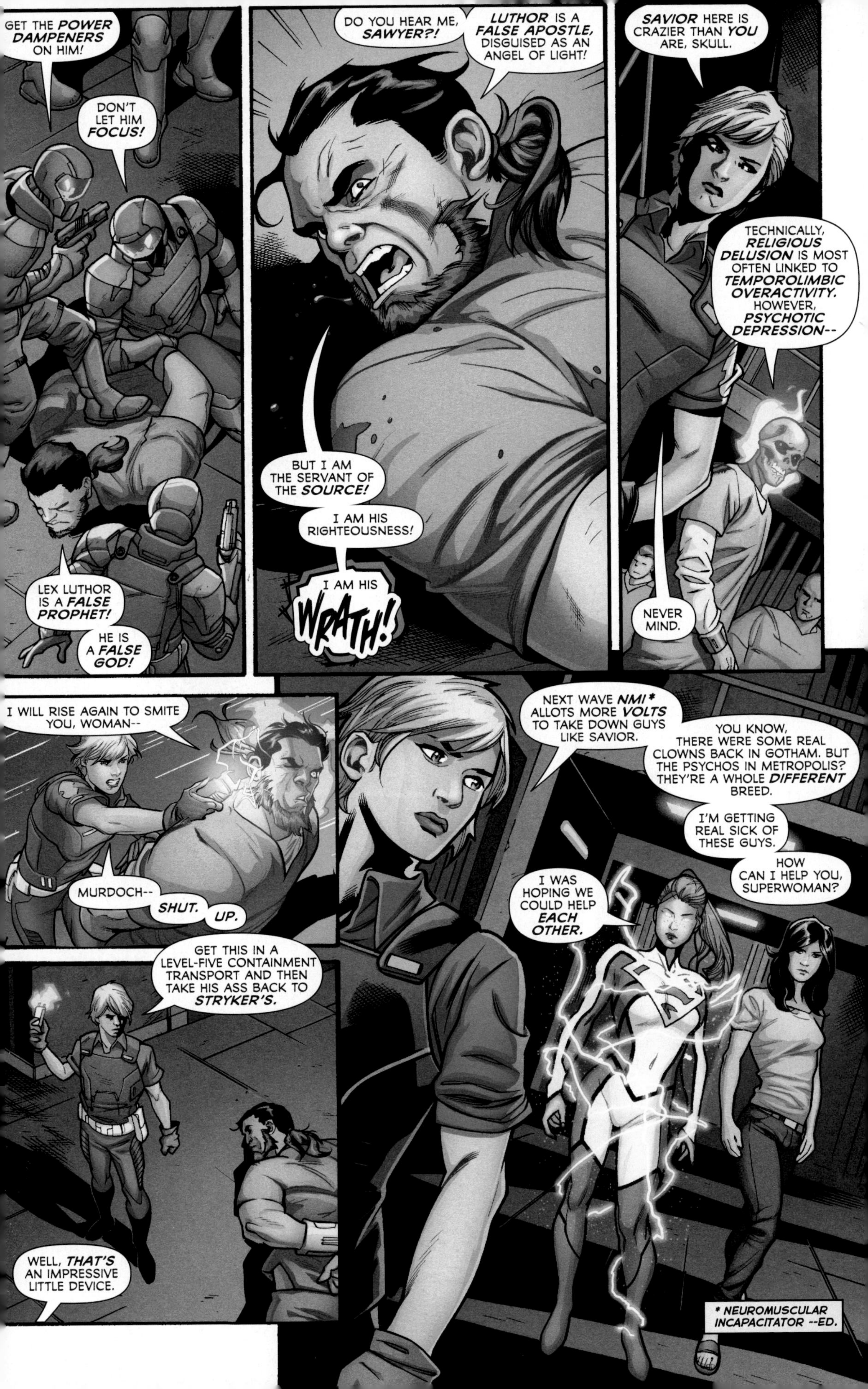
GET THE POWER DAMPENERS ON HIM!
DON'T LET HIM FOCUS!
LEX LUTHOR IS A FALSE PROPHET!
HE IS A FALSE GOD!
DO YOU HEAR ME, SAWYER?!
LUTHOR IS A FALSE APOSTLE, DISGUISED AS AN ANGEL OF LIGHT!
BUT I AM THE SERVANT OF THE SOURCE!
I AM HIS RIGHTEOUSNESS!
I AM HIS WRATH!
SAVIOR HERE IS CRAZIER THAN YOU ARE, SKULL.
TECHNICALLY, RELIGIOUS DELUSION IS MOST OFTEN LINKED TO TEMPOROLIMBIC OVERACTIVITY. HOWEVER, PSYCHOTIC DEPRESSION--
NEVER MIND.
I WILL RISE AGAIN TO SMITE YOU, WOMAN--
MURDOCH--
SHUT.
UP.
GET THIS IN A LEVEL-FIVE CONTAINMENT TRANSPORT AND THEN TAKE HIS ASS BACK TO STRYKER'S.
WELL, THAT'S AN IMPRESSIVE LITTLE DEVICE.
NEXT WAVE NMI* ALLOTS MORE VOLTS TO TAKE DOWN GUYS LIKE SAVIOR.
YOU KNOW, THERE WERE SOME REAL CLOWNS BACK IN GOTHAM. BUT THE PSYCHOS IN METROPOLIS? THEY'RE A WHOLE DIFFERENT BREED.
I'M GETTING REAL SICK OF THESE GUYS.
HOW CAN I HELP YOU, SUPERWOMAN?
I WAS HOPING WE COULD HELP EACH OTHER.
* NEUROMUSCULAR INCAPACITATOR --ED.

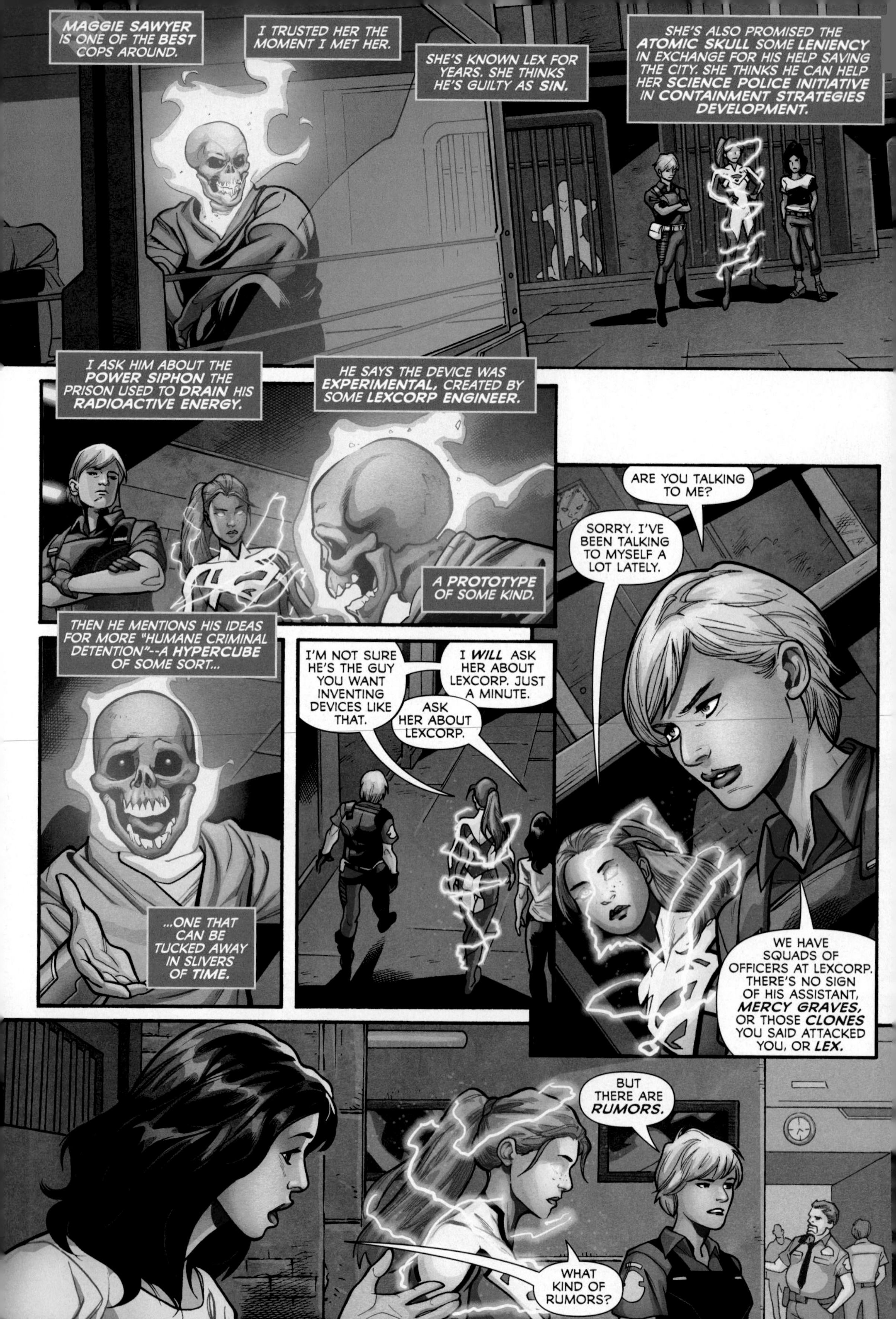

MAGGIE SAWYER IS ONE OF THE BEST COPS AROUND.
I TRUSTED HER THE MOMENT I MET HER.
SHE'S KNOWN LEX FOR YEARS. SHE THINKS HE'S GUILTY AS SIN.
SHE'S ALSO PROMISED THE ATOMIC SKULL SOME LENIENCY IN EXCHANGE FOR HIS HELP SAVING THE CITY. SHE THINKS HE CAN HELP HER SCIENCE POLICE INITIATIVE IN CONTAINMENT STRATEGIES DEVELOPMENT.
I ASK HIM ABOUT THE POWER SIPHON THE PRISON USED TO DRAIN HIS RADIOACTIVE ENERGY.
HE SAYS THE DEVICE WAS EXPERIMENTAL, CREATED BY SOME LEXCORP ENGINEER.
A PROTOTYPE OF SOME KIND.
ARE YOU TALKING TO ME?
SORRY. I'VE BEEN TALKING TO MYSELF A LOT LATELY.
THEN HE MENTIONS HIS IDEAS FOR MORE "HUMANE CRIMINAL DETENTION"--A HYPERCUBE OF SOME SORT...
...ONE THAT CAN BE TUCKED AWAY IN SLIVERS OF TIME.
I'M NOT SURE HE'S THE GUY YOU WANT INVENTING DEVICES LIKE THAT.
I WILL ASK HER ABOUT LEXCORP. JUST A MINUTE.
ASK HER ABOUT LEXCORP.
WE HAVE SQUADS OF OFFICERS AT LEXCORP. THERE'S NO SIGN OF HIS ASSISTANT, MERCY GRAVES, OR THOSE CLONES YOU SAID ATTACKED YOU, OR LEX.
BUT THERE ARE RUMORS.
WHAT KIND OF RUMORS?

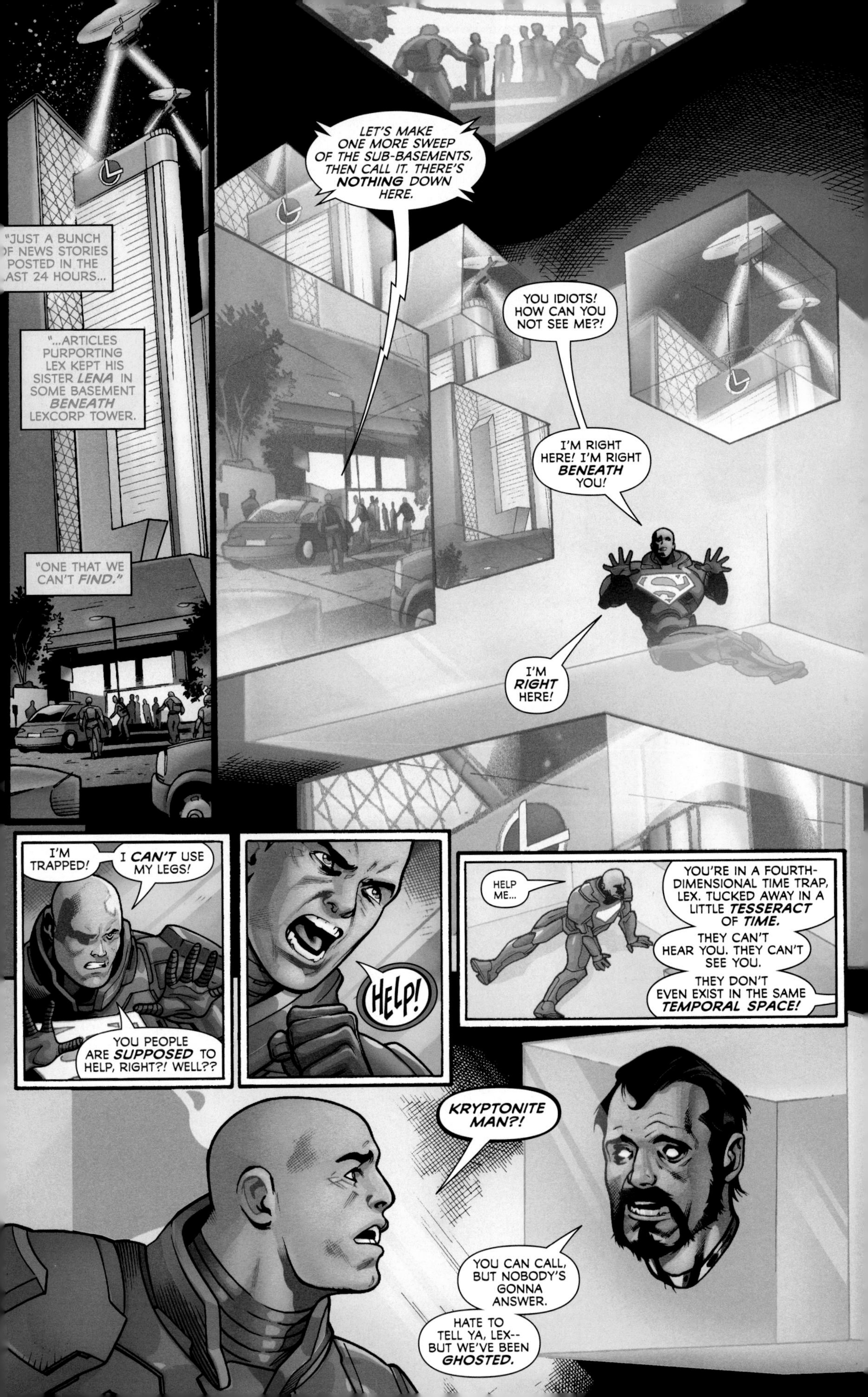
"JUST A BUNCH
OF NEWS STORIES POSTED IN THE LAST 24 HOURS...
"...ARTICLES PURPORTING LEX KEPT HIS SISTER LENA IN SOME BASEMENT BENEATH LEXCORP TOWER.
"ONE THAT WE CAN'T FIND."
LET'S MAKE ONE MORE SWEEP OF THE SUB-BASEMENTS, THEN CALL IT. THERE'S NOTHING DOWN HERE.
YOU IDIOTS! HOW CAN YOU NOT SEE ME?!
I'M RIGHT HERE! I'M RIGHT BENEATH YOU!
I'M RIGHT HERE!
I'M TRAPPED!
I CAN'T USE MY LEGS!
YOU PEOPLE ARE SUPPOSED TO HELP, RIGHT?! WELL??
HELP!
HELP ME...
YOU'RE IN A FOURTH-DIMENSIONAL TIME TRAP, LEX. TUCKED AWAY IN A LITTLE TESSERACT OF TIME.
THEY CAN'T HEAR YOU. THEY CAN'T SEE YOU.
THEY DON'T EVEN EXIST IN THE SAME TEMPORAL SPACE!
KRYPTONITE MAN?!
YOU CAN CALL, BUT NOBODY'S GONNA ANSWER.
HATE TO TELL YA, LEX-- BUT WE'VE BEEN GHOSTED.

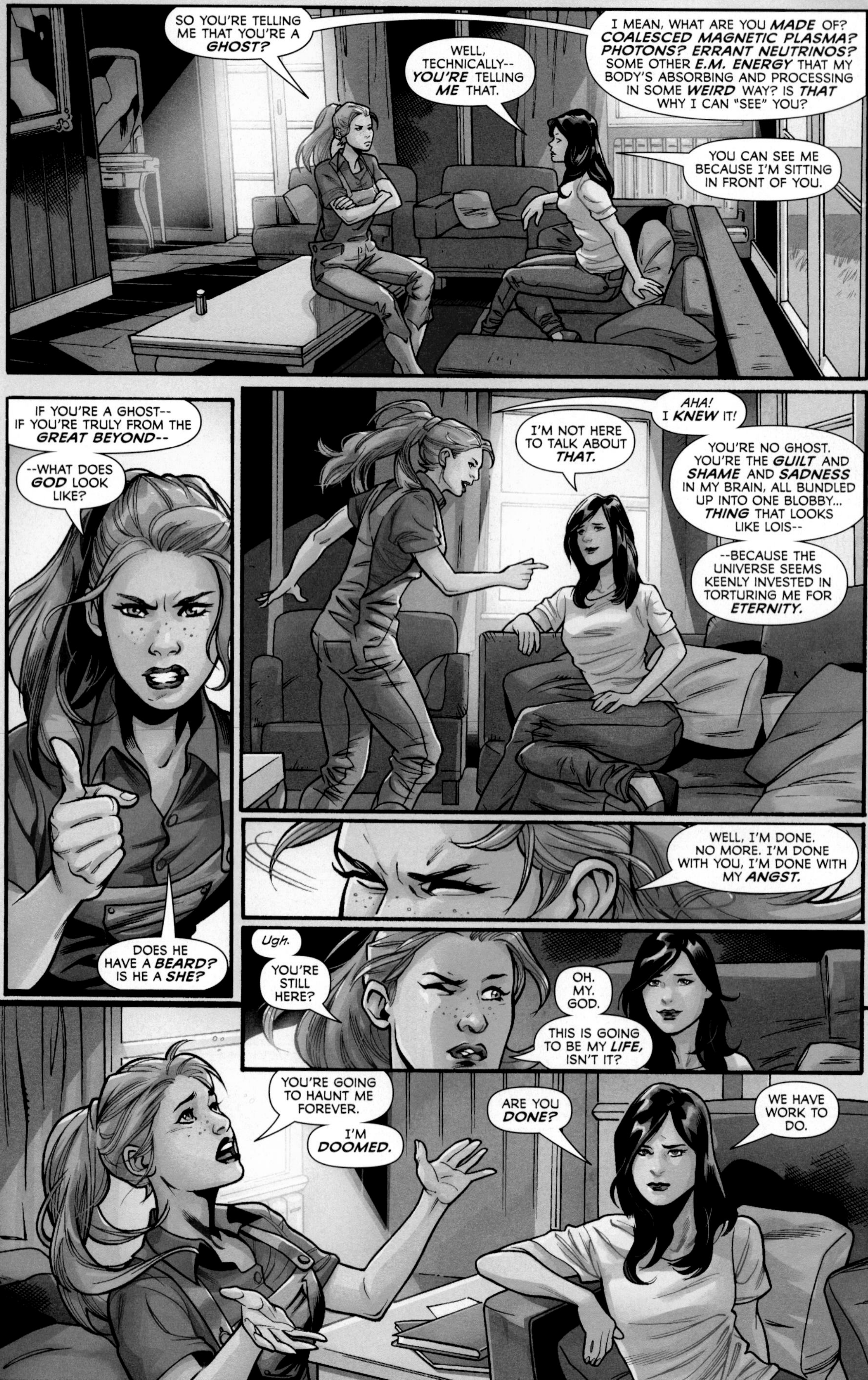
SO YOU'RE TELLING ME THAT YOU'RE A GHOST?
WELL, TECHNICALLY-- YOU'RE TELLING ME THAT.
I MEAN, WHAT ARE YOU MADE OF? COALESCED MAGNETIC PLASMA? PHOTONS? ERRANT NEUTRINOS? SOME OTHER E.M. ENERGY THAT MY BODY'S ABSORBING AND PROCESSING IN SOME WEIRD WAY? IS THAT WHY I CAN "SEE" YOU?
YOU CAN SEE ME BECAUSE I'M SITTING IN FRONT OF YOU.
IF YOU'RE A GHOST-- IF YOU'RE TRULY FROM THE GREAT BEYOND--
--WHAT DOES GOD LOOK LIKE?
DOES HE HAVE A BEARD? IS HE A SHE?
I'M NOT HERE TO TALK ABOUT THAT.
AHA! I KNEW IT!
YOU'RE NO GHOST. YOU'RE THE GUILT AND SHAME AND SADNESS IN MY BRAIN, ALL BUNDLED UP INTO ONE BLOBBY... THING THAT LOOKS LIKE LOIS--
--BECAUSE THE UNIVERSE SEEMS KEENLY INVESTED IN TORTURING ME FOR ETERNITY.
WELL, I'M DONE. NO MORE. I'M DONE WITH YOU, I'M DONE WITH MY ANGST.
Ugh.
YOU'RE STILL HERE?
OH. MY. GOD.
THIS IS GOING TO BE MY LIFE, ISN'T IT?
YOU'RE GOING TO HAUNT ME FOREVER.
I'M DOOMED.
ARE YOU DONE?
WE HAVE WORK TO DO.

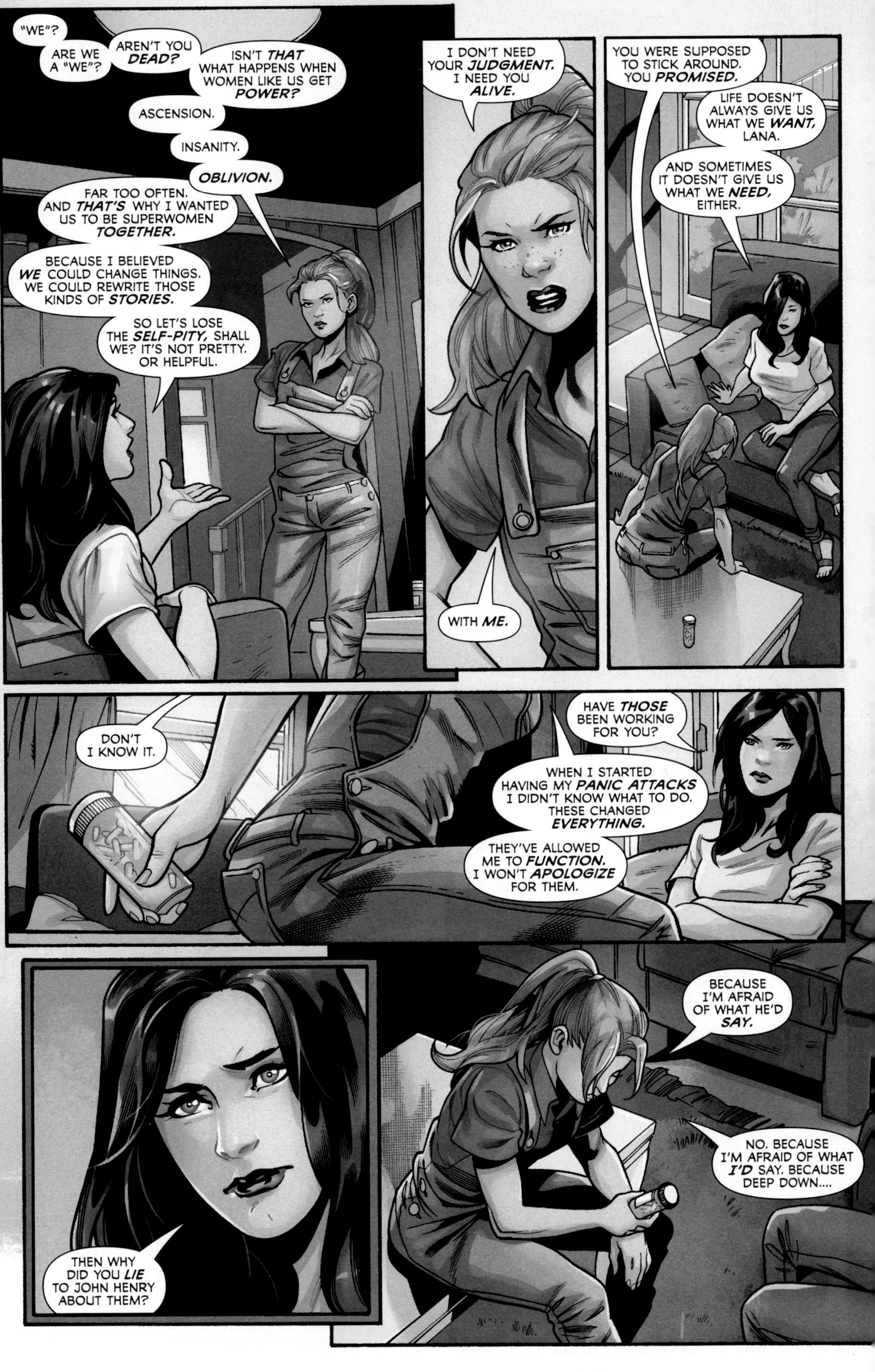
"WE"?
ARE WE A "WE"?
AREN'T YOU DEAD?
ISN'T THAT WHAT HAPPENS WHEN WOMEN LIKE US GET POWER?
ASCENSION.
INSANITY.
OBLIVION.
FAR TOO OFTEN. AND THAT'S WHY I WANTED US TO BE SUPERWOMEN TOGETHER.
BECAUSE I BELIEVED WE COULD CHANGE THINGS. WE COULD REWRITE THOSE KINDS OF STORIES.
SO LET'S LOSE THE SELF-PITY, SHALL WE? IT'S NOT PRETTY. OR HELPFUL.
I DON'T NEED YOUR JUDGMENT. I NEED YOU ALIVE.
WITH ME.
YOU WERE SUPPOSED TO STICK AROUND. YOU PROMISED.
LIFE DOESN'T ALWAYS GIVE US WHAT WE WANT, LANA.
AND SOMETIMES IT DOESN'T GIVE US WHAT WE NEED, EITHER.
DON'T I KNOW IT.
HAVE THOSE BEEN WORKING FOR YOU?
WHEN I STARTED HAVING MY PANIC ATTACKS I DIDN'T KNOW WHAT TO DO. THESE CHANGED EVERYTHING.
THEY'VE ALLOWED ME TO FUNCTION. I WON'T APOLOGIZE FOR THEM.
THEN WHY DID YOU LIE TO JOHN HENRY ABOUT THEM?
BECAUSE I'M AFRAID OF WHAT HE'D SAY.
NO. BECAUSE I'M AFRAID OF WHAT I'D SAY. BECAUSE DEEP DOWN....

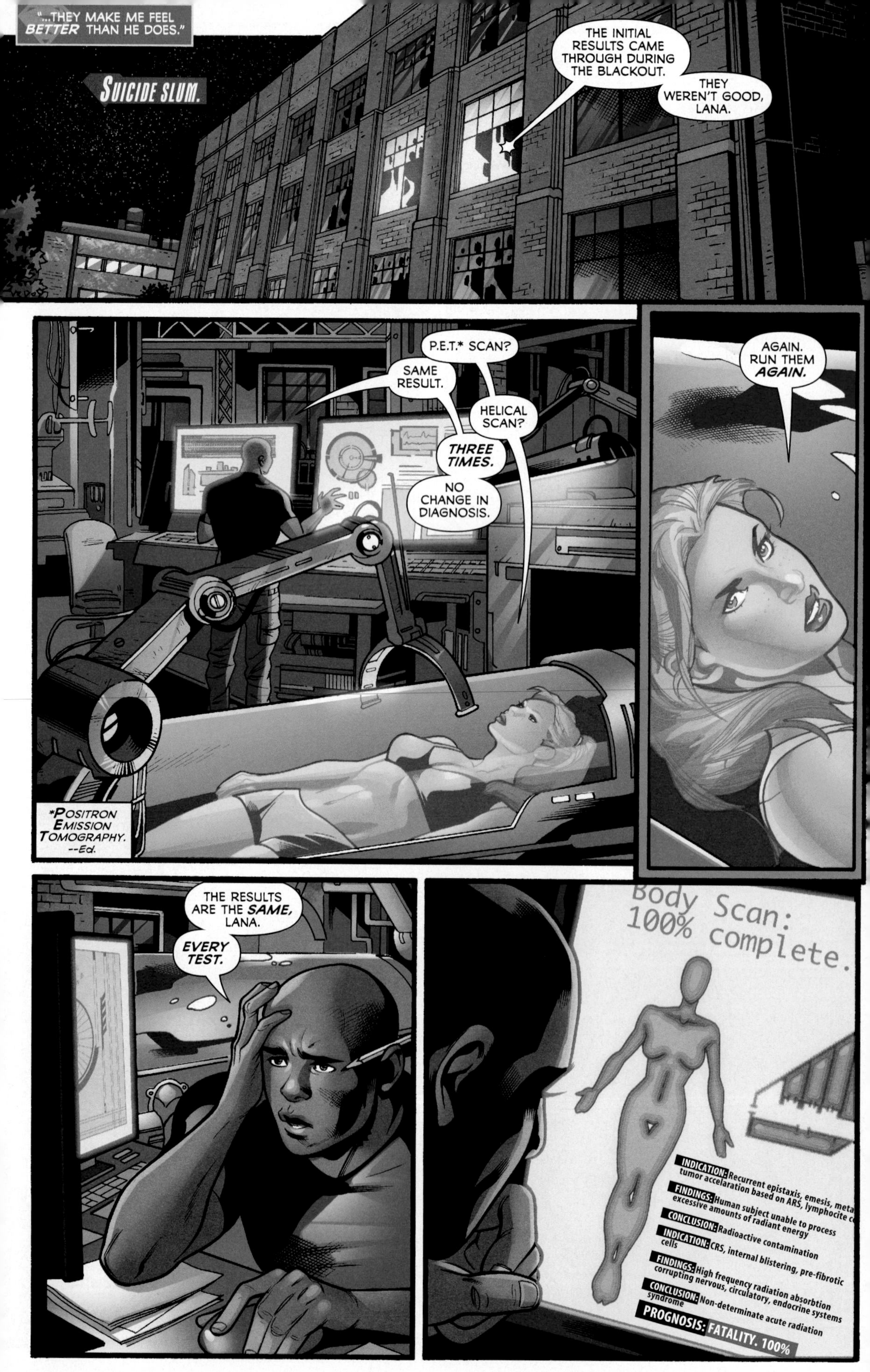
"...THEY MAKE ME FEEL BETTER THAN HE DOES."
SUICIDE SLUM.
THE INITIAL RESULTS CAME THROUGH DURING THE BLACKOUT.
THEY WEREN'T GOOD, LANA.
P.E.T.* SCAN?
SAME RESULT.
HELICAL SCAN?
THREE TIMES.
NO CHANGE IN DIAGNOSIS.
*POSITRON EMISSION TOMOGRAPHY. --Ed.
AGAIN. RUN THEM AGAIN.
THE RESULTS ARE THE SAME, LANA.
EVERY TEST.
Body Scan: 100% complete.
INDICATION: Recurrent epistaxis, emesis, meta tumor accelaration based on ARS, lymphocite c
FINDINGS: Human subject unable to process excessive amounts of radiant energy
CONCLUSION: Radioactive contamination
INDICATION: CRS, internal blistering, pre-fibrotic cells
FINDINGS: High frequency radiation absorbtion corrupting nervous, circulatory, endocrine systems
CONCLUSION: Non-determinate acute radiation syndrome
PROGNOSIS: FATALITY. 100%

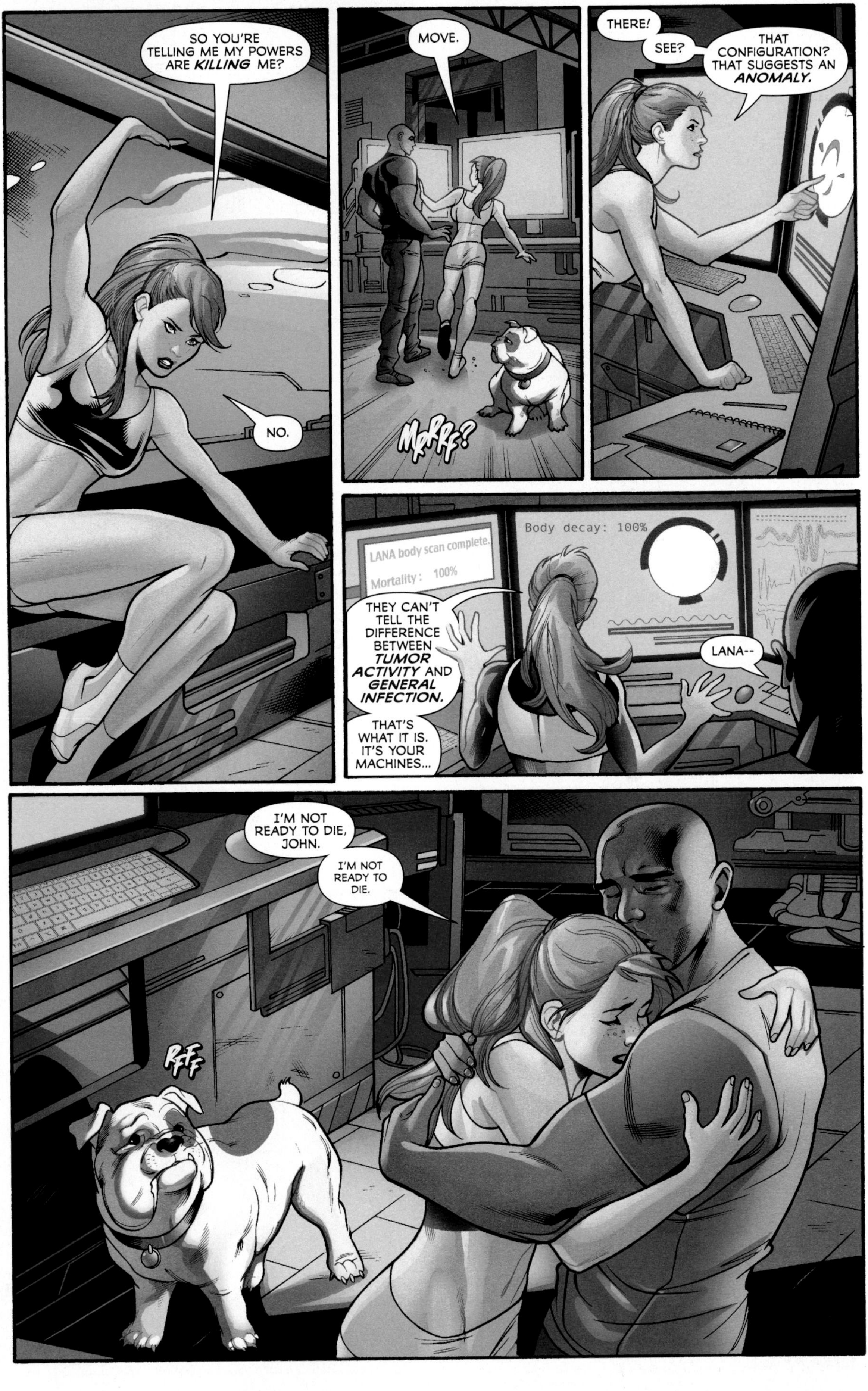
SO YOU'RE TELLING ME MY POWERS ARE *KILLING* ME?
NO.
MOVE.
MRRRF?
THERE!
SEE?
THAT CONFIGURATION? THAT SUGGESTS AN *ANOMALY.*
LANA body scan complete.
Mortality : 100%
Body decay: 100%
THEY CAN'T TELL THE DIFFERENCE BETWEEN *TUMOR ACTIVITY* AND *GENERAL INFECTION.*
THAT'S WHAT IT IS. IT'S YOUR MACHINES...
LANA--
I'M NOT READY TO DIE, JOHN.
I'M NOT READY TO DIE.
RFFF

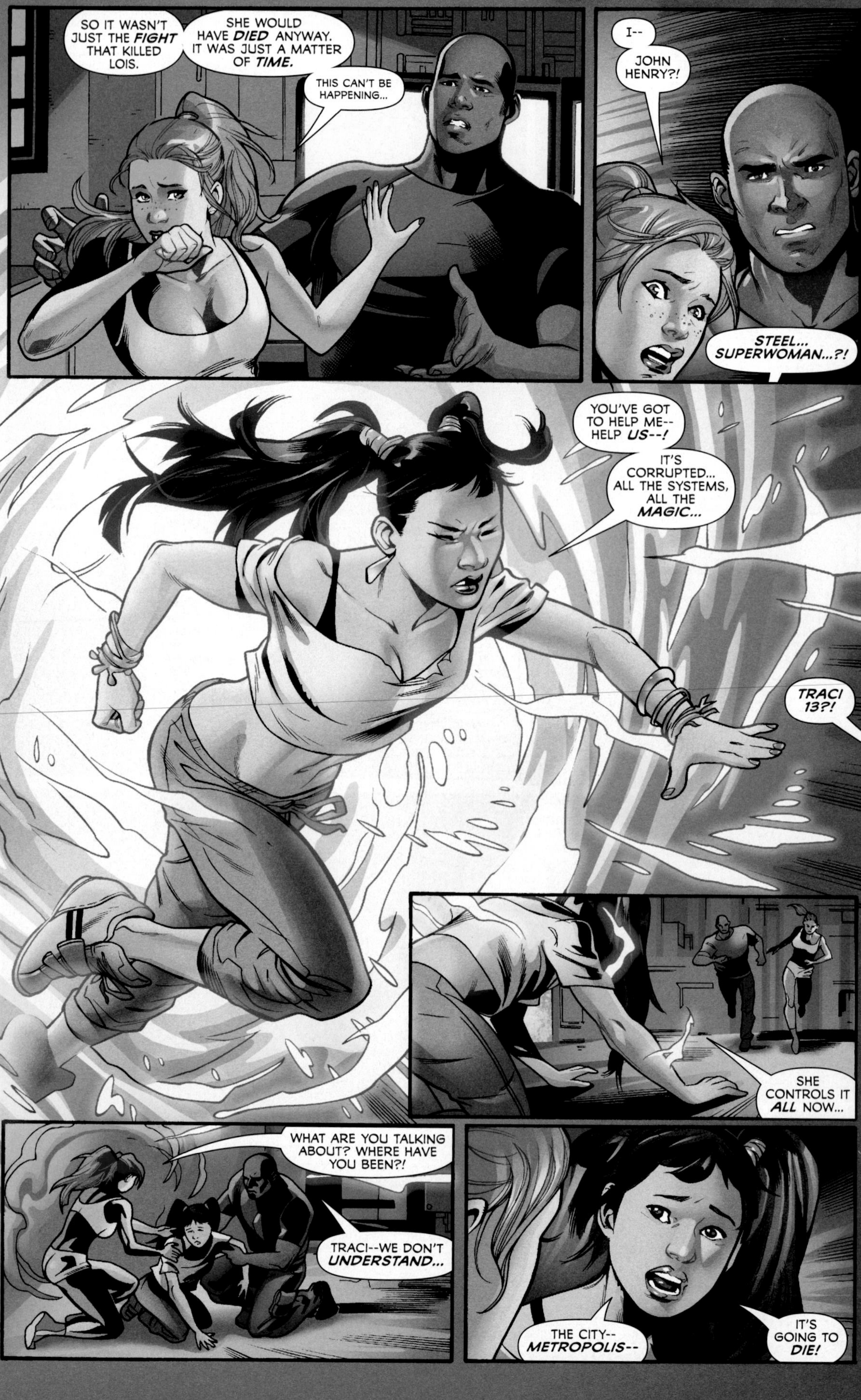
SO IT WASN'T JUST THE FIGHT THAT KILLED LOIS.
SHE WOULD HAVE DIED ANYWAY. IT WAS JUST A MATTER OF TIME.
THIS CAN'T BE HAPPENING...
I--
JOHN HENRY?!
STEEL... SUPERWOMAN...?!
YOU'VE GOT TO HELP ME-- HELP US--!
IT'S CORRUPTED... ALL THE SYSTEMS, ALL THE MAGIC...
TRACI 13?!
SHE CONTROLS IT ALL NOW...
WHAT ARE YOU TALKING ABOUT? WHERE HAVE YOU BEEN?!
TRACI--WE DON'T UNDERSTAND...
THE CITY-- METROPOLIS--
IT'S GOING TO DIE!

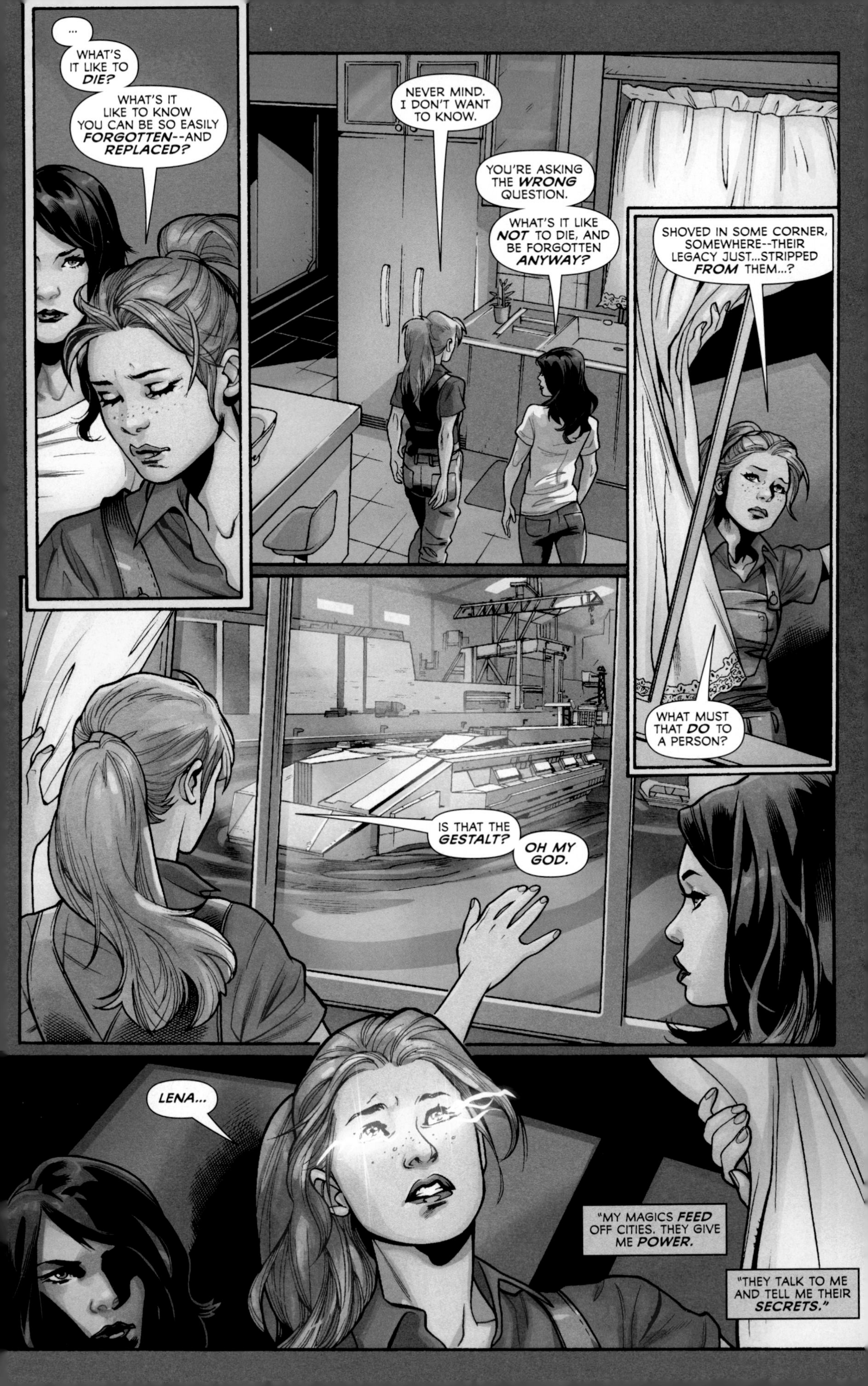
...
WHAT'S IT LIKE TO DIE?
WHAT'S IT LIKE TO KNOW YOU CAN BE SO EASILY FORGOTTEN--AND REPLACED?
NEVER MIND. I DON'T WANT TO KNOW.
YOU'RE ASKING THE WRONG QUESTION.
WHAT'S IT LIKE NOT TO DIE, AND BE FORGOTTEN ANYWAY?
SHOVED IN SOME CORNER, SOMEWHERE--THEIR LEGACY JUST...STRIPPED FROM THEM...?
WHAT MUST THAT DO TO A PERSON?
IS THAT THE GESTALT?
OH MY GOD.
LENA...
"MY MAGICS FEED OFF CITIES. THEY GIVE ME POWER.
"THEY TALK TO ME AND TELL ME THEIR SECRETS."

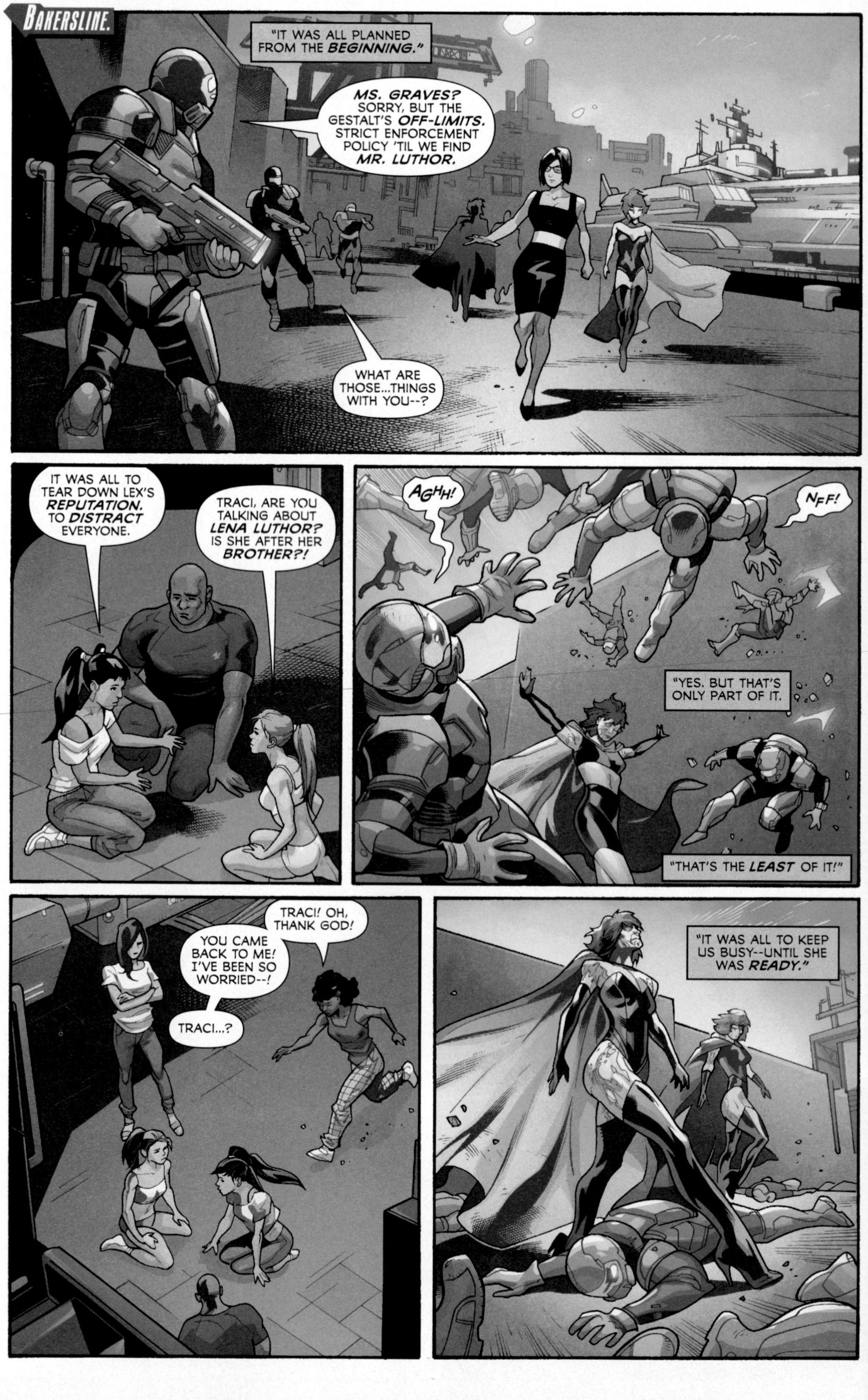
BAKERSLINE.
"IT WAS ALL PLANNED FROM THE BEGINNING."
MS. GRAVES? SORRY, BUT THE GESTALT'S OFF-LIMITS. STRICT ENFORCEMENT POLICY 'TIL WE FIND MR. LUTHOR.
WHAT ARE THOSE...THINGS WITH YOU--?
IT WAS ALL TO TEAR DOWN LEX'S REPUTATION. TO DISTRACT EVERYONE.
TRACI, ARE YOU TALKING ABOUT LENA LUTHOR? IS SHE AFTER HER BROTHER?!
AGHH!
NFF!
"YES. BUT THAT'S ONLY PART OF IT.
"THAT'S THE LEAST OF IT!"
TRACI! OH, THANK GOD!
YOU CAME BACK TO ME! I'VE BEEN SO WORRIED--!
TRACI...?
"IT WAS ALL TO KEEP US BUSY--UNTIL SHE WAS READY."

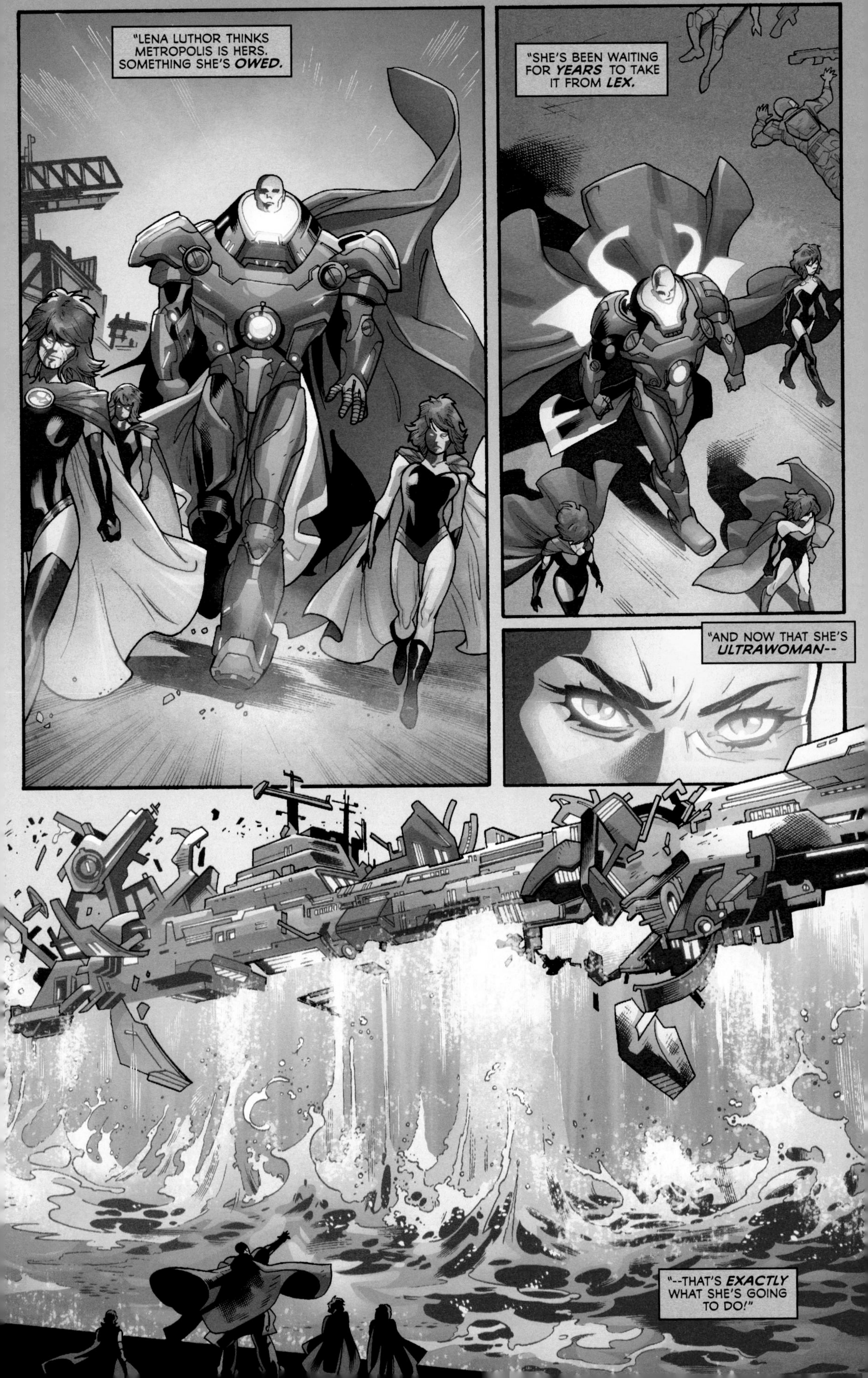
"LENA LUTHOR THINKS METROPOLIS IS HERS. SOMETHING SHE'S *OWED*.
"SHE'S BEEN WAITING FOR *YEARS* TO TAKE IT FROM *LEX*.
"AND NOW THAT SHE'S *ULTRAWOMAN*--
"--THAT'S *EXACTLY* WHAT SHE'S GOING TO DO!"

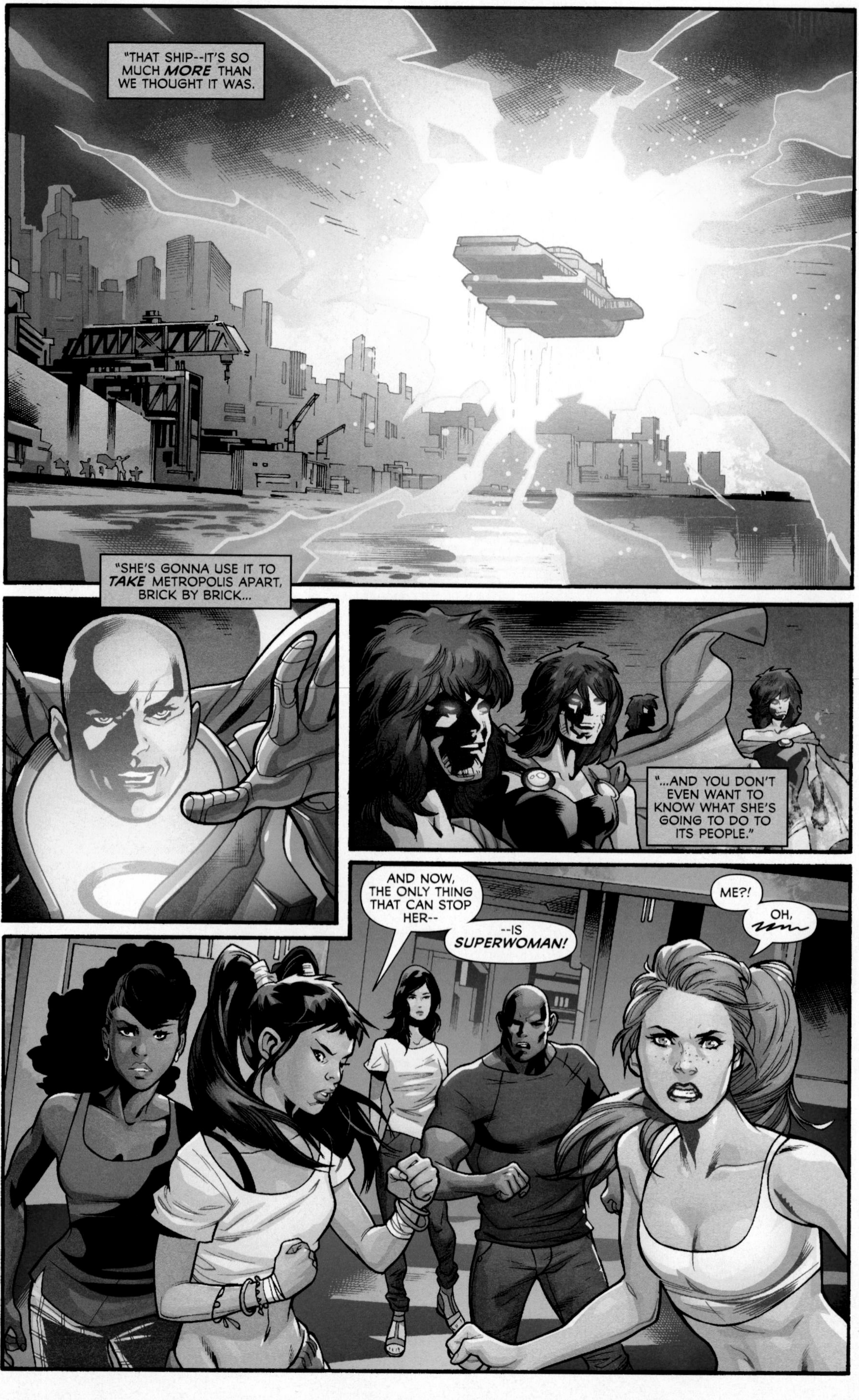
"THAT SHIP--IT'S SO MUCH *MORE* THAN WE THOUGHT IT WAS.
"SHE'S GONNA USE IT TO *TAKE* METROPOLIS APART, BRICK BY BRICK...
"...AND YOU DON'T EVEN WANT TO KNOW WHAT SHE'S GOING TO DO TO ITS PEOPLE."
AND NOW, THE ONLY THING THAT CAN STOP HER--
--IS *SUPERWOMAN!*
ME?!
OH,

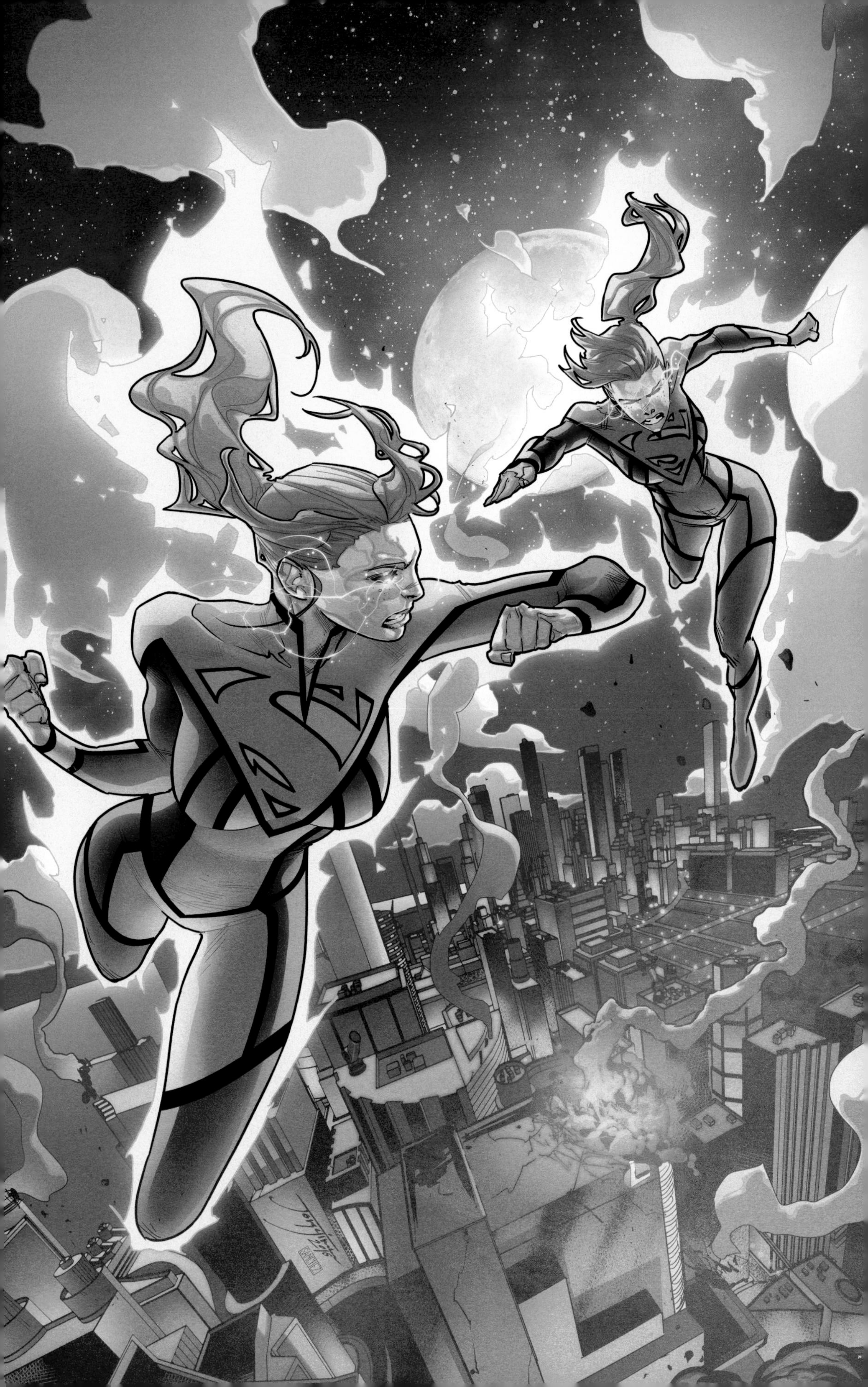

"WHO KILLED SUPERWOMAN? PART 5: IMPRESSIVE INSTANT"

PHIL JIMENEZ writer/penciller * MATT SANTORELLI inker

JEROMY COX and TONY AVINA colorists * cover by JORGE JIMENEZ and ALEJANDRO SANCHEZ

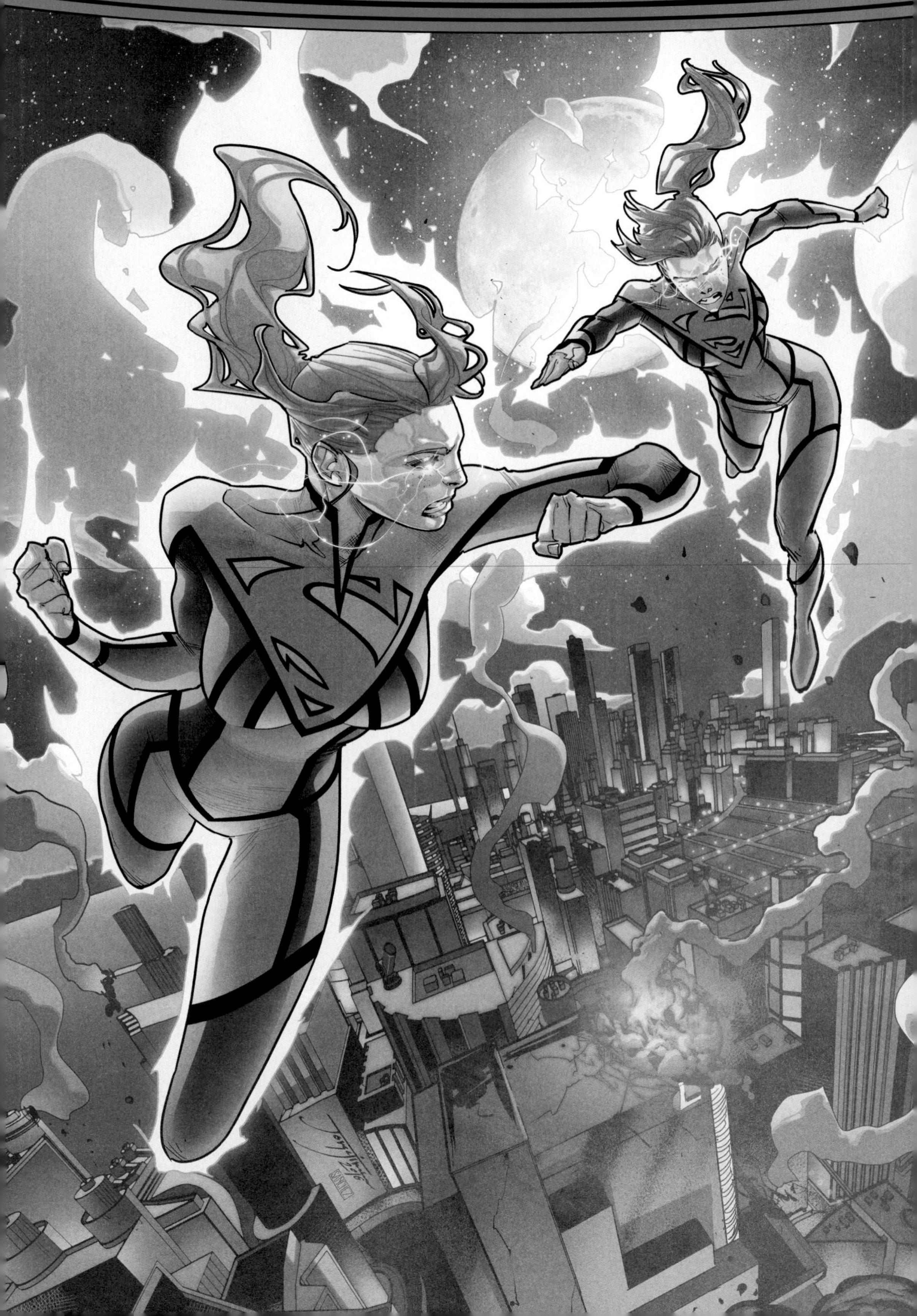

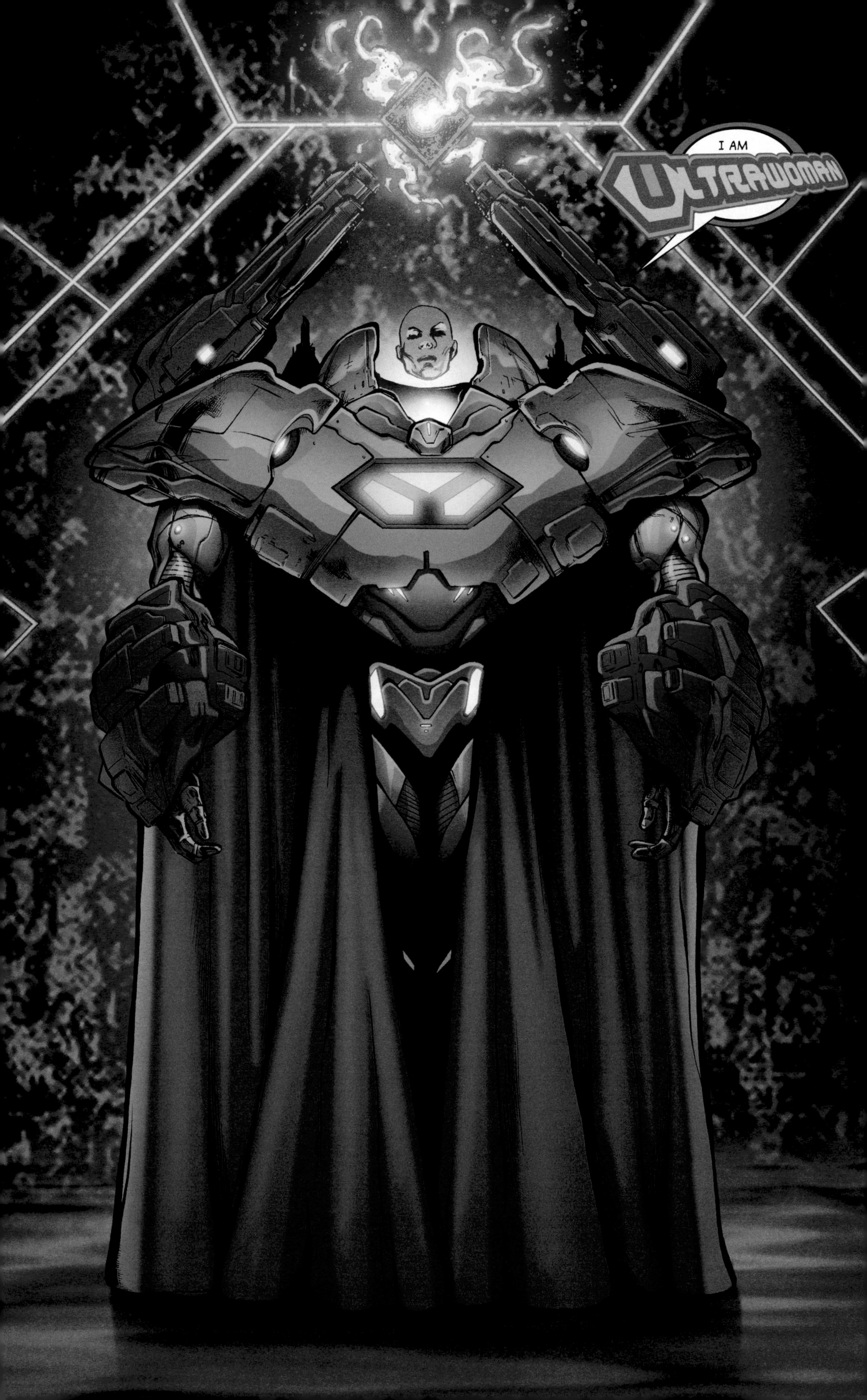
I AM ULTRAWOMAN

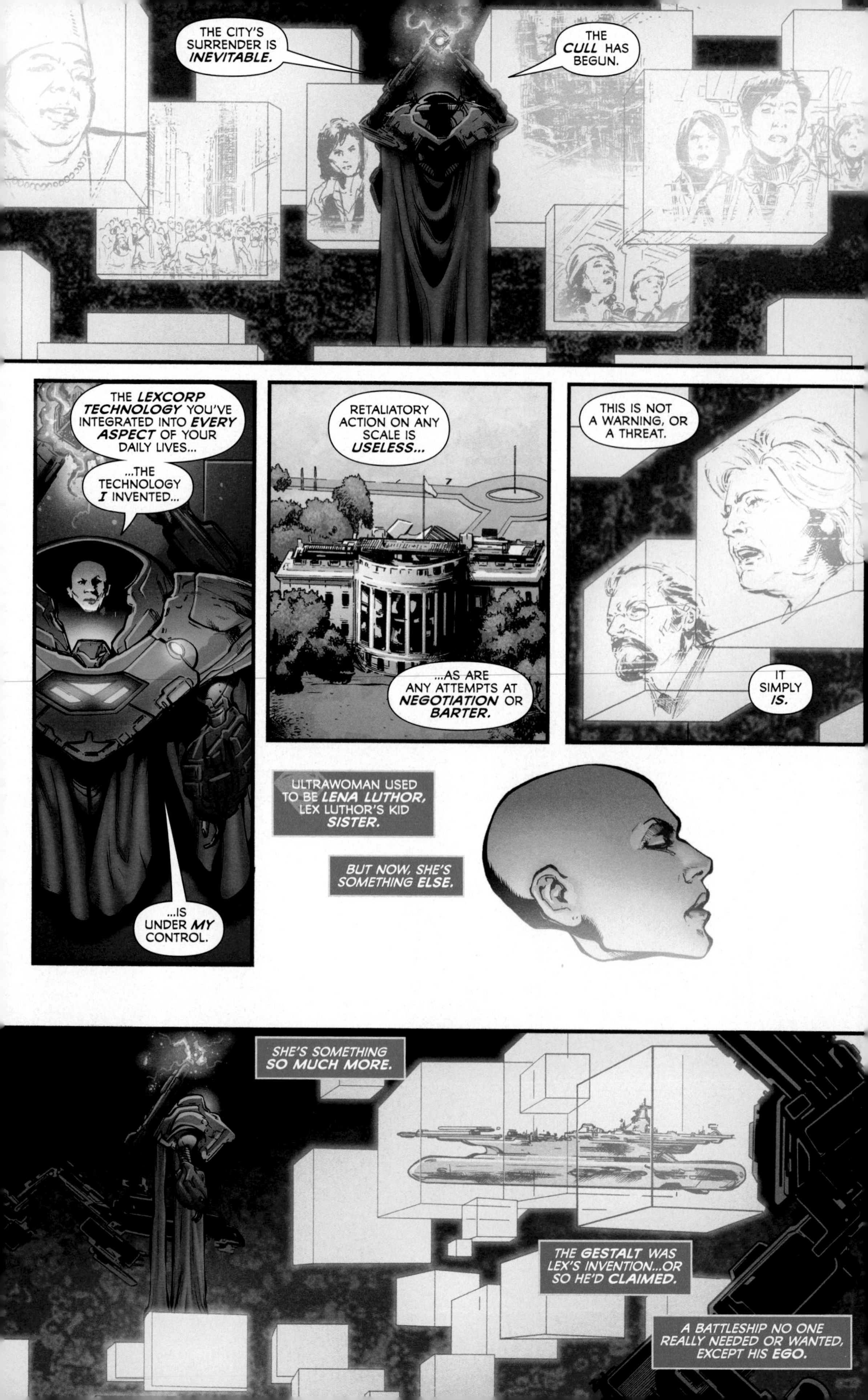
THE CITY'S SURRENDER IS INEVITABLE.
THE CULL HAS BEGUN.
THE LEXCORP TECHNOLOGY YOU'VE INTEGRATED INTO EVERY ASPECT OF YOUR DAILY LIVES...
...THE TECHNOLOGY I INVENTED...
...IS UNDER MY CONTROL.
RETALIATORY ACTION ON ANY SCALE IS USELESS...
...AS ARE ANY ATTEMPTS AT NEGOTIATION OR BARTER.
THIS IS NOT A WARNING, OR A THREAT.
IT SIMPLY IS.
ULTRAWOMAN USED TO BE LENA LUTHOR, LEX LUTHOR'S KID SISTER.
BUT NOW, SHE'S SOMETHING ELSE.
SHE'S SOMETHING SO MUCH MORE.
THE GESTALT WAS LEX'S INVENTION...OR SO HE'D CLAIMED.
A BATTLESHIP NO ONE REALLY NEEDED OR WANTED, EXCEPT HIS EGO.

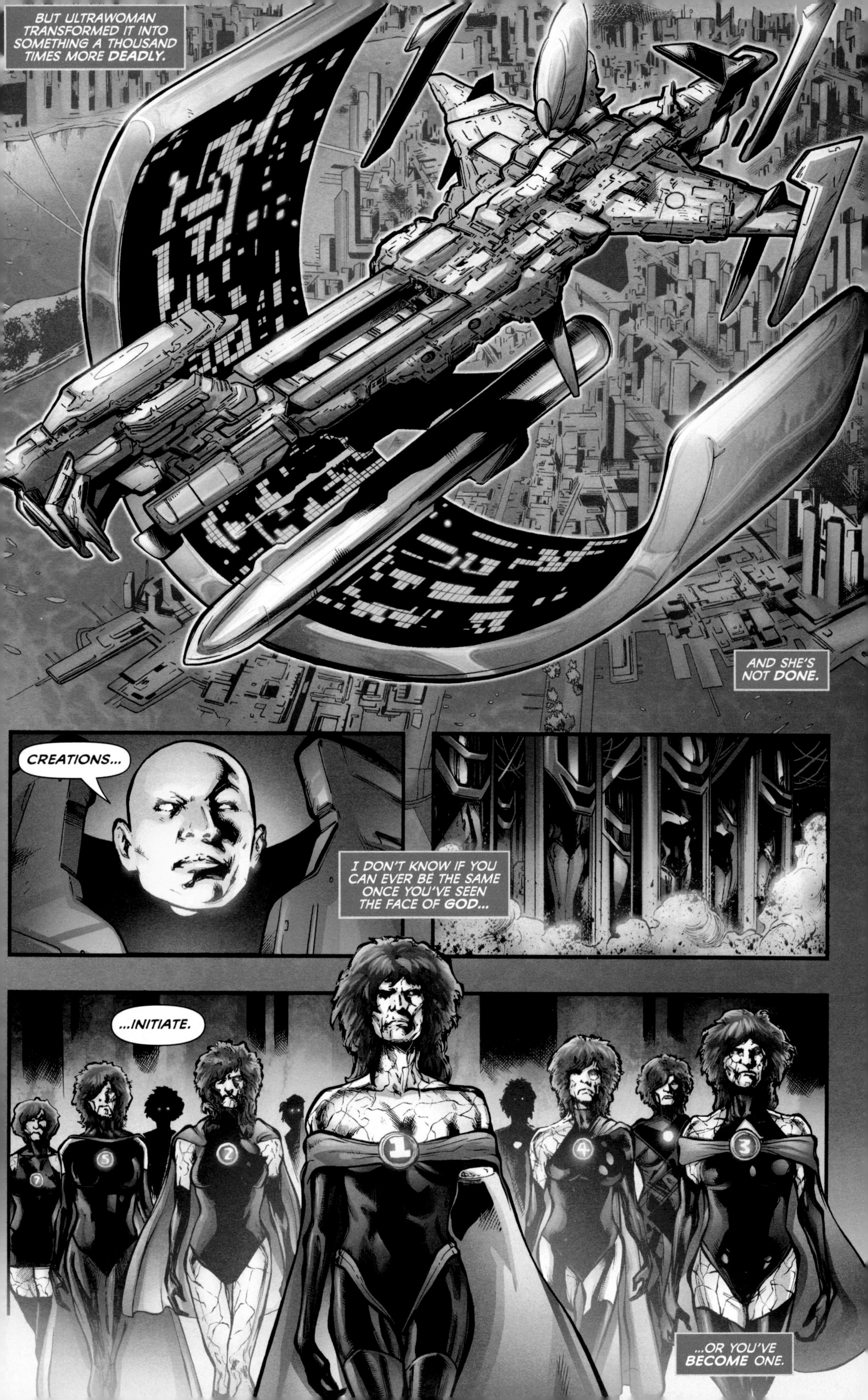
BUT ULTRAWOMAN TRANSFORMED IT INTO SOMETHING A THOUSAND TIMES MORE DEADLY.
AND SHE'S NOT DONE.
CREATIONS...
I DON'T KNOW IF YOU CAN EVER BE THE SAME ONCE YOU'VE SEEN THE FACE OF GOD...
...INITIATE.
...OR YOU'VE BECOME ONE.

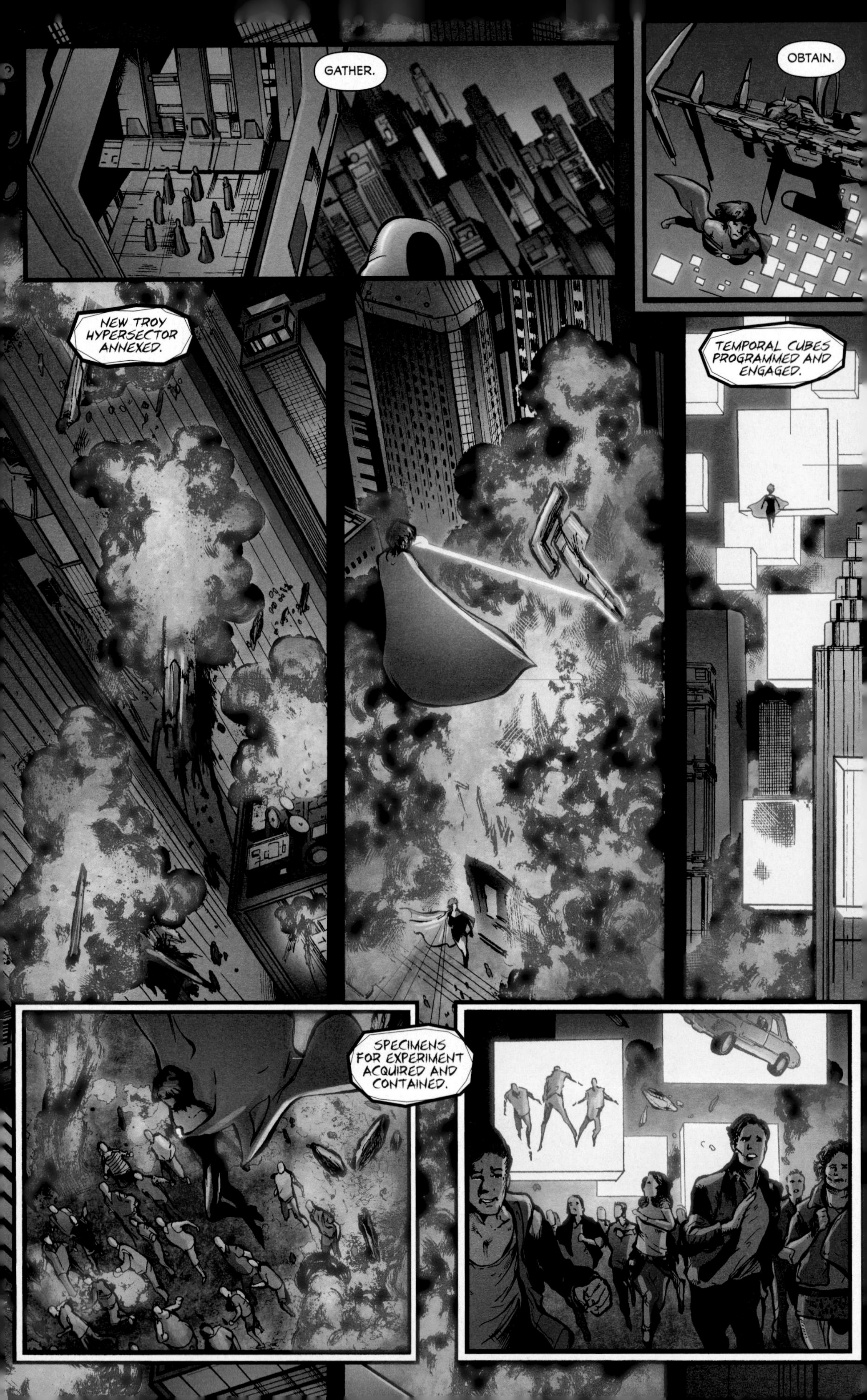
GATHER.
OBTAIN.
NEW TROY HYPERSECTOR ANNEXED.
TEMPORAL CUBES PROGRAMMED AND ENGAGED.
SPECIMENS FOR EXPERIMENT ACQUIRED AND CONTAINED.

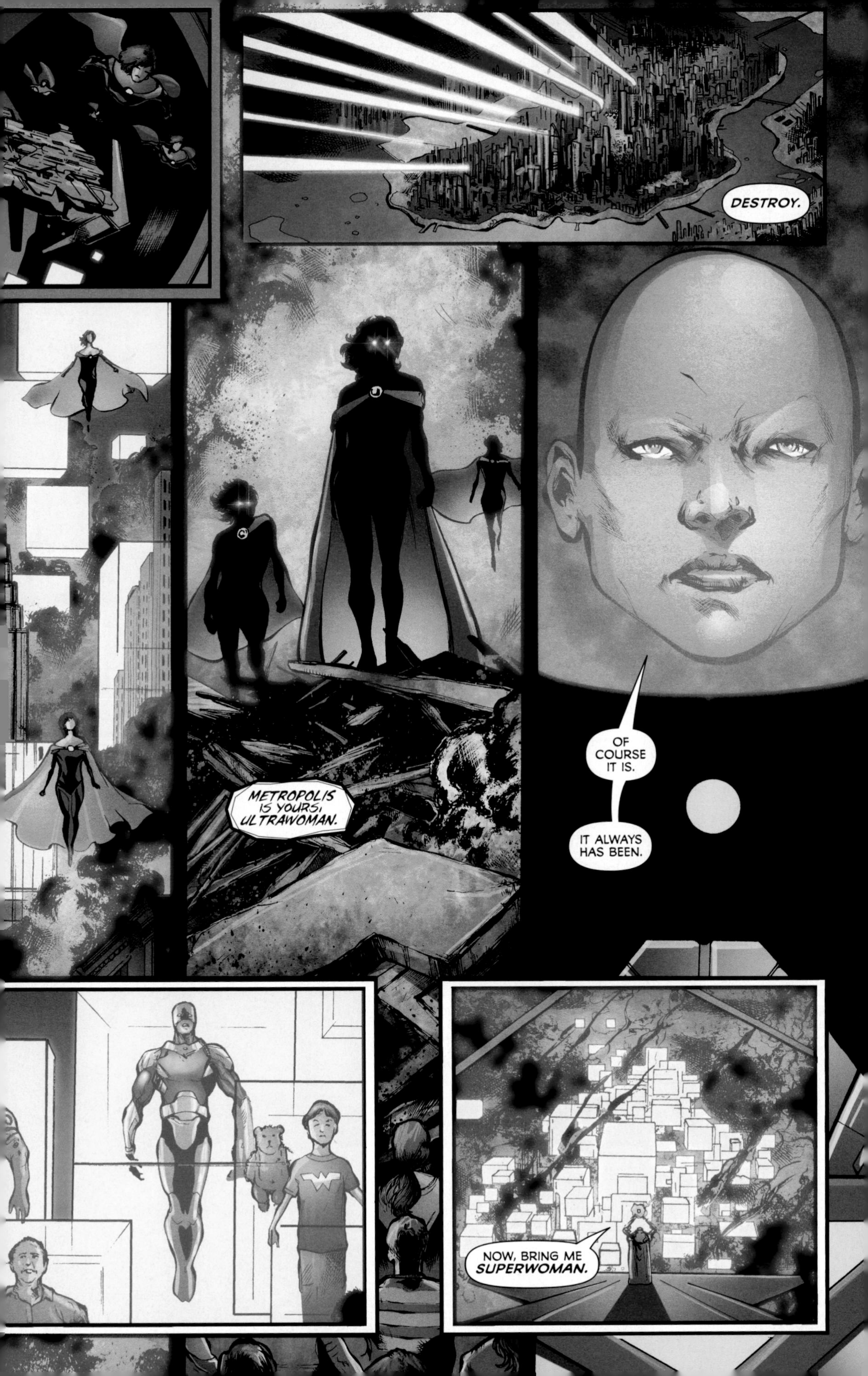
DESTROY.
METROPOLIS IS YOURS, ULTRAWOMAN.
OF COURSE IT IS.
IT ALWAYS HAS BEEN.
NOW, BRING ME SUPERWOMAN.

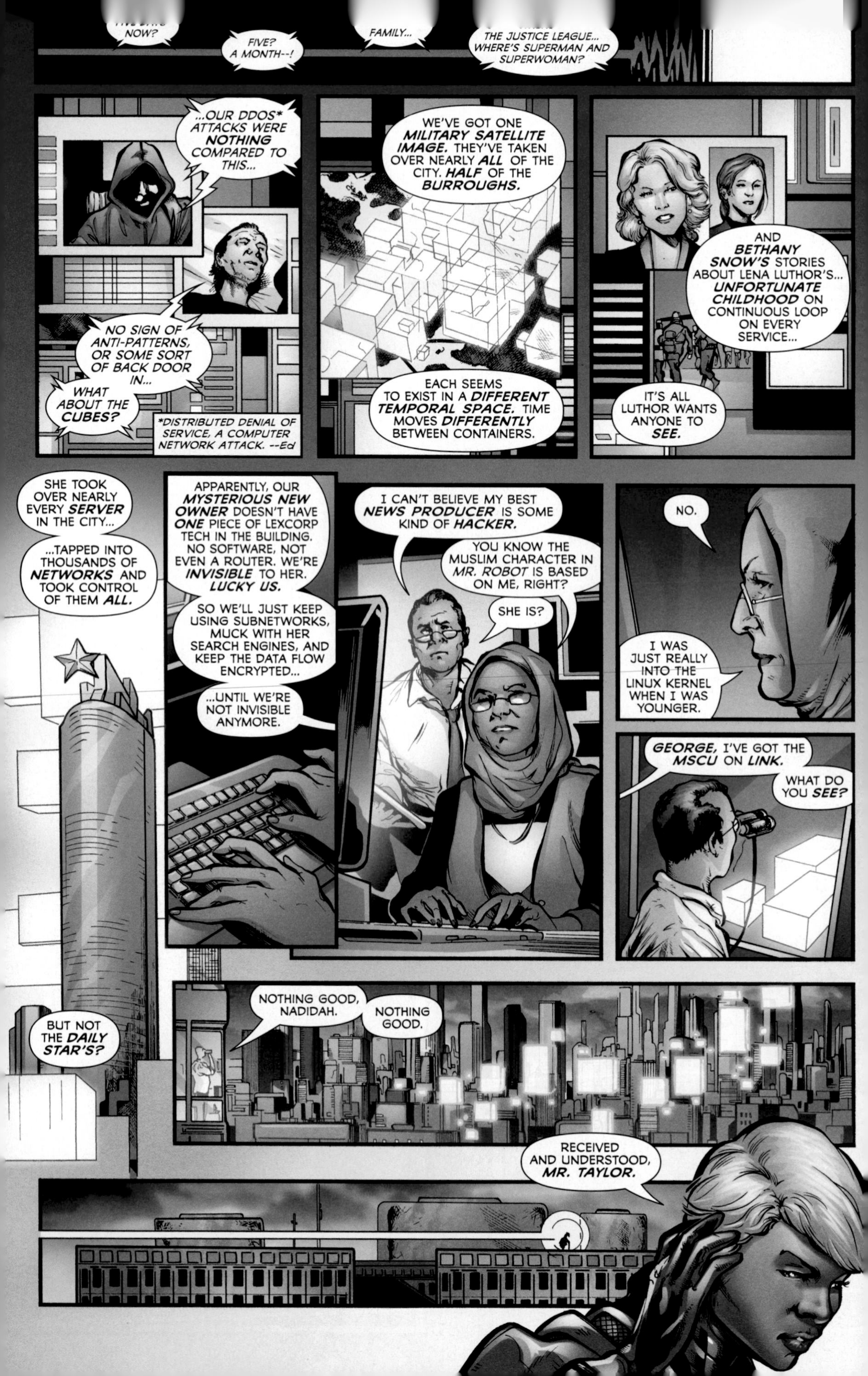
NOW?
FIVE? A MONTH--!
FAMILY...
THE JUSTICE LEAGUE... WHERE'S SUPERMAN AND SUPERWOMAN?
...OUR DDOS* ATTACKS WERE NOTHING COMPARED TO THIS...
NO SIGN OF ANTI-PATTERNS, OR SOME SORT OF BACK DOOR IN...
WHAT ABOUT THE CUBES?
*DISTRIBUTED DENIAL OF SERVICE, A COMPUTER NETWORK ATTACK. --Ed
WE'VE GOT ONE MILITARY SATELLITE IMAGE. THEY'VE TAKEN OVER NEARLY ALL OF THE CITY. HALF OF THE BURROUGHS.
EACH SEEMS TO EXIST IN A DIFFERENT TEMPORAL SPACE. TIME MOVES DIFFERENTLY BETWEEN CONTAINERS.
AND BETHANY SNOW'S STORIES ABOUT LENA LUTHOR'S... UNFORTUNATE CHILDHOOD ON CONTINUOUS LOOP ON EVERY SERVICE...
IT'S ALL LUTHOR WANTS ANYONE TO SEE.
SHE TOOK OVER NEARLY EVERY SERVER IN THE CITY...
...TAPPED INTO THOUSANDS OF NETWORKS AND TOOK CONTROL OF THEM ALL.
BUT NOT THE DAILY STAR'S?
APPARENTLY, OUR MYSTERIOUS NEW OWNER DOESN'T HAVE ONE PIECE OF LEXCORP TECH IN THE BUILDING. NO SOFTWARE, NOT EVEN A ROUTER. WE'RE INVISIBLE TO HER. LUCKY US.
SO WE'LL JUST KEEP USING SUBNETWORKS, MUCK WITH HER SEARCH ENGINES, AND KEEP THE DATA FLOW ENCRYPTED...
...UNTIL WE'RE NOT INVISIBLE ANYMORE.
I CAN'T BELIEVE MY BEST NEWS PRODUCER IS SOME KIND OF HACKER.
YOU KNOW THE MUSLIM CHARACTER IN MR. ROBOT IS BASED ON ME, RIGHT?
SHE IS?
NO.
I WAS JUST REALLY INTO THE LINUX KERNEL WHEN I WAS YOUNGER.
GEORGE, I'VE GOT THE MSCU ON LINK.
WHAT DO YOU SEE?
NOTHING GOOD, NADIDAH.
NOTHING GOOD.
RECEIVED AND UNDERSTOOD, MR. TAYLOR.

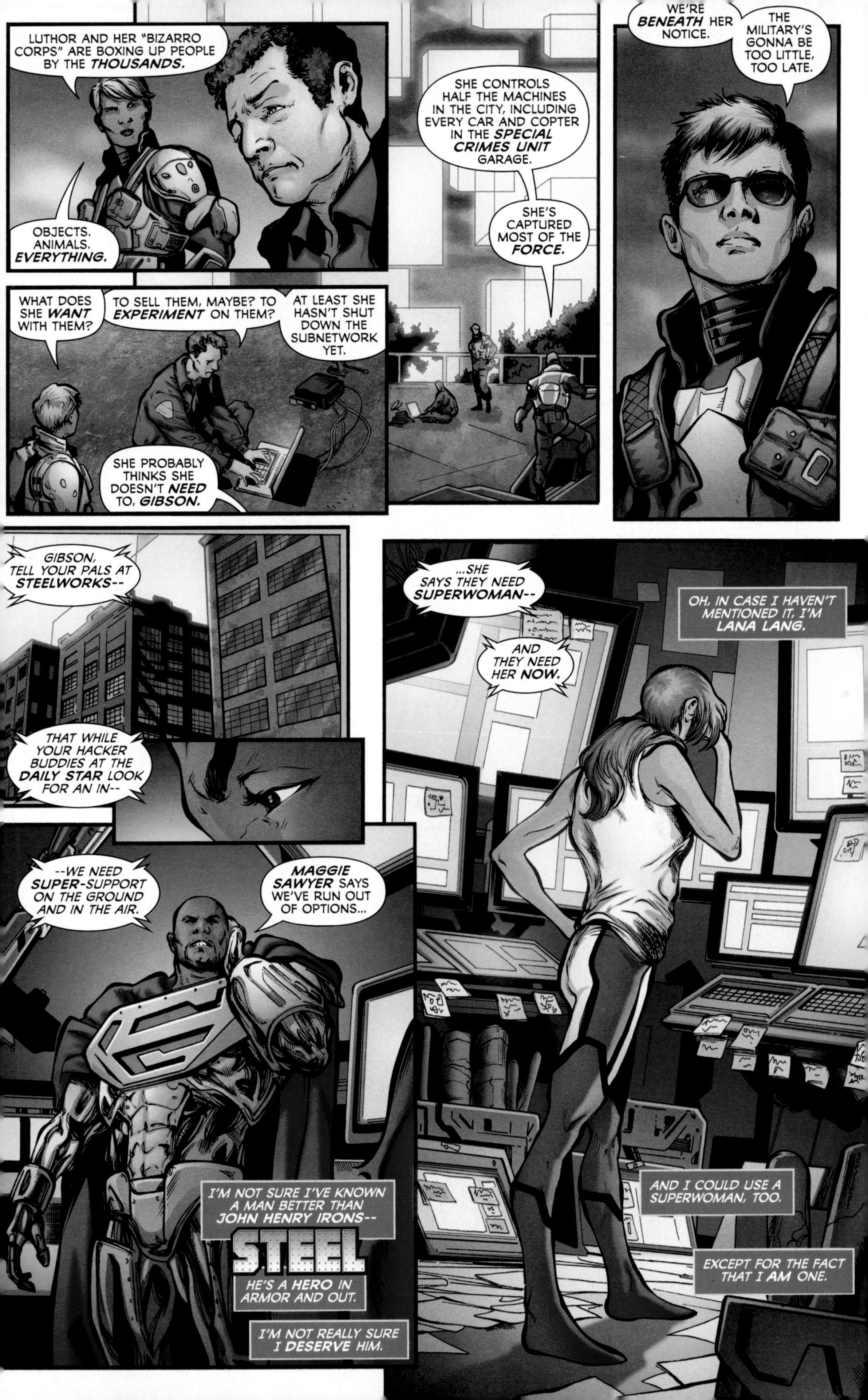
LUTHOR AND HER "BIZARRO CORPS" ARE BOXING UP PEOPLE BY THE THOUSANDS.
OBJECTS. ANIMALS. EVERYTHING.
SHE CONTROLS HALF THE MACHINES IN THE CITY, INCLUDING EVERY CAR AND COPTER IN THE SPECIAL CRIMES UNIT GARAGE.
SHE'S CAPTURED MOST OF THE FORCE.
WE'RE BENEATH HER NOTICE.
THE MILITARY'S GONNA BE TOO LITTLE, TOO LATE.
WHAT DOES SHE WANT WITH THEM?
TO SELL THEM, MAYBE? TO EXPERIMENT ON THEM?
AT LEAST SHE HASN'T SHUT DOWN THE SUBNETWORK YET.
SHE PROBABLY THINKS SHE DOESN'T NEED TO, GIBSON.
GIBSON, TELL YOUR PALS AT STEELWORKS--
THAT WHILE YOUR HACKER BUDDIES AT THE DAILY STAR LOOK FOR AN IN--
--WE NEED SUPER-SUPPORT ON THE GROUND AND IN THE AIR.
MAGGIE SAWYER SAYS WE'VE RUN OUT OF OPTIONS...
...SHE SAYS THEY NEED SUPERWOMAN--
AND THEY NEED HER NOW.
OH, IN CASE I HAVEN'T MENTIONED IT, I'M LANA LANG.
I'M NOT SURE I'VE KNOWN A MAN BETTER THAN JOHN HENRY IRONS--
STEEL
HE'S A HERO IN ARMOR AND OUT.
I'M NOT REALLY SURE I DESERVE HIM.
AND I COULD USE A SUPERWOMAN, TOO.
EXCEPT FOR THE FACT THAT I AM ONE.

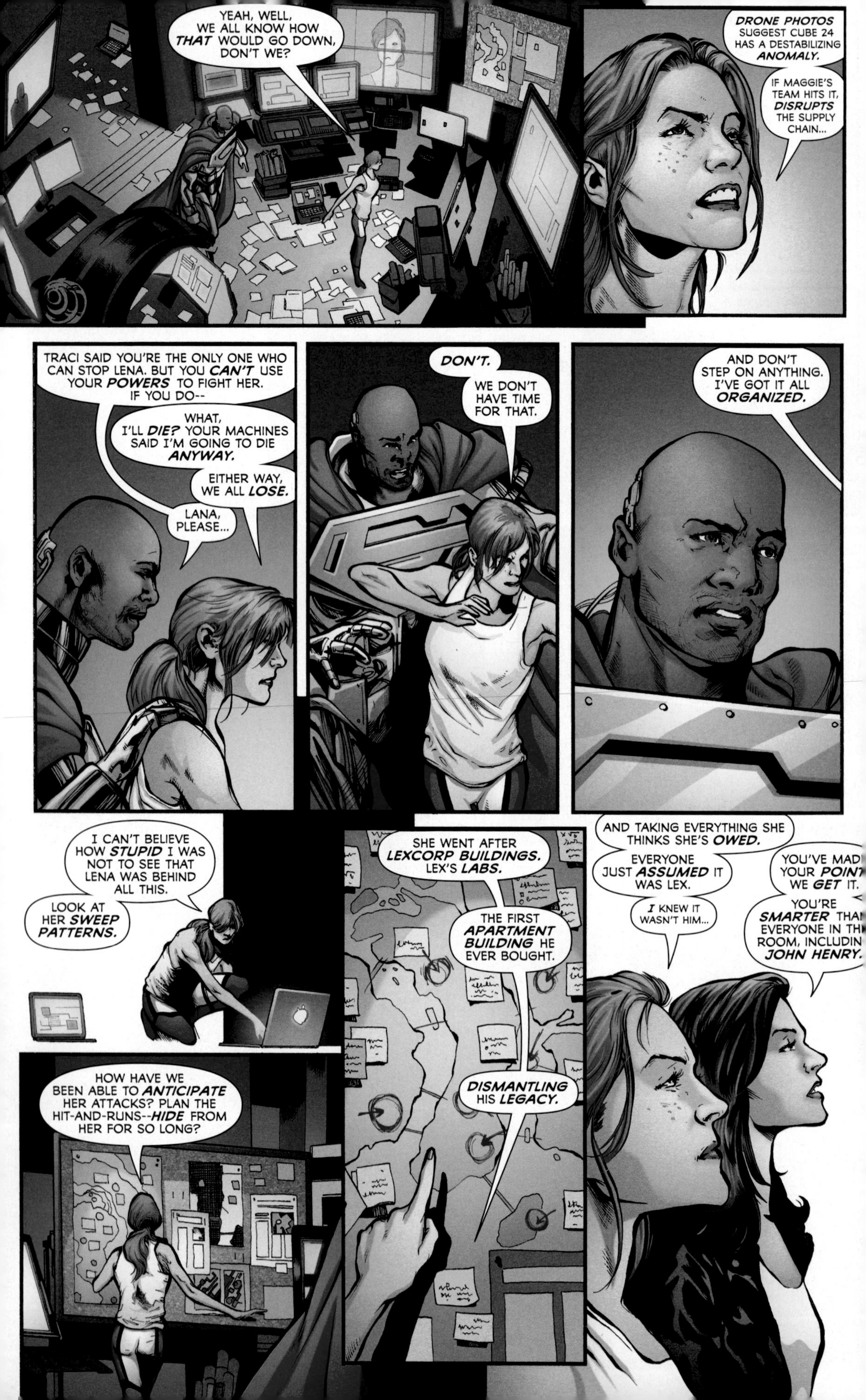

YEAH, WELL, WE ALL KNOW HOW THAT WOULD GO DOWN, DON'T WE?
DRONE PHOTOS SUGGEST CUBE 24 HAS A DESTABILIZING ANOMALY.
IF MAGGIE'S TEAM HITS IT, DISRUPTS THE SUPPLY CHAIN...
TRACI SAID YOU'RE THE ONLY ONE WHO CAN STOP LENA. BUT YOU CAN'T USE YOUR POWERS TO FIGHT HER. IF YOU DO--
WHAT, I'LL DIE? YOUR MACHINES SAID I'M GOING TO DIE ANYWAY.
EITHER WAY, WE ALL LOSE.
LANA, PLEASE...
DON'T.
WE DON'T HAVE TIME FOR THAT.
AND DON'T STEP ON ANYTHING. I'VE GOT IT ALL ORGANIZED.
I CAN'T BELIEVE HOW STUPID I WAS NOT TO SEE THAT LENA WAS BEHIND ALL THIS.
LOOK AT HER SWEEP PATTERNS.
HOW HAVE WE BEEN ABLE TO ANTICIPATE HER ATTACKS? PLAN THE HIT-AND-RUNS--HIDE FROM HER FOR SO LONG?
SHE WENT AFTER LEXCORP BUILDINGS. LEX'S LABS.
THE FIRST APARTMENT BUILDING HE EVER BOUGHT.
DISMANTLING HIS LEGACY.
AND TAKING EVERYTHING SHE THINKS SHE'S OWED.
EVERYONE JUST ASSUMED IT WAS LEX.
I KNEW IT WASN'T HIM...
YOU'VE MAD YOUR POINT WE GET IT.
YOU'RE SMARTER THA EVERYONE IN TH ROOM, INCLUDIN JOHN HENRY.

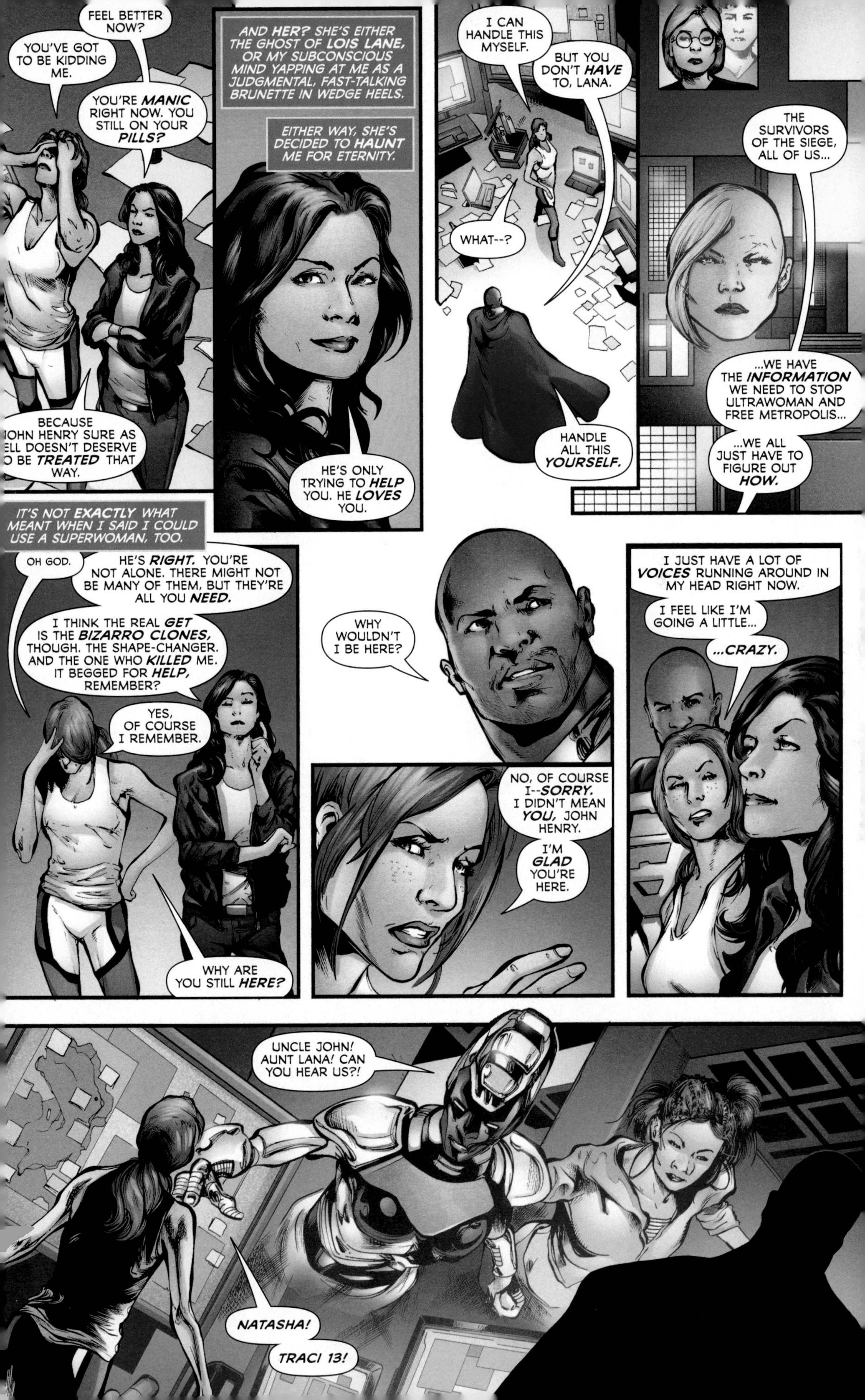

FEEL BETTER NOW?
YOU'VE GOT TO BE KIDDING ME.
YOU'RE MANIC RIGHT NOW. YOU STILL ON YOUR PILLS?
BECAUSE JOHN HENRY SURE AS ELL DOESN'T DESERVE O BE TREATED THAT WAY.
AND HER? SHE'S EITHER THE GHOST OF LOIS LANE, OR MY SUBCONSCIOUS MIND YAPPING AT ME AS A JUDGMENTAL, FAST-TALKING BRUNETTE IN WEDGE HEELS.
EITHER WAY, SHE'S DECIDED TO HAUNT ME FOR ETERNITY.
HE'S ONLY TRYING TO HELP YOU. HE LOVES YOU.
I CAN HANDLE THIS MYSELF.
BUT YOU DON'T HAVE TO, LANA.
WHAT--?
HANDLE ALL THIS YOURSELF.
THE SURVIVORS OF THE SIEGE, ALL OF US...
...WE HAVE THE INFORMATION WE NEED TO STOP ULTRAWOMAN AND FREE METROPOLIS...
...WE ALL JUST HAVE TO FIGURE OUT HOW.
IT'S NOT EXACTLY WHAT MEANT WHEN I SAID I COULD USE A SUPERWOMAN, TOO.
OH GOD.
HE'S RIGHT. YOU'RE NOT ALONE. THERE MIGHT NOT BE MANY OF THEM, BUT THEY'RE ALL YOU NEED.
I THINK THE REAL GET IS THE BIZARRO CLONES, THOUGH. THE SHAPE-CHANGER. AND THE ONE WHO KILLED ME. IT BEGGED FOR HELP, REMEMBER?
YES, OF COURSE I REMEMBER.
WHY ARE YOU STILL HERE?
WHY WOULDN'T I BE HERE?
NO, OF COURSE I--SORRY. I DIDN'T MEAN YOU, JOHN HENRY.
I'M GLAD YOU'RE HERE.
I JUST HAVE A LOT OF VOICES RUNNING AROUND IN MY HEAD RIGHT NOW.
I FEEL LIKE I'M GOING A LITTLE...
...CRAZY.
UNCLE JOHN! AUNT LANA! CAN YOU HEAR US?!
NATASHA!
TRACI 13!

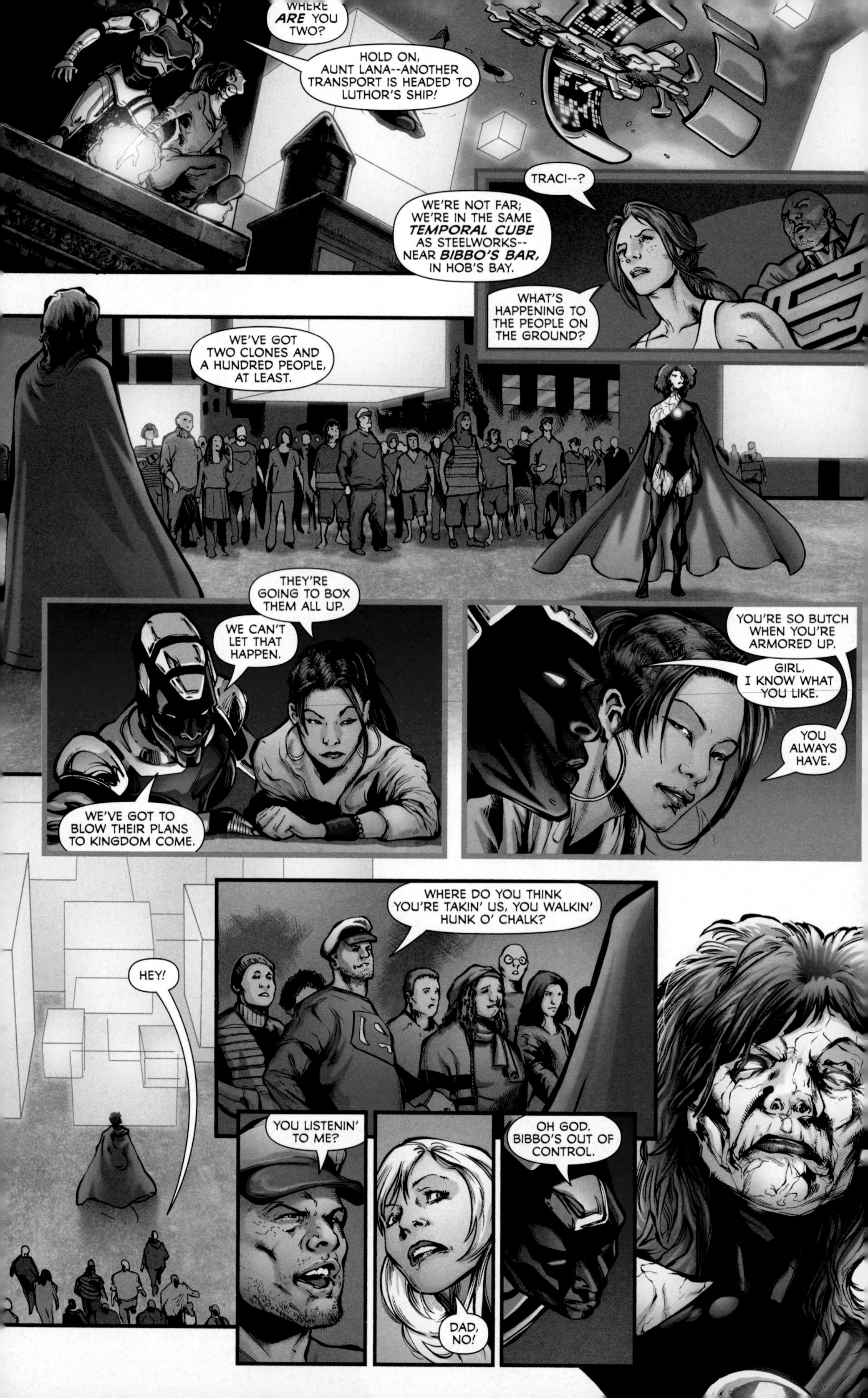
WHERE ARE YOU TWO?
HOLD ON, AUNT LANA--ANOTHER TRANSPORT IS HEADED TO LUTHOR'S SHIP!
TRACI--?
WE'RE NOT FAR; WE'RE IN THE SAME TEMPORAL CUBE AS STEELWORKS-- NEAR BIBBO'S BAR, IN HOB'S BAY.
WHAT'S HAPPENING TO THE PEOPLE ON THE GROUND?
WE'VE GOT TWO CLONES AND A HUNDRED PEOPLE, AT LEAST.
THEY'RE GOING TO BOX THEM ALL UP.
WE CAN'T LET THAT HAPPEN.
WE'VE GOT TO BLOW THEIR PLANS TO KINGDOM COME.
YOU'RE SO BUTCH WHEN YOU'RE ARMORED UP.
GIRL, I KNOW WHAT YOU LIKE.
YOU ALWAYS HAVE.
HEY!
WHERE DO YOU THINK YOU'RE TAKIN' US, YOU WALKIN' HUNK O' CHALK?
YOU LISTENIN' TO ME?
DAD, NO!
OH GOD. BIBBO'S OUT OF CONTROL.

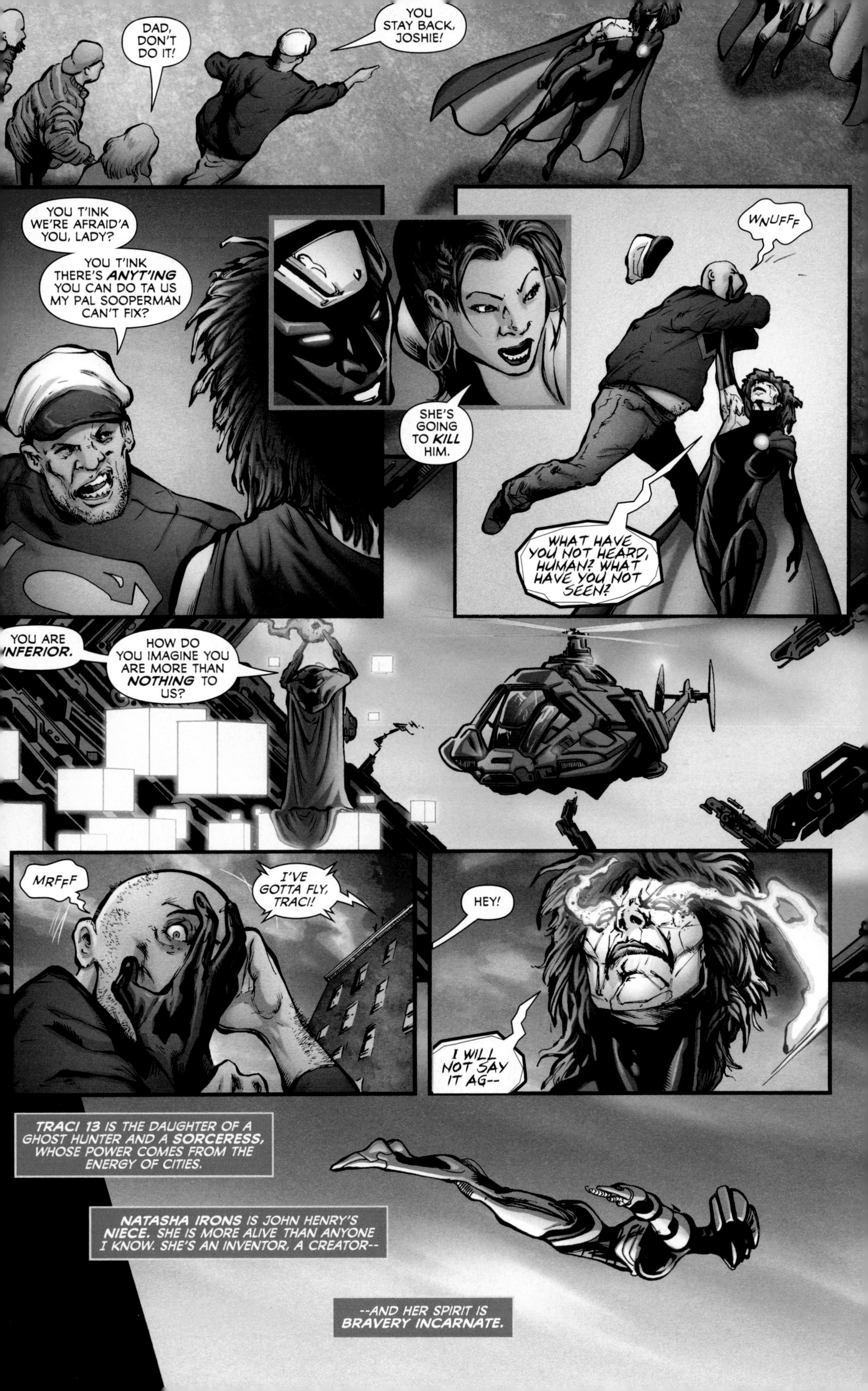
DAD, DON'T DO IT!
YOU STAY BACK, JOSHIE!
YOU T'INK WE'RE AFRAID'A YOU, LADY?
YOU T'INK THERE'S ANYT'ING YOU CAN DO TA US MY PAL SOOPERMAN CAN'T FIX?
SHE'S GOING TO KILL HIM.
WNUFFF
WHAT HAVE YOU NOT HEARD, HUMAN? WHAT HAVE YOU NOT SEEN?
YOU ARE INFERIOR.
HOW DO YOU IMAGINE YOU ARE MORE THAN NOTHING TO US?
MRFFF
I'VE GOTTA FLY, TRACI!
HEY!
I WILL NOT SAY IT AG--
TRACI 13 IS THE DAUGHTER OF A GHOST HUNTER AND A SORCERESS, WHOSE POWER COMES FROM THE ENERGY OF CITIES.
NATASHA IRONS IS JOHN HENRY'S NIECE. SHE IS MORE ALIVE THAN ANYONE I KNOW. SHE'S AN INVENTOR, A CREATOR--
--AND HER SPIRIT IS BRAVERY INCARNATE.

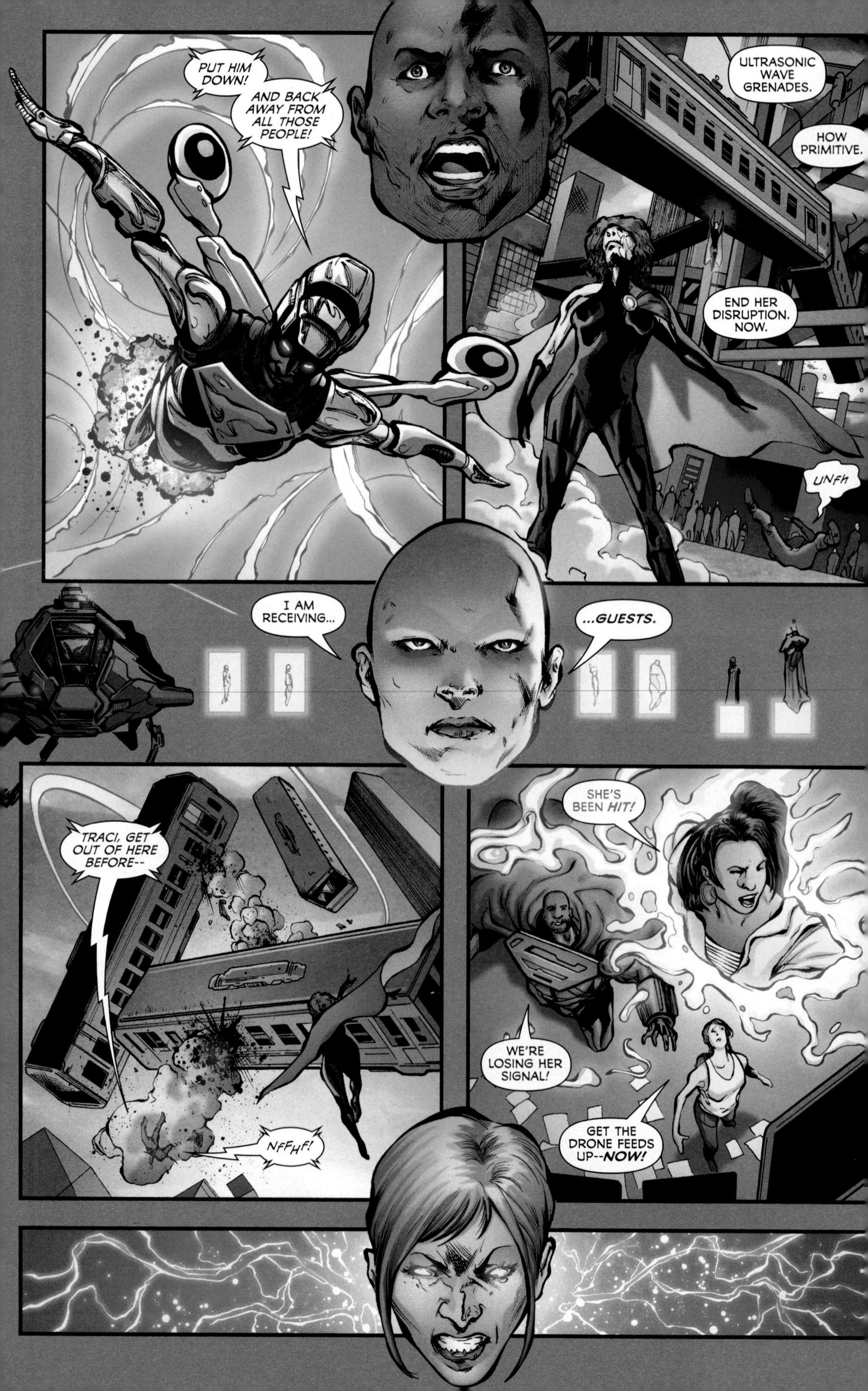
PUT HIM DOWN!
AND BACK AWAY FROM ALL THOSE PEOPLE!
ULTRASONIC WAVE GRENADES.
HOW PRIMITIVE.
END HER DISRUPTION. NOW.
UNFH
I AM RECEIVING...
...GUESTS.
TRACI, GET OUT OF HERE BEFORE--
NFFHF!
SHE'S BEEN HIT!
WE'RE LOSING HER SIGNAL!
GET THE DRONE FEEDS UP--NOW!

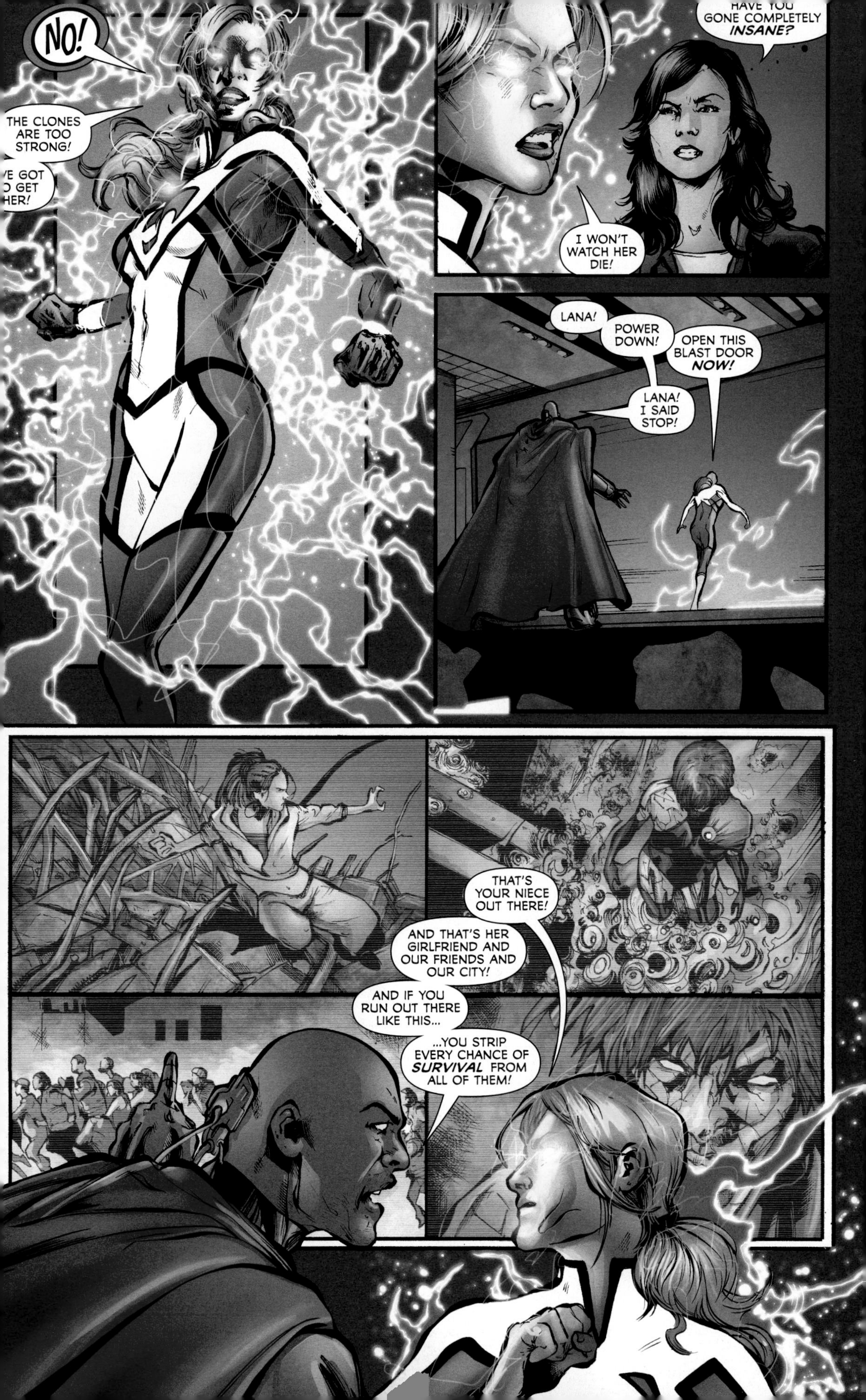
NO!
THE CLONES ARE TOO STRONG!
'E GOT O GET HER!
HAVE YOU GONE COMPLETELY INSANE?
I WON'T WATCH HER DIE!
LANA!
POWER DOWN!
OPEN THIS BLAST DOOR NOW!
LANA! I SAID STOP!
THAT'S YOUR NIECE OUT THERE!
AND THAT'S HER GIRLFRIEND AND OUR FRIENDS AND OUR CITY!
AND IF YOU RUN OUT THERE LIKE THIS...
...YOU STRIP EVERY CHANCE OF SURVIVAL FROM ALL OF THEM!

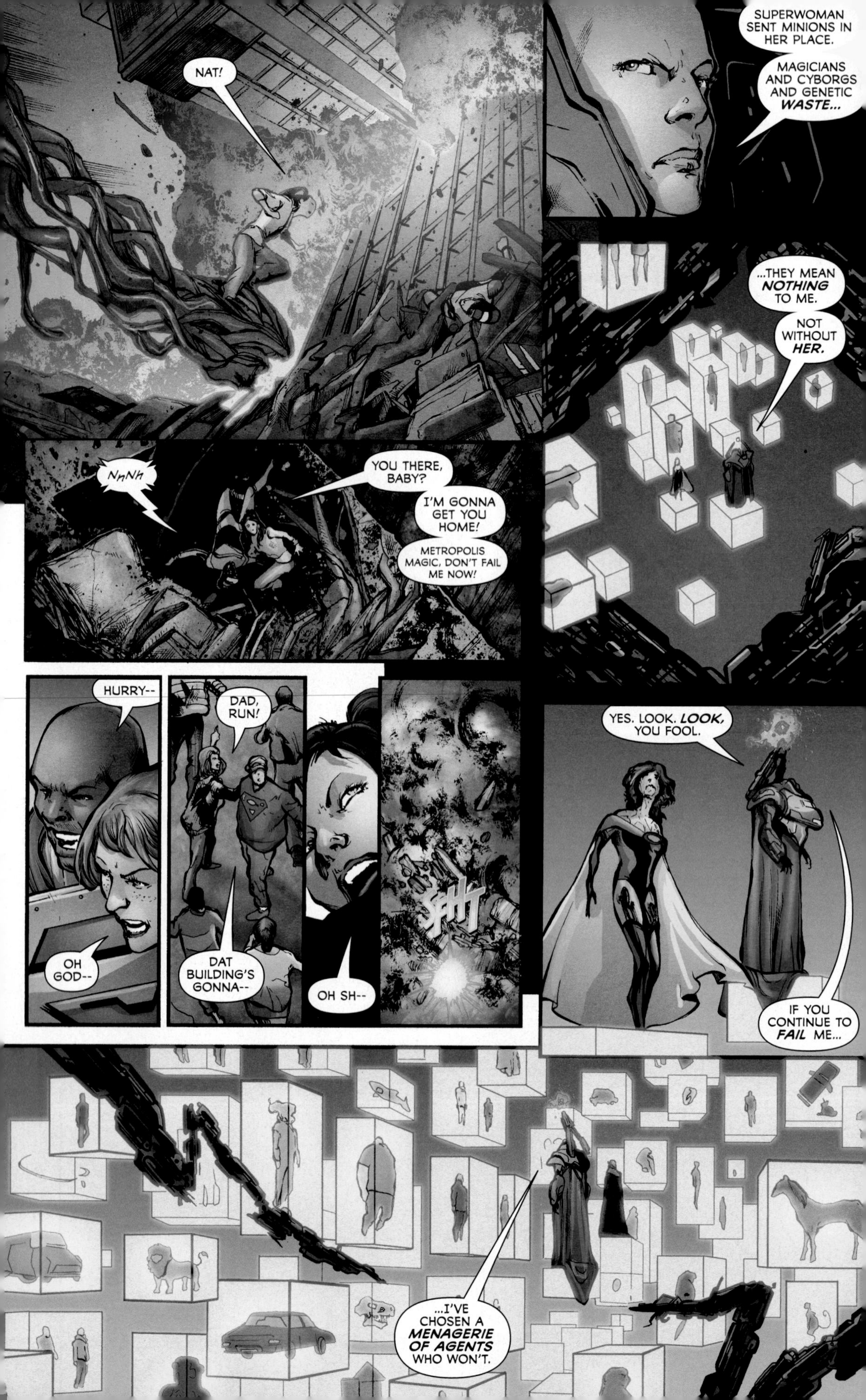
NAT!
SUPERWOMAN SENT MINIONS IN HER PLACE.
MAGICIANS AND CYBORGS AND GENETIC WASTE...
...THEY MEAN NOTHING TO ME.
NOT WITHOUT HER.
NnNh
YOU THERE, BABY?
I'M GONNA GET YOU HOME!
METROPOLIS MAGIC, DON'T FAIL ME NOW!
HURRY--
OH GOD--
DAD, RUN!
DAT BUILDING'S GONNA--
OH SH--
SFHT
YES. LOOK. LOOK, YOU FOOL.
IF YOU CONTINUE TO FAIL ME...
...I'VE CHOSEN A MENAGERIE OF AGENTS WHO WON'T.

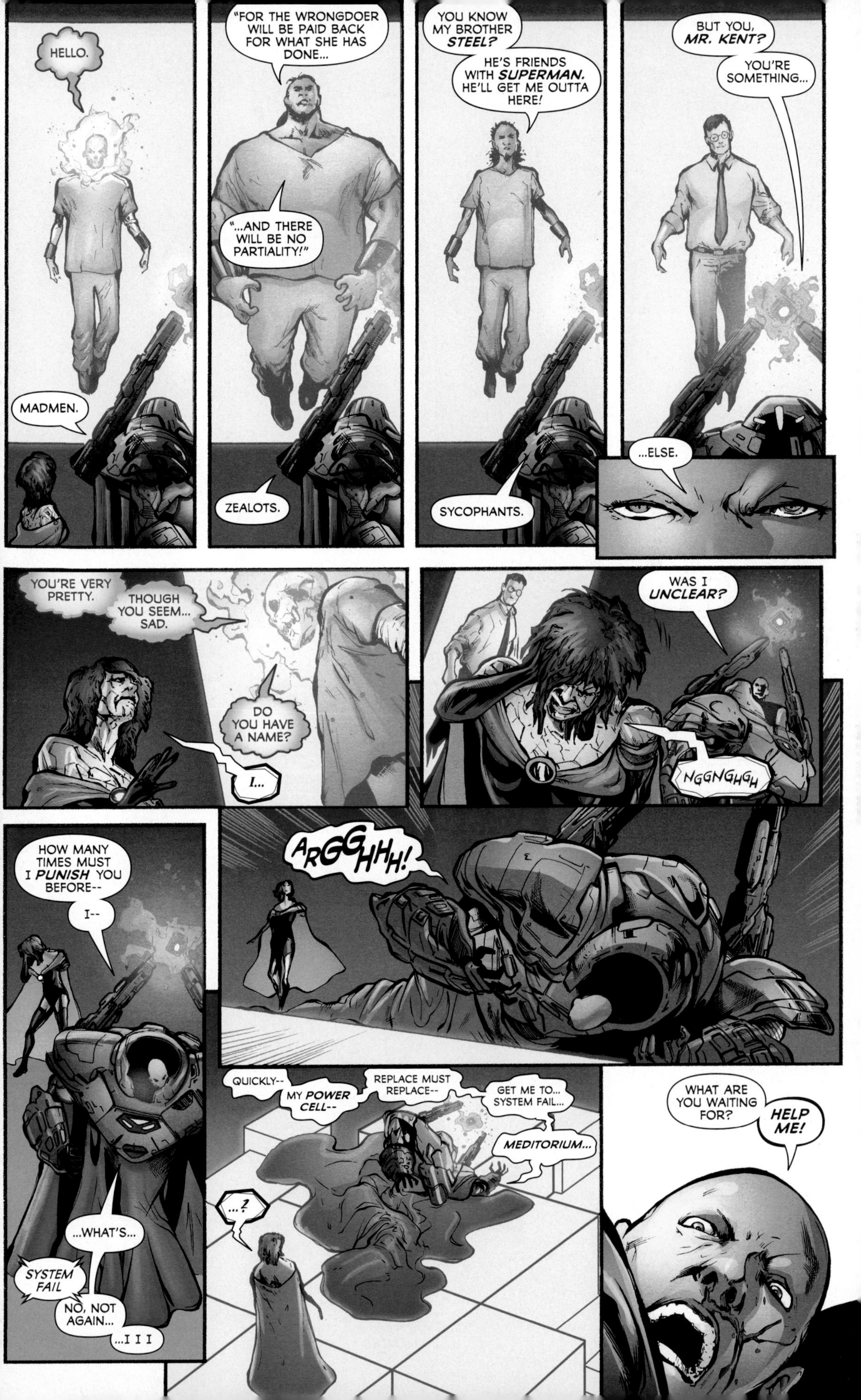
HELLO.
MADMEN.
"FOR THE WRONGDOER WILL BE PAID BACK FOR WHAT SHE HAS DONE...
"...AND THERE WILL BE NO PARTIALITY!"
ZEALOTS.
YOU KNOW MY BROTHER STEEL?
HE'S FRIENDS WITH SUPERMAN. HE'LL GET ME OUTTA HERE!
SYCOPHANTS.
BUT YOU, MR. KENT?
YOU'RE SOMETHING...
...ELSE.
YOU'RE VERY PRETTY.
THOUGH YOU SEEM... SAD.
DO YOU HAVE A NAME?
I...
WAS I UNCLEAR?
NGGNGHGH
HOW MANY TIMES MUST I PUNISH YOU BEFORE--
I--
ARGGHHH!
...WHAT'S...
SYSTEM FAIL
NO, NOT AGAIN...
...I I I
QUICKLY--
MY POWER CELL--
REPLACE MUST REPLACE--
GET ME TO... SYSTEM FAIL...
MEDITORIUM...
...?
WHAT ARE YOU WAITING FOR?
HELP ME!

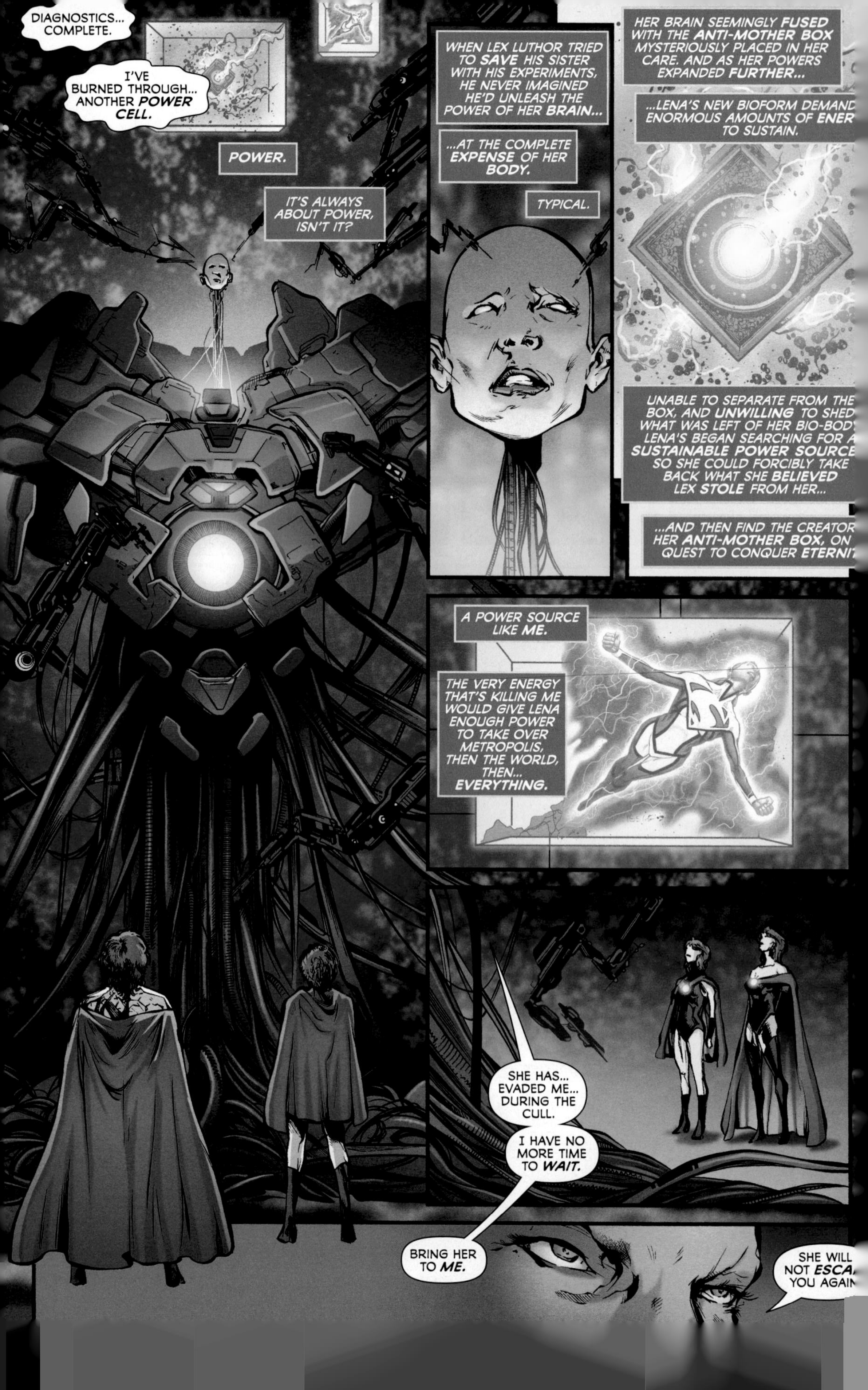

DIAGNOSTICS... COMPLETE.
I'VE BURNED THROUGH... ANOTHER POWER CELL.
POWER.
IT'S ALWAYS ABOUT POWER, ISN'T IT?
WHEN LEX LUTHOR TRIED TO SAVE HIS SISTER WITH HIS EXPERIMENTS, HE NEVER IMAGINED HE'D UNLEASH THE POWER OF HER BRAIN...
...AT THE COMPLETE EXPENSE OF HER BODY.
TYPICAL.
HER BRAIN SEEMINGLY FUSED WITH THE ANTI-MOTHER BOX MYSTERIOUSLY PLACED IN HER CARE. AND AS HER POWERS EXPANDED FURTHER...
...LENA'S NEW BIOFORM DEMAND ENORMOUS AMOUNTS OF ENER TO SUSTAIN.
UNABLE TO SEPARATE FROM THE BOX, AND UNWILLING TO SHED WHAT WAS LEFT OF HER BIO-BODY LENA'S BEGAN SEARCHING FOR A SUSTAINABLE POWER SOURCE SO SHE COULD FORCIBLY TAKE BACK WHAT SHE BELIEVED LEX STOLE FROM HER...
...AND THEN FIND THE CREATOR HER ANTI-MOTHER BOX, ON QUEST TO CONQUER ETERNIT
A POWER SOURCE LIKE ME.
THE VERY ENERGY THAT'S KILLING ME WOULD GIVE LENA ENOUGH POWER TO TAKE OVER METROPOLIS, THEN THE WORLD, THEN... EVERYTHING.
SHE HAS... EVADED ME... DURING THE CULL.
I HAVE NO MORE TIME TO WAIT.
BRING HER TO ME.
SHE WILL NOT ESCA YOU AGAI

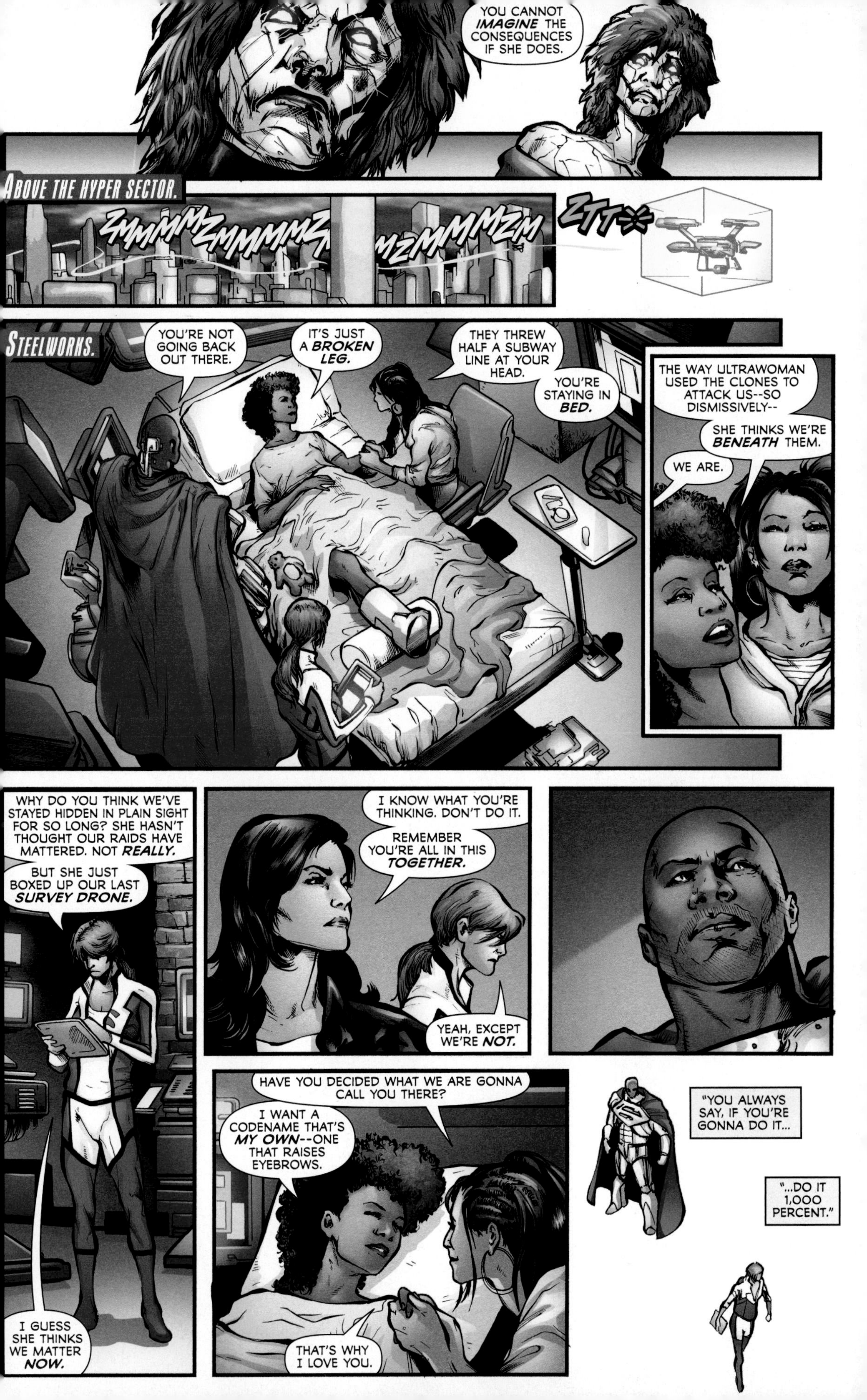
YOU CANNOT IMAGINE THE CONSEQUENCES IF SHE DOES.
ABOVE THE HYPER SECTOR.
ZMMMMZMMMMMZMMZMMMMZM
ZTTT
STEELWORKS.
YOU'RE NOT GOING BACK OUT THERE.
IT'S JUST A BROKEN LEG.
THEY THREW HALF A SUBWAY LINE AT YOUR HEAD.
YOU'RE STAYING IN BED.
THE WAY ULTRAWOMAN USED THE CLONES TO ATTACK US--SO DISMISSIVELY--
SHE THINKS WE'RE BENEATH THEM.
WE ARE.
WHY DO YOU THINK WE'VE STAYED HIDDEN IN PLAIN SIGHT FOR SO LONG? SHE HASN'T THOUGHT OUR RAIDS HAVE MATTERED. NOT REALLY.
BUT SHE JUST BOXED UP OUR LAST SURVEY DRONE.
I GUESS SHE THINKS WE MATTER NOW.
I KNOW WHAT YOU'RE THINKING. DON'T DO IT.
REMEMBER YOU'RE ALL IN THIS TOGETHER.
YEAH, EXCEPT WE'RE NOT.
HAVE YOU DECIDED WHAT WE ARE GONNA CALL YOU THERE?
I WANT A CODENAME THAT'S MY OWN--ONE THAT RAISES EYEBROWS.
THAT'S WHY I LOVE YOU.
"YOU ALWAYS SAY, IF YOU'RE GONNA DO IT...
"...DO IT 1,000 PERCENT."

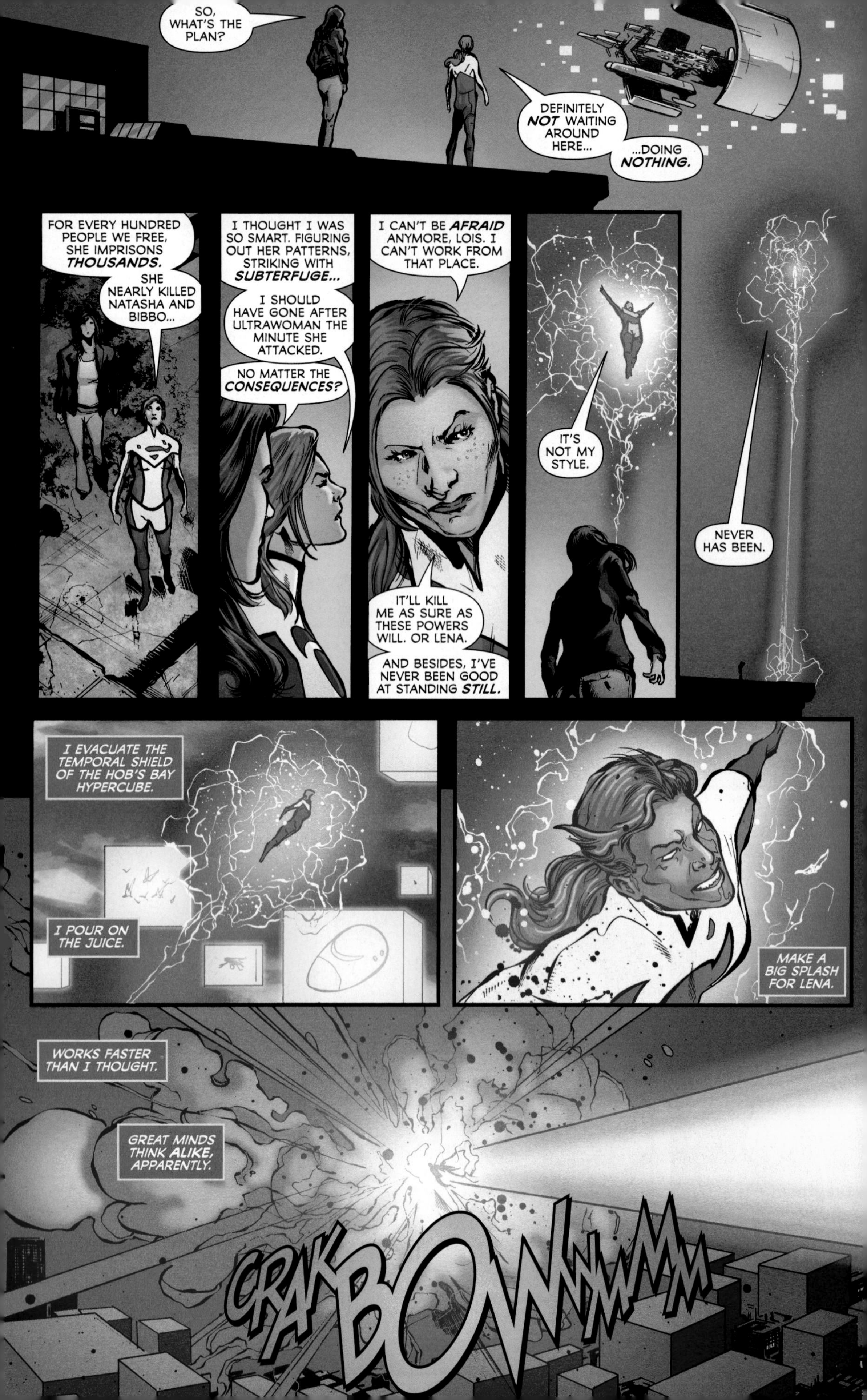
SO, WHAT'S THE PLAN?
DEFINITELY NOT WAITING AROUND HERE...
...DOING NOTHING.
FOR EVERY HUNDRED PEOPLE WE FREE, SHE IMPRISONS THOUSANDS.
SHE NEARLY KILLED NATASHA AND BIBBO...
I THOUGHT I WAS SO SMART. FIGURING OUT HER PATTERNS, STRIKING WITH SUBTERFUGE...
I SHOULD HAVE GONE AFTER ULTRAWOMAN THE MINUTE SHE ATTACKED.
NO MATTER THE CONSEQUENCES?
I CAN'T BE AFRAID ANYMORE, LOIS. I CAN'T WORK FROM THAT PLACE.
IT'LL KILL ME AS SURE AS THESE POWERS WILL. OR LENA.
AND BESIDES, I'VE NEVER BEEN GOOD AT STANDING STILL.
IT'S NOT MY STYLE.
NEVER HAS BEEN.
I EVACUATE THE TEMPORAL SHIELD OF THE HOB'S BAY HYPERCUBE.
I POUR ON THE JUICE.
MAKE A BIG SPLASH FOR LENA.
WORKS FASTER THAN I THOUGHT.
GREAT MINDS THINK ALIKE, APPARENTLY.
CRAKBOMMMMM

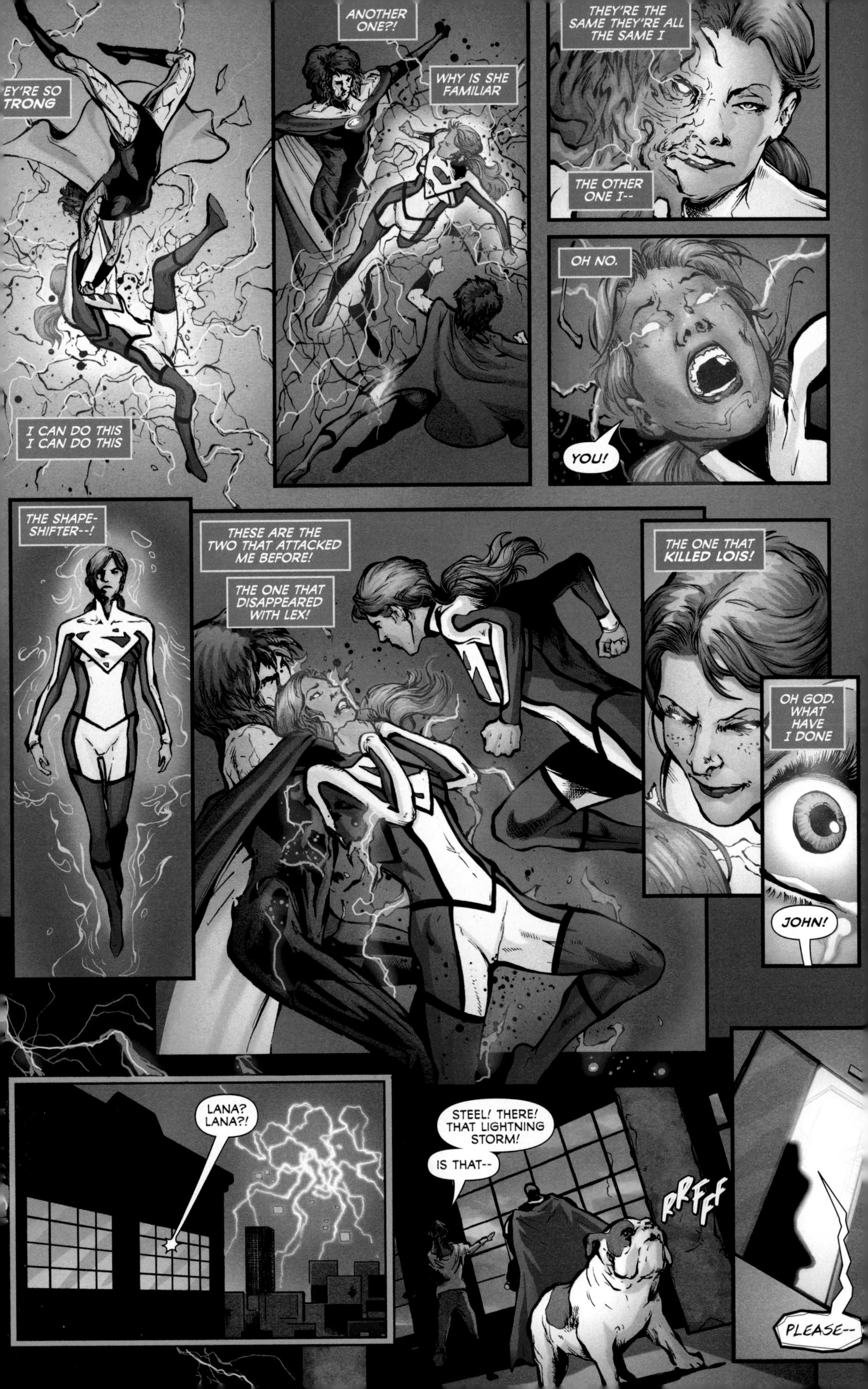
EY'RE SO
TRONG
I CAN DO THIS
I CAN DO THIS
ANOTHER ONE?!
WHY IS SHE FAMILIAR
THEY'RE THE SAME THEY'RE ALL THE SAME I
THE OTHER ONE I--
OH NO.
YOU!
THE SHAPE-SHIFTER--!
THESE ARE THE TWO THAT ATTACKED ME BEFORE!
THE ONE THAT DISAPPEARED WITH LEX!
THE ONE THAT KILLED LOIS!
OH GOD. WHAT HAVE I DONE
JOHN!
LANA? LANA?!
STEEL! THERE! THAT LIGHTNING STORM!
IS THAT--
RRFFF
PLEASE--

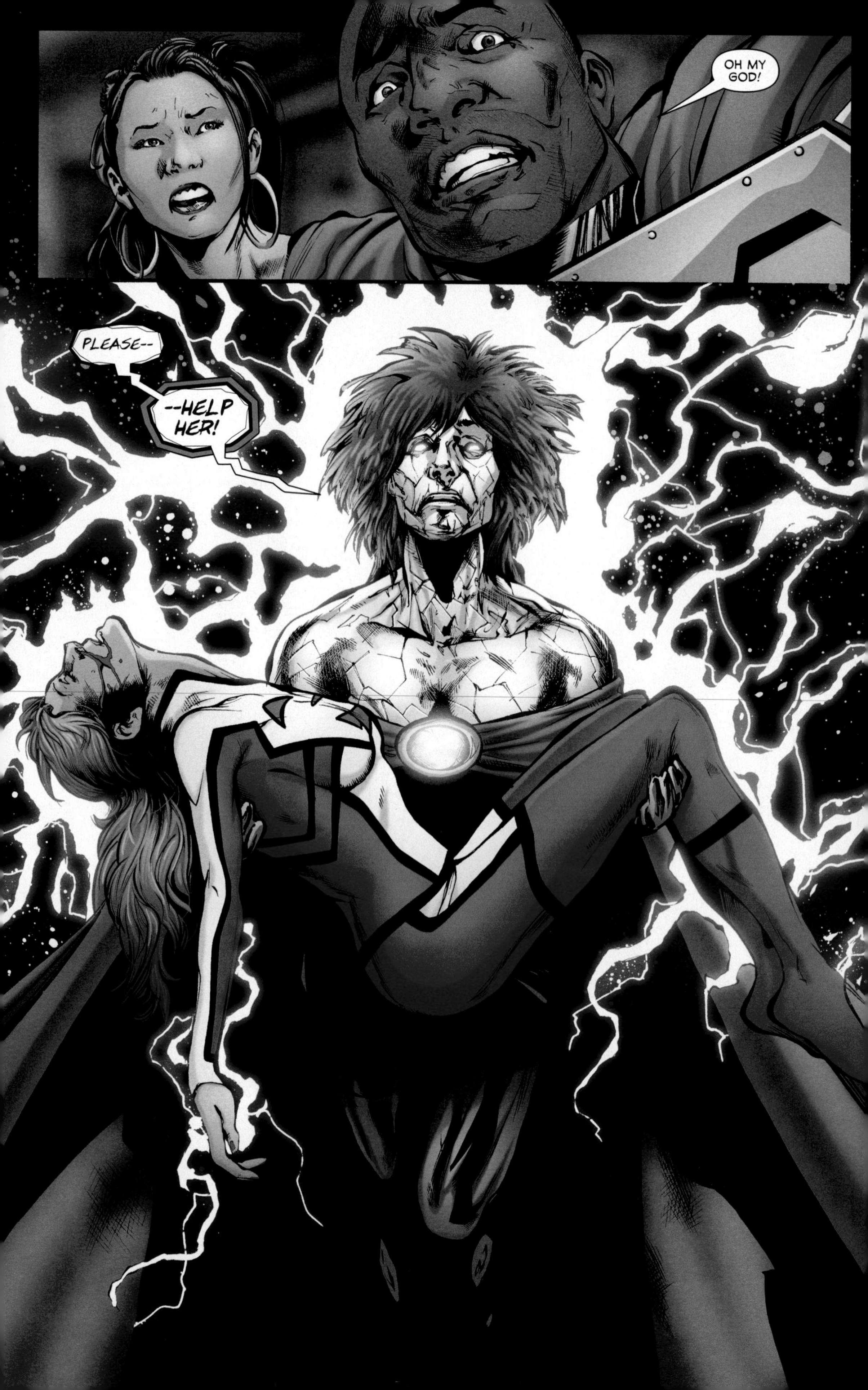
OH MY GOD!
PLEASE--
--HELP HER!

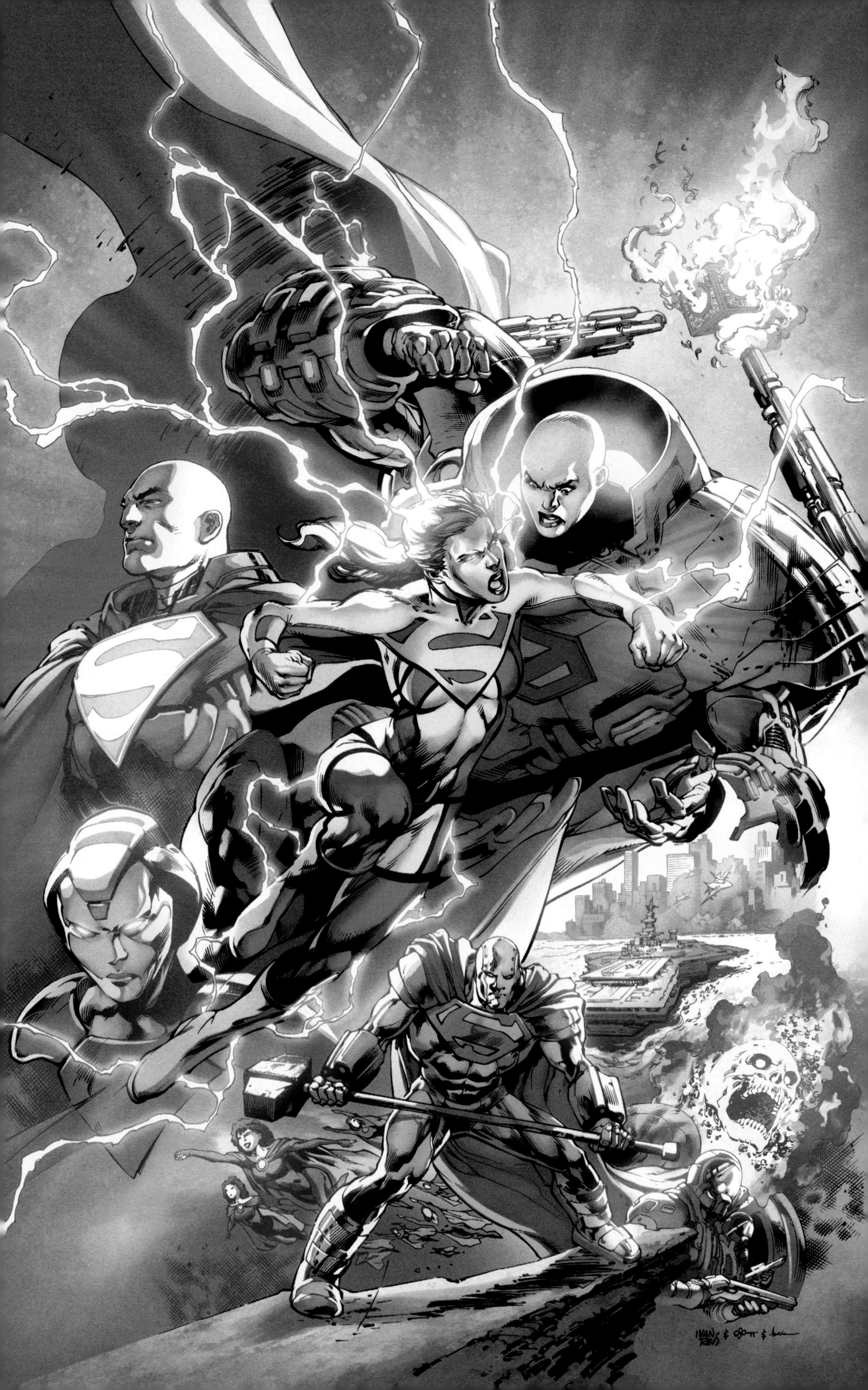

"WHO KILLED SUPERWOMAN? PART 6: COME DANCING"

PHIL JIMENEZ writer/penciller ∗ MATT SANTORELLI JACK HERBERT artists
HI-FI colorist ∗ cover by IVAN REIS, JOE PRADO and MARCELO MAIOLO

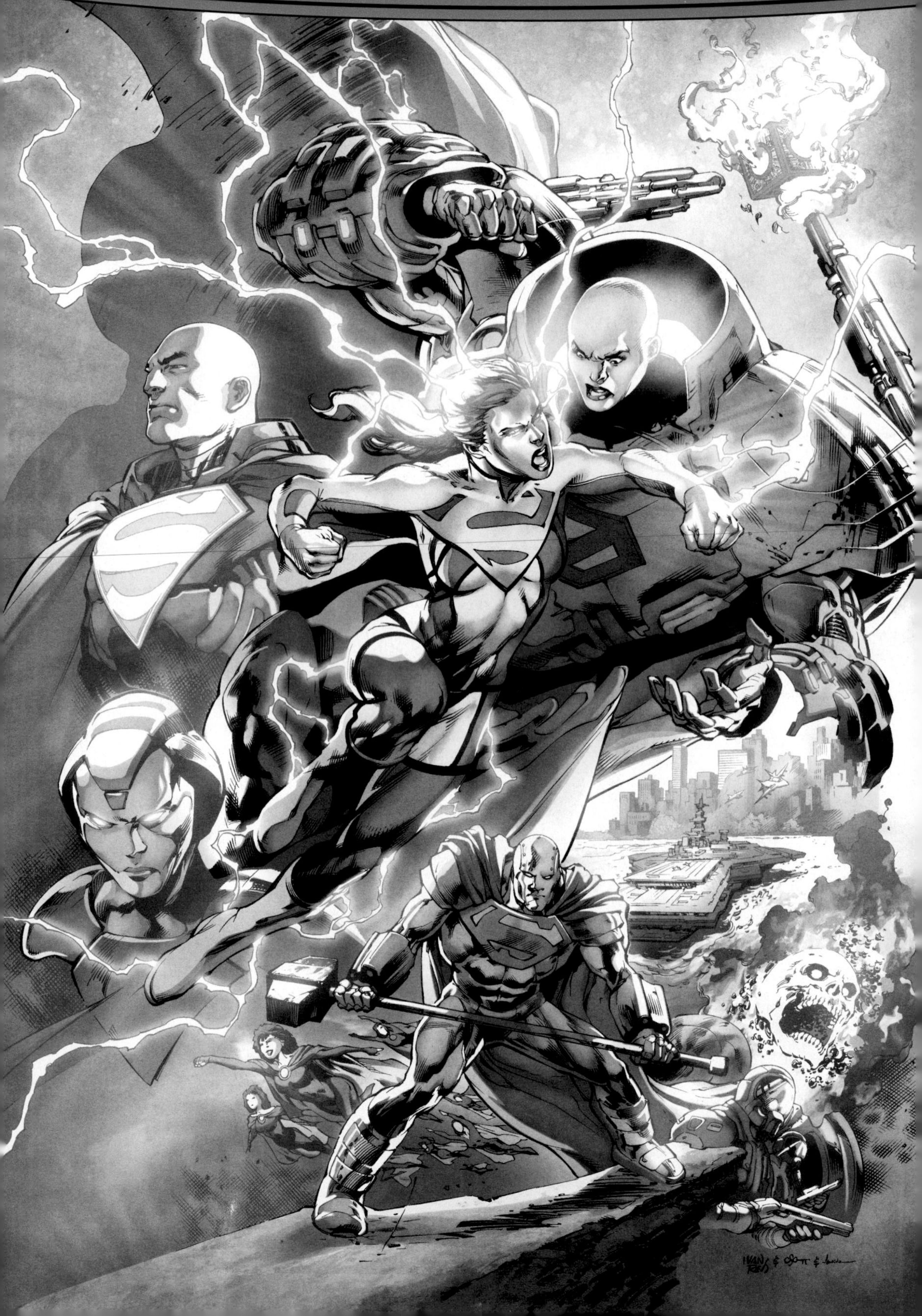

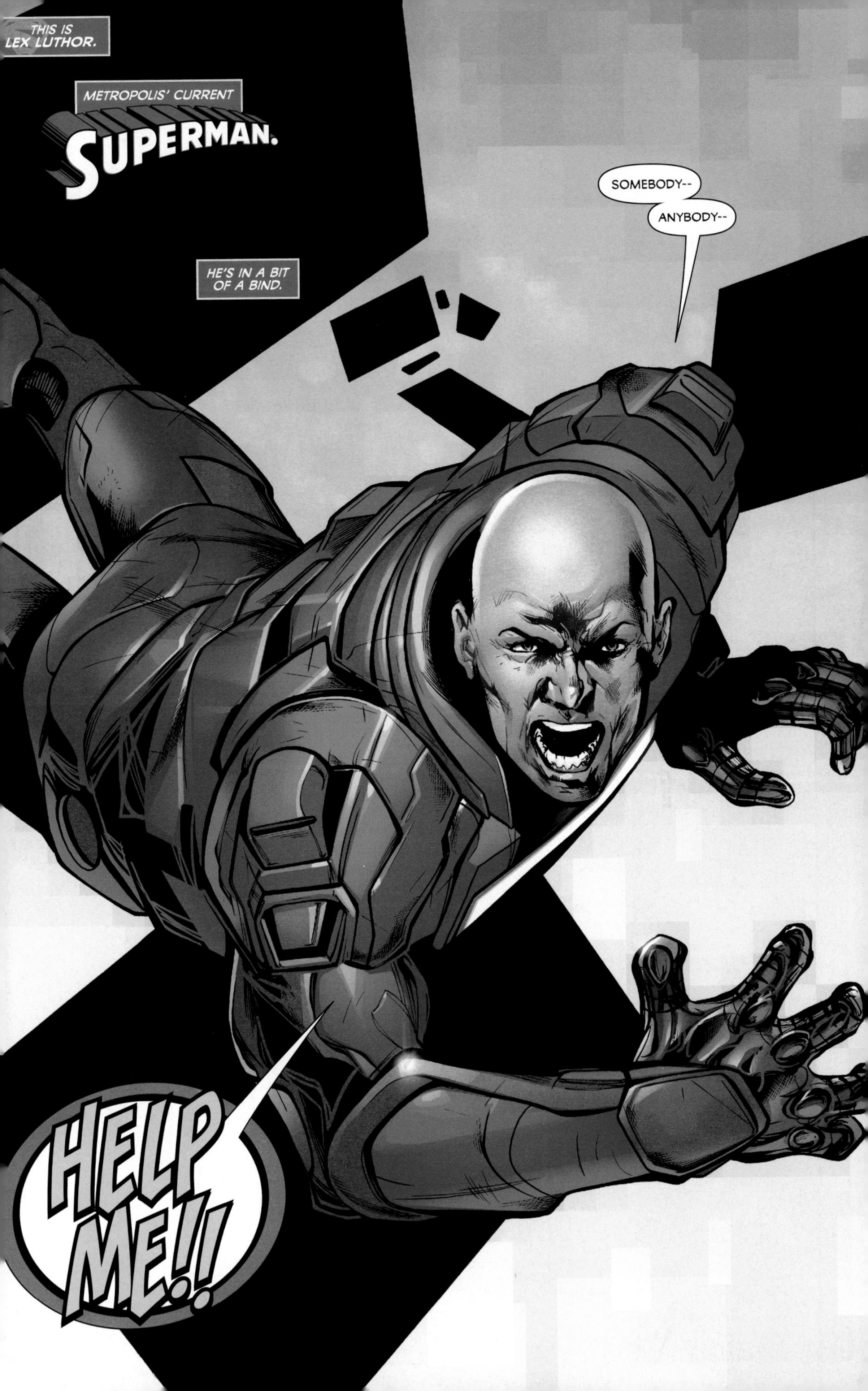
THIS IS LEX LUTHOR.
METROPOLIS' CURRENT
SUPERMAN.
HE'S IN A BIT OF A BIND.
SOMEBODY--
ANYBODY--
HELP ME!!

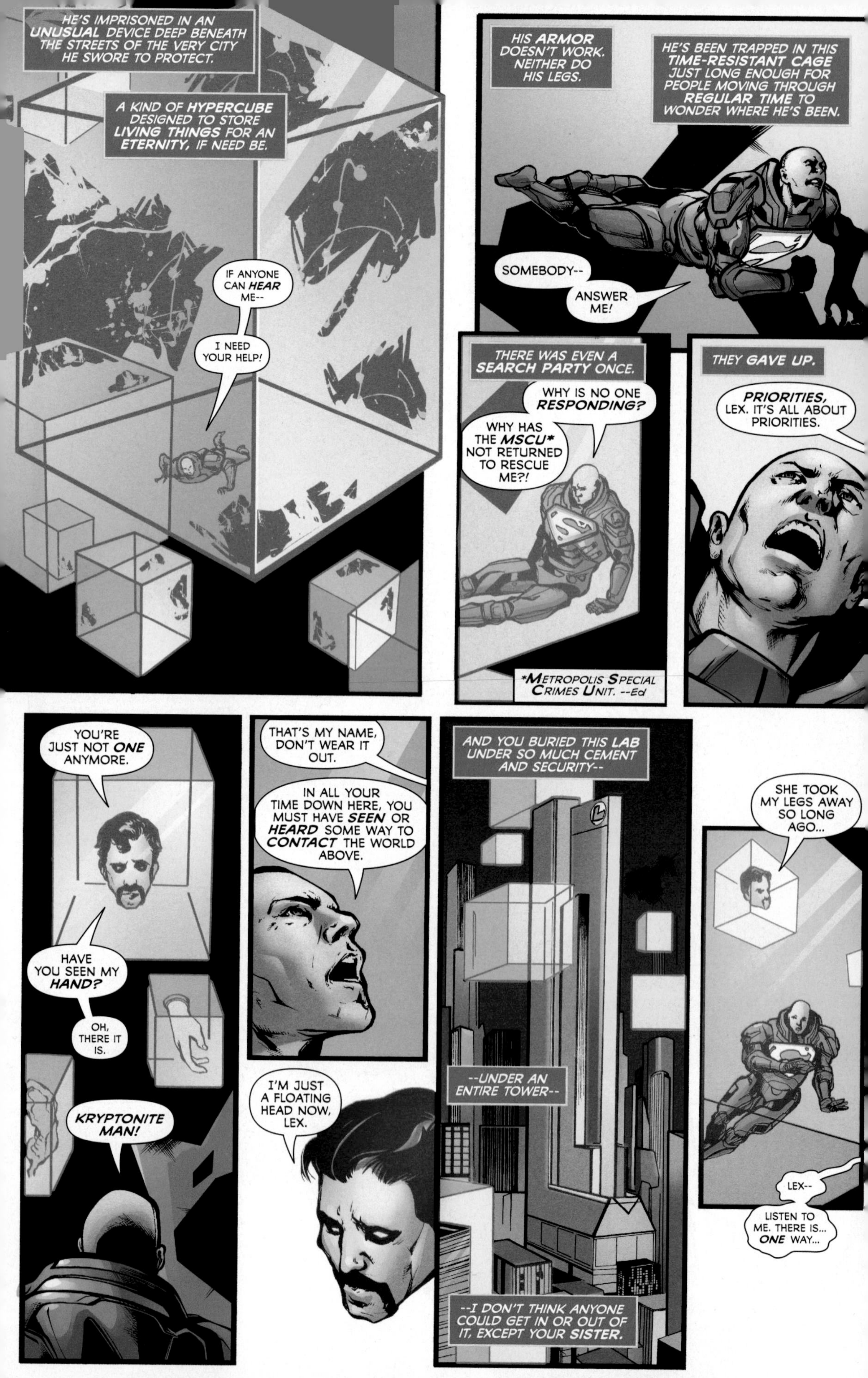

HE'S IMPRISONED IN AN UNUSUAL DEVICE DEEP BENEATH THE STREETS OF THE VERY CITY HE SWORE TO PROTECT.
A KIND OF HYPERCUBE DESIGNED TO STORE LIVING THINGS FOR AN ETERNITY, IF NEED BE.
IF ANYONE CAN HEAR ME--
I NEED YOUR HELP!
HIS ARMOR DOESN'T WORK. NEITHER DO HIS LEGS.
HE'S BEEN TRAPPED IN THIS TIME-RESISTANT CAGE JUST LONG ENOUGH FOR PEOPLE MOVING THROUGH REGULAR TIME TO WONDER WHERE HE'S BEEN.
SOMEBODY--
ANSWER ME!
THERE WAS EVEN A SEARCH PARTY ONCE.
WHY IS NO ONE RESPONDING?
WHY HAS THE MSCU* NOT RETURNED TO RESCUE ME?!
*METROPOLIS SPECIAL CRIMES UNIT. --Ed
THEY GAVE UP.
PRIORITIES, LEX. IT'S ALL ABOUT PRIORITIES.
YOU'RE JUST NOT ONE ANYMORE.
HAVE YOU SEEN MY HAND?
OH, THERE IT IS.
KRYPTONITE MAN!
THAT'S MY NAME, DON'T WEAR IT OUT.
IN ALL YOUR TIME DOWN HERE, YOU MUST HAVE SEEN OR HEARD SOME WAY TO CONTACT THE WORLD ABOVE.
I'M JUST A FLOATING HEAD NOW, LEX.
AND YOU BURIED THIS LAB UNDER SO MUCH CEMENT AND SECURITY--
--UNDER AN ENTIRE TOWER--
--I DON'T THINK ANYONE COULD GET IN OR OUT OF IT, EXCEPT YOUR SISTER.
SHE TOOK MY LEGS AWAY SO LONG AGO...
LEX--
LISTEN TO ME. THERE IS... ONE WAY...

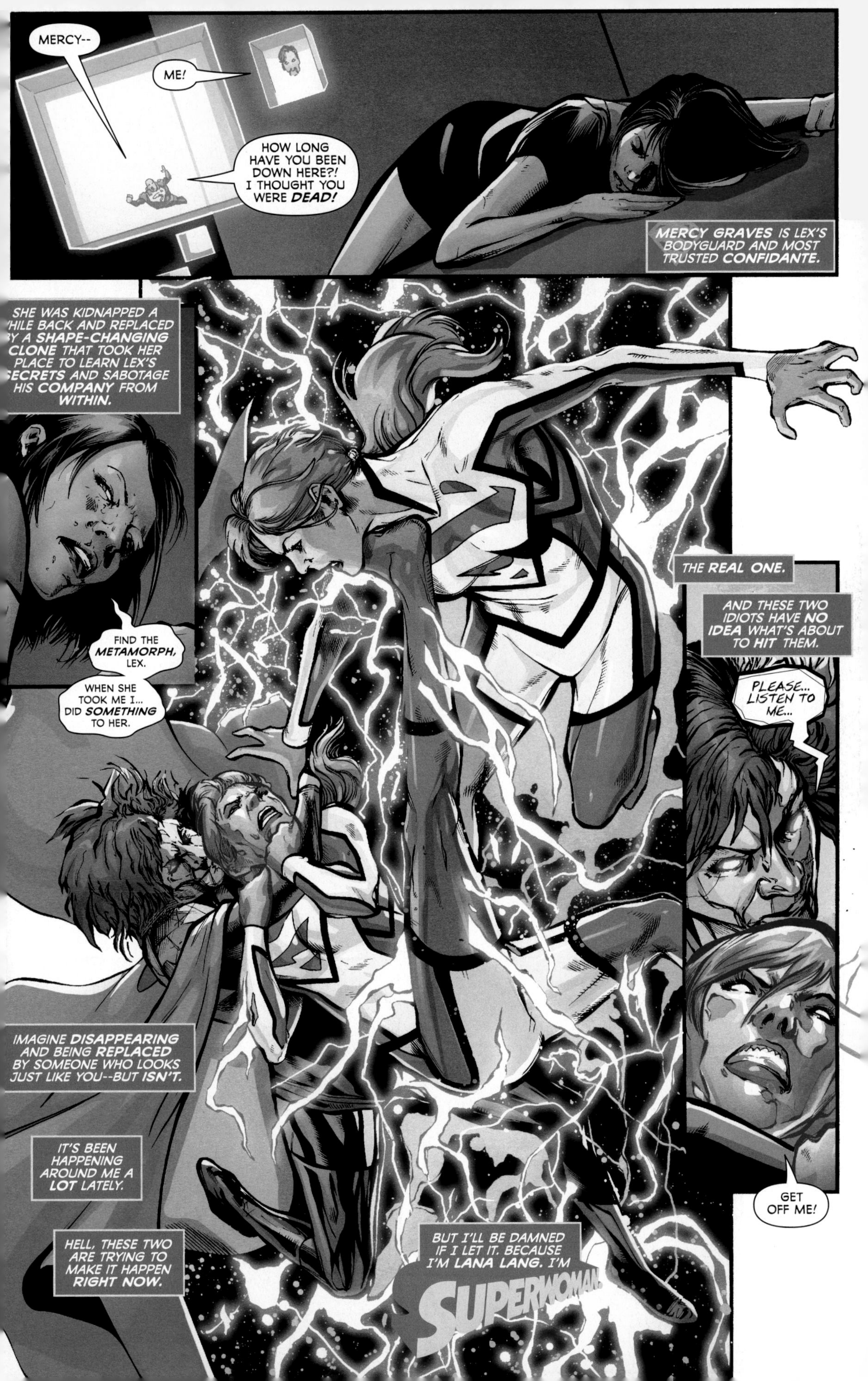
MERCY--
ME!
HOW LONG HAVE YOU BEEN DOWN HERE?! I THOUGHT YOU WERE DEAD!
MERCY GRAVES IS LEX'S BODYGUARD AND MOST TRUSTED CONFIDANTE.
SHE WAS KIDNAPPED A WHILE BACK AND REPLACED BY A SHAPE-CHANGING CLONE THAT TOOK HER PLACE TO LEARN LEX'S SECRETS AND SABOTAGE HIS COMPANY FROM WITHIN.
FIND THE METAMORPH, LEX.
WHEN SHE TOOK ME I... DID SOMETHING TO HER.
THE REAL ONE.
AND THESE TWO IDIOTS HAVE NO IDEA WHAT'S ABOUT TO HIT THEM.
PLEASE... LISTEN TO ME...
IMAGINE DISAPPEARING AND BEING REPLACED BY SOMEONE WHO LOOKS JUST LIKE YOU--BUT ISN'T.
IT'S BEEN HAPPENING AROUND ME A LOT LATELY.
GET OFF ME!
HELL, THESE TWO ARE TRYING TO MAKE IT HAPPEN RIGHT NOW.
BUT I'LL BE DAMNED IF I LET IT. BECAUSE I'M LANA LANG. I'M
SUPERWOMAN.

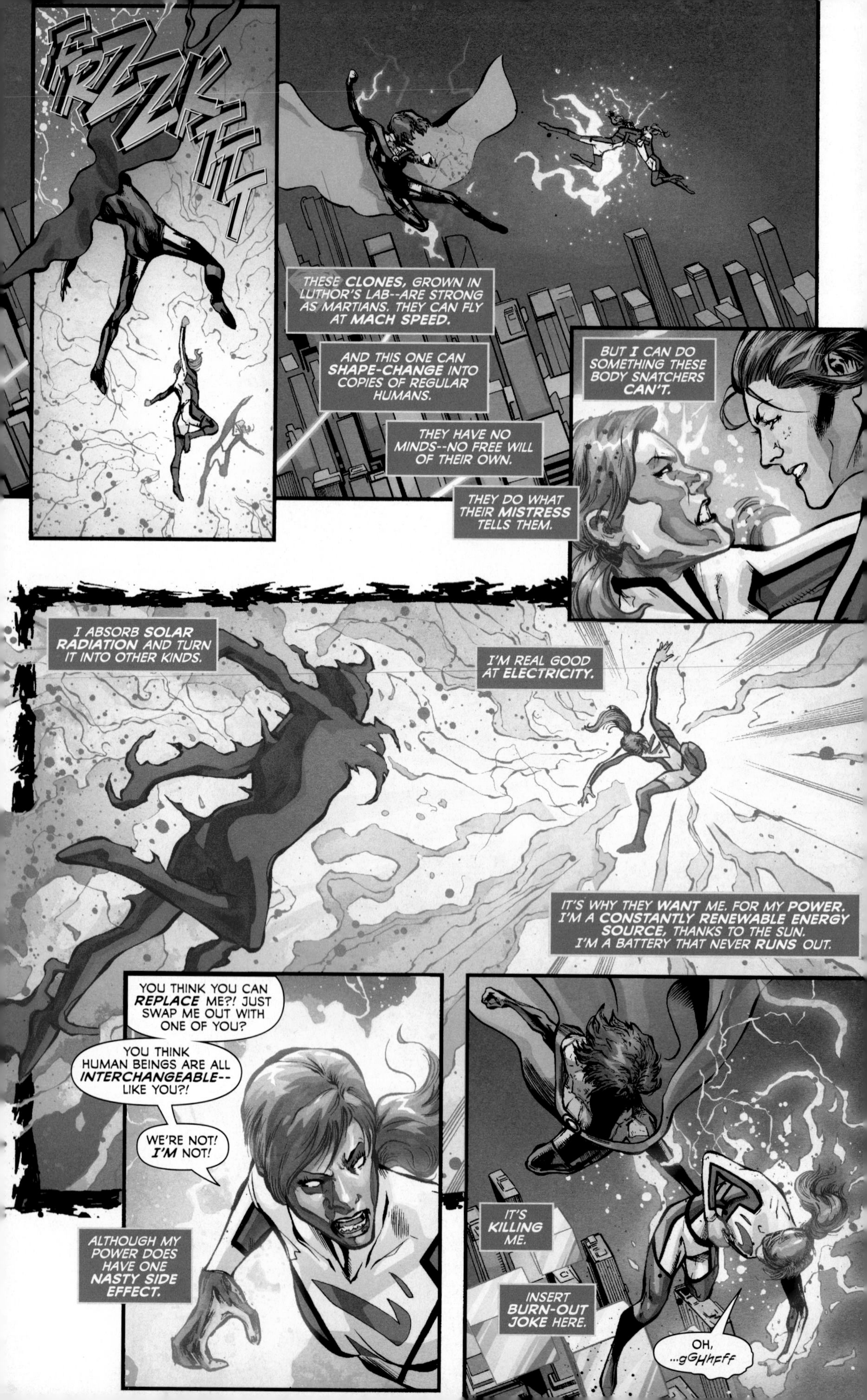
FRZZZK KRZZK
THESE CLONES, GROWN IN LUTHOR'S LAB--ARE STRONG AS MARTIANS. THEY CAN FLY AT MACH SPEED.
AND THIS ONE CAN SHAPE-CHANGE INTO COPIES OF REGULAR HUMANS.
THEY HAVE NO MINDS--NO FREE WILL OF THEIR OWN.
THEY DO WHAT THEIR MISTRESS TELLS THEM.
BUT I CAN DO SOMETHING THESE BODY SNATCHERS CAN'T.
I ABSORB SOLAR RADIATION AND TURN IT INTO OTHER KINDS.
I'M REAL GOOD AT ELECTRICITY.
IT'S WHY THEY WANT ME. FOR MY POWER. I'M A CONSTANTLY RENEWABLE ENERGY SOURCE, THANKS TO THE SUN. I'M A BATTERY THAT NEVER RUNS OUT.
YOU THINK YOU CAN REPLACE ME?! JUST SWAP ME OUT WITH ONE OF YOU?
YOU THINK HUMAN BEINGS ARE ALL INTERCHANGEABLE-- LIKE YOU?!
WE'RE NOT! I'M NOT!
ALTHOUGH MY POWER DOES HAVE ONE NASTY SIDE EFFECT.
IT'S KILLING ME.
INSERT BURN-OUT JOKE HERE.
OH, ...gGHhFFF

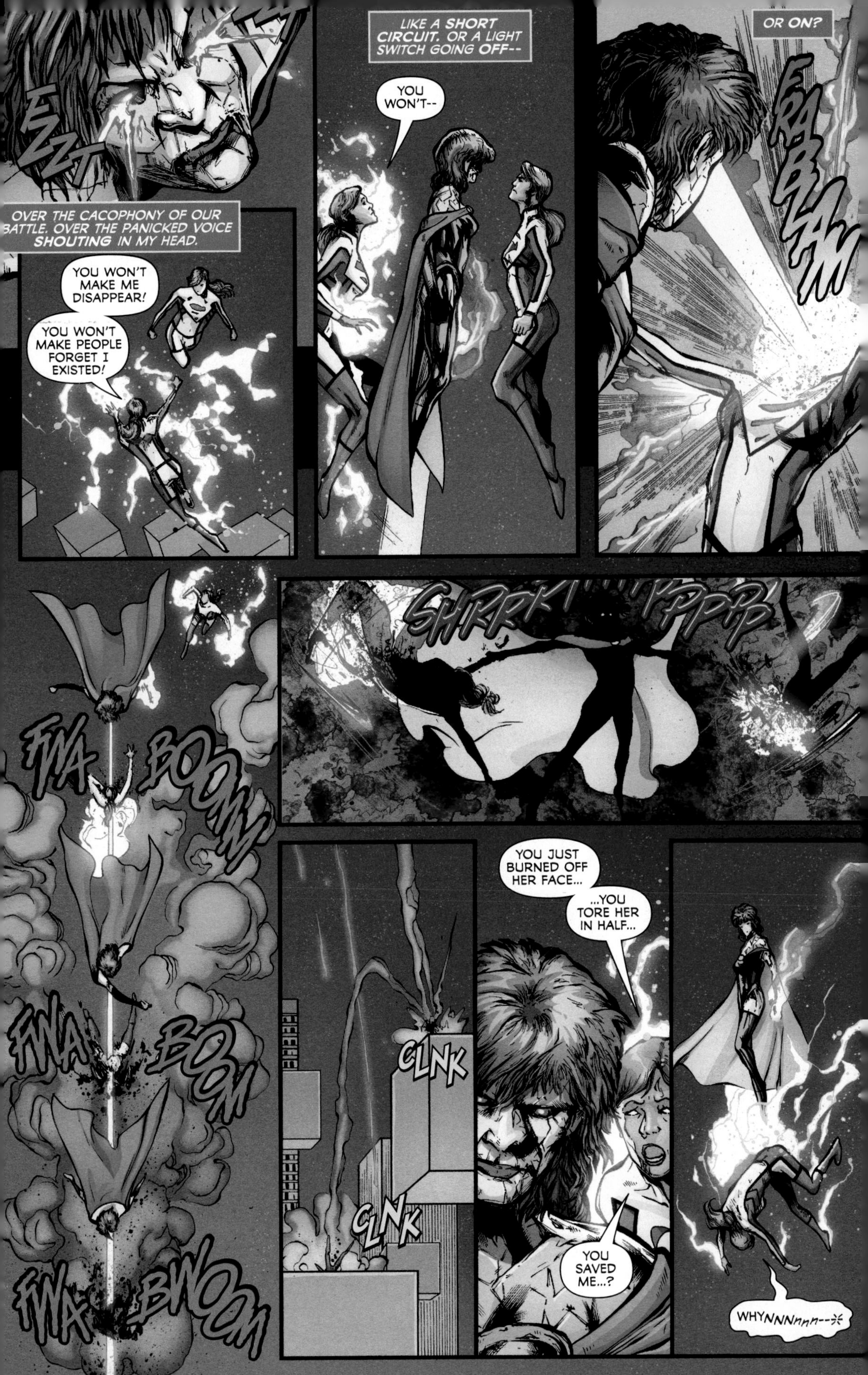
EZZZT
OVER THE CACOPHONY OF OUR BATTLE. OVER THE PANICKED VOICE SHOUTING IN MY HEAD.
YOU WON'T MAKE ME DISAPPEAR!
YOU WON'T MAKE PEOPLE FORGET I EXISTED!
LIKE A SHORT CIRCUIT. OR A LIGHT SWITCH GOING OFF--
YOU WON'T--
OR ON?
FRABLAM
FWA BOOOM
FWA BOOM
FWA BWOOM
SHRRKTTTTPPPP
CLNK
CLNK
YOU JUST BURNED OFF HER FACE...
...YOU TORE HER IN HALF...
YOU SAVED ME...?
WHYNNNnnn--

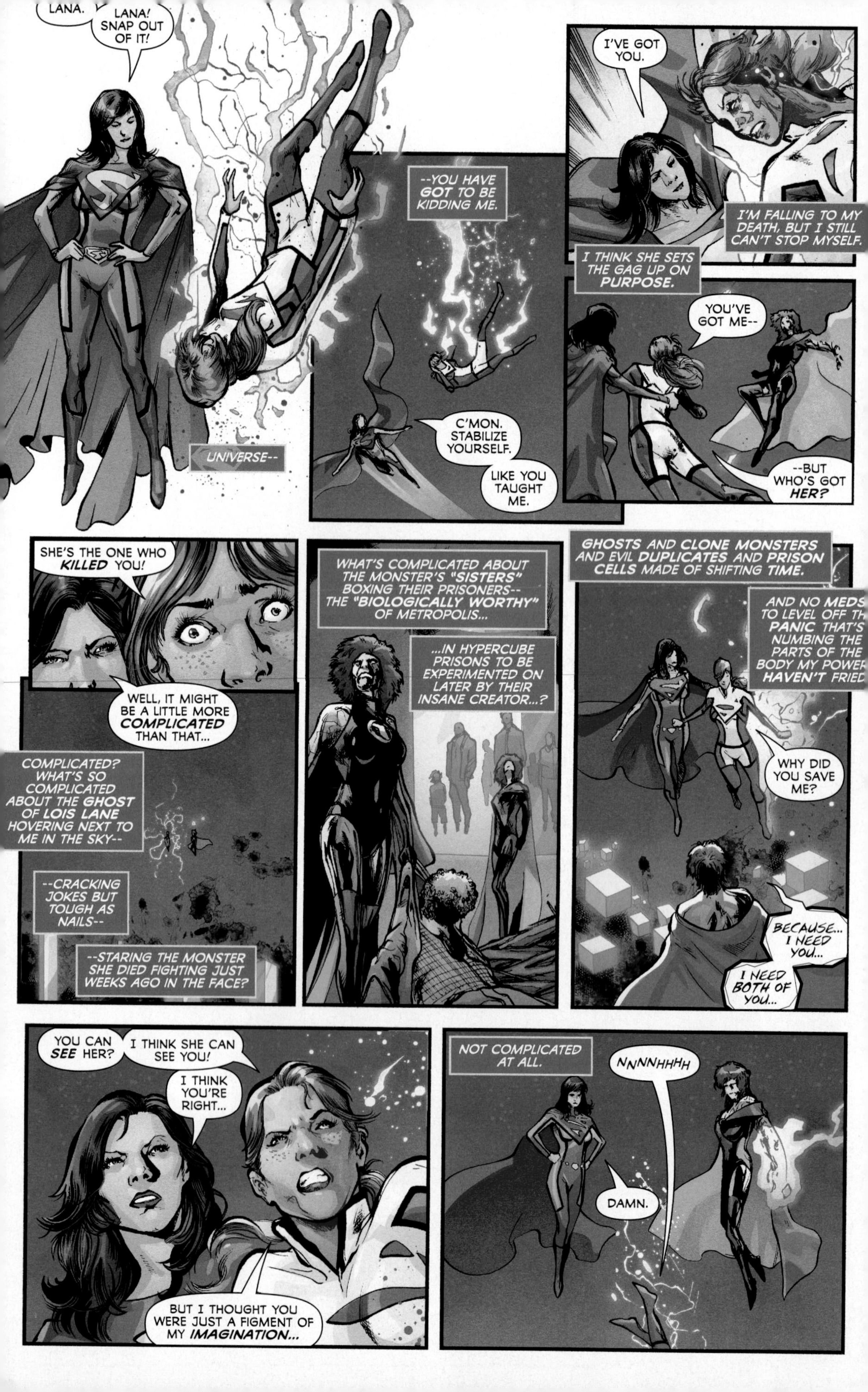
LANA.
LANA! SNAP OUT OF IT!
UNIVERSE--
--YOU HAVE GOT TO BE KIDDING ME.
C'MON. STABILIZE YOURSELF.
LIKE YOU TAUGHT ME.
I'VE GOT YOU.
I'M FALLING TO MY DEATH, BUT I STILL CAN'T STOP MYSELF.
I THINK SHE SETS THE GAG UP ON PURPOSE.
YOU'VE GOT ME--
--BUT WHO'S GOT HER?
SHE'S THE ONE WHO KILLED YOU!
WELL, IT MIGHT BE A LITTLE MORE COMPLICATED THAN THAT...
COMPLICATED? WHAT'S SO COMPLICATED ABOUT THE GHOST OF LOIS LANE HOVERING NEXT TO ME IN THE SKY--
--CRACKING JOKES BUT TOUGH AS NAILS--
--STARING THE MONSTER SHE DIED FIGHTING JUST WEEKS AGO IN THE FACE?
WHAT'S COMPLICATED ABOUT THE MONSTER'S "SISTERS" BOXING THEIR PRISONERS-- THE "BIOLOGICALLY WORTHY" OF METROPOLIS...
...IN HYPERCUBE PRISONS TO BE EXPERIMENTED ON LATER BY THEIR INSANE CREATOR...?
GHOSTS AND CLONE MONSTERS AND EVIL DUPLICATES AND PRISON CELLS MADE OF SHIFTING TIME.
AND NO MEDS TO LEVEL OFF TH PANIC THAT'S NUMBING THE PARTS OF THE BODY MY POWER HAVEN'T FRIED
WHY DID YOU SAVE ME?
BECAUSE... I NEED YOU...
I NEED BOTH OF YOU...
YOU CAN SEE HER?
I THINK SHE CAN SEE YOU!
I THINK YOU'RE RIGHT...
BUT I THOUGHT YOU WERE JUST A FIGMENT OF MY IMAGINATION...
NOT COMPLICATED AT ALL.
NNNNHHHH
DAMN.

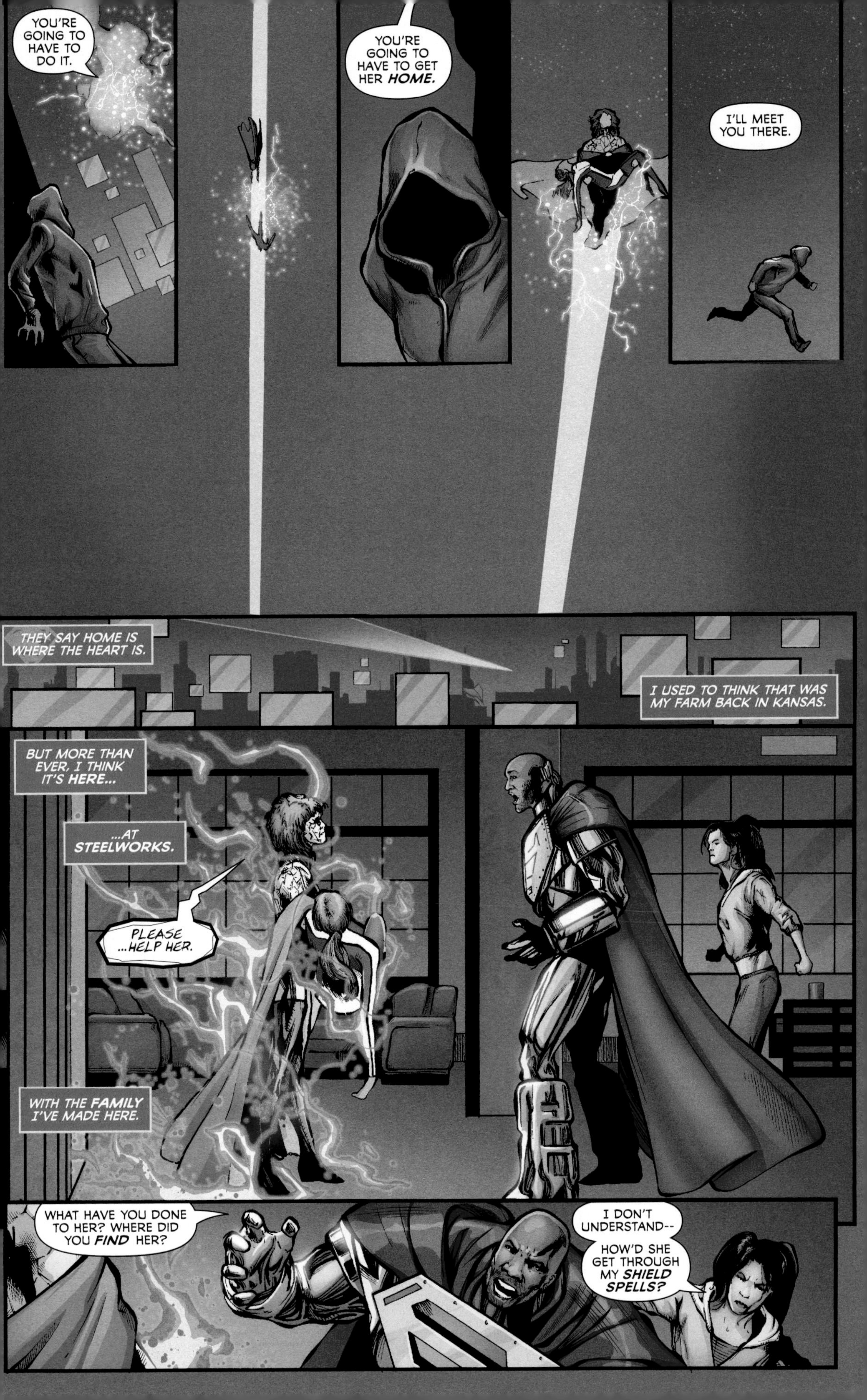
YOU'RE GOING TO HAVE TO DO IT.
YOU'RE GOING TO HAVE TO GET HER HOME.
I'LL MEET YOU THERE.
THEY SAY HOME IS WHERE THE HEART IS.
I USED TO THINK THAT WAS MY FARM BACK IN KANSAS.
BUT MORE THAN EVER, I THINK IT'S HERE...
...AT STEELWORKS.
PLEASE ...HELP HER.
WITH THE FAMILY I'VE MADE HERE.
WHAT HAVE YOU DONE TO HER? WHERE DID YOU FIND HER?
I DON'T UNDERSTAND--
HOW'D SHE GET THROUGH MY SHIELD SPELLS?

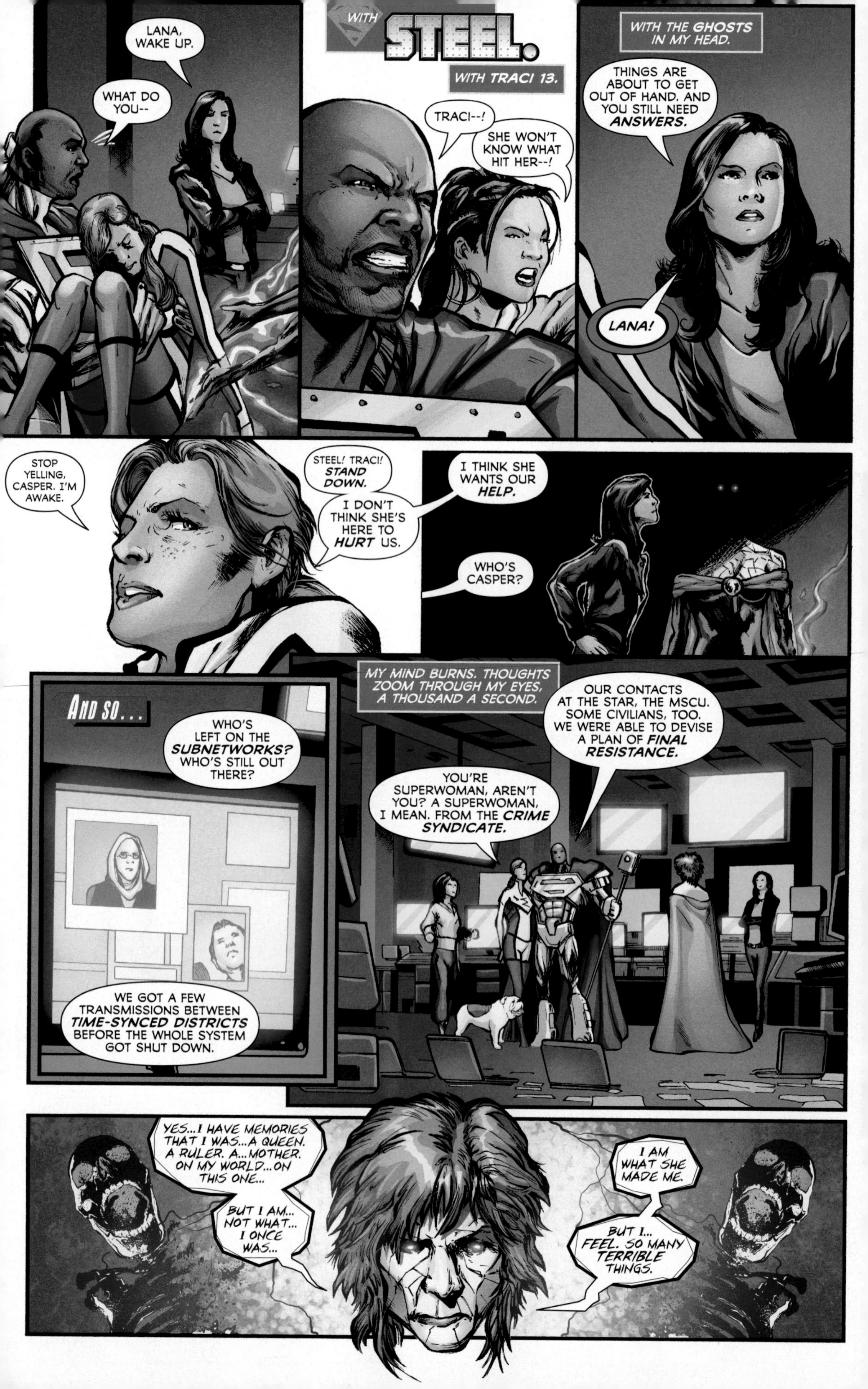

WITH STEEL.
WITH TRACI 13.
WITH THE GHOSTS IN MY HEAD.
LANA, WAKE UP.
WHAT DO YOU--
TRACI--!
SHE WON'T KNOW WHAT HIT HER--!
THINGS ARE ABOUT TO GET OUT OF HAND. AND YOU STILL NEED ANSWERS.
LANA!
STOP YELLING, CASPER. I'M AWAKE.
STEEL! TRACI! STAND DOWN.
I DON'T THINK SHE'S HERE TO HURT US.
I THINK SHE WANTS OUR HELP.
WHO'S CASPER?
AND SO...
WHO'S LEFT ON THE SUBNETWORKS? WHO'S STILL OUT THERE?
WE GOT A FEW TRANSMISSIONS BETWEEN TIME-SYNCED DISTRICTS BEFORE THE WHOLE SYSTEM GOT SHUT DOWN.
MY MIND BURNS. THOUGHTS ZOOM THROUGH MY EYES, A THOUSAND A SECOND.
OUR CONTACTS AT THE STAR, THE MSCU. SOME CIVILIANS, TOO. WE WERE ABLE TO DEVISE A PLAN OF FINAL RESISTANCE.
YOU'RE SUPERWOMAN, AREN'T YOU? A SUPERWOMAN, I MEAN. FROM THE CRIME SYNDICATE.
YES...I HAVE MEMORIES THAT I WAS...A QUEEN. A RULER. A...MOTHER. ON MY WORLD...ON THIS ONE...
BUT I AM... NOT WHAT... I ONCE WAS...
I AM WHAT SHE MADE ME.
BUT I... FEEL. SO MANY TERRIBLE THINGS.

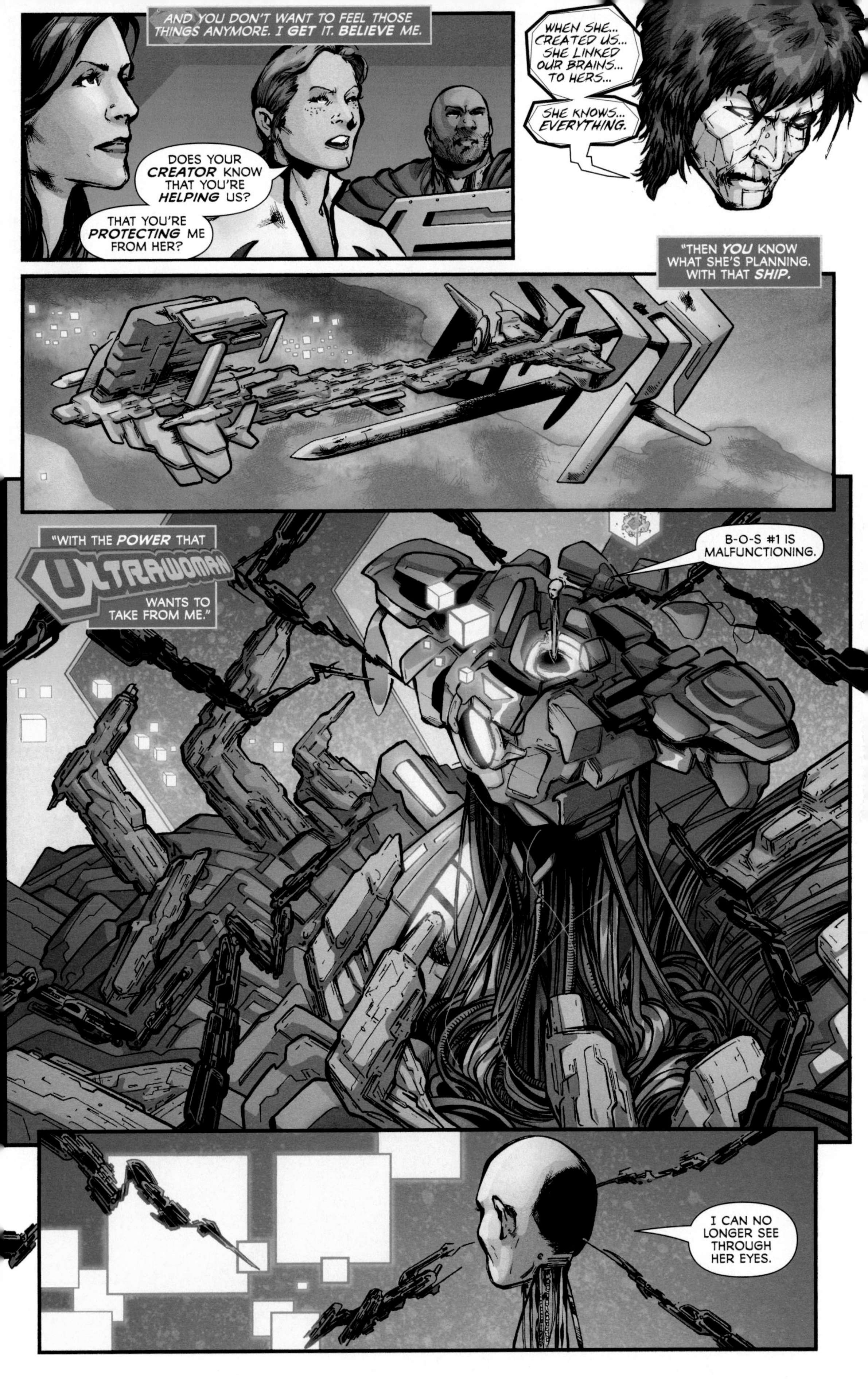
AND YOU DON'T WANT TO FEEL THOSE THINGS ANYMORE. I GET IT. BELIEVE ME.
DOES YOUR CREATOR KNOW THAT YOU'RE HELPING US?
THAT YOU'RE PROTECTING ME FROM HER?
WHEN SHE... CREATED US... SHE LINKED OUR BRAINS... TO HERS...
SHE KNOWS... EVERYTHING.
"THEN YOU KNOW WHAT SHE'S PLANNING. WITH THAT SHIP.
"WITH THE POWER THAT
ULTRAWOMAN
WANTS TO TAKE FROM ME."
B-O-S #1 IS MALFUNCTIONING.
I CAN NO LONGER SEE THROUGH HER EYES.

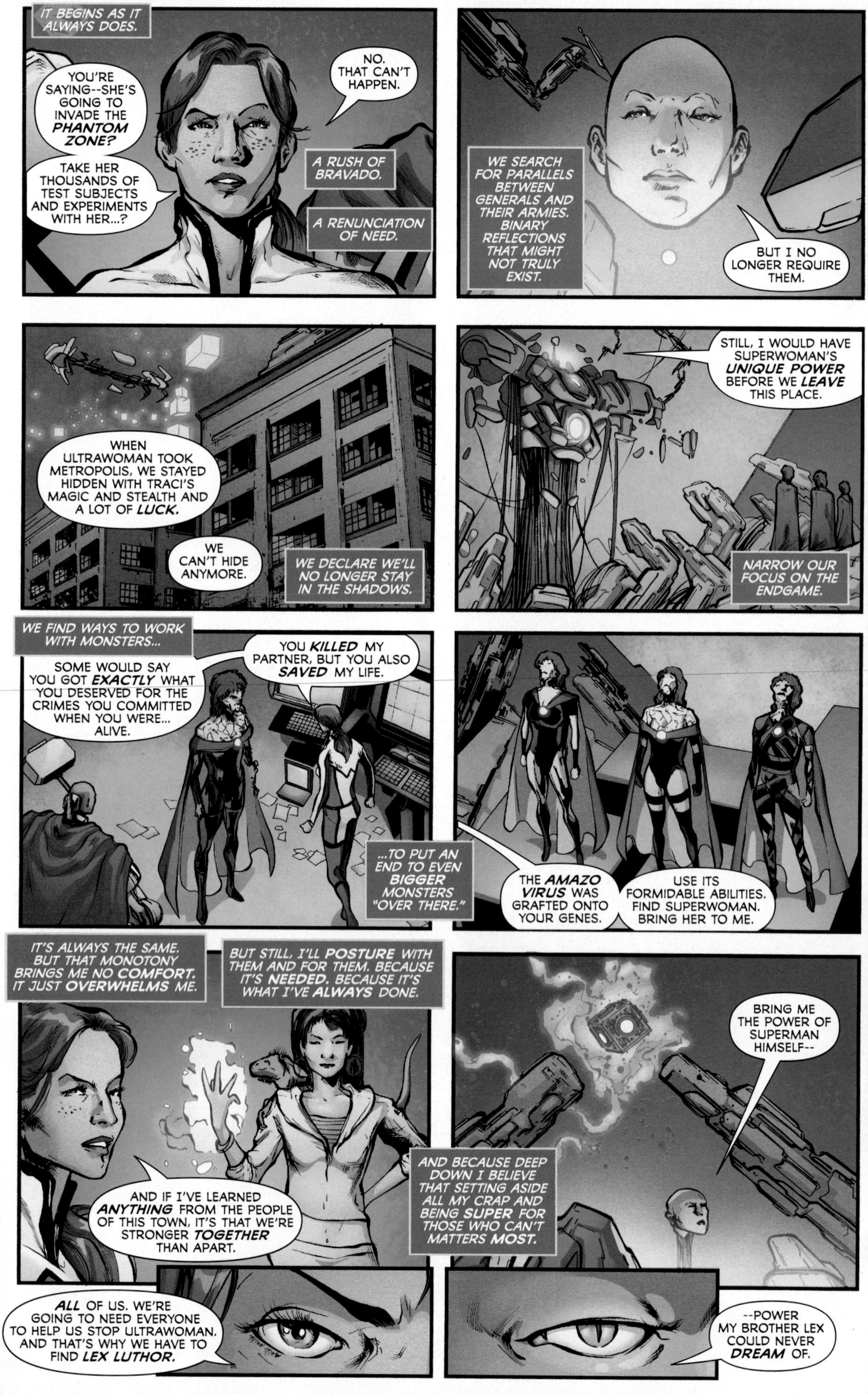
IT BEGINS AS IT ALWAYS DOES.
YOU'RE SAYING--SHE'S GOING TO INVADE THE PHANTOM ZONE?
TAKE HER THOUSANDS OF TEST SUBJECTS AND EXPERIMENTS WITH HER...?
NO. THAT CAN'T HAPPEN.
A RUSH OF BRAVADO.
A RENUNCIATION OF NEED.
WE SEARCH FOR PARALLELS BETWEEN GENERALS AND THEIR ARMIES. BINARY REFLECTIONS THAT MIGHT NOT TRULY EXIST.
BUT I NO LONGER REQUIRE THEM.
WHEN ULTRAWOMAN TOOK METROPOLIS, WE STAYED HIDDEN WITH TRACI'S MAGIC AND STEALTH AND A LOT OF LUCK.
WE CAN'T HIDE ANYMORE.
WE DECLARE WE'LL NO LONGER STAY IN THE SHADOWS.
STILL, I WOULD HAVE SUPERWOMAN'S UNIQUE POWER BEFORE WE LEAVE THIS PLACE.
NARROW OUR FOCUS ON THE ENDGAME.
WE FIND WAYS TO WORK WITH MONSTERS...
SOME WOULD SAY YOU GOT EXACTLY WHAT YOU DESERVED FOR THE CRIMES YOU COMMITTED WHEN YOU WERE... ALIVE.
YOU KILLED MY PARTNER, BUT YOU ALSO SAVED MY LIFE.
...TO PUT AN END TO EVEN BIGGER MONSTERS "OVER THERE."
THE AMAZO VIRUS WAS GRAFTED ONTO YOUR GENES.
USE ITS FORMIDABLE ABILITIES. FIND SUPERWOMAN. BRING HER TO ME.
IT'S ALWAYS THE SAME, BUT THAT MONOTONY BRINGS ME NO COMFORT. IT JUST OVERWHELMS ME.
BUT STILL, I'LL POSTURE WITH THEM AND FOR THEM. BECAUSE IT'S NEEDED. BECAUSE IT'S WHAT I'VE ALWAYS DONE.
AND IF I'VE LEARNED ANYTHING FROM THE PEOPLE OF THIS TOWN, IT'S THAT WE'RE STRONGER TOGETHER THAN APART.
AND BECAUSE DEEP DOWN I BELIEVE THAT SETTING ASIDE ALL MY CRAP AND BEING SUPER FOR THOSE WHO CAN'T MATTERS MOST.
BRING ME THE POWER OF SUPERMAN HIMSELF--
ALL OF US. WE'RE GOING TO NEED EVERYONE TO HELP US STOP ULTRAWOMAN. AND THAT'S WHY WE HAVE TO FIND LEX LUTHOR.
--POWER MY BROTHER LEX COULD NEVER DREAM OF.

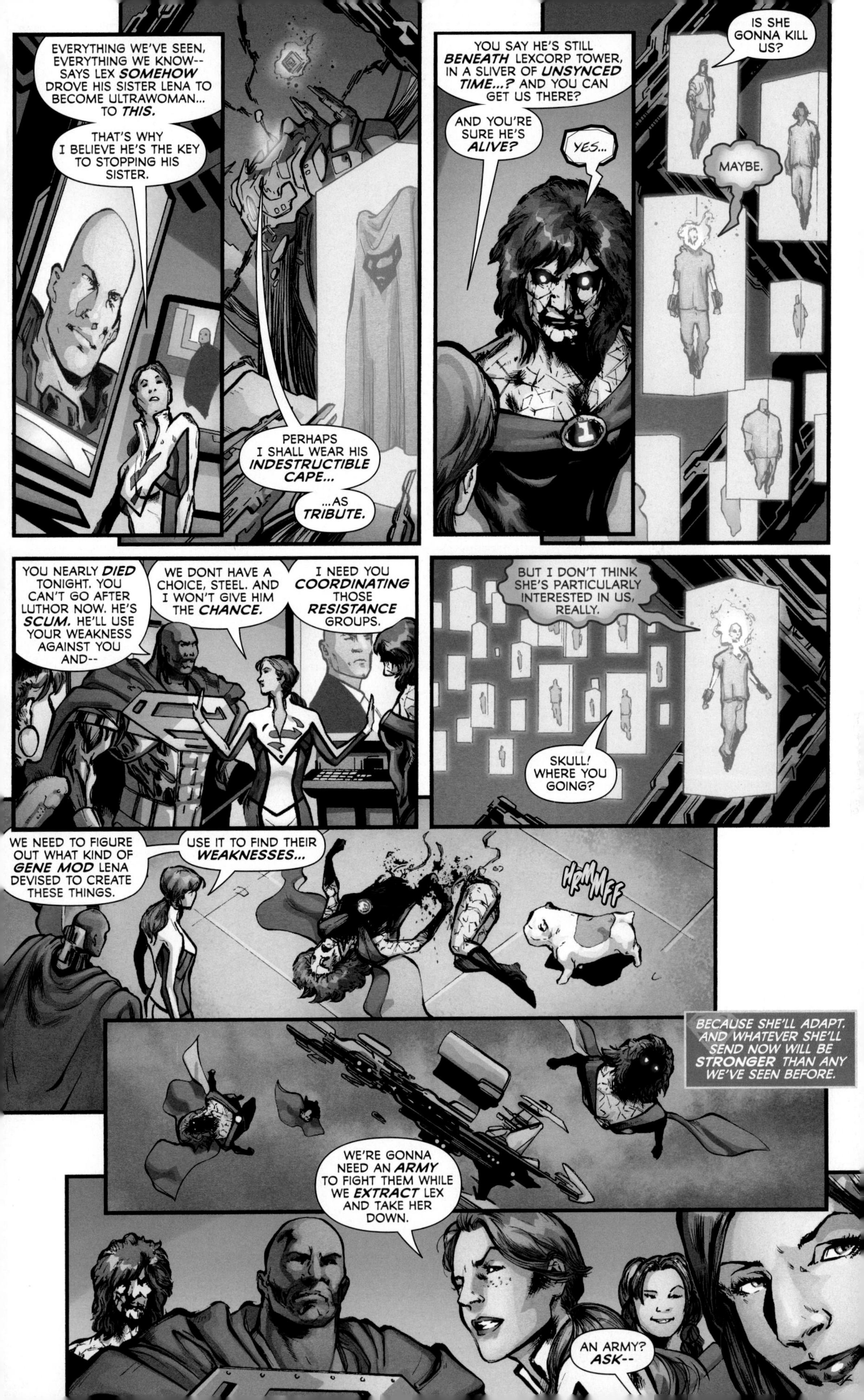
EVERYTHING WE'VE SEEN, EVERYTHING WE KNOW-- SAYS LEX *SOMEHOW* DROVE HIS SISTER LENA TO BECOME ULTRAWOMAN... TO *THIS.*
THAT'S WHY I BELIEVE HE'S THE KEY TO STOPPING HIS SISTER.
PERHAPS I SHALL WEAR HIS *INDESTRUCTIBLE CAPE...*
...AS *TRIBUTE.*
YOU SAY HE'S STILL *BENEATH* LEXCORP TOWER, IN A SLIVER OF *UNSYNCED TIME...?* AND YOU CAN GET US THERE?
AND YOU'RE SURE HE'S *ALIVE?*
YES...
IS SHE GONNA KILL US?
MAYBE.
YOU NEARLY *DIED* TONIGHT. YOU CAN'T GO AFTER LUTHOR NOW. HE'S *SCUM.* HE'LL USE YOUR WEAKNESS AGAINST YOU AND--
WE DONT HAVE A CHOICE, STEEL. AND I WON'T GIVE HIM THE *CHANCE.*
I NEED YOU *COORDINATING* THOSE *RESISTANCE* GROUPS.
BUT I DON'T THINK SHE'S PARTICULARLY INTERESTED IN US, REALLY.
SKULL! WHERE YOU GOING?
WE NEED TO FIGURE OUT WHAT KIND OF *GENE MOD* LENA DEVISED TO CREATE THESE THINGS.
USE IT TO FIND THEIR *WEAKNESSES...*
HRMMFF
BECAUSE SHE'LL ADAPT. AND WHATEVER SHE'LL SEND NOW WILL BE STRONGER THAN ANY WE'VE SEEN BEFORE.
WE'RE GONNA NEED AN *ARMY* TO FIGHT THEM WHILE WE *EXTRACT* LEX AND TAKE HER DOWN.
AN ARMY? *ASK--*

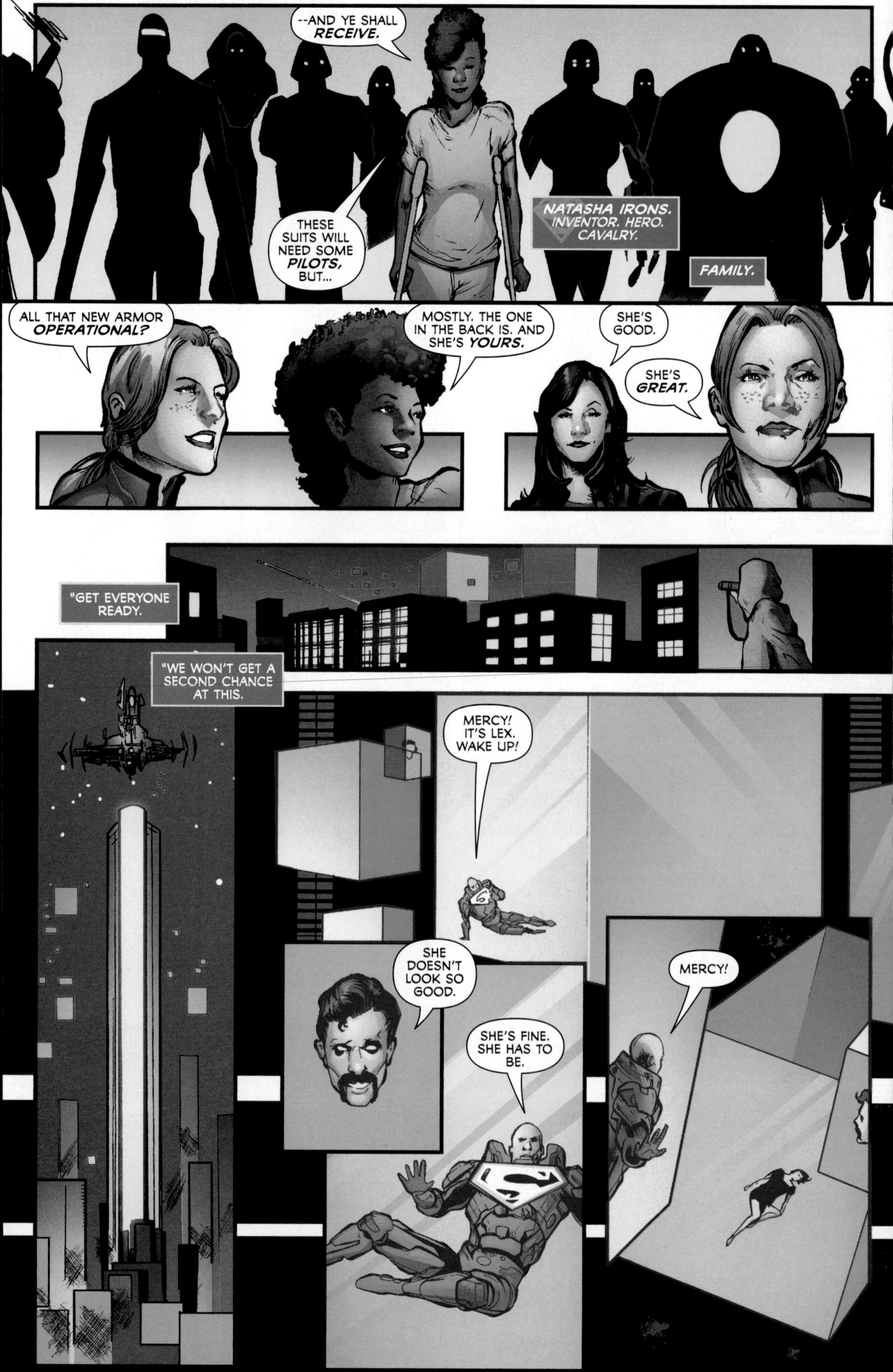
--AND YE SHALL RECEIVE.
THESE SUITS WILL NEED SOME PILOTS, BUT...
NATASHA IRONS. INVENTOR. HERO. CAVALRY.
FAMILY.
ALL THAT NEW ARMOR OPERATIONAL?
MOSTLY. THE ONE IN THE BACK IS. AND SHE'S YOURS.
SHE'S GOOD.
SHE'S GREAT.
"GET EVERYONE READY.
"WE WON'T GET A SECOND CHANCE AT THIS.
MERCY! IT'S LEX. WAKE UP!
SHE DOESN'T LOOK SO GOOD.
SHE'S FINE. SHE HAS TO BE.
MERCY!

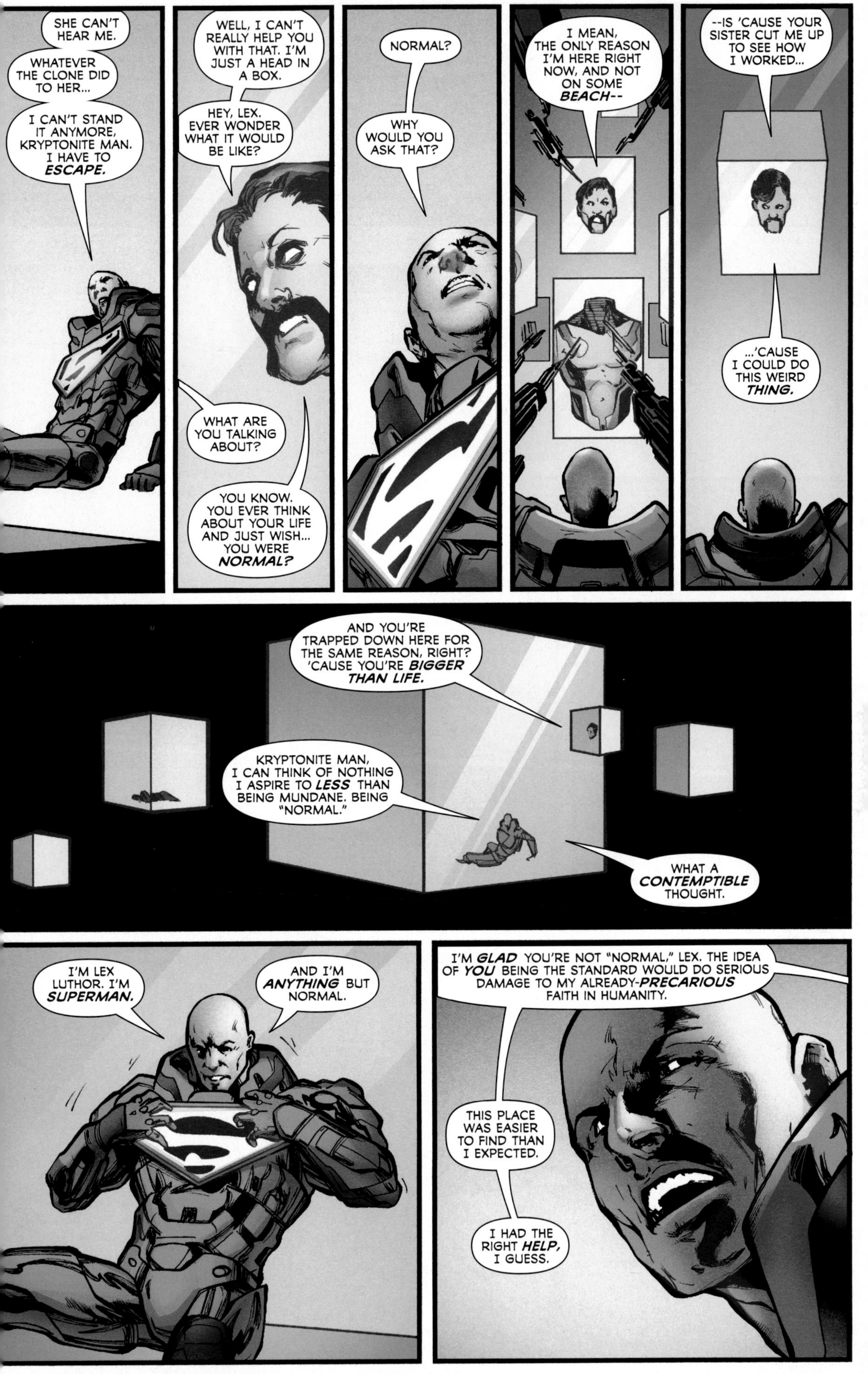
SHE CAN'T HEAR ME.
WHATEVER THE CLONE DID TO HER...
I CAN'T STAND IT ANYMORE, KRYPTONITE MAN. I HAVE TO ESCAPE.
WELL, I CAN'T REALLY HELP YOU WITH THAT. I'M JUST A HEAD IN A BOX.
HEY, LEX. EVER WONDER WHAT IT WOULD BE LIKE?
WHAT ARE YOU TALKING ABOUT?
YOU KNOW. YOU EVER THINK ABOUT YOUR LIFE AND JUST WISH... YOU WERE NORMAL?
NORMAL?
WHY WOULD YOU ASK THAT?
I MEAN, THE ONLY REASON I'M HERE RIGHT NOW, AND NOT ON SOME BEACH--
--IS 'CAUSE YOUR SISTER CUT ME UP TO SEE HOW I WORKED...
...'CAUSE I COULD DO THIS WEIRD THING.
AND YOU'RE TRAPPED DOWN HERE FOR THE SAME REASON, RIGHT? 'CAUSE YOU'RE BIGGER THAN LIFE.
KRYPTONITE MAN, I CAN THINK OF NOTHING I ASPIRE TO LESS THAN BEING MUNDANE. BEING "NORMAL."
WHAT A CONTEMPTIBLE THOUGHT.
I'M LEX LUTHOR. I'M SUPERMAN.
AND I'M ANYTHING BUT NORMAL.
I'M GLAD YOU'RE NOT "NORMAL," LEX. THE IDEA OF YOU BEING THE STANDARD WOULD DO SERIOUS DAMAGE TO MY ALREADY-PRECARIOUS FAITH IN HUMANITY.
THIS PLACE WAS EASIER TO FIND THAN I EXPECTED.
I HAD THE RIGHT HELP, I GUESS.

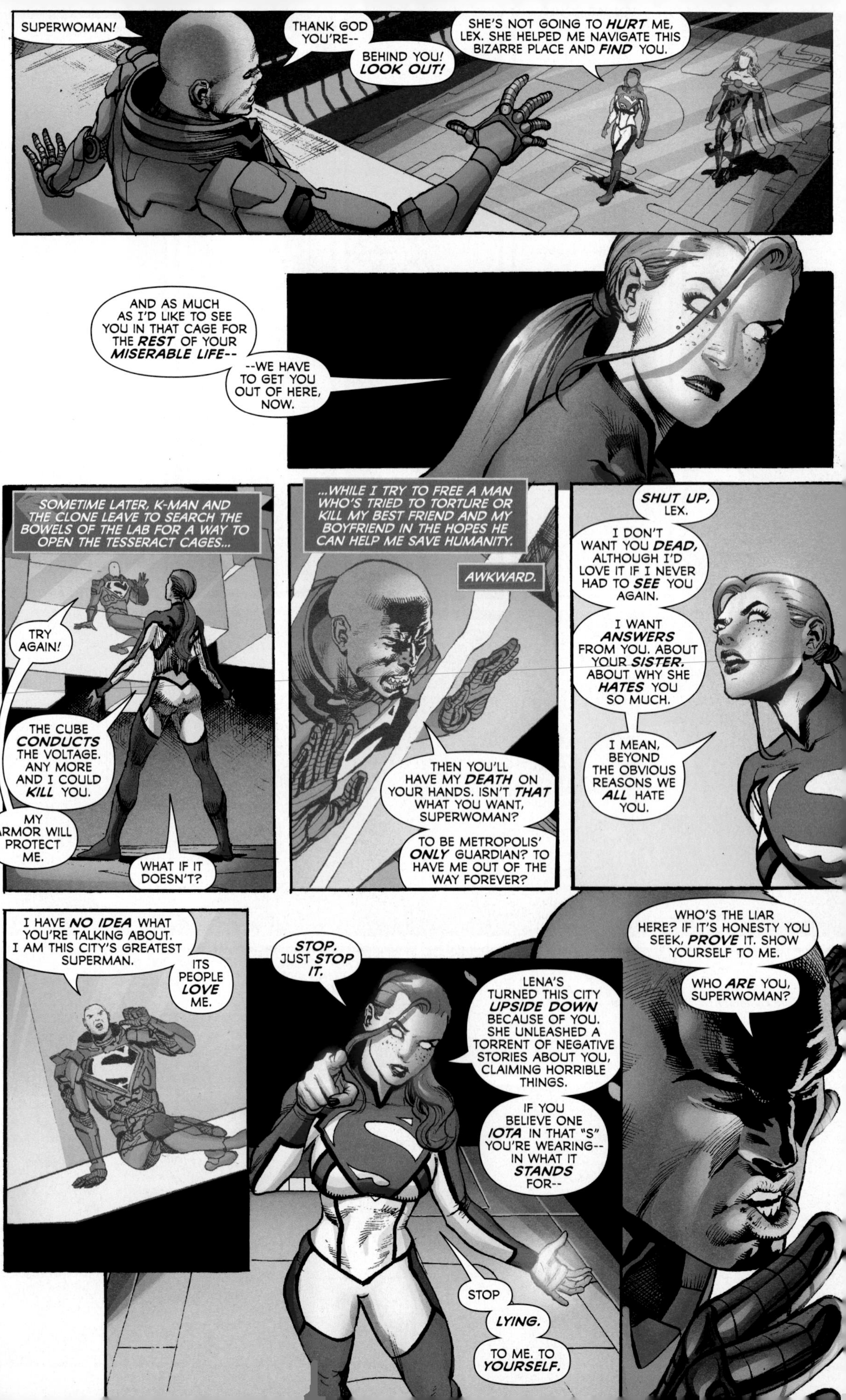

SUPERWOMAN!
THANK GOD YOU'RE--
BEHIND YOU! LOOK OUT!
SHE'S NOT GOING TO HURT ME, LEX. SHE HELPED ME NAVIGATE THIS BIZARRE PLACE AND FIND YOU.
AND AS MUCH AS I'D LIKE TO SEE YOU IN THAT CAGE FOR THE REST OF YOUR MISERABLE LIFE--
--WE HAVE TO GET YOU OUT OF HERE, NOW.
SOMETIME LATER, K-MAN AND THE CLONE LEAVE TO SEARCH THE BOWELS OF THE LAB FOR A WAY TO OPEN THE TESSERACT CAGES...
TRY AGAIN!
THE CUBE CONDUCTS THE VOLTAGE. ANY MORE AND I COULD KILL YOU.
MY ARMOR WILL PROTECT ME.
WHAT IF IT DOESN'T?
...WHILE I TRY TO FREE A MAN WHO'S TRIED TO TORTURE OR KILL MY BEST FRIEND AND MY BOYFRIEND IN THE HOPES HE CAN HELP ME SAVE HUMANITY.
AWKWARD.
THEN YOU'LL HAVE MY DEATH ON YOUR HANDS. ISN'T THAT WHAT YOU WANT, SUPERWOMAN?
TO BE METROPOLIS' ONLY GUARDIAN? TO HAVE ME OUT OF THE WAY FOREVER?
SHUT UP, LEX.
I DON'T WANT YOU DEAD, ALTHOUGH I'D LOVE IT IF I NEVER HAD TO SEE YOU AGAIN.
I WANT ANSWERS FROM YOU. ABOUT YOUR SISTER. ABOUT WHY SHE HATES YOU SO MUCH.
I MEAN, BEYOND THE OBVIOUS REASONS WE ALL HATE YOU.
I HAVE NO IDEA WHAT YOU'RE TALKING ABOUT. I AM THIS CITY'S GREATEST SUPERMAN.
ITS PEOPLE LOVE ME.
STOP. JUST STOP IT.
LENA'S TURNED THIS CITY UPSIDE DOWN BECAUSE OF YOU. SHE UNLEASHED A TORRENT OF NEGATIVE STORIES ABOUT YOU, CLAIMING HORRIBLE THINGS.
IF YOU BELIEVE ONE IOTA IN THAT "S" YOU'RE WEARING-- IN WHAT IT STANDS FOR--
STOP
LYING.
TO ME. TO YOURSELF.
WHO'S THE LIAR HERE? IF IT'S HONESTY YOU SEEK, PROVE IT. SHOW YOURSELF TO ME.
WHO ARE YOU, SUPERWOMAN?

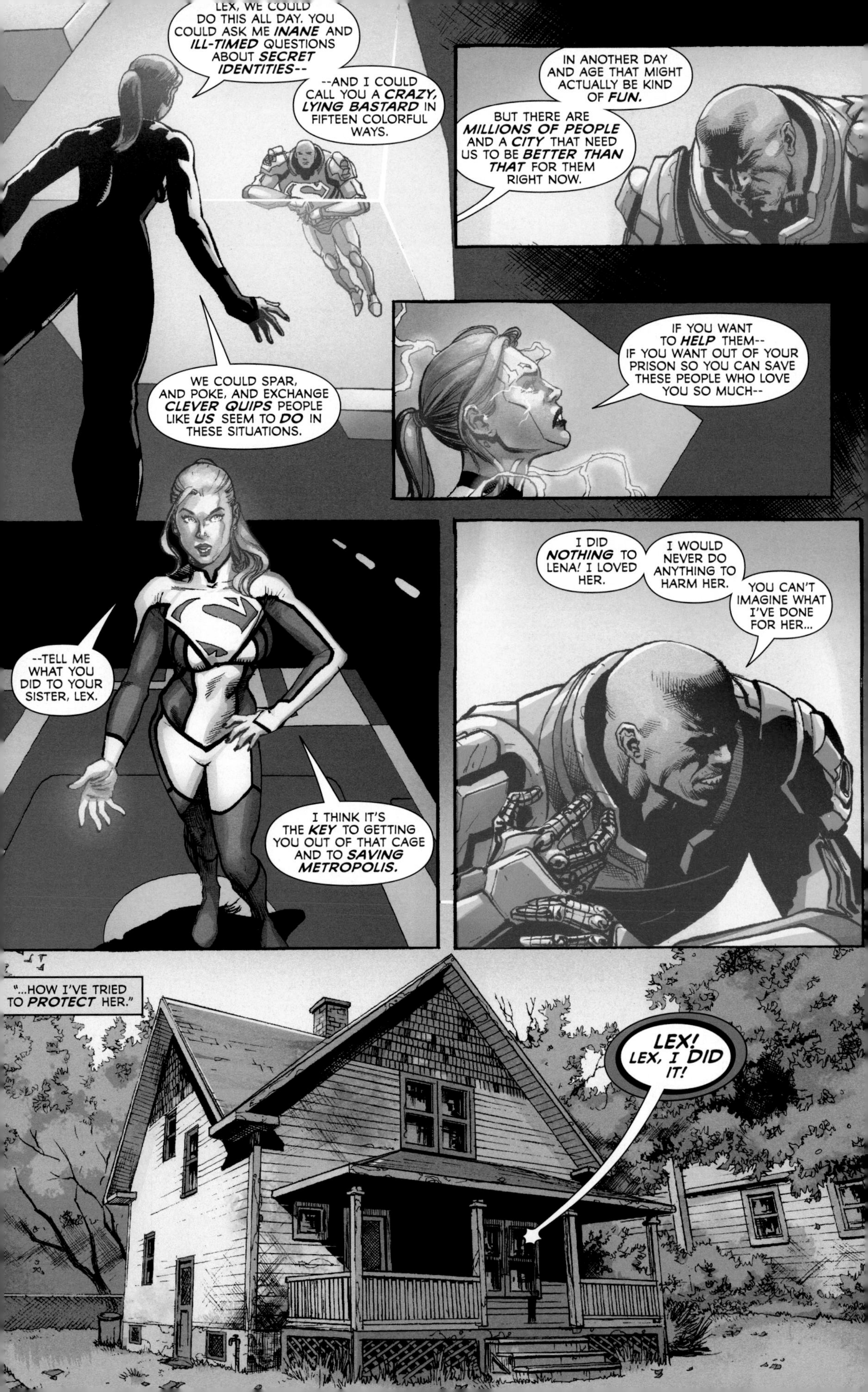
LEX, WE COULD DO THIS ALL DAY. YOU COULD ASK ME *INANE* AND *ILL-TIMED* QUESTIONS ABOUT *SECRET IDENTITIES*--
--AND I COULD CALL YOU A *CRAZY, LYING BASTARD* IN FIFTEEN COLORFUL WAYS.
IN ANOTHER DAY AND AGE THAT MIGHT ACTUALLY BE KIND OF *FUN.*
BUT THERE ARE *MILLIONS OF PEOPLE* AND A *CITY* THAT NEED US TO BE *BETTER THAN THAT* FOR THEM RIGHT NOW.
WE COULD SPAR, AND POKE, AND EXCHANGE *CLEVER QUIPS* PEOPLE LIKE *US* SEEM TO *DO* IN THESE SITUATIONS.
IF YOU WANT TO *HELP* THEM-- IF YOU WANT OUT OF YOUR PRISON SO YOU CAN SAVE THESE PEOPLE WHO LOVE YOU SO MUCH--
--TELL ME WHAT YOU DID TO YOUR SISTER, LEX.
I THINK IT'S THE *KEY* TO GETTING YOU OUT OF THAT CAGE AND TO *SAVING METROPOLIS.*
I DID *NOTHING* TO LENA! I LOVED HER.
I WOULD NEVER DO ANYTHING TO HARM HER.
YOU CAN'T IMAGINE WHAT I'VE DONE FOR HER...
"...HOW I'VE TRIED TO *PROTECT* HER."
LEX! LEX, I DID IT!

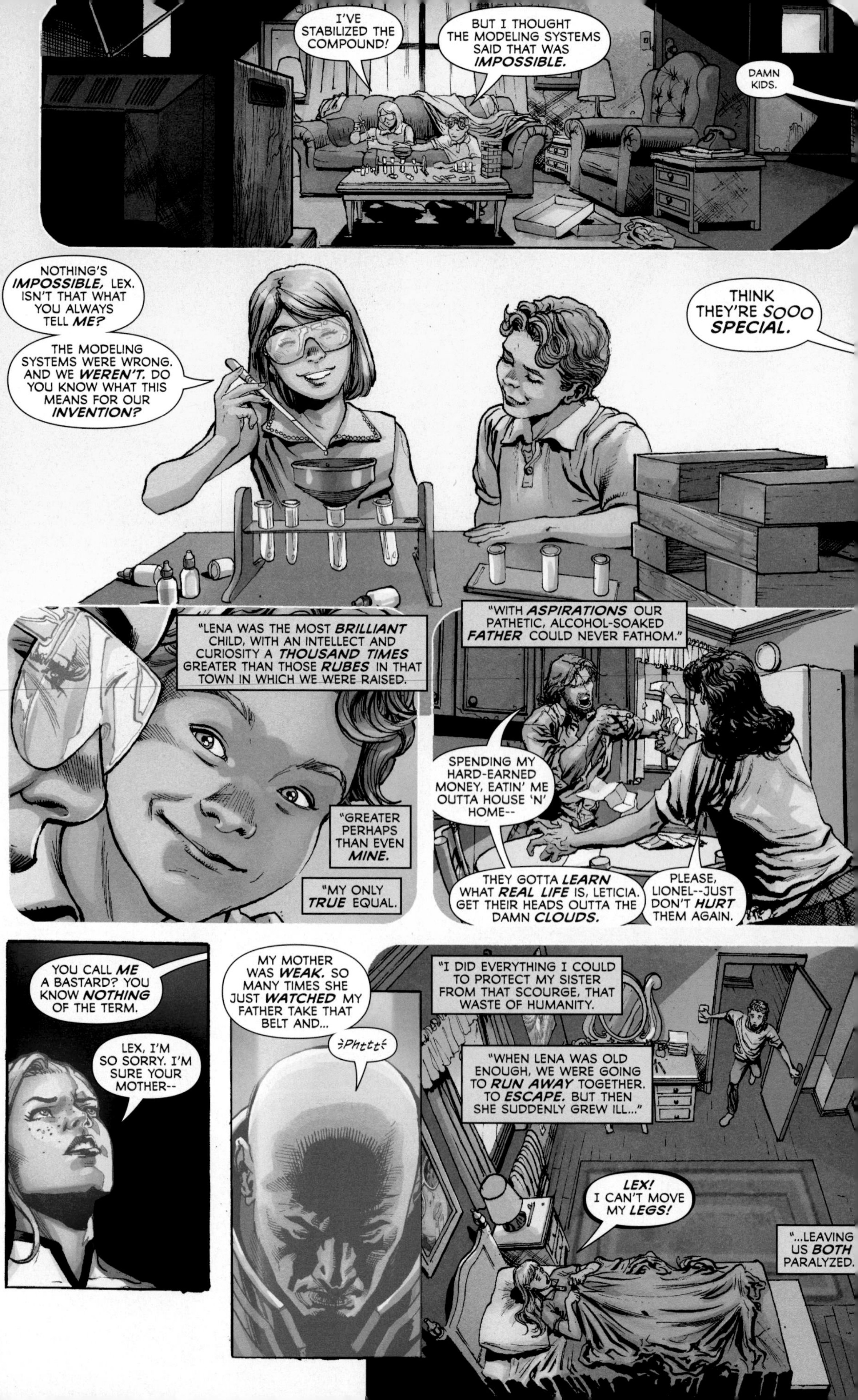
I'VE STABILIZED THE COMPOUND!
BUT I THOUGHT THE MODELING SYSTEMS SAID THAT WAS IMPOSSIBLE.
DAMN KIDS.
NOTHING'S IMPOSSIBLE, LEX. ISN'T THAT WHAT YOU ALWAYS TELL ME?
THE MODELING SYSTEMS WERE WRONG. AND WE WEREN'T. DO YOU KNOW WHAT THIS MEANS FOR OUR INVENTION?
THINK THEY'RE SOOO SPECIAL.
"LENA WAS THE MOST BRILLIANT CHILD, WITH AN INTELLECT AND CURIOSITY A THOUSAND TIMES GREATER THAN THOSE RUBES IN THAT TOWN IN WHICH WE WERE RAISED.
"GREATER PERHAPS THAN EVEN MINE.
"MY ONLY TRUE EQUAL.
"WITH ASPIRATIONS OUR PATHETIC, ALCOHOL-SOAKED FATHER COULD NEVER FATHOM."
SPENDING MY HARD-EARNED MONEY, EATIN' ME OUTTA HOUSE 'N' HOME--
THEY GOTTA LEARN WHAT REAL LIFE IS, LETICIA. GET THEIR HEADS OUTTA THE DAMN CLOUDS.
PLEASE, LIONEL--JUST DON'T HURT THEM AGAIN.
YOU CALL ME A BASTARD? YOU KNOW NOTHING OF THE TERM.
LEX, I'M SO SORRY. I'M SURE YOUR MOTHER--
MY MOTHER WAS WEAK. SO MANY TIMES SHE JUST WATCHED MY FATHER TAKE THAT BELT AND...
Phttt
"I DID EVERYTHING I COULD TO PROTECT MY SISTER FROM THAT SCOURGE, THAT WASTE OF HUMANITY.
"WHEN LENA WAS OLD ENOUGH, WE WERE GOING TO RUN AWAY TOGETHER. TO ESCAPE. BUT THEN SHE SUDDENLY GREW ILL..."
LEX! I CAN'T MOVE MY LEGS!
"...LEAVING US BOTH PARALYZED.

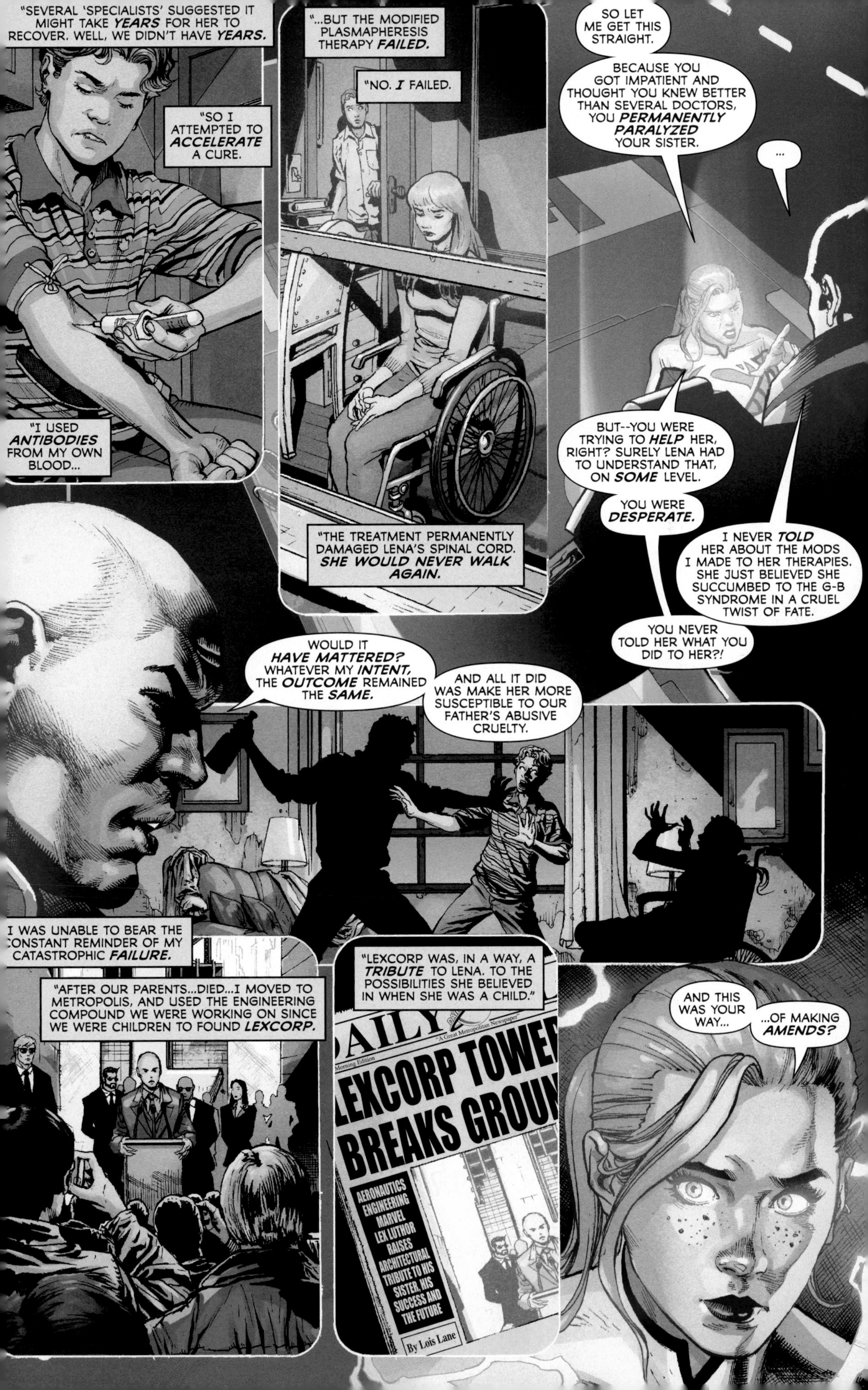
"SEVERAL 'SPECIALISTS' SUGGESTED IT MIGHT TAKE YEARS FOR HER TO RECOVER. WELL, WE DIDN'T HAVE YEARS.
"SO I ATTEMPTED TO ACCELERATE A CURE.
"I USED ANTIBODIES FROM MY OWN BLOOD...
"...BUT THE MODIFIED PLASMAPHERESIS THERAPY FAILED.
"NO. I FAILED.
"THE TREATMENT PERMANENTLY DAMAGED LENA'S SPINAL CORD. SHE WOULD NEVER WALK AGAIN.
SO LET ME GET THIS STRAIGHT.
BECAUSE YOU GOT IMPATIENT AND THOUGHT YOU KNEW BETTER THAN SEVERAL DOCTORS, YOU PERMANENTLY PARALYZED YOUR SISTER.
...
BUT--YOU WERE TRYING TO HELP HER, RIGHT? SURELY LENA HAD TO UNDERSTAND THAT, ON SOME LEVEL.
YOU WERE DESPERATE.
I NEVER TOLD HER ABOUT THE MODS I MADE TO HER THERAPIES. SHE JUST BELIEVED SHE SUCCUMBED TO THE G-B SYNDROME IN A CRUEL TWIST OF FATE.
YOU NEVER TOLD HER WHAT YOU DID TO HER?!
WOULD IT HAVE MATTERED? WHATEVER MY INTENT, THE OUTCOME REMAINED THE SAME.
AND ALL IT DID WAS MAKE HER MORE SUSCEPTIBLE TO OUR FATHER'S ABUSIVE CRUELTY.
I WAS UNABLE TO BEAR THE CONSTANT REMINDER OF MY CATASTROPHIC FAILURE.
"AFTER OUR PARENTS...DIED...I MOVED TO METROPOLIS, AND USED THE ENGINEERING COMPOUND WE WERE WORKING ON SINCE WE WERE CHILDREN TO FOUND LEXCORP.
"LEXCORP WAS, IN A WAY, A TRIBUTE TO LENA. TO THE POSSIBILITIES SHE BELIEVED IN WHEN SHE WAS A CHILD."
DAILY
"A Great Metropolitan Newspaper"
Morning Edition
LEXCORP TOWE
BREAKS GROUN
AERONAUTICS ENGINEERING MARVEL LEX LUTHOR RAISES ARCHITECTURAL TRIBUTE TO HIS SISTER, HIS SUCCESS AND THE FUTURE
By Lois Lane
AND THIS WAS YOUR WAY...
...OF MAKING AMENDS?

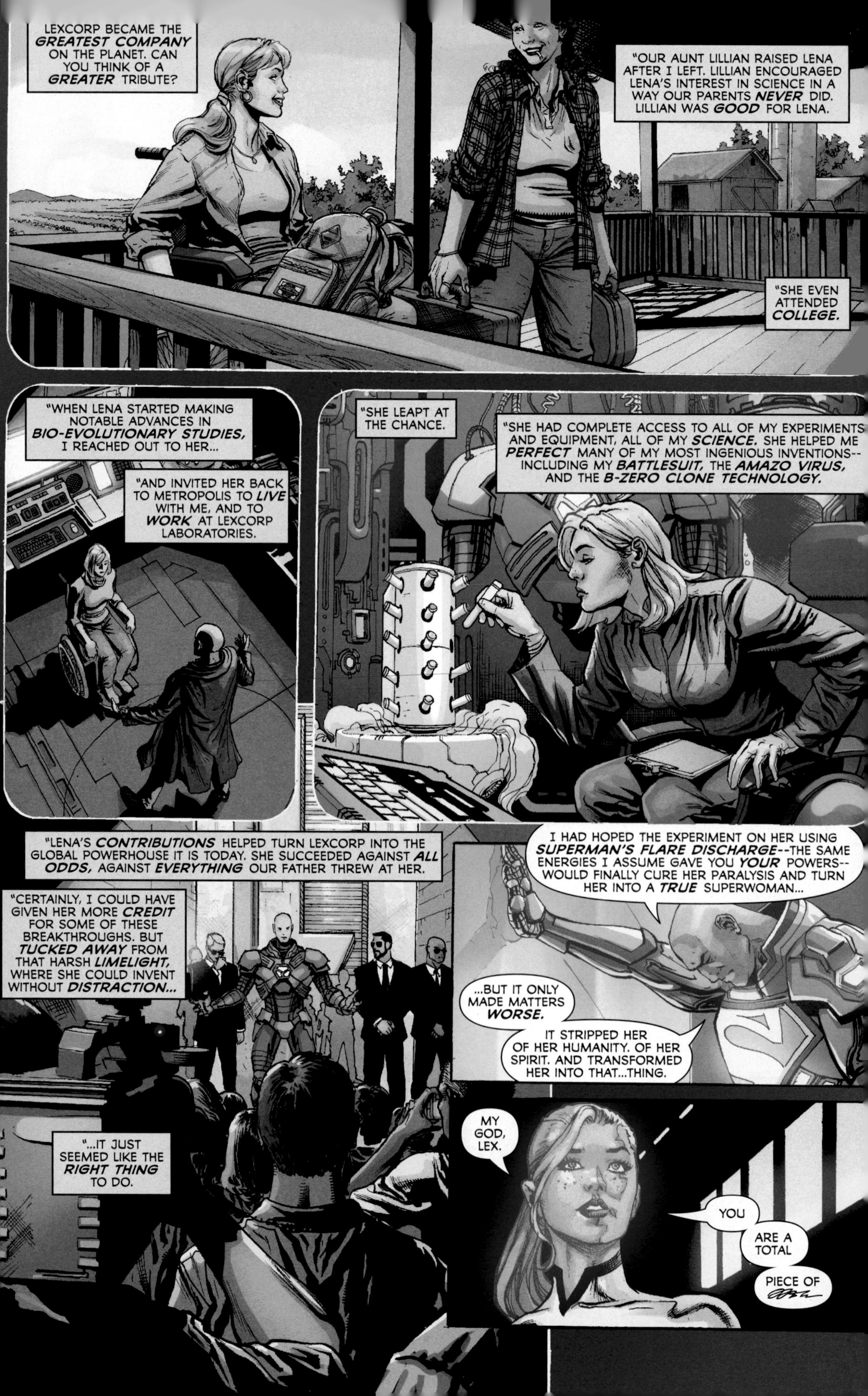
LEXCORP BECAME THE GREATEST COMPANY ON THE PLANET. CAN YOU THINK OF A GREATER TRIBUTE?
"OUR AUNT LILLIAN RAISED LENA AFTER I LEFT. LILLIAN ENCOURAGED LENA'S INTEREST IN SCIENCE IN A WAY OUR PARENTS NEVER DID. LILLIAN WAS GOOD FOR LENA.
"SHE EVEN ATTENDED COLLEGE.
"WHEN LENA STARTED MAKING NOTABLE ADVANCES IN BIO-EVOLUTIONARY STUDIES, I REACHED OUT TO HER...
"AND INVITED HER BACK TO METROPOLIS TO LIVE WITH ME, AND TO WORK AT LEXCORP LABORATORIES.
"SHE LEAPT AT THE CHANCE.
"SHE HAD COMPLETE ACCESS TO ALL OF MY EXPERIMENTS AND EQUIPMENT, ALL OF MY SCIENCE. SHE HELPED ME PERFECT MANY OF MY MOST INGENIOUS INVENTIONS-- INCLUDING MY BATTLESUIT, THE AMAZO VIRUS, AND THE B-ZERO CLONE TECHNOLOGY.
"LENA'S CONTRIBUTIONS HELPED TURN LEXCORP INTO THE GLOBAL POWERHOUSE IT IS TODAY. SHE SUCCEEDED AGAINST ALL ODDS, AGAINST EVERYTHING OUR FATHER THREW AT HER.
"CERTAINLY, I COULD HAVE GIVEN HER MORE CREDIT FOR SOME OF THESE BREAKTHROUGHS. BUT TUCKED AWAY FROM THAT HARSH LIMELIGHT, WHERE SHE COULD INVENT WITHOUT DISTRACTION...
"...IT JUST SEEMED LIKE THE RIGHT THING TO DO.
I HAD HOPED THE EXPERIMENT ON HER USING SUPERMAN'S FLARE DISCHARGE--THE SAME ENERGIES I ASSUME GAVE YOU YOUR POWERS--WOULD FINALLY CURE HER PARALYSIS AND TURN HER INTO A TRUE SUPERWOMAN...
...BUT IT ONLY MADE MATTERS WORSE.
IT STRIPPED HER OF HER HUMANITY. OF HER SPIRIT. AND TRANSFORMED HER INTO THAT...THING.
MY GOD, LEX.
YOU
ARE A TOTAL
PIECE OF

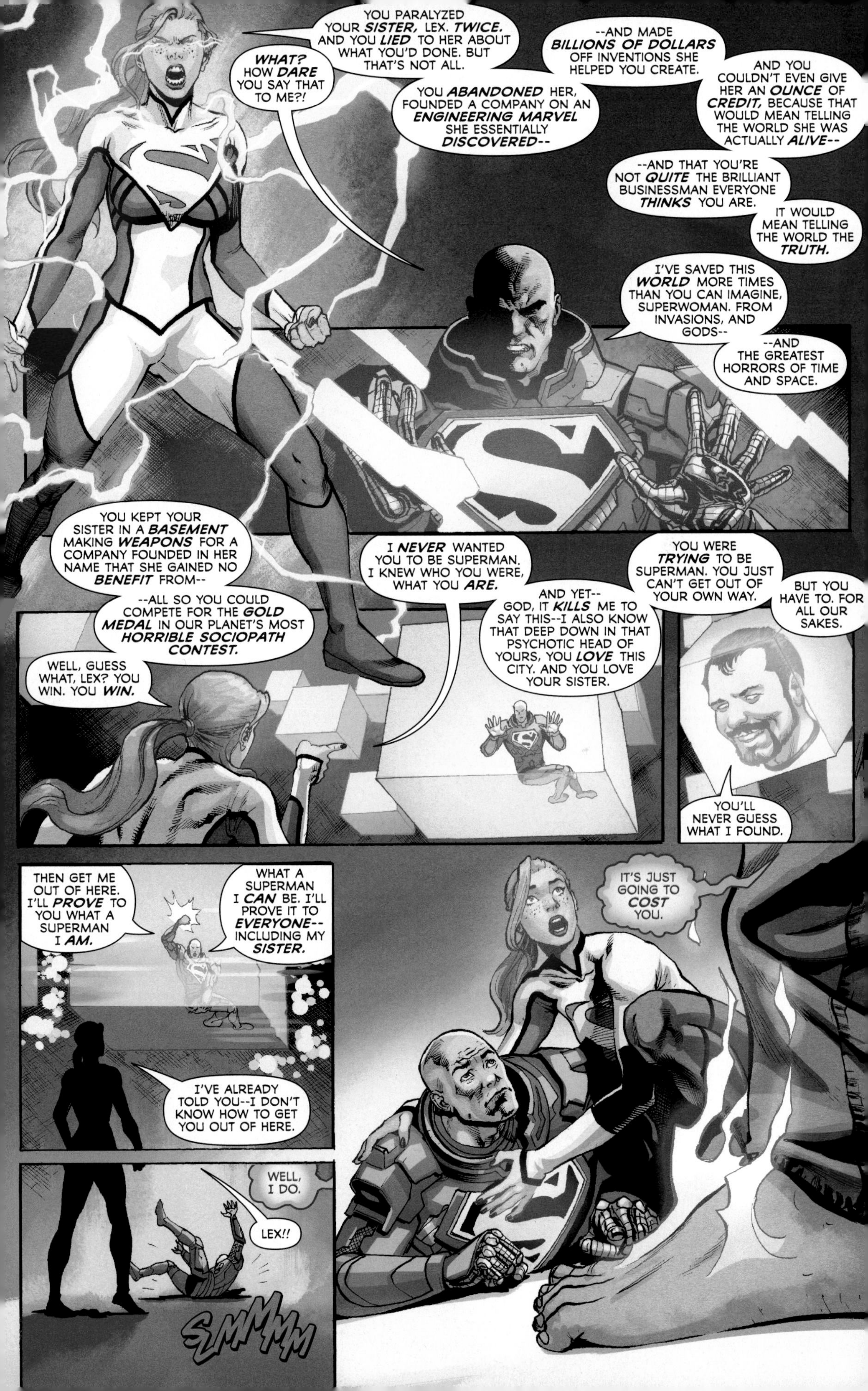
YOU PARALYZED YOUR SISTER, LEX. TWICE. AND YOU LIED TO HER ABOUT WHAT YOU'D DONE. BUT THAT'S NOT ALL.
WHAT? HOW DARE YOU SAY THAT TO ME?!
YOU ABANDONED HER, FOUNDED A COMPANY ON AN ENGINEERING MARVEL SHE ESSENTIALLY DISCOVERED--
--AND MADE BILLIONS OF DOLLARS OFF INVENTIONS SHE HELPED YOU CREATE.
AND YOU COULDN'T EVEN GIVE HER AN OUNCE OF CREDIT, BECAUSE THAT WOULD MEAN TELLING THE WORLD SHE WAS ACTUALLY ALIVE--
--AND THAT YOU'RE NOT QUITE THE BRILLIANT BUSINESSMAN EVERYONE THINKS YOU ARE.
IT WOULD MEAN TELLING THE WORLD THE TRUTH.
I'VE SAVED THIS WORLD MORE TIMES THAN YOU CAN IMAGINE, SUPERWOMAN. FROM INVASIONS, AND GODS--
--AND THE GREATEST HORRORS OF TIME AND SPACE.
YOU KEPT YOUR SISTER IN A BASEMENT MAKING WEAPONS FOR A COMPANY FOUNDED IN HER NAME THAT SHE GAINED NO BENEFIT FROM--
--ALL SO YOU COULD COMPETE FOR THE GOLD MEDAL IN OUR PLANET'S MOST HORRIBLE SOCIOPATH CONTEST.
WELL, GUESS WHAT, LEX? YOU WIN. YOU WIN.
I NEVER WANTED YOU TO BE SUPERMAN. I KNEW WHO YOU WERE, WHAT YOU ARE.
AND YET-- GOD, IT KILLS ME TO SAY THIS--I ALSO KNOW THAT DEEP DOWN IN THAT PSYCHOTIC HEAD OF YOURS, YOU LOVE THIS CITY. AND YOU LOVE YOUR SISTER.
YOU WERE TRYING TO BE SUPERMAN. YOU JUST CAN'T GET OUT OF YOUR OWN WAY.
BUT YOU HAVE TO. FOR ALL OUR SAKES.
YOU'LL NEVER GUESS WHAT I FOUND.
THEN GET ME OUT OF HERE. I'LL PROVE TO YOU WHAT A SUPERMAN I AM.
WHAT A SUPERMAN I CAN BE. I'LL PROVE IT TO EVERYONE-- INCLUDING MY SISTER.
I'VE ALREADY TOLD YOU--I DON'T KNOW HOW TO GET YOU OUT OF HERE.
WELL, I DO.
LEX!!
SLMMMM
IT'S JUST GOING TO COST YOU.

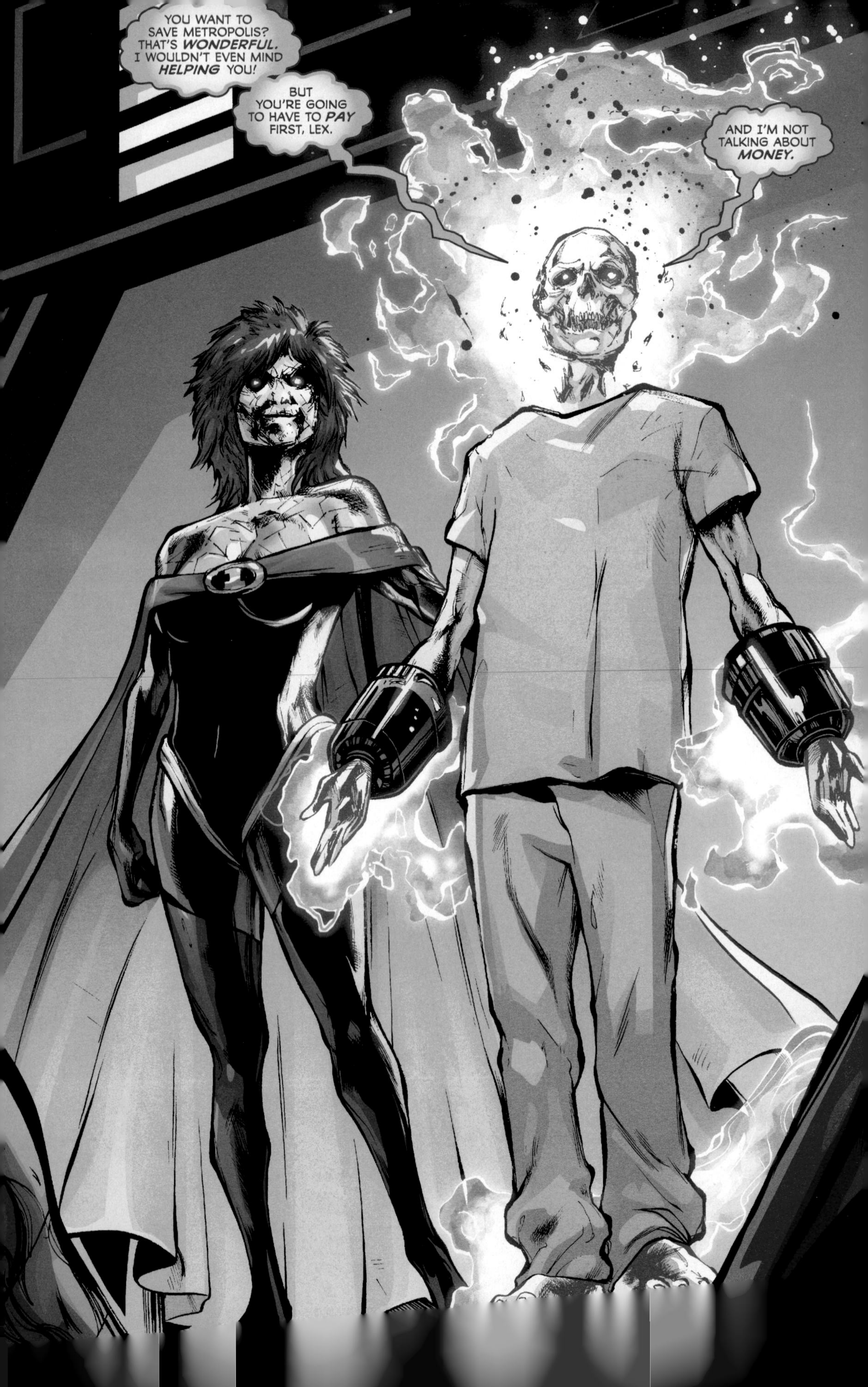
YOU WANT TO SAVE METROPOLIS? THAT'S **WONDERFUL.** I WOULDN'T EVEN MIND **HELPING** YOU!
BUT YOU'RE GOING TO HAVE TO **PAY** FIRST, LEX.
AND I'M NOT TALKING ABOUT **MONEY.**

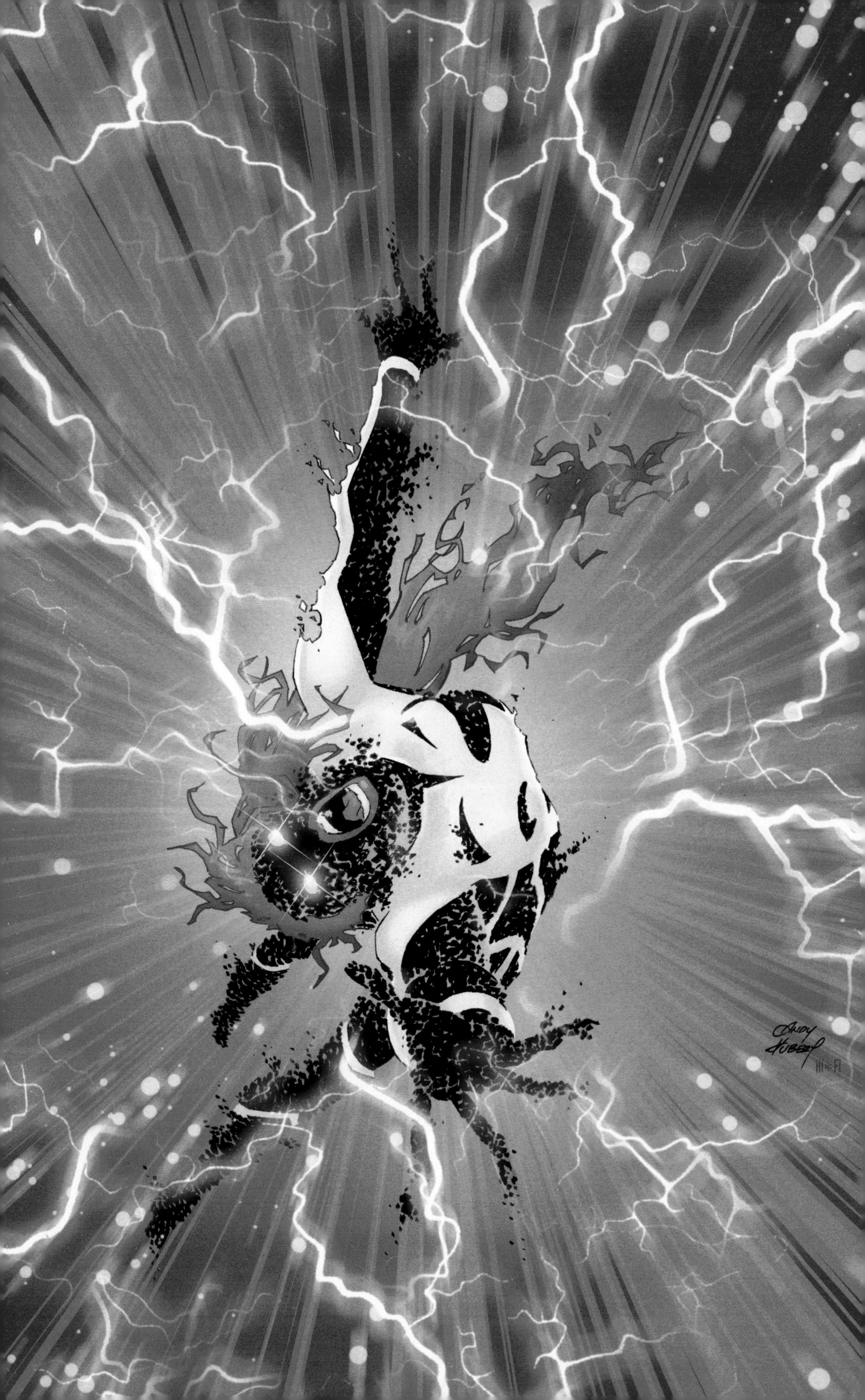

"WHO KILLED SUPERWOMAN? CONCLUSION: NEVER BE SATISFIED"

PHIL JIMENEZ writer/penciller * MATT SANTORELLI JACK HERBERT artists

HI-FI colorist * cover by ANDY KUBERT and HI-FI

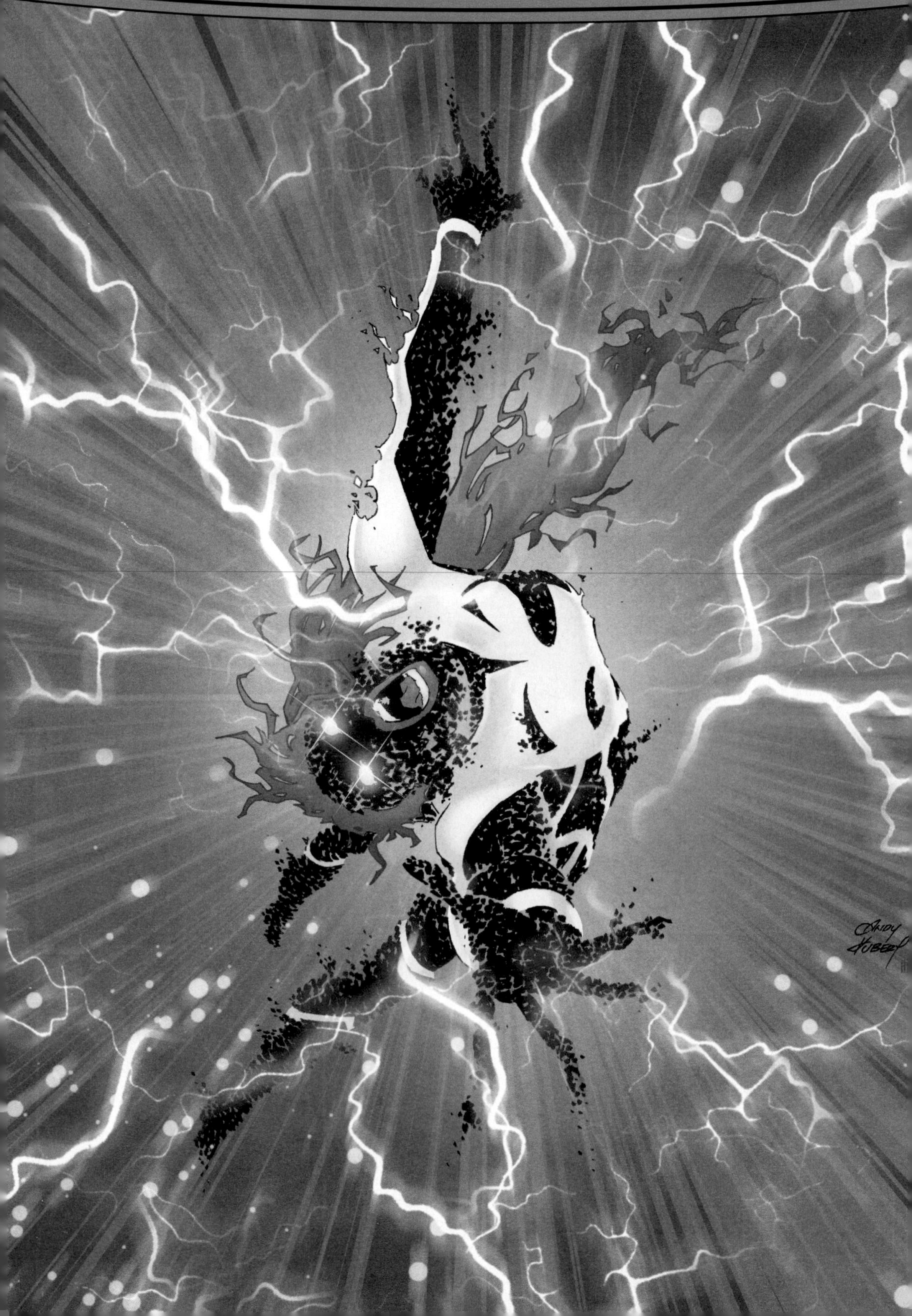
ANDY KUBERT

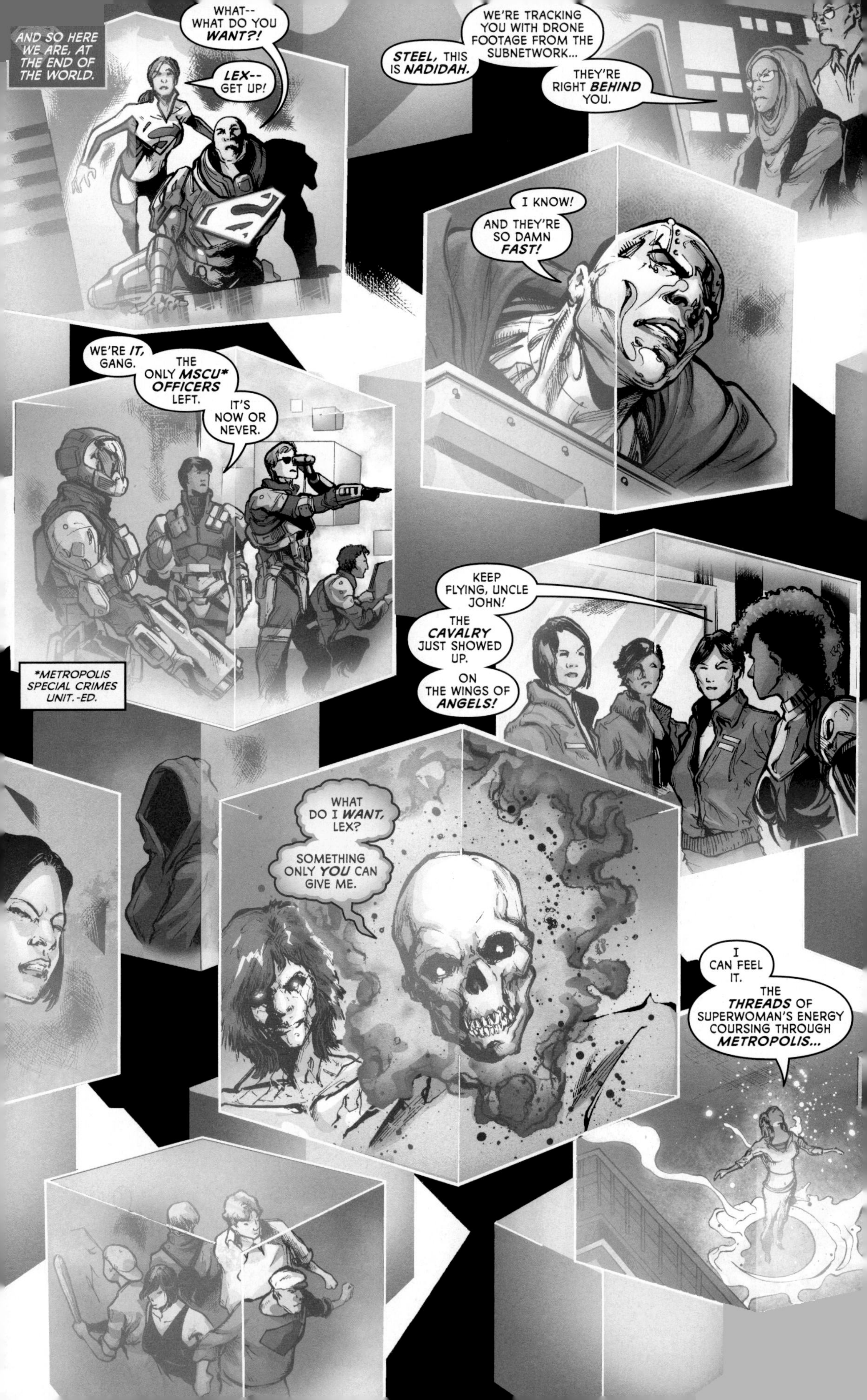
AND SO HERE WE ARE, AT THE END OF THE WORLD.
WHAT-- WHAT DO YOU WANT?!
LEX-- GET UP!
STEEL, THIS IS NADIDAH.
WE'RE TRACKING YOU WITH DRONE FOOTAGE FROM THE SUBNETWORK...
THEY'RE RIGHT BEHIND YOU.
I KNOW!
AND THEY'RE SO DAMN FAST!
WE'RE IT, GANG.
THE ONLY MSCU* OFFICERS LEFT.
IT'S NOW OR NEVER.
*METROPOLIS SPECIAL CRIMES UNIT. -ED.
KEEP FLYING, UNCLE JOHN!
THE CAVALRY JUST SHOWED UP.
ON THE WINGS OF ANGELS!
WHAT DO I WANT, LEX?
SOMETHING ONLY YOU CAN GIVE ME.
I CAN FEEL IT.
THE THREADS OF SUPERWOMAN'S ENERGY COURSING THROUGH METROPOLIS...

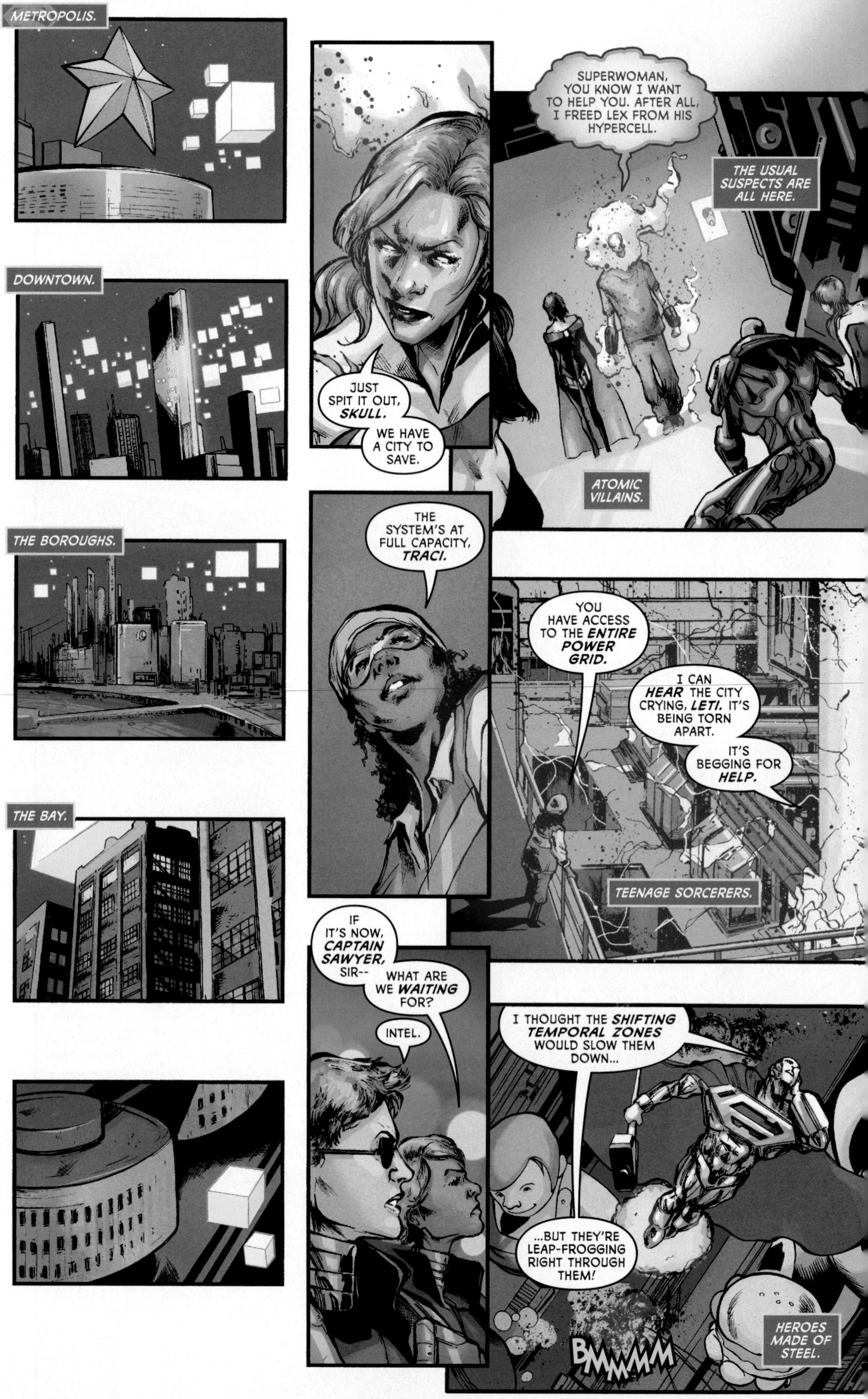
METROPOLIS.
DOWNTOWN.
THE BOROUGHS.
THE BAY.
SUPERWOMAN, YOU KNOW I WANT TO HELP YOU. AFTER ALL, I FREED LEX FROM HIS HYPERCELL.
THE USUAL SUSPECTS ARE ALL HERE.
JUST SPIT IT OUT, SKULL.
WE HAVE A CITY TO SAVE.
ATOMIC VILLAINS.
THE SYSTEM'S AT FULL CAPACITY, TRACI.
YOU HAVE ACCESS TO THE ENTIRE POWER GRID.
I CAN HEAR THE CITY CRYING, LETI. IT'S BEING TORN APART.
IT'S BEGGING FOR HELP.
TEENAGE SORCERERS.
IF IT'S NOW, CAPTAIN SAWYER, SIR--
WHAT ARE WE WAITING FOR?
INTEL.
I THOUGHT THE SHIFTING TEMPORAL ZONES WOULD SLOW THEM DOWN...
...BUT THEY'RE LEAP-FROGGING RIGHT THROUGH THEM!
BMMMM
HEROES MADE OF STEEL.

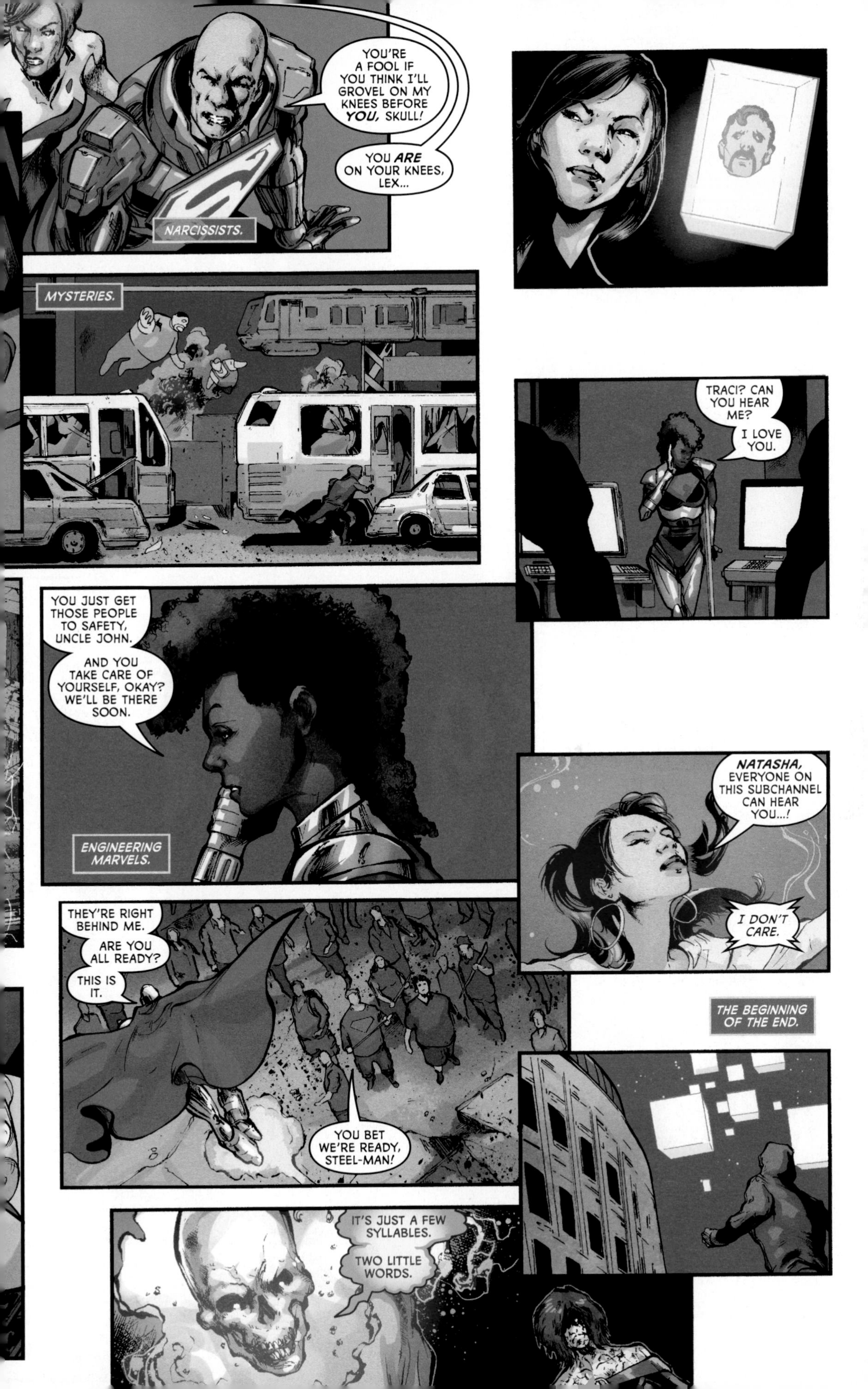
YOU'RE A FOOL IF YOU THINK I'LL GROVEL ON MY KNEES BEFORE YOU, SKULL!
YOU ARE ON YOUR KNEES, LEX...
NARCISSISTS.
MYSTERIES.
TRACI? CAN YOU HEAR ME?
I LOVE YOU.
YOU JUST GET THOSE PEOPLE TO SAFETY, UNCLE JOHN.
AND YOU TAKE CARE OF YOURSELF, OKAY? WE'LL BE THERE SOON.
ENGINEERING MARVELS.
NATASHA, EVERYONE ON THIS SUBCHANNEL CAN HEAR YOU...!
I DON'T CARE.
THEY'RE RIGHT BEHIND ME.
ARE YOU ALL READY?
THIS IS IT.
YOU BET WE'RE READY, STEEL-MAN!
THE BEGINNING OF THE END.
IT'S JUST A FEW SYLLABLES.
TWO LITTLE WORDS.

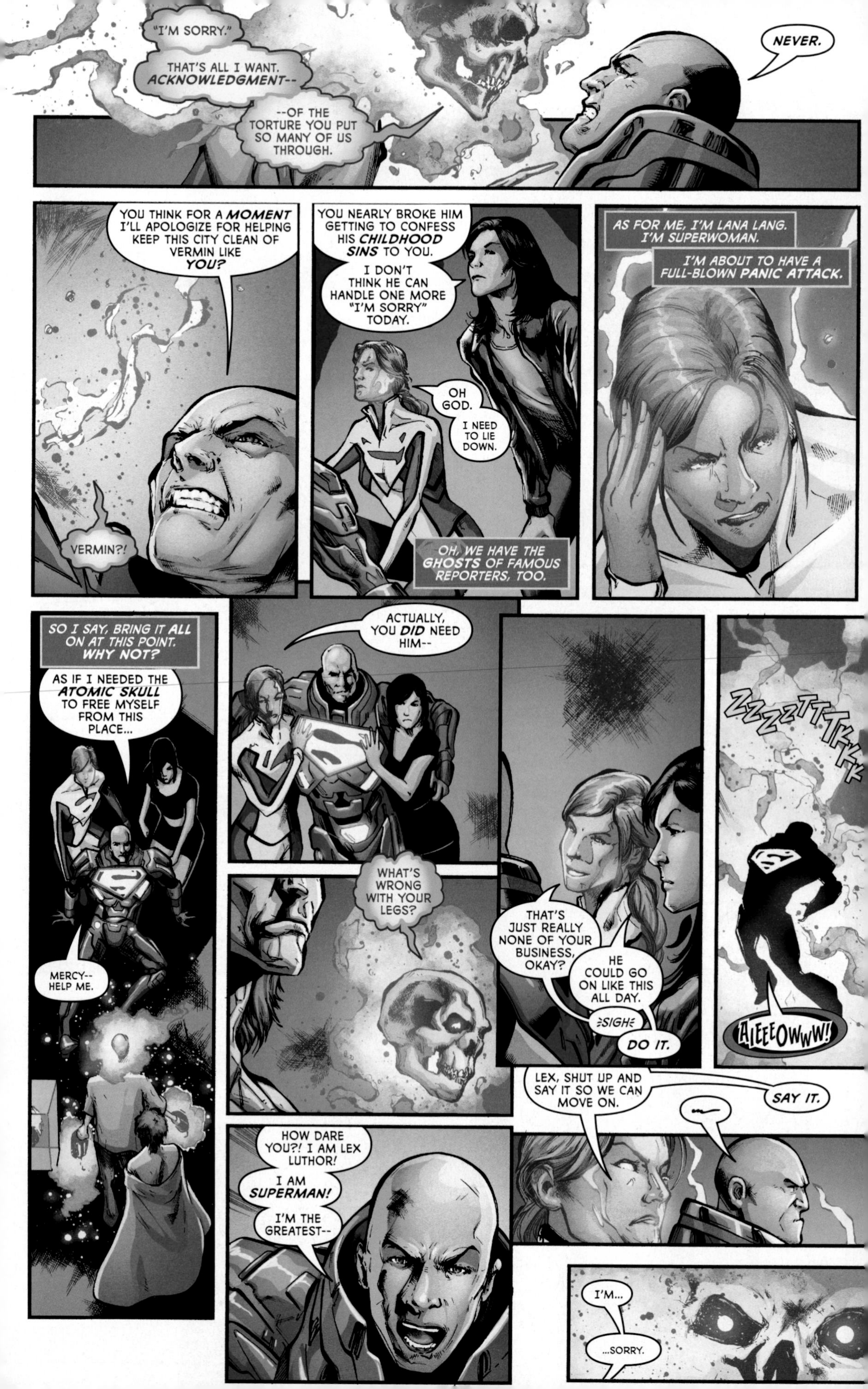

"I'M SORRY."
THAT'S ALL I WANT. ACKNOWLEDGMENT--
--OF THE TORTURE YOU PUT SO MANY OF US THROUGH.
NEVER.
YOU THINK FOR A MOMENT I'LL APOLOGIZE FOR HELPING KEEP THIS CITY CLEAN OF VERMIN LIKE YOU?
VERMIN?!
YOU NEARLY BROKE HIM GETTING TO CONFESS HIS CHILDHOOD SINS TO YOU.
I DON'T THINK HE CAN HANDLE ONE MORE "I'M SORRY" TODAY.
OH GOD.
I NEED TO LIE DOWN.
OH, WE HAVE THE GHOSTS OF FAMOUS REPORTERS, TOO.
AS FOR ME, I'M LANA LANG. I'M SUPERWOMAN.
I'M ABOUT TO HAVE A FULL-BLOWN PANIC ATTACK.
SO I SAY, BRING IT ALL ON AT THIS POINT. WHY NOT?
AS IF I NEEDED THE ATOMIC SKULL TO FREE MYSELF FROM THIS PLACE...
MERCY-- HELP ME.
ACTUALLY, YOU DID NEED HIM--
WHAT'S WRONG WITH YOUR LEGS?
THAT'S JUST REALLY NONE OF YOUR BUSINESS, OKAY?
HE COULD GO ON LIKE THIS ALL DAY.
SIGH
DO IT.
ZZZZTTTKKK
AIEEEOWWW!
HOW DARE YOU?! I AM LEX LUTHOR!
I AM SUPERMAN!
I'M THE GREATEST--
LEX, SHUT UP AND SAY IT SO WE CAN MOVE ON.
SAY IT.
I'M...
...SORRY.

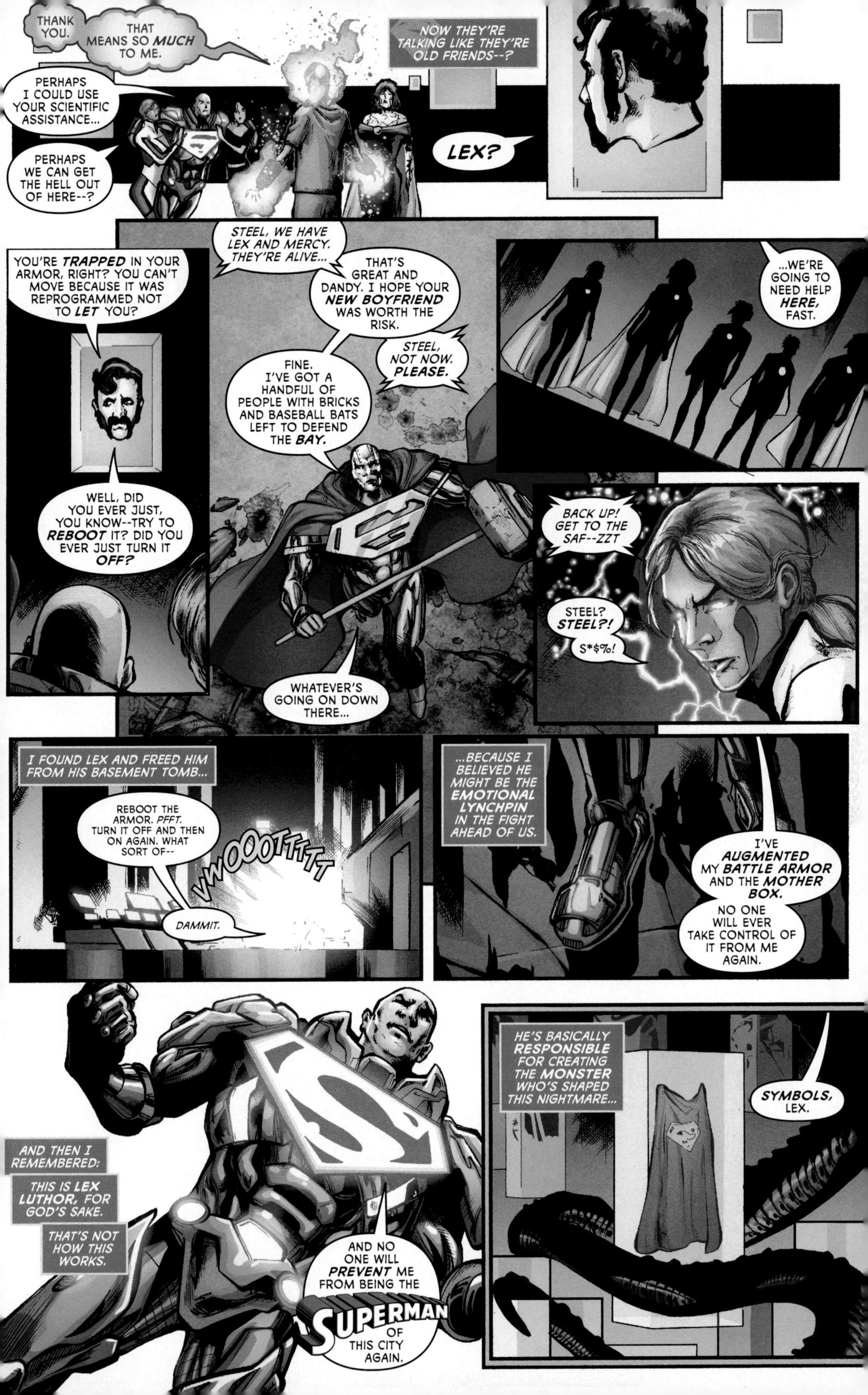
THANK YOU.
THAT MEANS SO MUCH TO ME.
NOW THEY'RE TALKING LIKE THEY'RE OLD FRIENDS--?
PERHAPS I COULD USE YOUR SCIENTIFIC ASSISTANCE...
PERHAPS WE CAN GET THE HELL OUT OF HERE--?
LEX?
YOU'RE TRAPPED IN YOUR ARMOR, RIGHT? YOU CAN'T MOVE BECAUSE IT WAS REPROGRAMMED NOT TO LET YOU?
WELL, DID YOU EVER JUST, YOU KNOW--TRY TO REBOOT IT? DID YOU EVER JUST TURN IT OFF?
STEEL, WE HAVE LEX AND MERCY. THEY'RE ALIVE...
THAT'S GREAT AND DANDY. I HOPE YOUR NEW BOYFRIEND WAS WORTH THE RISK.
STEEL, NOT NOW. PLEASE.
FINE. I'VE GOT A HANDFUL OF PEOPLE WITH BRICKS AND BASEBALL BATS LEFT TO DEFEND THE BAY.
WHATEVER'S GOING ON DOWN THERE...
...WE'RE GOING TO NEED HELP HERE, FAST.
BACK UP! GET TO THE SAF--ZZT
STEEL? STEEL?!
S*$%!
I FOUND LEX AND FREED HIM FROM HIS BASEMENT TOMB...
REBOOT THE ARMOR. PFFT. TURN IT OFF AND THEN ON AGAIN. WHAT SORT OF--
VWOOOTTTTT
DAMMIT.
...BECAUSE I BELIEVED HE MIGHT BE THE EMOTIONAL LYNCHPIN IN THE FIGHT AHEAD OF US.
I'VE AUGMENTED MY BATTLE ARMOR AND THE MOTHER BOX.
NO ONE WILL EVER TAKE CONTROL OF IT FROM ME AGAIN.
AND THEN I REMEMBERED:
THIS IS LEX LUTHOR, FOR GOD'S SAKE.
THAT'S NOT HOW THIS WORKS.
AND NO ONE WILL PREVENT ME FROM BEING THE SUPERMAN OF THIS CITY AGAIN.
HE'S BASICALLY RESPONSIBLE FOR CREATING THE MONSTER WHO'S SHAPED THIS NIGHTMARE...
SYMBOLS, LEX.

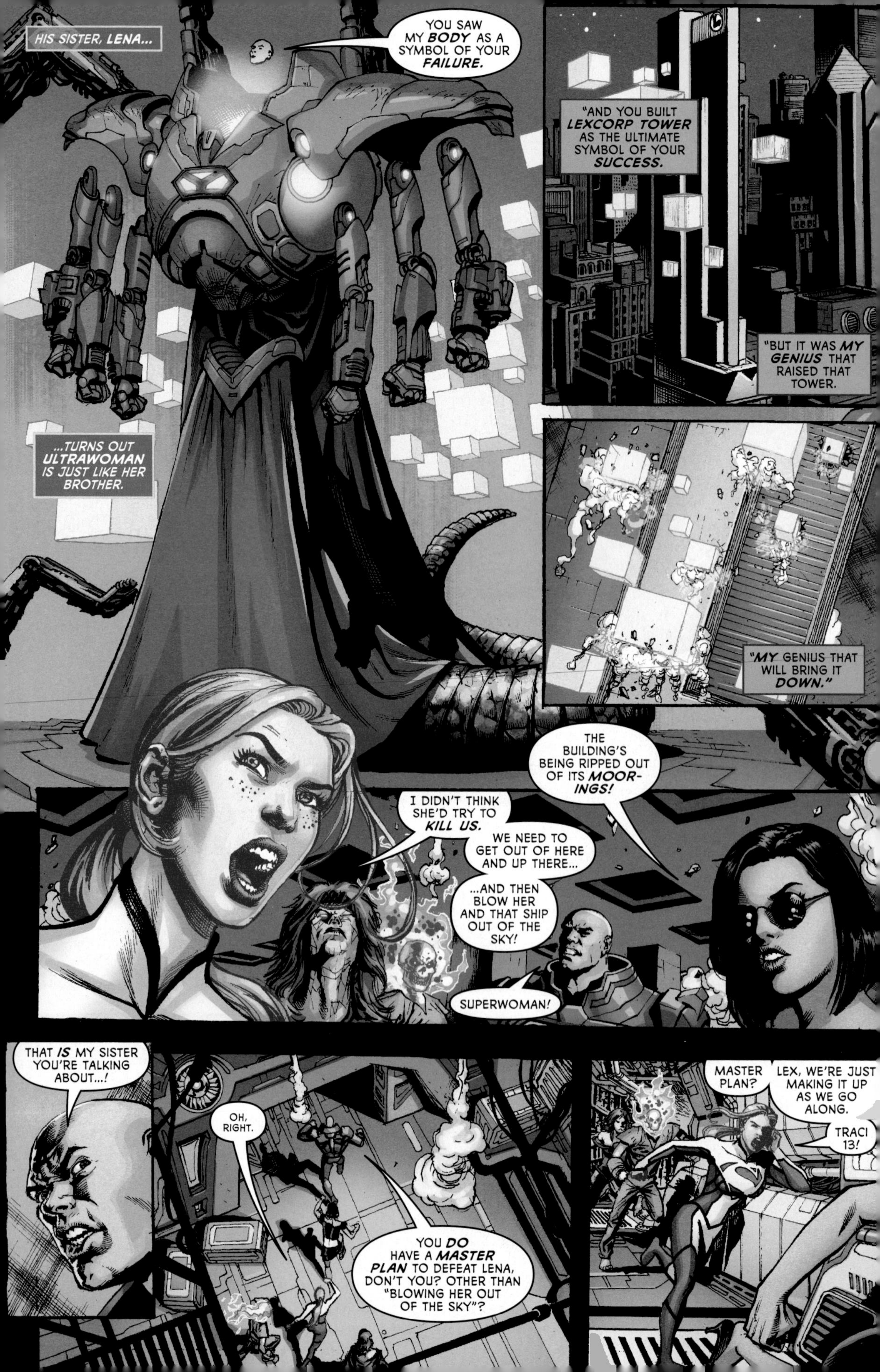
HIS SISTER, LENA...
YOU SAW MY BODY AS A SYMBOL OF YOUR FAILURE.
"AND YOU BUILT LEXCORP TOWER AS THE ULTIMATE SYMBOL OF YOUR SUCCESS.
"BUT IT WAS MY GENIUS THAT RAISED THAT TOWER.
...TURNS OUT ULTRAWOMAN IS JUST LIKE HER BROTHER.
"MY GENIUS THAT WILL BRING IT DOWN."
THE BUILDING'S BEING RIPPED OUT OF ITS MOORINGS!
I DIDN'T THINK SHE'D TRY TO KILL US.
WE NEED TO GET OUT OF HERE AND UP THERE...
...AND THEN BLOW HER AND THAT SHIP OUT OF THE SKY!
SUPERWOMAN!
THAT IS MY SISTER YOU'RE TALKING ABOUT...!
OH, RIGHT.
YOU DO HAVE A MASTER PLAN TO DEFEAT LENA, DON'T YOU? OTHER THAN "BLOWING HER OUT OF THE SKY"?
MASTER PLAN?
LEX, WE'RE JUST MAKING IT UP AS WE GO ALONG.
TRACI 13!

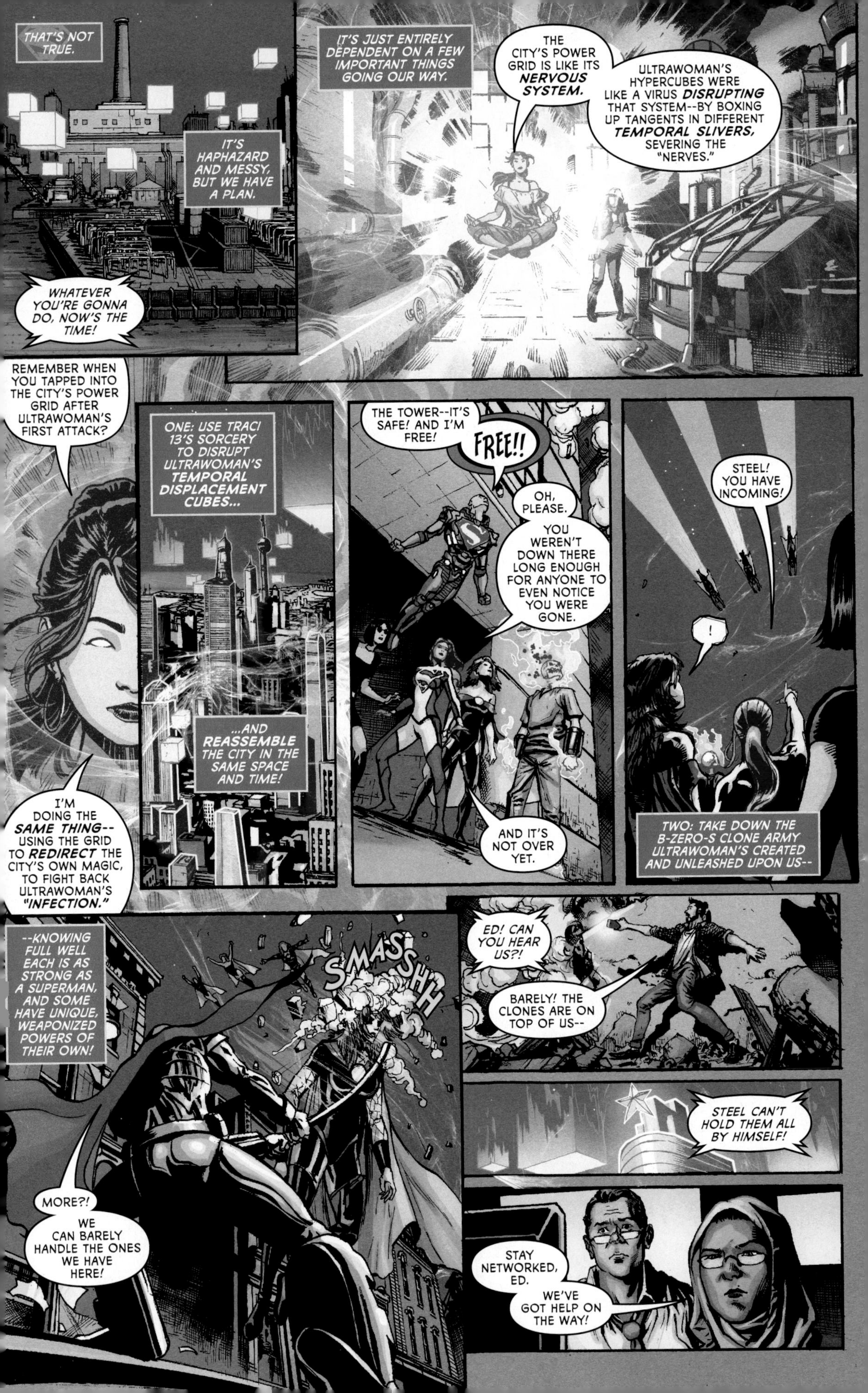
THAT'S NOT TRUE.
IT'S HAPHAZARD AND MESSY, BUT WE HAVE A PLAN.
WHATEVER YOU'RE GONNA DO, NOW'S THE TIME!
IT'S JUST ENTIRELY DEPENDENT ON A FEW IMPORTANT THINGS GOING OUR WAY.
THE CITY'S POWER GRID IS LIKE ITS NERVOUS SYSTEM.
ULTRAWOMAN'S HYPERCUBES WERE LIKE A VIRUS DISRUPTING THAT SYSTEM--BY BOXING UP TANGENTS IN DIFFERENT TEMPORAL SLIVERS, SEVERING THE "NERVES."
REMEMBER WHEN YOU TAPPED INTO THE CITY'S POWER GRID AFTER ULTRAWOMAN'S FIRST ATTACK?
I'M DOING THE SAME THING--USING THE GRID TO REDIRECT THE CITY'S OWN MAGIC, TO FIGHT BACK ULTRAWOMAN'S "INFECTION."
ONE: USE TRACI 13'S SORCERY TO DISRUPT ULTRAWOMAN'S TEMPORAL DISPLACEMENT CUBES...
...AND REASSEMBLE THE CITY IN THE SAME SPACE AND TIME!
THE TOWER--IT'S SAFE! AND I'M FREE!
FREE!!
OH, PLEASE.
YOU WEREN'T DOWN THERE LONG ENOUGH FOR ANYONE TO EVEN NOTICE YOU WERE GONE.
AND IT'S NOT OVER YET.
STEEL! YOU HAVE INCOMING!
!
TWO: TAKE DOWN THE B-ZERO-S CLONE ARMY ULTRAWOMAN'S CREATED AND UNLEASHED UPON US--
--KNOWING FULL WELL EACH IS AS STRONG AS A SUPERMAN, AND SOME HAVE UNIQUE, WEAPONIZED POWERS OF THEIR OWN!
SMASSHH
MORE?! WE CAN BARELY HANDLE THE ONES WE HAVE HERE!
ED! CAN YOU HEAR US?!
BARELY! THE CLONES ARE ON TOP OF US--
STEEL CAN'T HOLD THEM ALL BY HIMSELF!
STAY NETWORKED, ED.
WE'VE GOT HELP ON THE WAY!

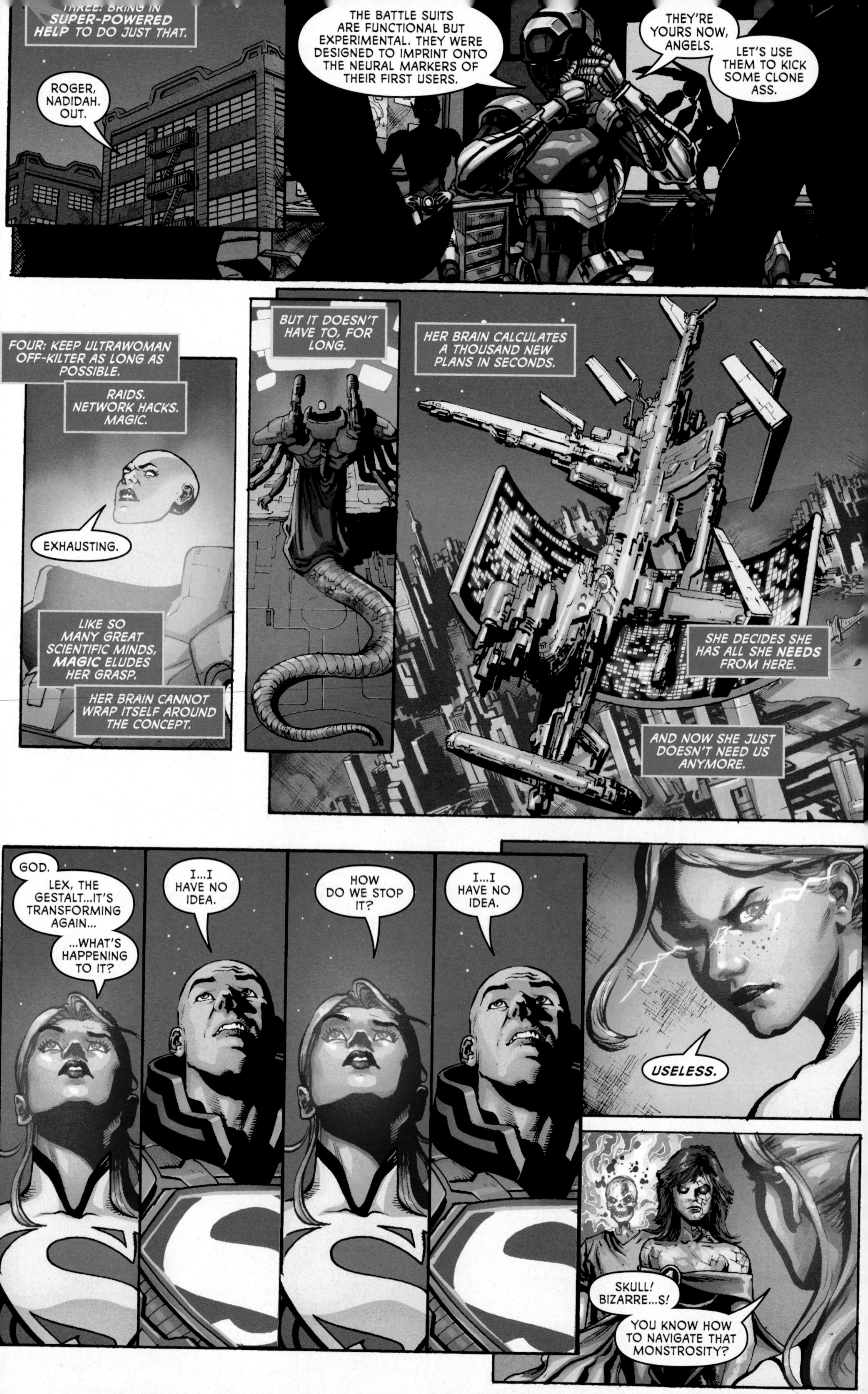
THREE: BRING IN SUPER-POWERED HELP TO DO JUST THAT.
ROGER, NADIDAH. OUT.
THE BATTLE SUITS ARE FUNCTIONAL BUT EXPERIMENTAL. THEY WERE DESIGNED TO IMPRINT ONTO THE NEURAL MARKERS OF THEIR FIRST USERS.
THEY'RE YOURS NOW, ANGELS.
LET'S USE THEM TO KICK SOME CLONE ASS.
FOUR: KEEP ULTRAWOMAN OFF-KILTER AS LONG AS POSSIBLE.
RAIDS. NETWORK HACKS. MAGIC.
EXHAUSTING.
LIKE SO MANY GREAT SCIENTIFIC MINDS, MAGIC ELUDES HER GRASP.
HER BRAIN CANNOT WRAP ITSELF AROUND THE CONCEPT.
BUT IT DOESN'T HAVE TO, FOR LONG.
HER BRAIN CALCULATES A THOUSAND NEW PLANS IN SECONDS.
SHE DECIDES SHE HAS ALL SHE NEEDS FROM HERE.
AND NOW SHE JUST DOESN'T NEED US ANYMORE.
GOD.
LEX, THE GESTALT...IT'S TRANSFORMING AGAIN...
...WHAT'S HAPPENING TO IT?
I...I HAVE NO IDEA.
HOW DO WE STOP IT?
I...I HAVE NO IDEA.
USELESS.
SKULL! BIZARRE...S!
YOU KNOW HOW TO NAVIGATE THAT MONSTROSITY?

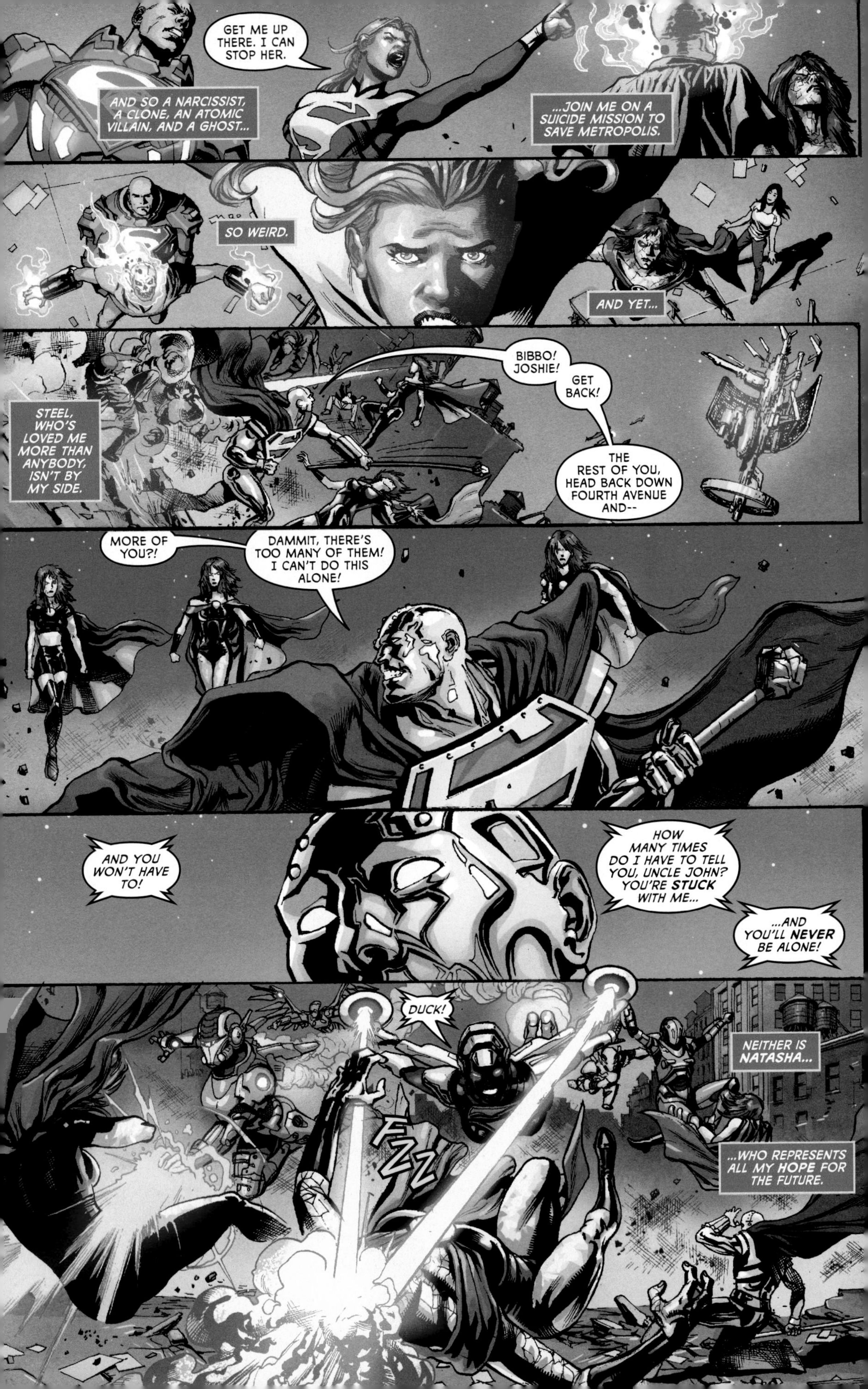
GET ME UP THERE. I CAN STOP HER.
AND SO A NARCISSIST, A CLONE, AN ATOMIC VILLAIN, AND A GHOST...
...JOIN ME ON A SUICIDE MISSION TO SAVE METROPOLIS.
SO WEIRD.
AND YET...
STEEL, WHO'S LOVED ME MORE THAN ANYBODY, ISN'T BY MY SIDE.
BIBBO! JOSHIE!
GET BACK!
THE REST OF YOU, HEAD BACK DOWN FOURTH AVENUE AND--
MORE OF YOU?!
DAMMIT, THERE'S TOO MANY OF THEM! I CAN'T DO THIS ALONE!
AND YOU WON'T HAVE TO!
HOW MANY TIMES DO I HAVE TO TELL YOU, UNCLE JOHN? YOU'RE STUCK WITH ME...
...AND YOU'LL NEVER BE ALONE!
DUCK!
FZZ
NEITHER IS NATASHA...
...WHO REPRESENTS ALL MY HOPE FOR THE FUTURE.

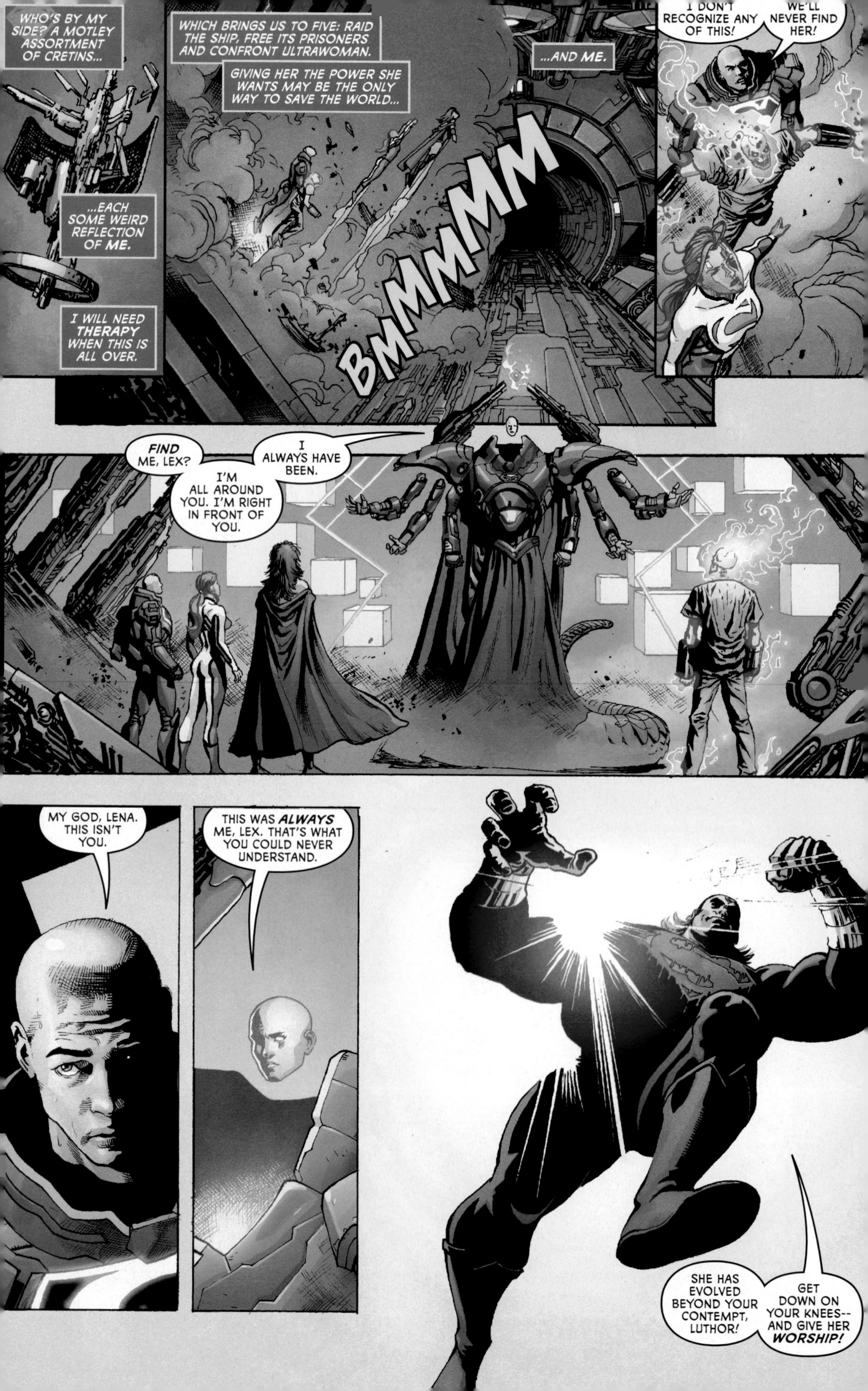
WHO'S BY MY SIDE? A MOTLEY ASSORTMENT OF CRETINS...
...EACH SOME WEIRD REFLECTION OF ME.
I WILL NEED THERAPY WHEN THIS IS ALL OVER.
WHICH BRINGS US TO FIVE: RAID THE SHIP, FREE ITS PRISONERS AND CONFRONT ULTRAWOMAN.
GIVING HER THE POWER SHE WANTS MAY BE THE ONLY WAY TO SAVE THE WORLD...
...AND ME.
BMMMMM
I DON'T RECOGNIZE ANY OF THIS!
WE'LL NEVER FIND HER!
FIND ME, LEX?
I'M ALL AROUND YOU. I'M RIGHT IN FRONT OF YOU.
I ALWAYS HAVE BEEN.
MY GOD, LENA. THIS ISN'T YOU.
THIS WAS ALWAYS ME, LEX. THAT'S WHAT YOU COULD NEVER UNDERSTAND.
SHE HAS EVOLVED BEYOND YOUR CONTEMPT, LUTHOR!
GET DOWN ON YOUR KNEES-- AND GIVE HER WORSHIP!

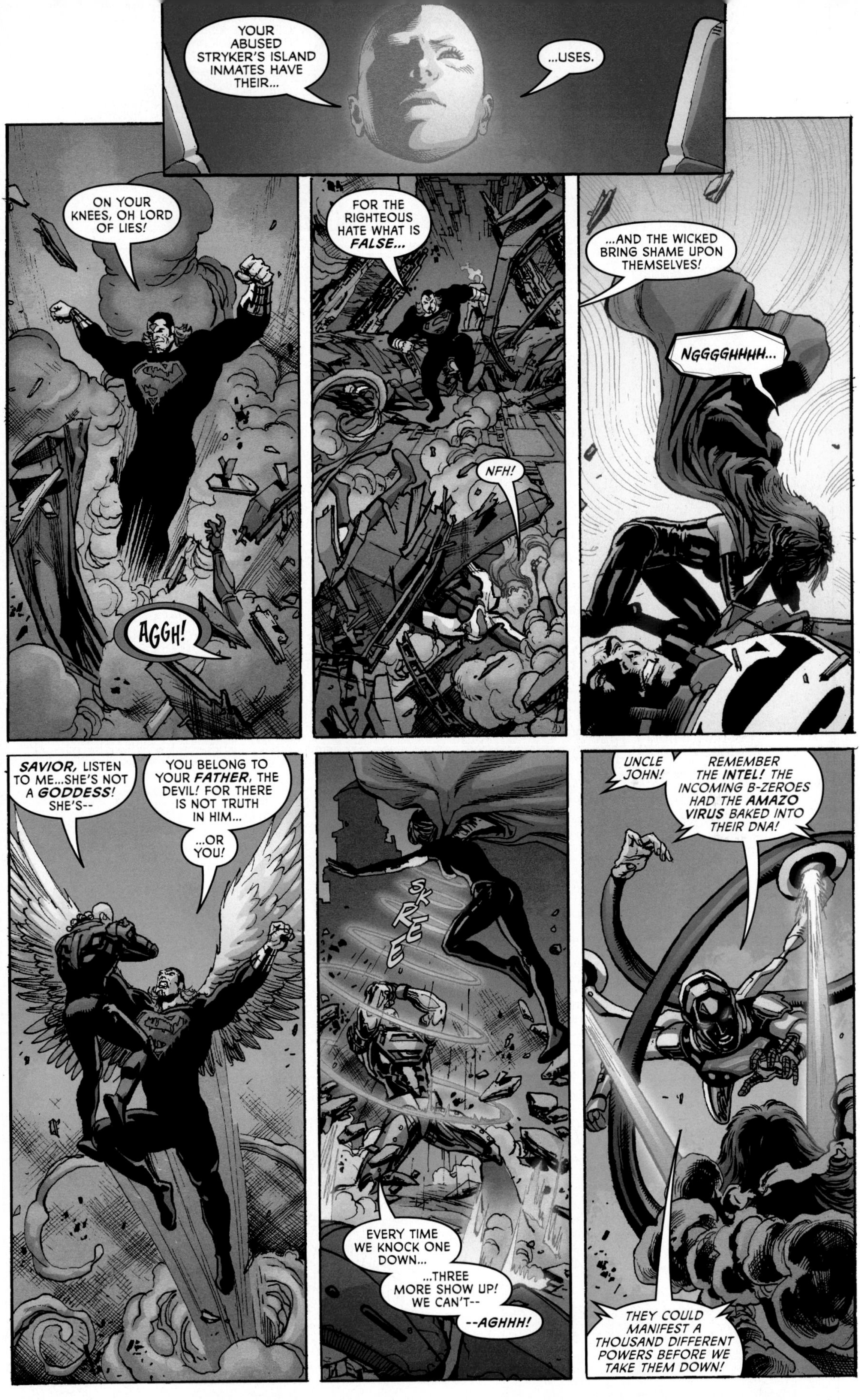
YOUR ABUSED STRYKER'S ISLAND INMATES HAVE THEIR...
...USES.
ON YOUR KNEES, OH LORD OF LIES!
AGGH!
FOR THE RIGHTEOUS HATE WHAT IS FALSE...
NFH!
...AND THE WICKED BRING SHAME UPON THEMSELVES!
NGGGGHHHH...
SAVIOR, LISTEN TO ME...SHE'S NOT A GODDESS! SHE'S--
YOU BELONG TO YOUR FATHER, THE DEVIL! FOR THERE IS NOT TRUTH IN HIM...
...OR YOU!
SKREEE
EVERY TIME WE KNOCK ONE DOWN...
...THREE MORE SHOW UP! WE CAN'T--
--AGHHH!
UNCLE JOHN!
REMEMBER THE INTEL! THE INCOMING B-ZEROES HAD THE AMAZO VIRUS BAKED INTO THEIR DNA!
THEY COULD MANIFEST A THOUSAND DIFFERENT POWERS BEFORE WE TAKE THEM DOWN!

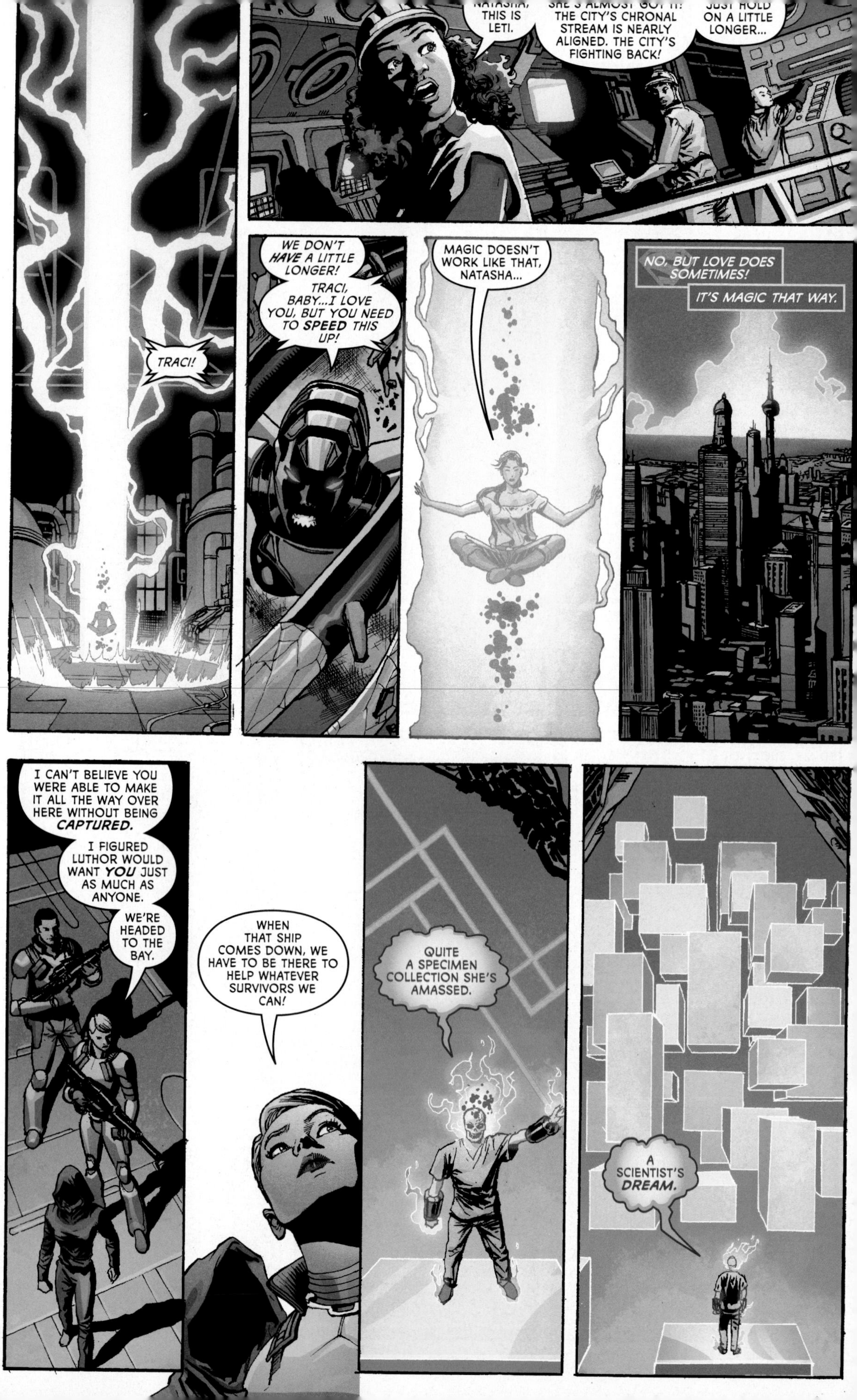
THIS IS LETI.
THE CITY'S CHRONAL STREAM IS NEARLY ALIGNED. THE CITY'S FIGHTING BACK!
ON A LITTLE LONGER...
TRACI!
WE DON'T HAVE A LITTLE LONGER!
TRACI, BABY...I LOVE YOU, BUT YOU NEED TO SPEED THIS UP!
MAGIC DOESN'T WORK LIKE THAT, NATASHA...
NO, BUT LOVE DOES SOMETIMES!
IT'S MAGIC THAT WAY.
I CAN'T BELIEVE YOU WERE ABLE TO MAKE IT ALL THE WAY OVER HERE WITHOUT BEING CAPTURED.
I FIGURED LUTHOR WOULD WANT YOU JUST AS MUCH AS ANYONE.
WE'RE HEADED TO THE BAY.
WHEN THAT SHIP COMES DOWN, WE HAVE TO BE THERE TO HELP WHATEVER SURVIVORS WE CAN!
QUITE A SPECIMEN COLLECTION SHE'S AMASSED.
A SCIENTIST'S DREAM.

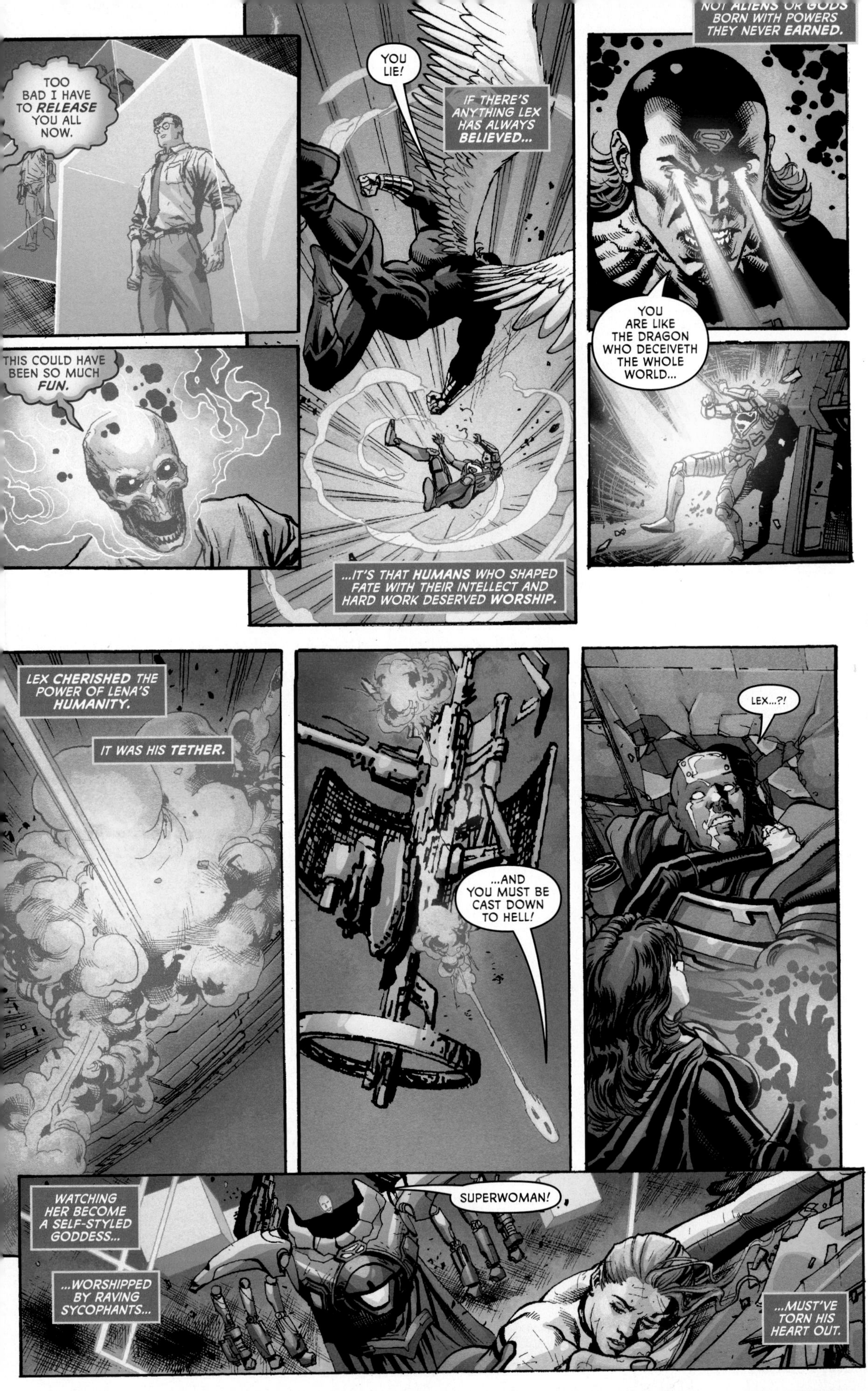
NOT ALIENS OR GODS BORN WITH POWERS THEY NEVER EARNED.
TOO BAD I HAVE TO RELEASE YOU ALL NOW.
THIS COULD HAVE BEEN SO MUCH FUN.
YOU LIE!
IF THERE'S ANYTHING LEX HAS ALWAYS BELIEVED...
...IT'S THAT HUMANS WHO SHAPED FATE WITH THEIR INTELLECT AND HARD WORK DESERVED WORSHIP.
YOU ARE LIKE THE DRAGON WHO DECEIVETH THE WHOLE WORLD...
LEX CHERISHED THE POWER OF LENA'S HUMANITY.
IT WAS HIS TETHER.
...AND YOU MUST BE CAST DOWN TO HELL!
LEX...?!
WATCHING HER BECOME A SELF-STYLED GODDESS...
SUPERWOMAN!
...WORSHIPPED BY RAVING SYCOPHANTS...
...MUST'VE TORN HIS HEART OUT.

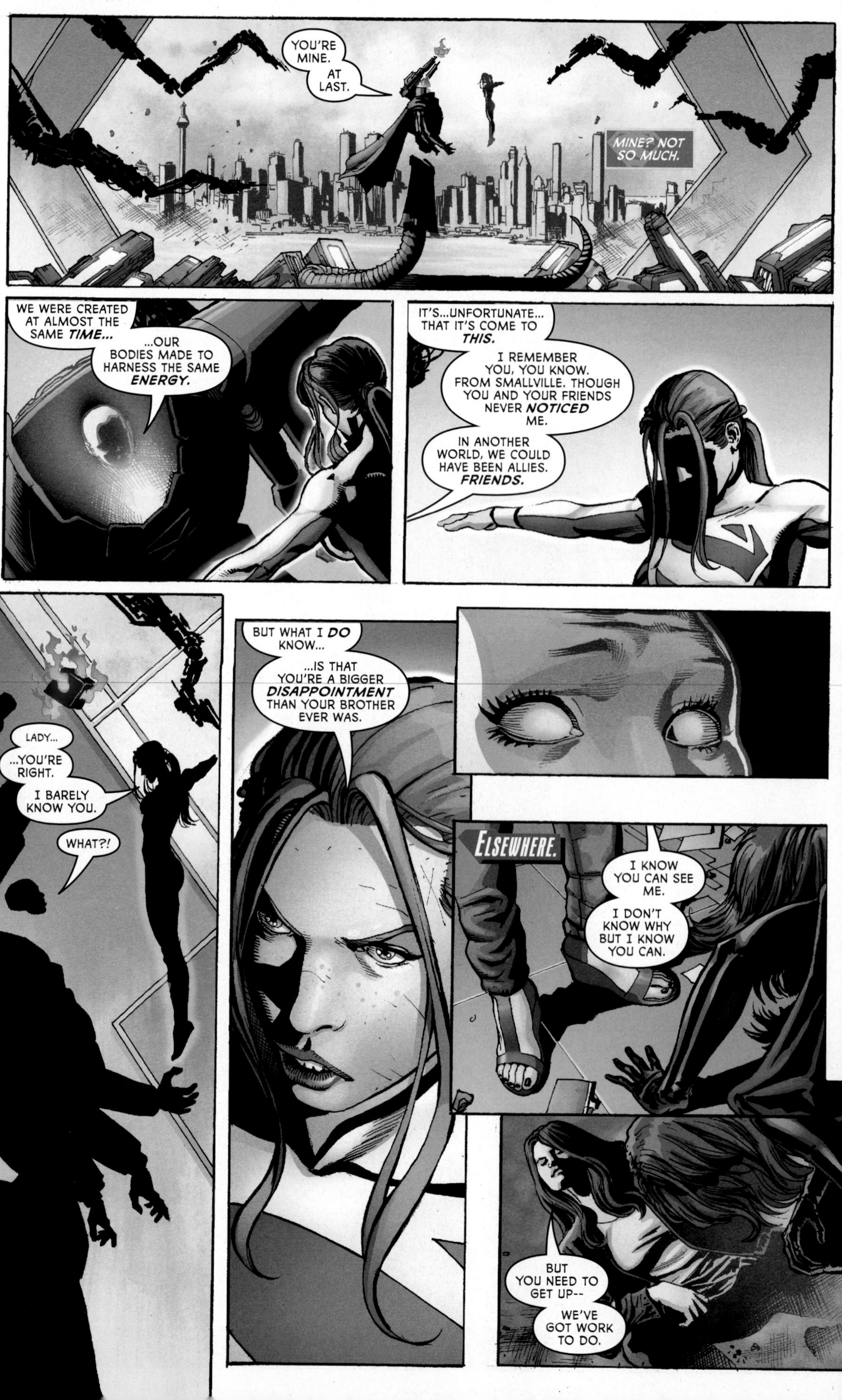

YOU'RE MINE.
AT LAST.
MINE? NOT SO MUCH.
WE WERE CREATED AT ALMOST THE SAME TIME...
...OUR BODIES MADE TO HARNESS THE SAME ENERGY.
IT'S...UNFORTUNATE... THAT IT'S COME TO THIS.
I REMEMBER YOU, YOU KNOW. FROM SMALLVILLE. THOUGH YOU AND YOUR FRIENDS NEVER NOTICED ME.
IN ANOTHER WORLD, WE COULD HAVE BEEN ALLIES. FRIENDS.
LADY...
...YOU'RE RIGHT.
I BARELY KNOW YOU.
WHAT?!
BUT WHAT I DO KNOW...
...IS THAT YOU'RE A BIGGER DISAPPOINTMENT THAN YOUR BROTHER EVER WAS.
ELSEWHERE.
I KNOW YOU CAN SEE ME.
I DON'T KNOW WHY BUT I KNOW YOU CAN.
BUT YOU NEED TO GET UP--
WE'VE GOT WORK TO DO.

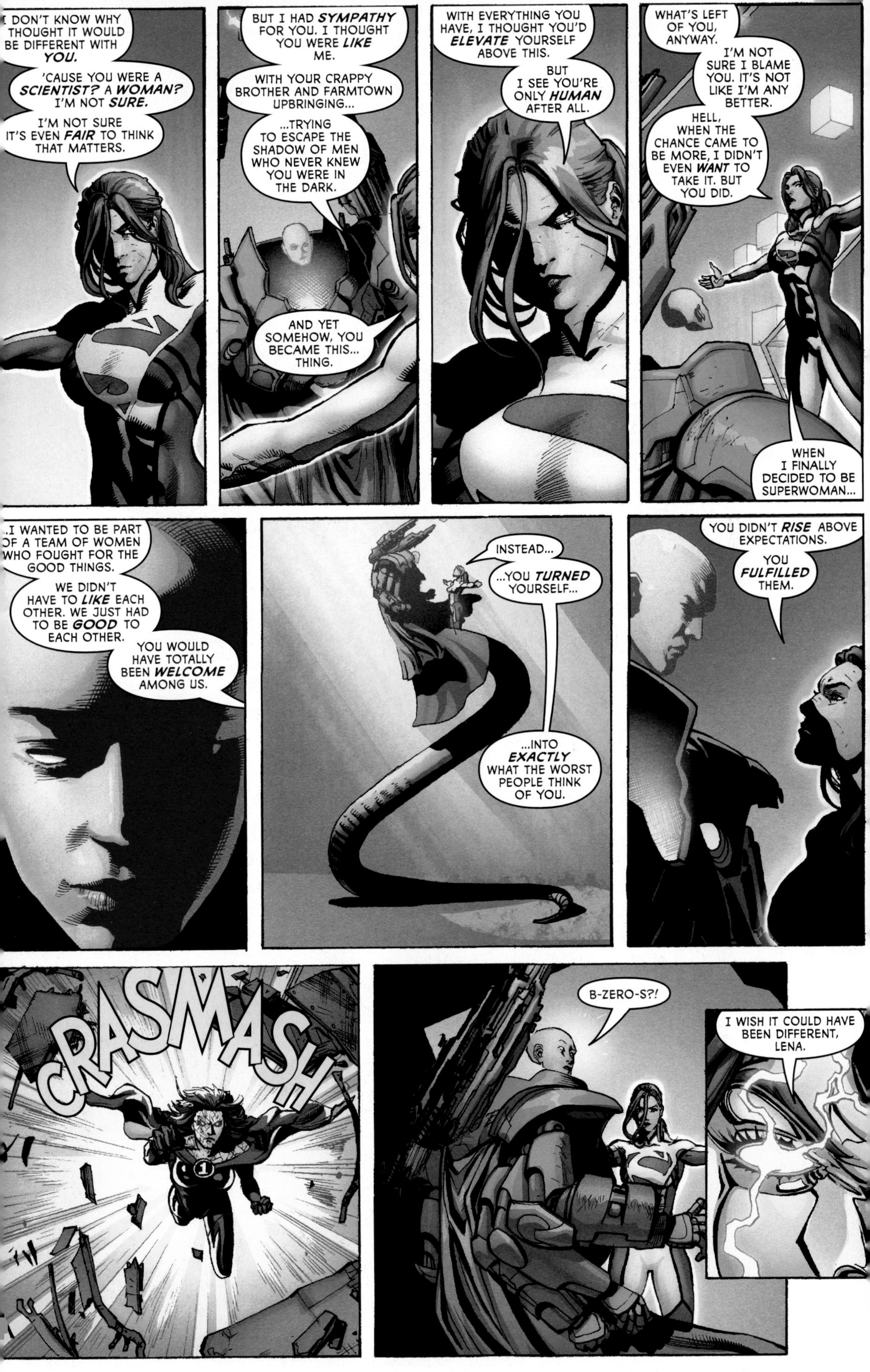
I DON'T KNOW WHY I THOUGHT IT WOULD BE DIFFERENT WITH YOU.
'CAUSE YOU WERE A SCIENTIST? A WOMAN? I'M NOT SURE.
I'M NOT SURE IT'S EVEN FAIR TO THINK THAT MATTERS.
BUT I HAD SYMPATHY FOR YOU. I THOUGHT YOU WERE LIKE ME.
WITH YOUR CRAPPY BROTHER AND FARMTOWN UPBRINGING...
...TRYING TO ESCAPE THE SHADOW OF MEN WHO NEVER KNEW YOU WERE IN THE DARK.
AND YET SOMEHOW, YOU BECAME THIS... THING.
WITH EVERYTHING YOU HAVE, I THOUGHT YOU'D ELEVATE YOURSELF ABOVE THIS.
BUT I SEE YOU'RE ONLY HUMAN AFTER ALL.
WHAT'S LEFT OF YOU, ANYWAY.
I'M NOT SURE I BLAME YOU. IT'S NOT LIKE I'M ANY BETTER.
HELL, WHEN THE CHANCE CAME TO BE MORE, I DIDN'T EVEN WANT TO TAKE IT. BUT YOU DID.
WHEN I FINALLY DECIDED TO BE SUPERWOMAN...
...I WANTED TO BE PART OF A TEAM OF WOMEN WHO FOUGHT FOR THE GOOD THINGS.
WE DIDN'T HAVE TO LIKE EACH OTHER. WE JUST HAD TO BE GOOD TO EACH OTHER.
YOU WOULD HAVE TOTALLY BEEN WELCOME AMONG US.
INSTEAD...
...YOU TURNED YOURSELF...
...INTO EXACTLY WHAT THE WORST PEOPLE THINK OF YOU.
YOU DIDN'T RISE ABOVE EXPECTATIONS.
YOU FULFILLED THEM.
CRASMASH
B-ZERO-S?!
I WISH IT COULD HAVE BEEN DIFFERENT, LENA.

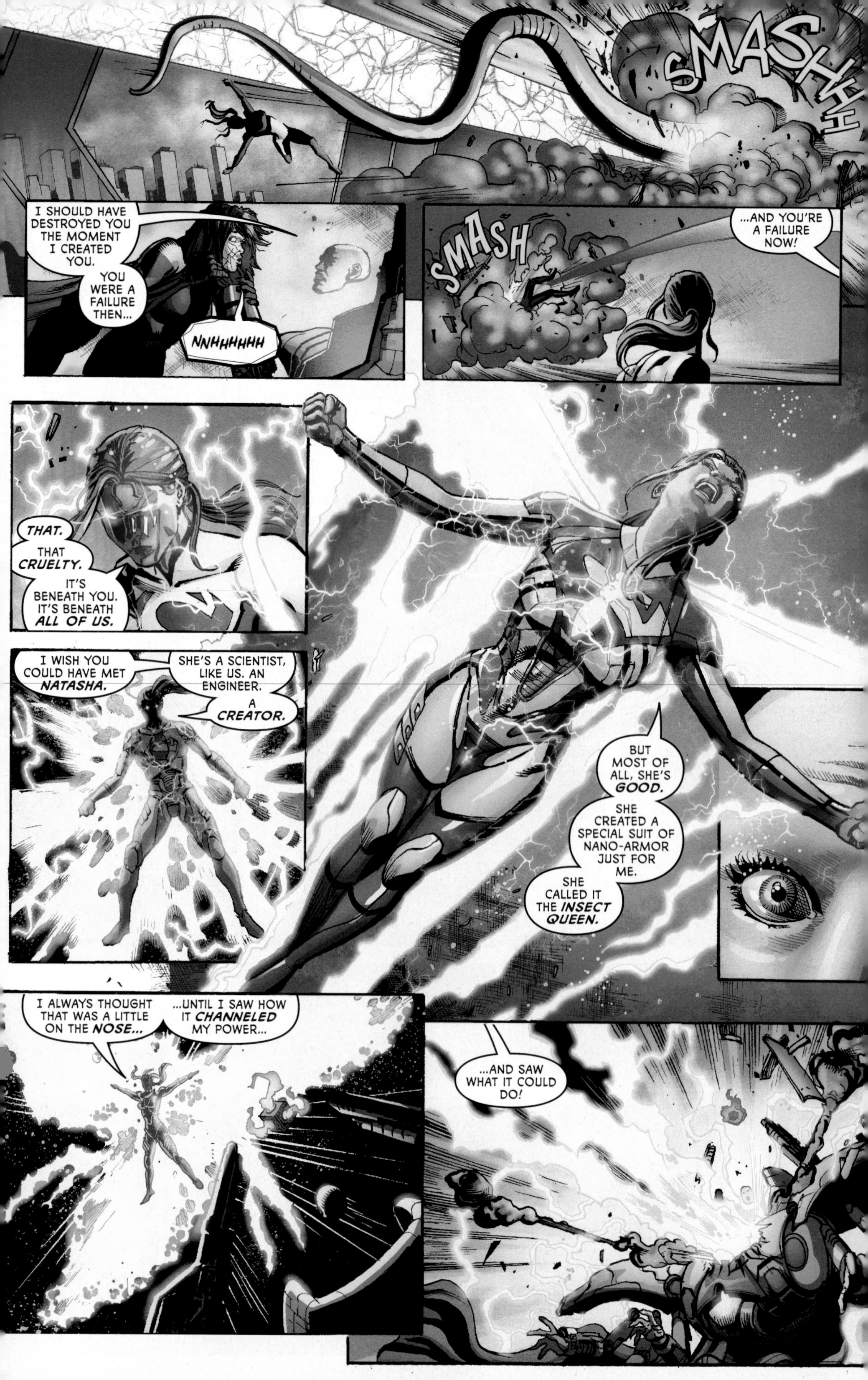
SMASHHH
I SHOULD HAVE DESTROYED YOU THE MOMENT I CREATED YOU.
YOU WERE A FAILURE THEN...
NNHHHHHH
SMASH
...AND YOU'RE A FAILURE NOW!
THAT.
THAT CRUELTY.
IT'S BENEATH YOU. IT'S BENEATH ALL OF US.
I WISH YOU COULD HAVE MET NATASHA.
SHE'S A SCIENTIST, LIKE US. AN ENGINEER.
A CREATOR.
BUT MOST OF ALL, SHE'S GOOD.
SHE CREATED A SPECIAL SUIT OF NANO-ARMOR JUST FOR ME.
SHE CALLED IT THE INSECT QUEEN.
I ALWAYS THOUGHT THAT WAS A LITTLE ON THE NOSE...
...UNTIL I SAW HOW IT CHANNELED MY POWER...
...AND SAW WHAT IT COULD DO!

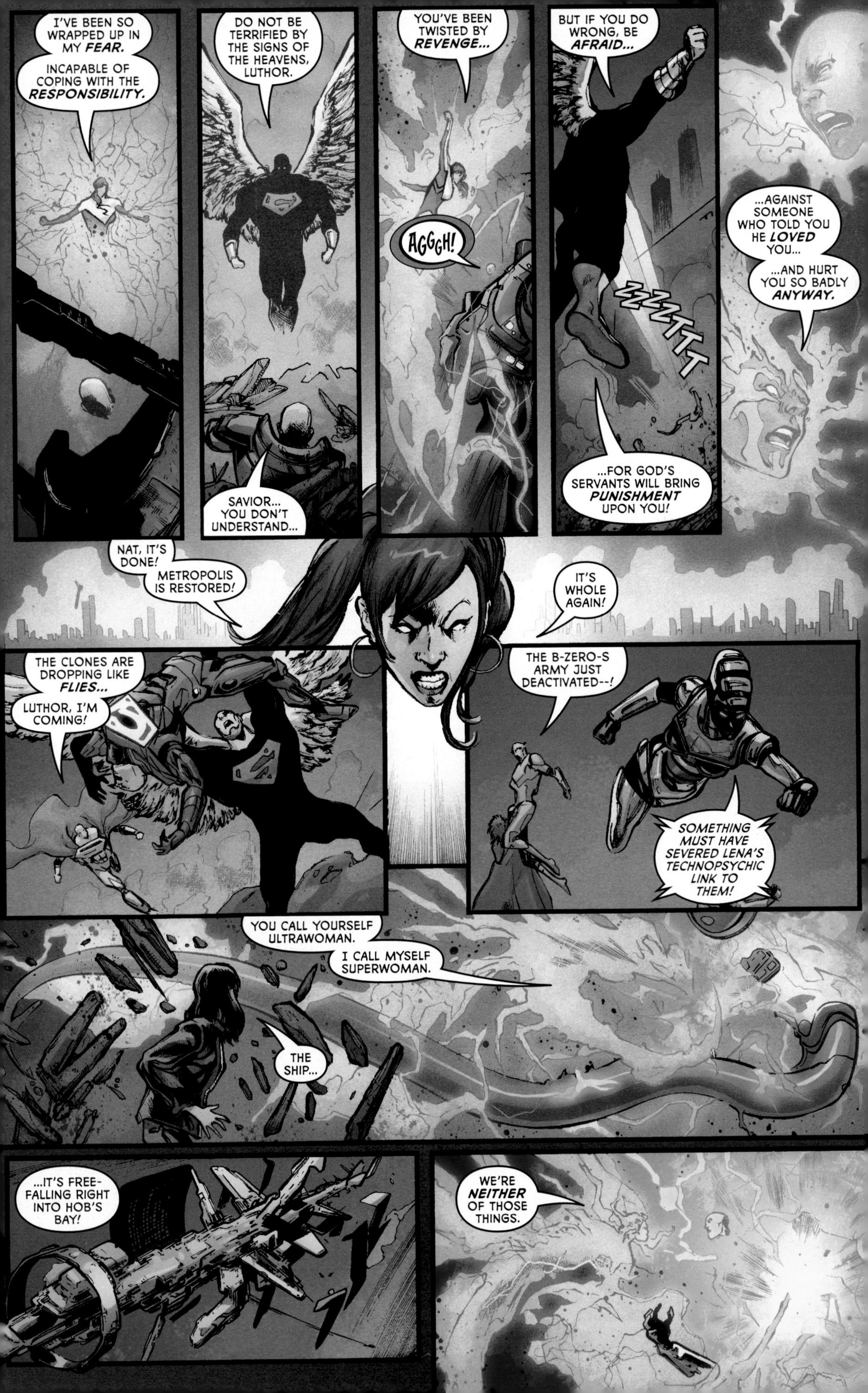
I'VE BEEN SO WRAPPED UP IN MY FEAR.
INCAPABLE OF COPING WITH THE RESPONSIBILITY.
DO NOT BE TERRIFIED BY THE SIGNS OF THE HEAVENS, LUTHOR.
SAVIOR... YOU DON'T UNDERSTAND...
YOU'VE BEEN TWISTED BY REVENGE...
AGGGH!
BUT IF YOU DO WRONG, BE AFRAID...
ZZZZTTT
...FOR GOD'S SERVANTS WILL BRING PUNISHMENT UPON YOU!
...AGAINST SOMEONE WHO TOLD YOU HE LOVED YOU...
...AND HURT YOU SO BADLY ANYWAY.
NAT, IT'S DONE!
METROPOLIS IS RESTORED!
IT'S WHOLE AGAIN!
THE CLONES ARE DROPPING LIKE FLIES...
LUTHOR, I'M COMING!
THE B-ZERO-S ARMY JUST DEACTIVATED--!
SOMETHING MUST HAVE SEVERED LENA'S TECHNOPSYCHIC LINK TO THEM!
YOU CALL YOURSELF ULTRAWOMAN.
I CALL MYSELF SUPERWOMAN.
THE SHIP...
...IT'S FREE-FALLING RIGHT INTO HOB'S BAY!
WE'RE NEITHER OF THOSE THINGS.

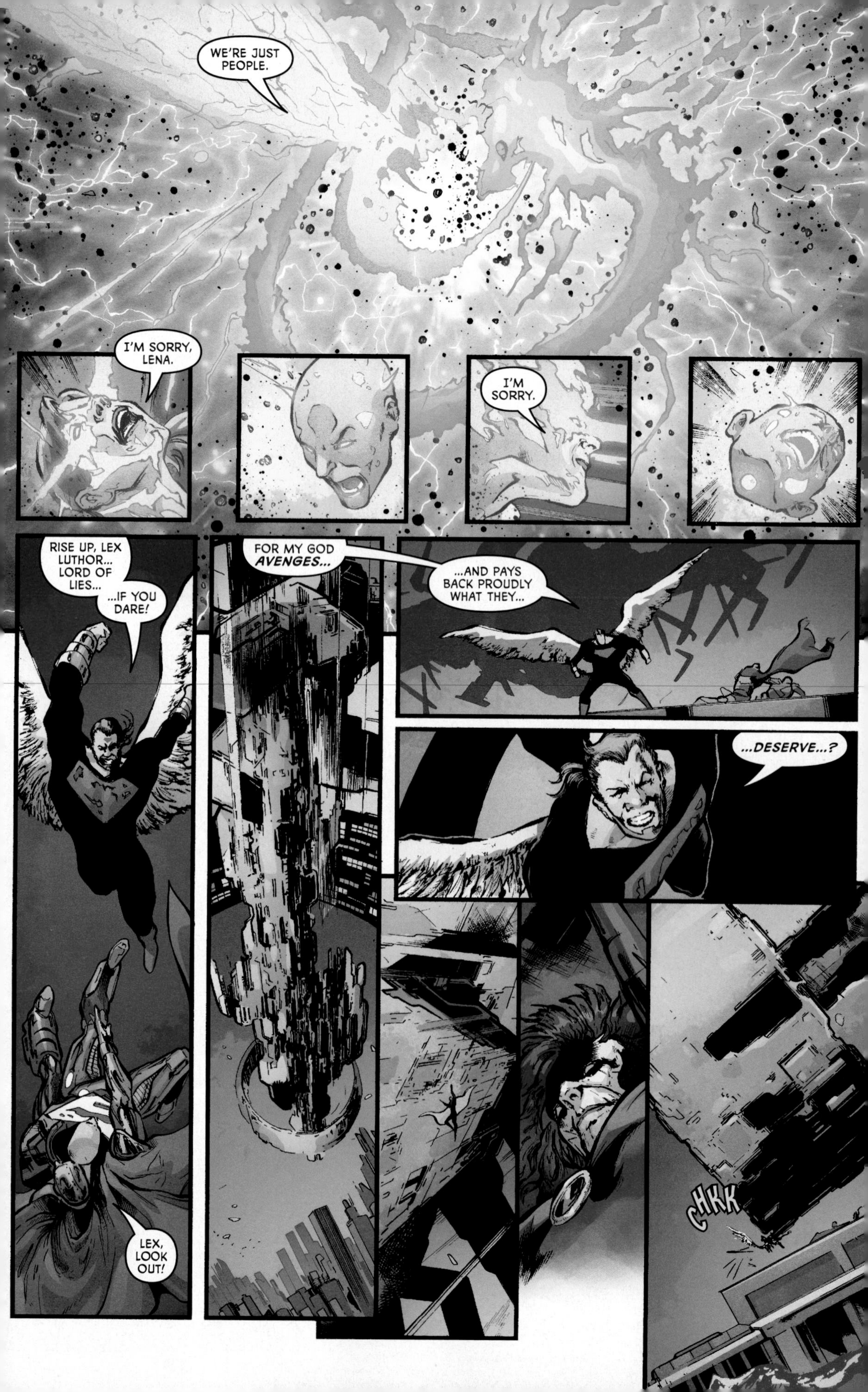
WE'RE JUST PEOPLE.
I'M SORRY, LENA.
I'M SORRY.
RISE UP, LEX LUTHOR... LORD OF LIES...
...IF YOU DARE!
LEX, LOOK OUT!
FOR MY GOD AVENGES...
...AND PAYS BACK PROUDLY WHAT THEY...
...DESERVE...?
CHKK

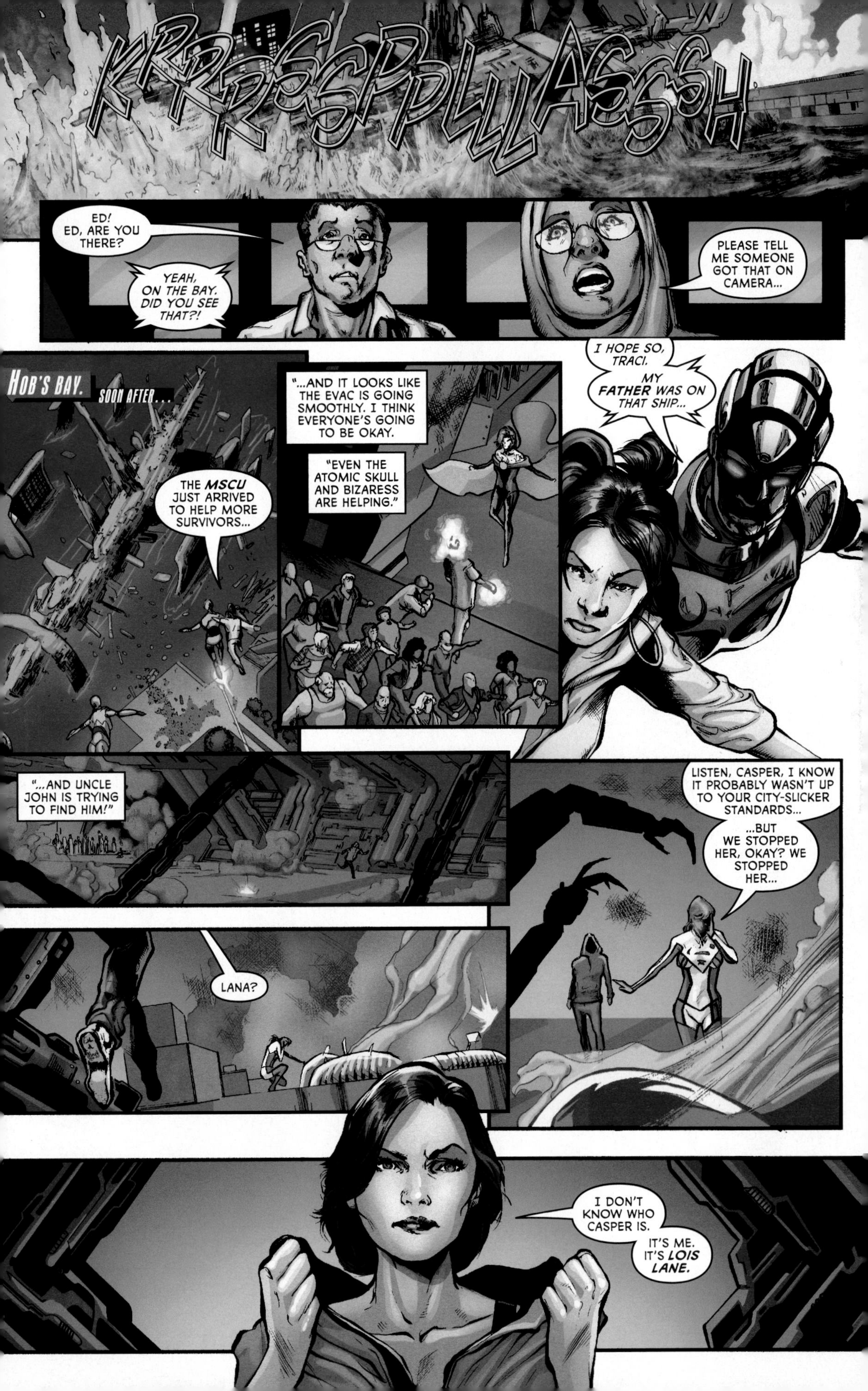
KRRRSSPPLLLASSSH
ED! ED, ARE YOU THERE?
YEAH, ON THE BAY. DID YOU SEE THAT?!
PLEASE TELL ME SOMEONE GOT THAT ON CAMERA...
HOB'S BAY. SOON AFTER...
THE MSCU JUST ARRIVED TO HELP MORE SURVIVORS...
"...AND IT LOOKS LIKE THE EVAC IS GOING SMOOTHLY. I THINK EVERYONE'S GOING TO BE OKAY.
"EVEN THE ATOMIC SKULL AND BIZARESS ARE HELPING."
I HOPE SO, TRACI.
MY FATHER WAS ON THAT SHIP...
"...AND UNCLE JOHN IS TRYING TO FIND HIM!"
LISTEN, CASPER, I KNOW IT PROBABLY WASN'T UP TO YOUR CITY-SLICKER STANDARDS...
...BUT WE STOPPED HER, OKAY? WE STOPPED HER...
LANA?
I DON'T KNOW WHO CASPER IS.
IT'S ME. IT'S LOIS LANE.

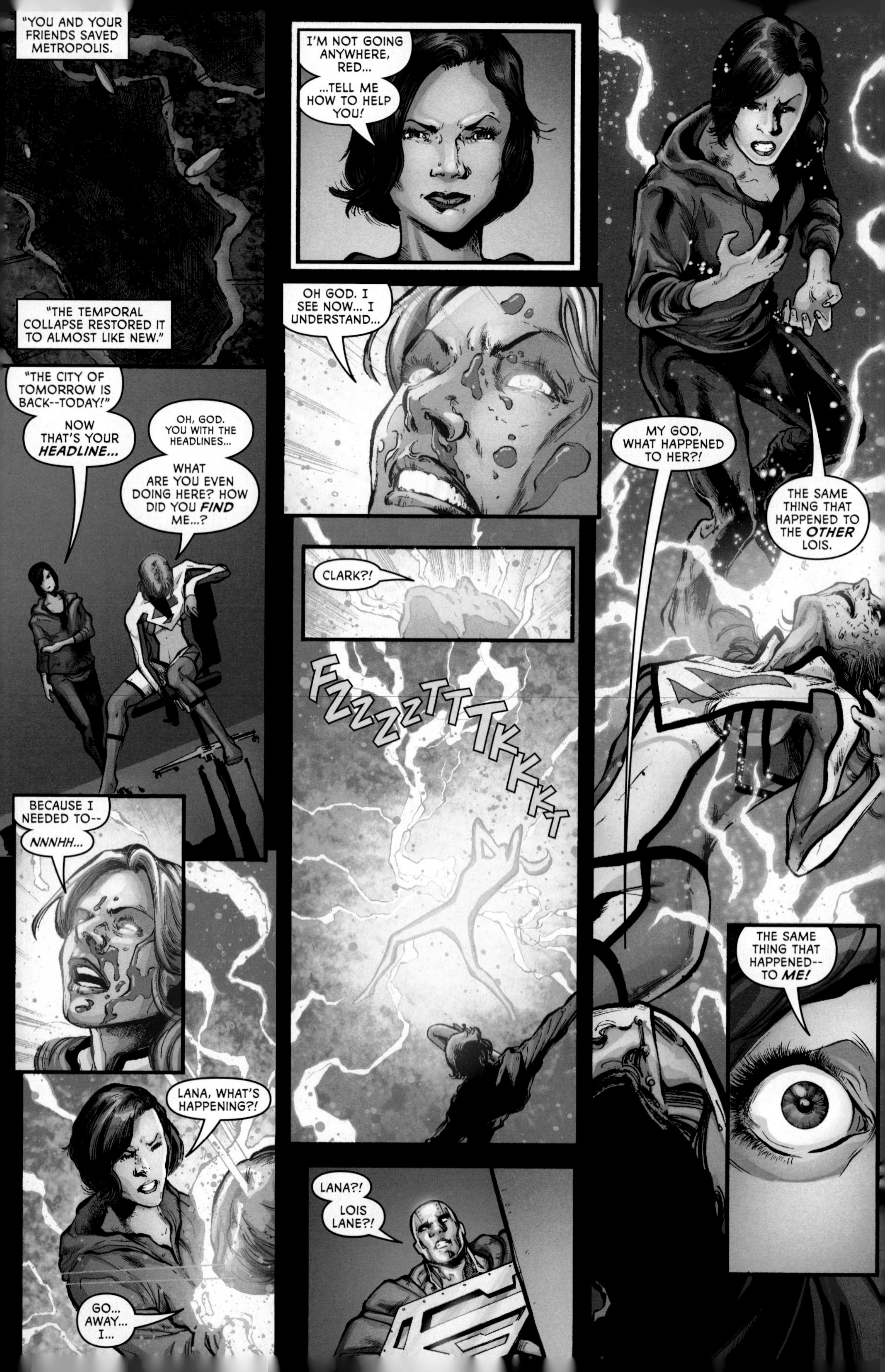
"YOU AND YOUR FRIENDS SAVED METROPOLIS.
"THE TEMPORAL COLLAPSE RESTORED IT TO ALMOST LIKE NEW."
"THE CITY OF TOMORROW IS BACK--TODAY!"
NOW THAT'S YOUR *HEADLINE...*
OH, GOD. YOU WITH THE HEADLINES...
WHAT ARE YOU EVEN DOING HERE? HOW DID YOU *FIND* ME...?
BECAUSE I NEEDED TO--
NNNHH...
LANA, WHAT'S HAPPENING?!
GO... AWAY... I...
I'M NOT GOING ANYWHERE, RED...
...TELL ME HOW TO HELP YOU!
OH GOD. I SEE NOW... I UNDERSTAND...
CLARK?!
FZZZZZTTTKKKKT
LANA?!
LOIS LANE?!
MY GOD, WHAT HAPPENED TO HER?!
THE SAME THING THAT HAPPENED TO THE *OTHER* LOIS.
THE SAME THING THAT HAPPENED-- TO *ME!*

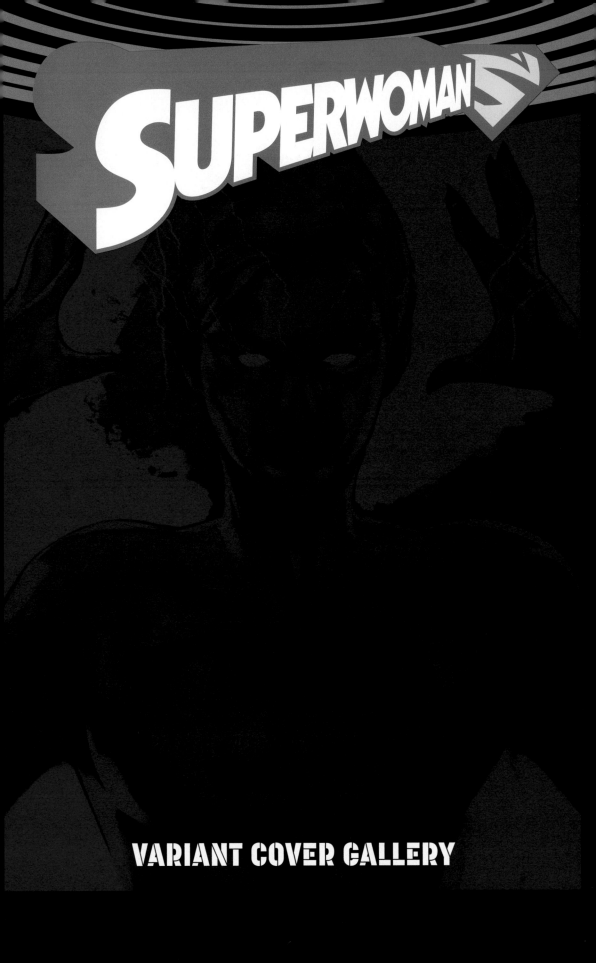

SUPERWOMAN

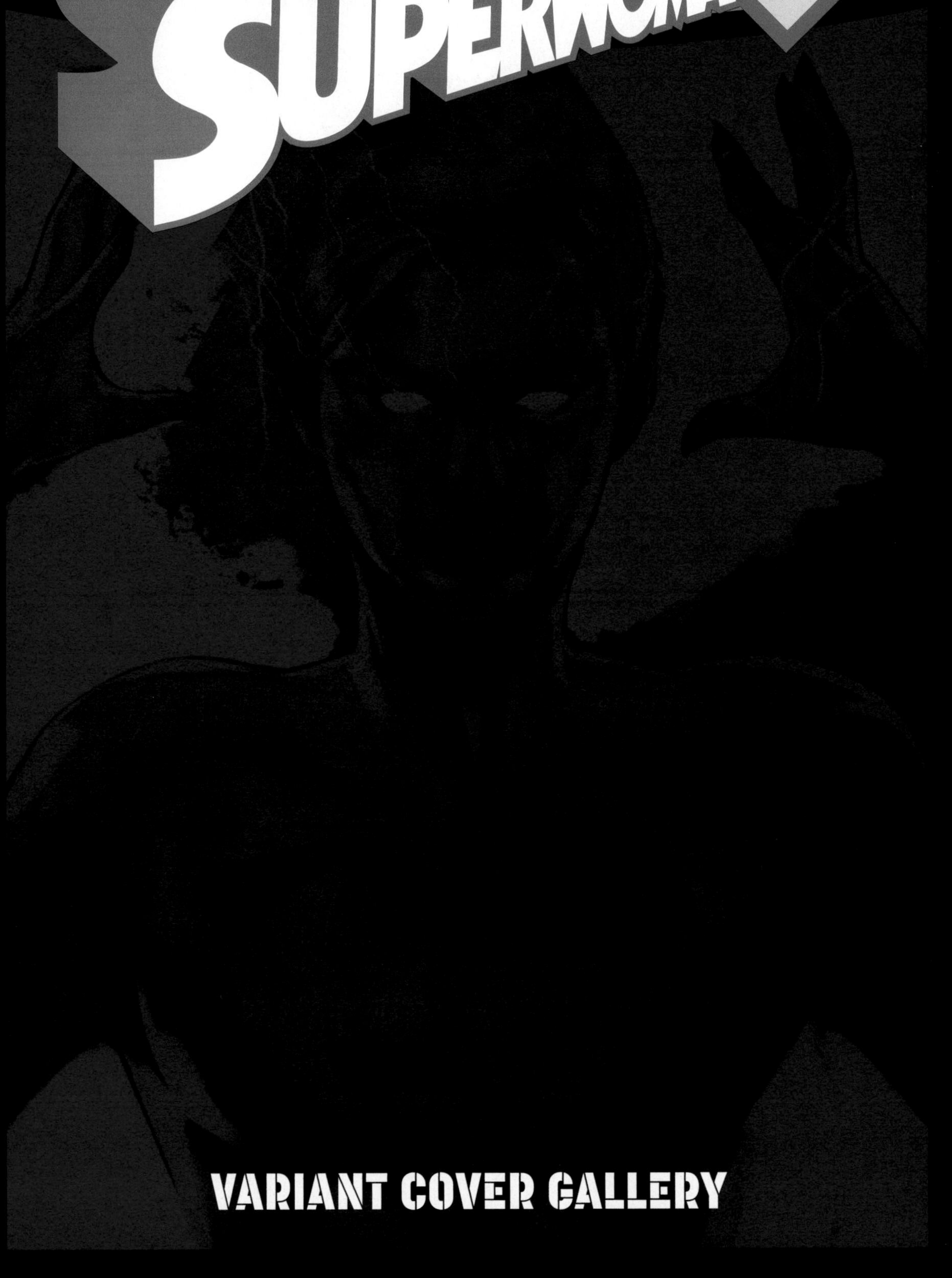

VARIANT COVER GALLERY

SUPERWOMAN #1 variant by TERRY DODSON and RACHEL DODSON

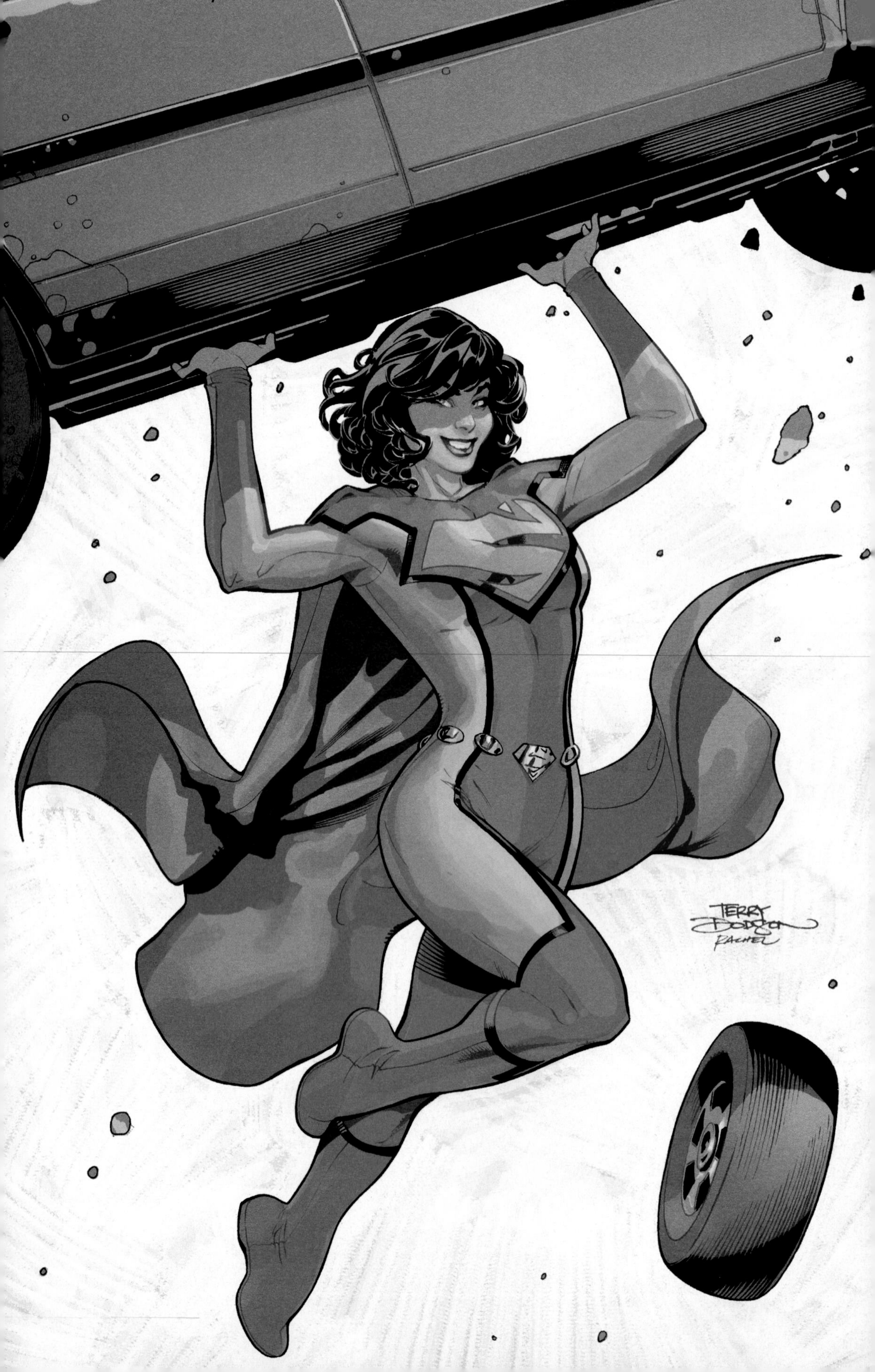
TERRY DODSON
RACHEL

SUPERWOMAN #2 variant by TERRY DODSON and RACHEL DODSON

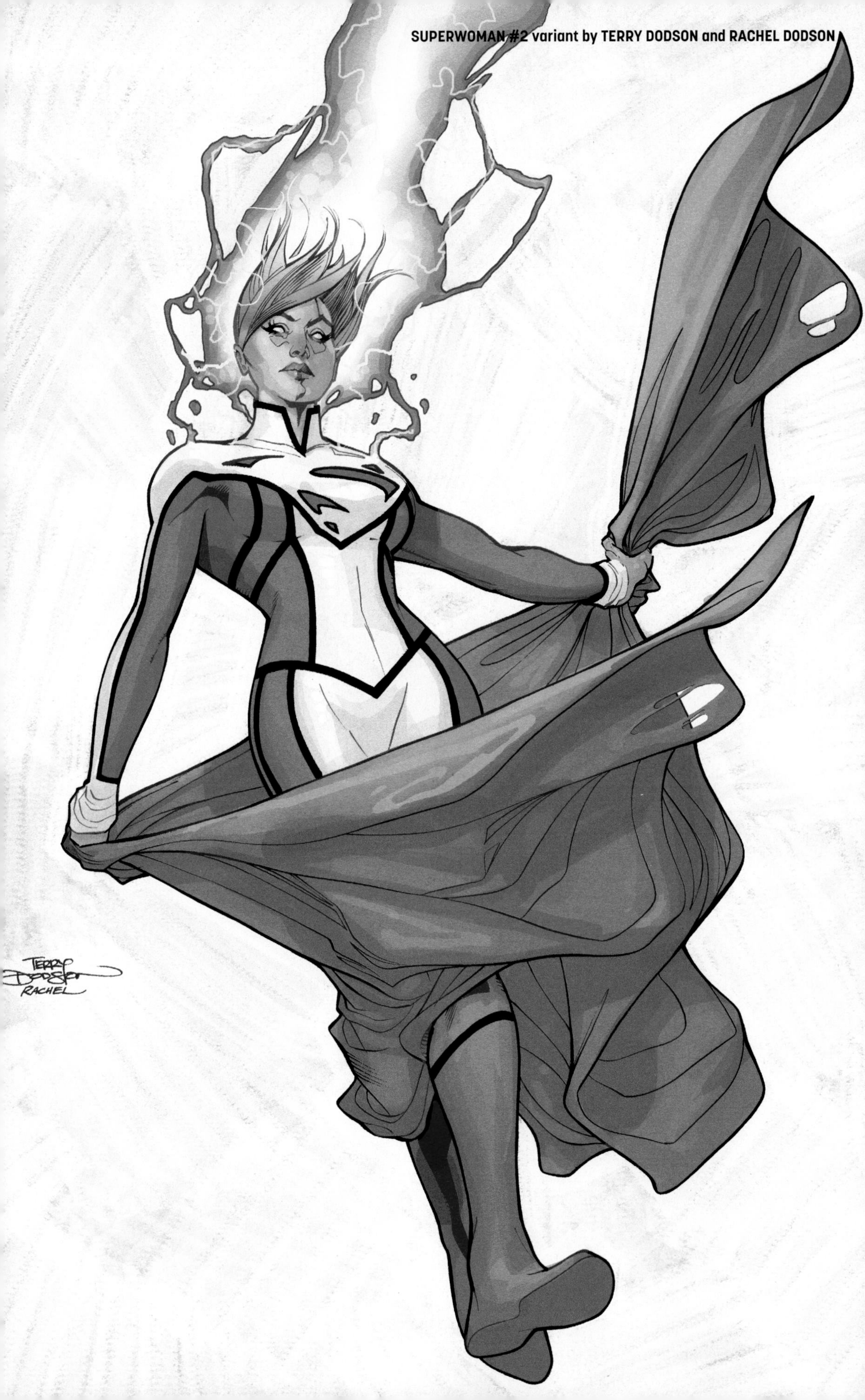
TERRY DODSON
RACHEL

SUPERWOMAN #3 variant by TERRY DODSON and RACHEL DODSON

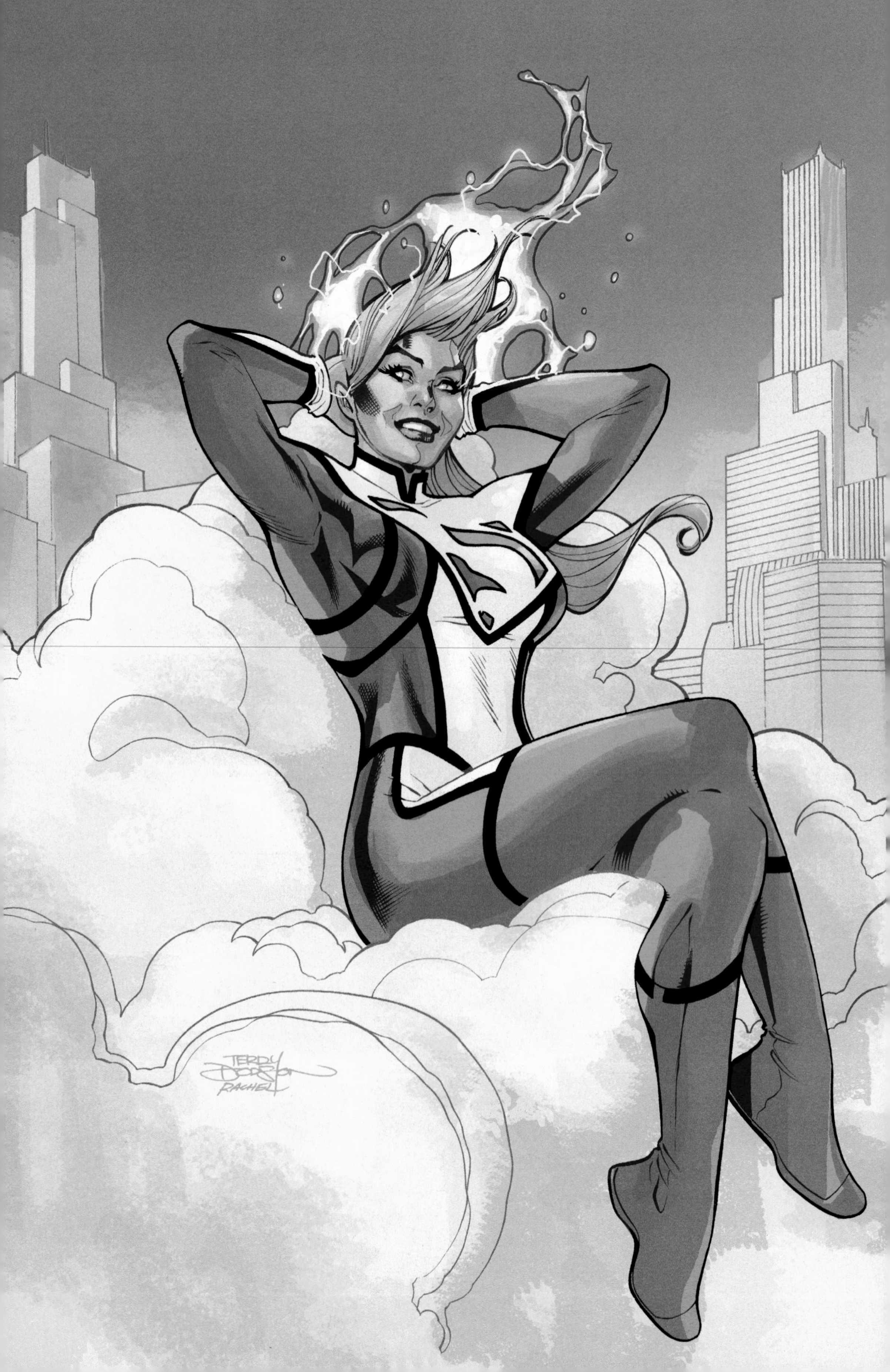
TERRY DODSON
RACHEL

SUPERWOMAN #4 variant by BEN OLIVER

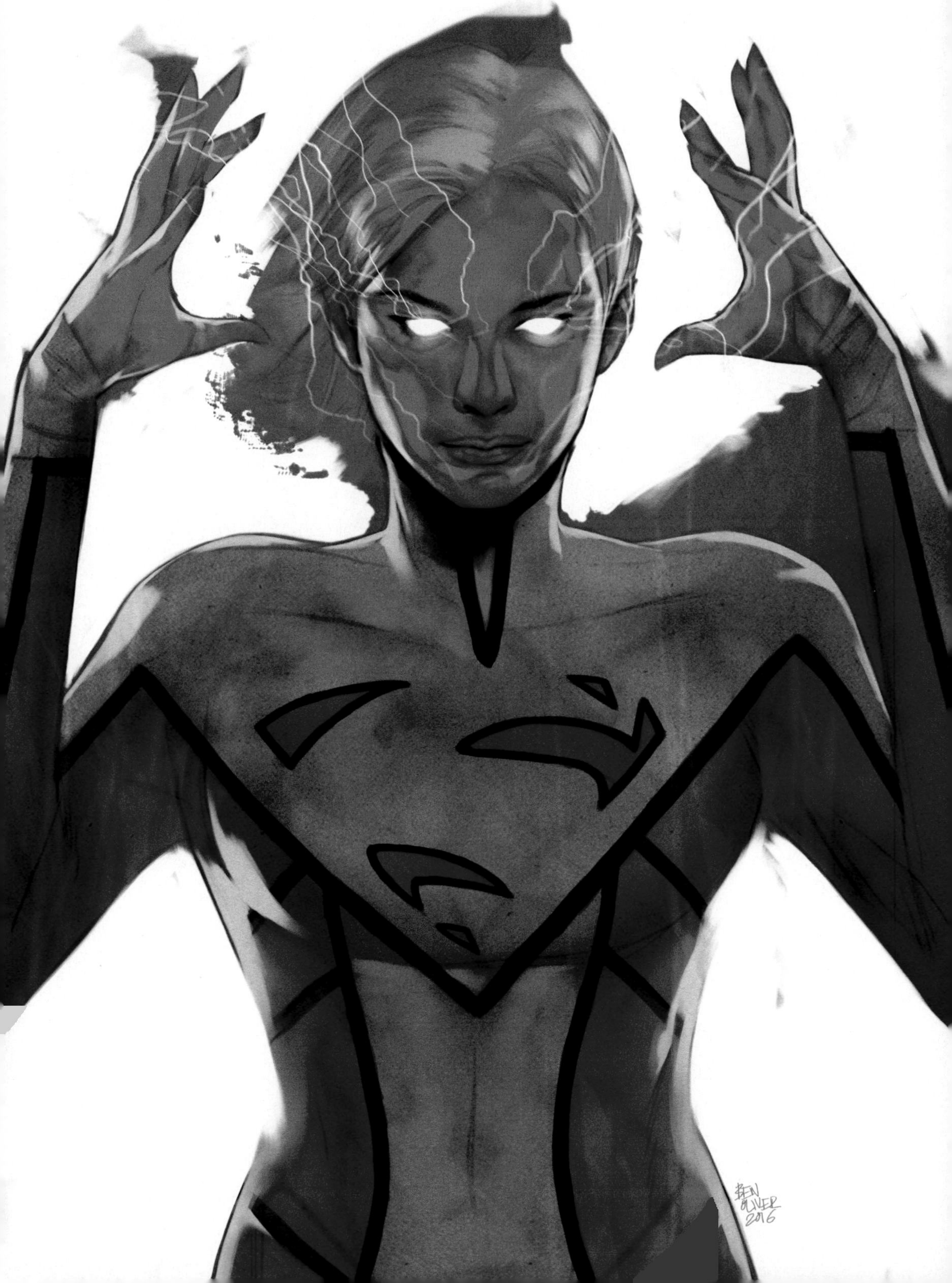
BEN
OLIVER
2016

SUPERWOMAN #5 variant by BEN OLIVER

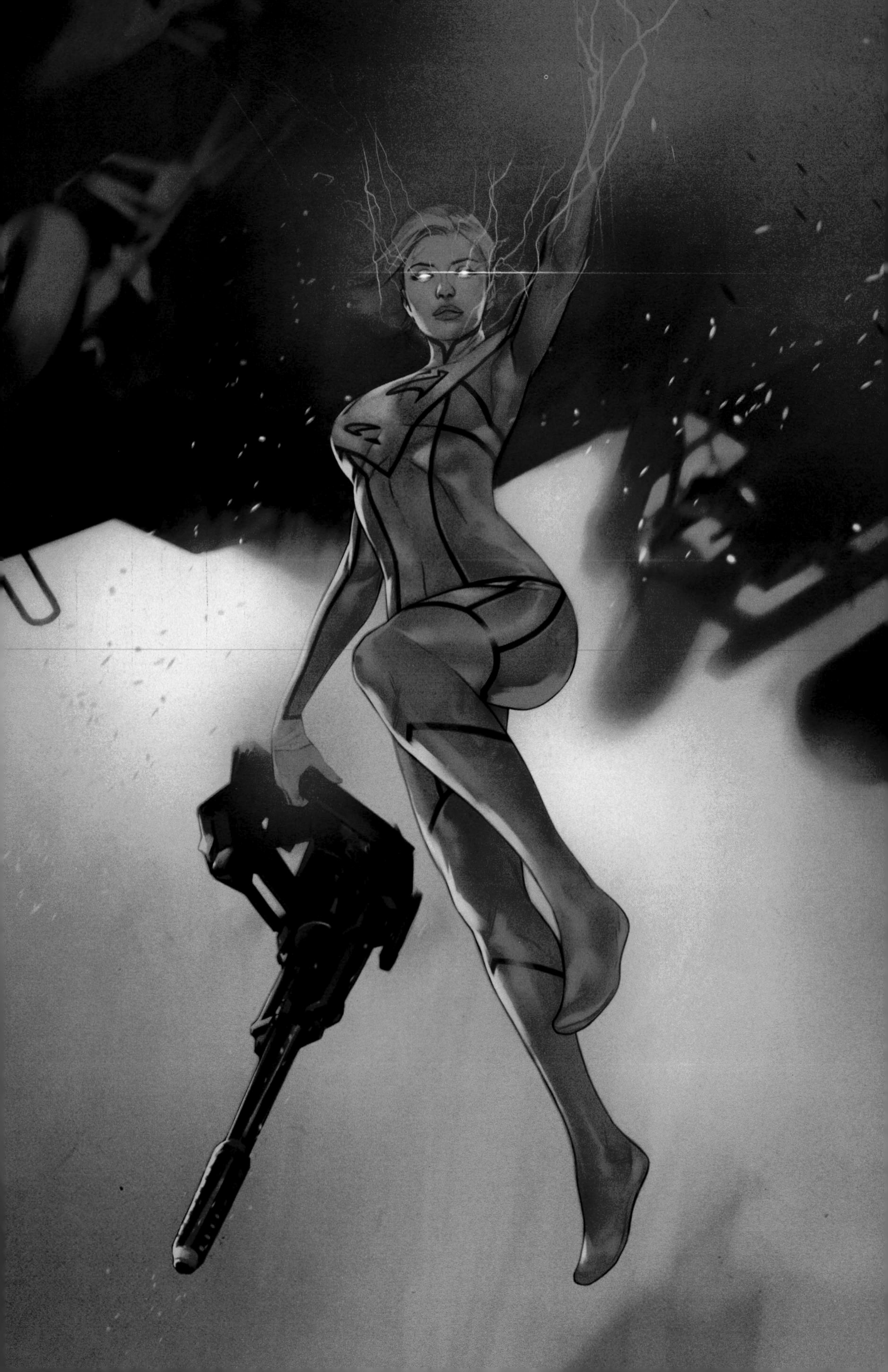

SUPERWOMAN #6 variant
by DREW JOHNSON and ROMULO FAJARDO JR.

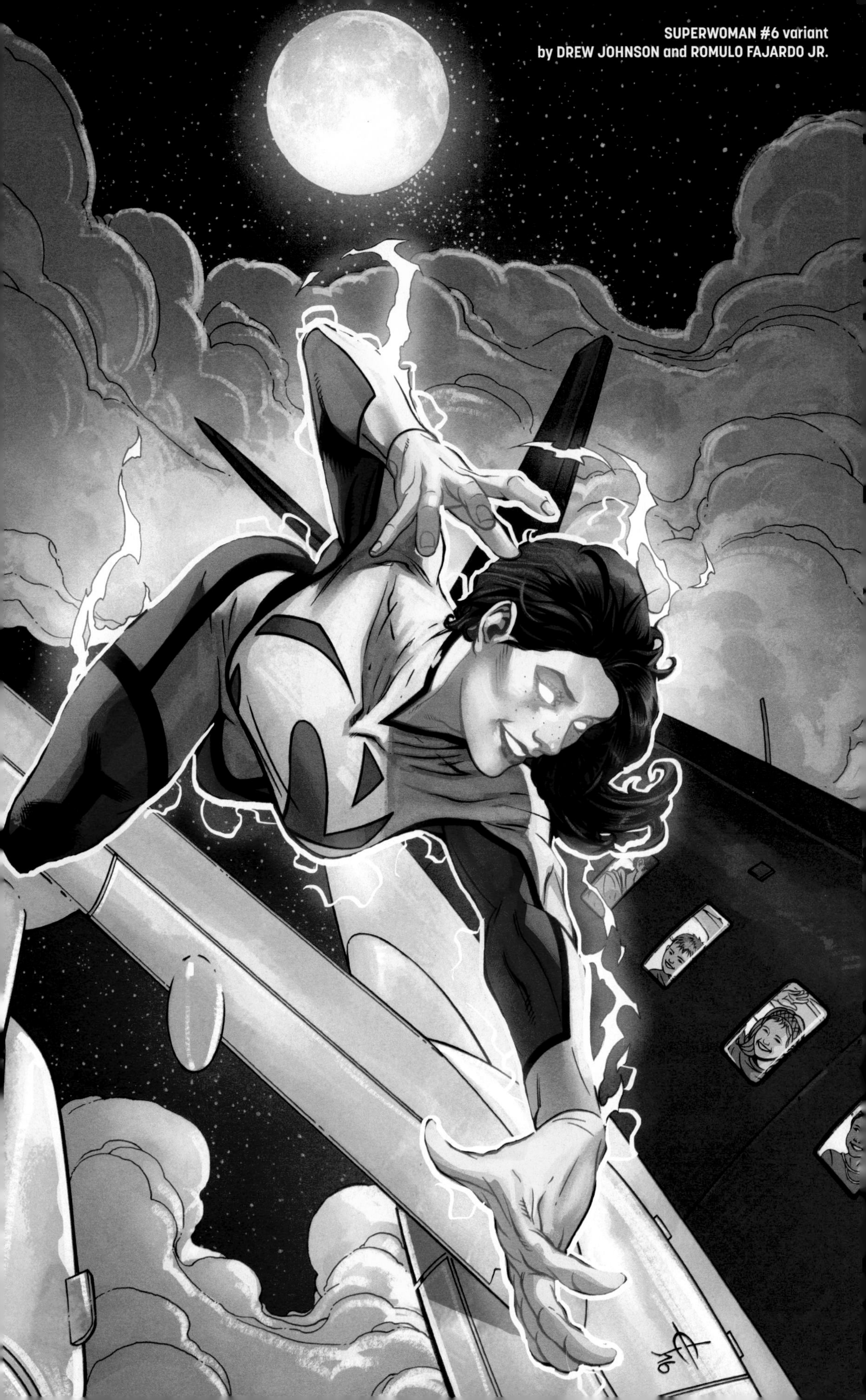

SUPERWOMAN #7 variant by ANDY KUBERT

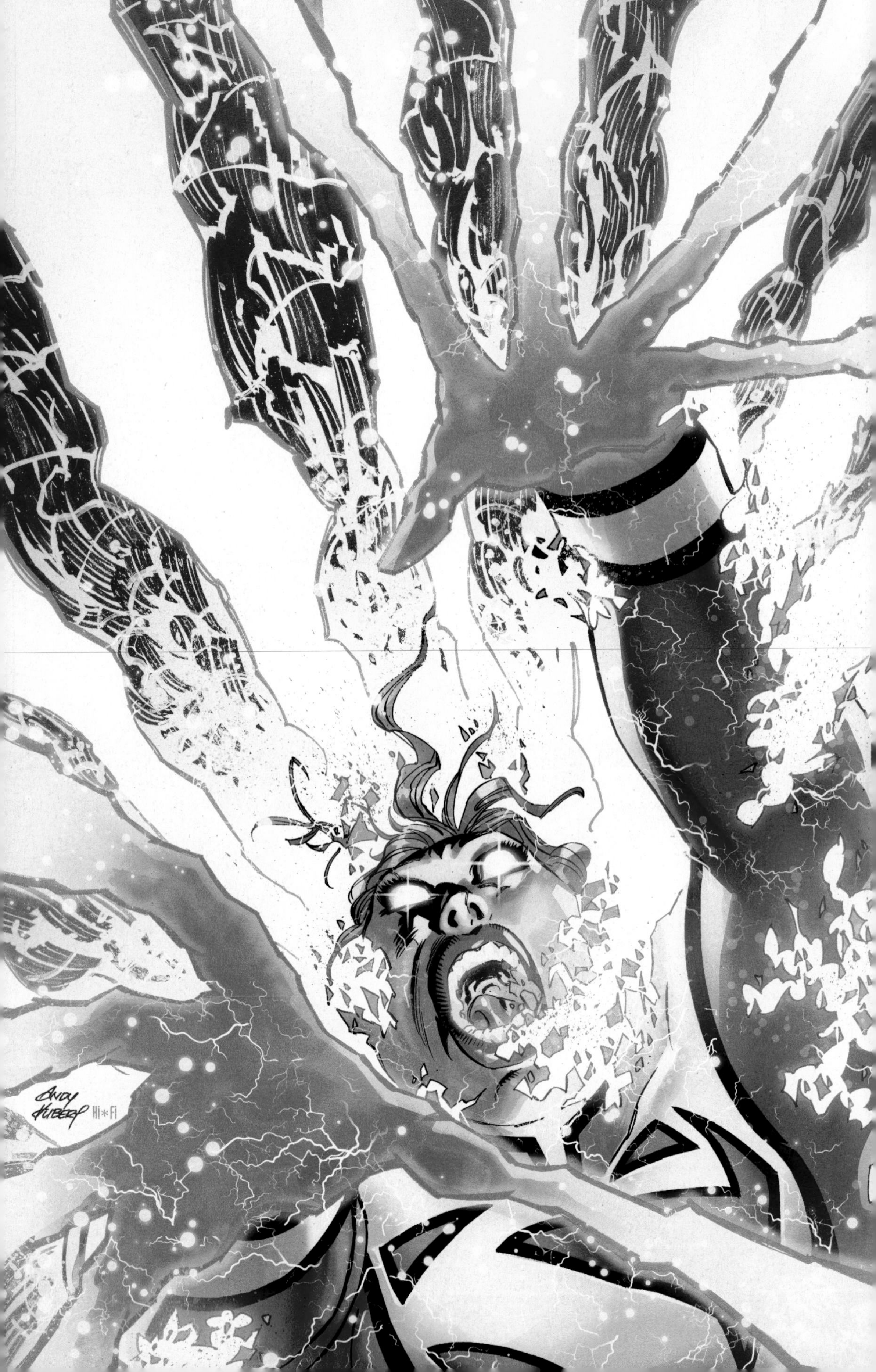

DC UNIVERSE REBIRTH

WONDER WOMAN

VOL. 1: THE LIES

GREG RUCKA with LIAM SHARP

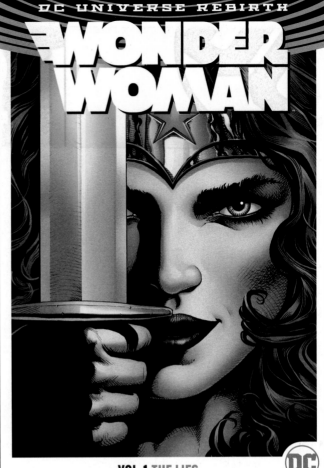

VOL.1 THE LIES
GREG RUCKA ∗ LIAM SHARP ∗ LAURA MARTIN

VOL.1 THE EXTINCTION MACHINES
BRYAN HITCH ∗ TONY S. DANIEL ∗ SANDU FLOREA ∗ TOMEU MOREY

JUSTICE LEAGUE VOL. 1: THE EXTINCTION MACHINES

VOL.1 REIGN OF THE SUPERMEN
STEVE ORLANDO ∗ BRIAN CHING ∗ MIKE ATIYEH

SUPERGIRL VOL. 1: REIGN OF THE SUPERMEN

VOL.1 BEYOND BURNSIDE
HOPE LARSON ∗ RAFAEL ALBUQUERQUE

BATGIRL VOL. 1: BEYOND BURNSIDE

"That gorgeous spectacle is an undeniable part of Superman's appeal, but the family dynamics are what make it such an engaging read."
– A.V. CLUB

"Head and shoulders above the rest."
– NEWSARAMA

DC UNIVERSE REBIRTH

SUPERMAN

VOL. 1: SON OF SUPERMAN

PETER J. TOMASI with PATRICK GLEASON, DOUG MAHNKE & JORGE JIMENEZ

VOL.1 SON OF SUPERMAN
PETER J.TOMASI * PATRICK GLEASON * DOUG MAHNKE * JORGE JIMENEZ * MICK GRAY

VOL.1 REIGN OF THE SUPERMEN
STEVE ORLANDO * BRIAN CHING * MIKE ATIYEH

**SUPERGIRL VOL. 1:
REIGN OF THE SUPERMEN**

VOL.1 PATH OF DOOM
DAN JURGENS * PATRICK ZIRCHER * TYLER KIRKHAM * STEPHEN SEGOVIA * TOM GRUMMETT

**ACTION COMICS VOL. 1:
PATH OF DOOM**

VOL.1 I AM GOTHAM
TOM KING * DAVID FINCH

**BATMAN VOL. 1:
I AM GOTHAM**

Get more DC graphic novels wherever comics and books are sold!